Food Economics

D0145796

Food and food markets still enjoy a pivotal role in the world economy, and the international food industry is moving towards greater consolidation and globalization, with increased vertical integration and changes to market structure. Companies grow bigger in order to obtain economies of scale, and issues such as food security and quality, obesity and health are ever important factors.

This book describes the link between food markets and food companies from a theoretical and a business economics perspective. The relationships, trends and impacts on the international food market are presented, and the topic is related to actual business conditions.

Each chapter is accompanied by questions and assignments designed to help students in their learning.

Henning Otte Hansen is Senior Advisor in the Institute of Food and Resource Economics / Section for Production, Markets and Policy Unit at Copenhagen University, Denmark.

Routledge textbooks in environmental and agricultural economics

Food Economics

Industry and markets

Henning Otte Hansen

Routledge
Taylor & Francis Group

LONDON AND NEW YORK

First published 2013
by Routledge
2 Park Square, Milton Park, Abingdon, Oxon OX14 4RN

Simultaneously published in the USA and Canada
by Routledge
711 Third Avenue, New York, NY 10017

Routledge is an imprint of the Taylor & Francis Group, an informa business

British Library Cataloguing in Publication Data
A catalogue record for this book is available from the British Library

Library of Congress Cataloging in Publication Data
Hansen, Henning Otte, 1959–
Food economics / Henning O. Hansen.
    p. cm. – (Routledge textbooks in environmental and agricultural economics)
1. Food industry and trade.   2. Produce trade.   3. Food supply –
Political aspects.   4. Globalization – Economic aspects.   I. Title.
    HD9000.5.H363 2013
    381'.41 – dc23

2012032224

ISBN: 978-0-415-60459-8 (hbk)
ISBN: 978-0-415-60461-1 (pbk)
ISBN: 978-0-203-06647-8 (ebk)

Typeset in Times New Roman
by RefineCatch Limited, Bungay, Suffolk

MIX
Paper from
responsible sources
FSC
www.fsc.org   FSC® C018575

Printed and bound in Great Britain by MPG Printgroup

Contents

Figures

Tables

Preface

The food industry and markets are currently undergoing major and rapid change. The business environment is changing, and influence of the outside world can be both unpredictable and fateful for food companies. Food markets develop under special conditions, which in many ways are unique. The relationship between food markets and the food industry is becoming more and more complex and, at the same time, both markets and companies are becoming more and more globalised.

Developments on the international food markets have a major influence on the food industry's development, but the entire food product chain, food cluster and consumers are also affected. In addition, important issues such as food security, food supply, trade policy, development aid and globalisation also play a significant role.

This book describes the link between food markets and food companies from a theoretical and business economics perspective. The ambition is to survey the relationships, trends and influences, and to relate these to actual business conditions.

I would like to thank 'Andelsfonden' and the Institute of Resource Economics and Food Policy, University of Copenhagen for their support with preparing this book. Thanks also to Stuart Wright for help with the translation of the original Danish text. Finally, I would also like to thank my children, David, Louise and Maria for their moral support and patience.

Henning Otte Hansen
Copenhagen, August 2012

1 The uniqueness of food markets

Food and food markets are subject to specific conditions which, for better or for worse, are different from those elsewhere. The natural conditions are special, but also the supply and demand conditions and the sector's structure, adaptability, etc. are significantly different. These distinct and significant conditions form the critical foundation for the analyses of the sector and the markets which are continuously made. Moreover, they have great importance for development, which the food sector and the markets experience in line with economic growth.

There are also, however, signs that the food sector's special conditions in several areas are becoming less distinctive: all the links in the value chain are becoming industrialised and can increasingly be compared with the conditions in other industries.

This chapter discusses some of the special conditions which exist throughout the food value chain and on the food markets.

Introduction

All industries and sectors are subject to specific conditions. However, in the case of food, these are so distinctive that it is possible to talk about the 'food sector's special conditions'.

The food sector's distinctive conditions can be more or less special compared to other sectors. In some areas, the differences are becoming fewer and fewer, while, in other areas, the differences are so fundamental and physical that they do not change much.

Other industries also have their own special conditions, but they are rarely as distinctive as agriculture's. Therefore, one can generally say that the food sector operates under special circumstances in several important areas.

Some of the food sector's special conditions only apply to parts of the food sector, particularly in agriculture. Since the food sector can be considered as one vertically integrated and connected value chain, the special conditions in one link can affect the other links in the chain. For example, instability in agriculture can have a significant influence on all the subsequent links in the value chain, with the recent food crises being obvious examples.

One can divide the special conditions into three categories: 1) biological and physical conditions; 2) structural conditions; and 3) market and economic conditions. However, the division is not unambiguous in all cases. Some conditions may be, e.g., market-related, but also the result of biological factors.

The special conditions are thus linked. The biological conditions may be the reason for the particular market conditions, while the structural conditions may also be coupled to the biological and market circumstances.

Box 1.1 presents an overview of the food sector's specific characteristics divided into three categories.

Box 1.1 Overview of agriculture's special conditions

Biological and physical conditions

- agricultural production is unstable from year to year
- limited potential for storage
- seasonality
- biological lags in production
- cyclical fluctuations and cobweb phenomena
- the tie to the land makes it necessary to spread agricultural production geographically
- agricultural land is a scarce resource
- huge potential for increasing efficiency
- food is a basic necessity good which is consumed every day by all consumers
- the agricultural and food sectors' conditions vary considerably from country to country
- food production has an inevitable impact on nature and the environment.

Structural conditions

- agriculture's structure is distinctive
- the structure of the food industry is distinctive
- significant need for capital and investment
- competitive conditions and price setting in the food sector are distinctive
- vertical integration.

Market-related and economic conditions

- the price of agricultural products is unstable and fluctuates greatly over time
- fluctuating and low incomes
- fixed resources – adaptability (fixed assets)

- the agricultural treadmill
- the agricultural terms of trade deteriorate over time
- the food sector declines in importance as the economy grows
- demand depends on income
- trade policy restrictions and subsidy schemes
- world trade in agricultural and food products is small
- world trade in agriculture and food grows slowly.

Biological and physical conditions

The biological and physical conditions encompass a number of special natural characteristics, which present the food sector with a number of challenges.

Agricultural production is unstable from year to year

Agricultural production is affected by many factors in each year, which farmers cannot fully control, e.g. the weather, pests and diseases. The result is large annual fluctuations in production, primarily in crop production.

Although drought in all agricultural countries at the same time is very rare, there is still too much instability in total global production. As can be seen in Figure 1.1, the world's total production of grain has experienced annual fluctuations of between −4 and 10 per cent in recent decades.

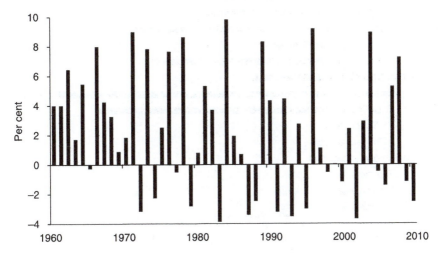

Figure 1.1 Annual changes in the world's total grain production.

Source: Author's calculations based on FAO (2012).

Annual fluctuations of 5–10 per cent in grain production are significant compared to the fluctuations in the total output of the economy. In the Western world, the development of gross domestic product (GDP) is relatively stable and fluctuations of more than a few per cent per year are rare. Agriculture is one of the industries which experiences the largest annual fluctuations in GDP at factor cost (value of production minus value of inputs).

Limited opportunities for reserves

In contrast to a number of industries, agriculture has limited opportunities for storing products and thereby limited opportunities for managing, optimising or evening out supply.

There are several sides to the problem of the storage of agricultural products. It is simply not possible to store some agricultural products for a long period (e.g. fruit and fresh food), while, for other agricultural products, storage involves significant costs. The size of stocks therefore depends on the natural qualities of agricultural products, which dictate the opportunities for storage and stockpiling (see Figure 1.2).

As can be seen in Figure 1.2, grain stocks correspond to approximately 20 per cent of production, which equates to just two months' production or consumption. Given that stocks play a very important role in the stability of the entire grain market, and the global food supply, the reserves seem relatively low.

For livestock products, however, stocks are much lower.

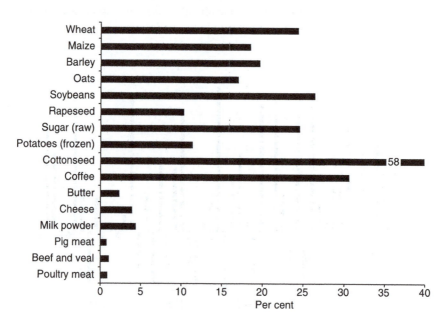

Figure 1.2 The size of stocks (percentage of production, 2008).

Source: Author's calculations based on USDA (2009).

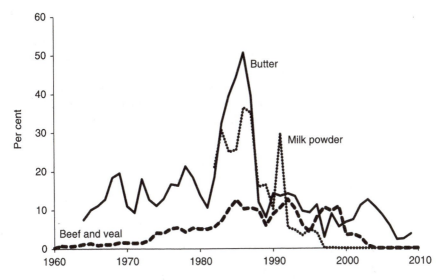

Figure 1.3 The EU's stocks for selected agricultural products (percentage of production).
Source: Author's calculations based on USDA (2009).

The size of stocks fluctuates considerably over time, which can be positive, since reserves have to act as a buffer, which can be increased or reduced depending on the market situation.

Agricultural stocks can also, to a greater or lesser extent, be an indication of overproduction, and thus storage is a way of removing production that cannot be sold at the normal market price in either the short or long term. The developments in the European Union (EU)'s stocks of, e.g., dairy products in the 1980s is an example of the results of overproduction (see Figure 1.3).

In line with the increasing market orientation of the EU's agricultural policy, the need for storage and intervention is becoming much smaller, and thus reserves have been reduced considerably. The EU's grain stocks are today relatively low when compared with the EU's grain consumption.

Seasonality

Seasonal variation due to climatic conditions is another special condition in agricultural production, which does not exist to the same extent in other industries.

Seasonal movements or seasonal fluctuations are generally understood as the variation that occurs in one row of data within a calendar year.

Seasonal fluctuations are annually recurring fluctuations, which are often caused by the climate. Seasonal fluctuations are also seen in livestock production, e.g. milk production, which is climate-dependent and experiences distinct seasonal swings depending on fluctuations in crop and feed production (see Box 1.2).

Box 1.2 Seasonality in milk production

Milk production varies greatly from year to year, especially in regions where access to feed is at times an important limiting factor. In New Zealand (Figure 1.4), where cows usually graze outside throughout the year, where grass production is very low in the winter and where coarse fodder is not widely produced for winter feeding, milk production is very low in winter. Also in Argentina (Figure 1.5) there are significant seasonal

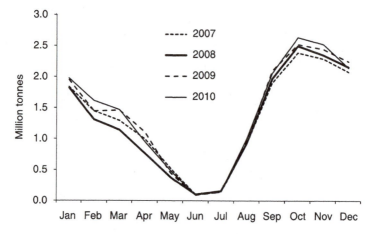

Figure 1.4 Monthly milk production in New Zealand.

Source: DCANZ (2012).

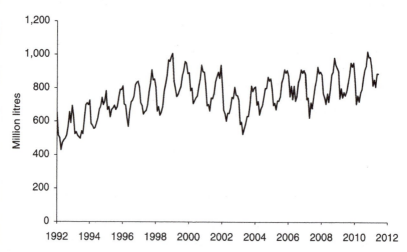

Figure 1.5 Monthly milk production in Argentina.

Source: Arlimentos Argentinos (2012).

fluctuations, while fluctuations in the USA (Figure 1.6) are more limited (typically 10–15 per cent). In Denmark (Figure 1.7), fluctuations have declined from around 50 per cent in the 1970s to only about 15 per cent today. While the consumption of milk and dairy products is much more stable over time, the task for the dairy industry is to control the processing and refinement of raw milk delivered by farmers, so that the varying quantities are optimally used at any one time.

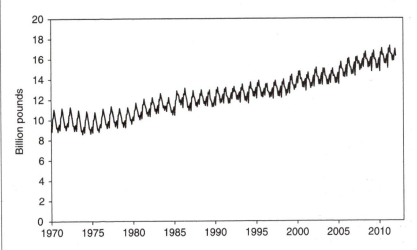

Figure 1.6 Monthly milk production in the USA.

Source: NASS (several years).

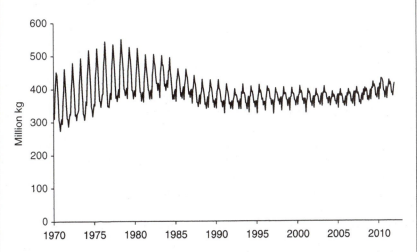

Figure 1.7 Monthly milk production in Denmark.

Source: Statistics Denmark (several years and 2012).

Biological lags in production

Biological conditions also mean that there are significant lags (time shifts) in production.

For example, a certain period of time elapses from the initial planning of the year's land use until harvest, owing to limitations which are set by nature. It is thus not possible in any significant way to speed up or slow down production, as is possible in other industries.

The time lag naturally varies from production sector to production sector. When it comes to the production of fruit, Christmas trees and the like, the time lags involve many years, but also in livestock production several years elapse from the decision to expand production significantly to the actual realisation of an increase in supply.

Cyclical fluctuations and cobweb phenomena

The previously discussed lags in production, along with other conditions, mean that cyclical fluctuations in prices and the supply of agricultural products occur in certain places.

Cyclic fluctuations are a well-known phenomenon in the agricultural production sector. These movements are basically sine functions, which therefore have a constant period but, in practice, of course, we are dealing with approximations of varying volatility and duration. As a result of these random fluctuations, the cycles are usually not sufficiently stable to be reliably described by a mathematical function.

The primary cause of the cyclical variations is that the size of production in many cases follows a particular course with regard to prices, supply and demand (see the pattern determined by cobweb theory, described below). The supply of agricultural crops especially appears to follow the theory's assumptions, but certain parts of animal production also exhibit clear cyclical movements.

If agricultural production and agricultural prices are not completely controlled or stabilised by different policy instruments, the price and production of many agricultural products will exhibit periodic fluctuations corresponding to the so-called cobweb phenomenon. The cyclic variations are usually interpreted as a distinctive agricultural phenomenon.

Cobweb theory was developed in the 1930s (see Ezekiel, 1938) and has proved to be particularly suitable for explaining the periodic fluctuations of many agricultural commodities, especially pig production.

Cobweb theory is based on the following assumptions:

- The production period has a certain duration, so that there is a time lag before production responds to a change in price.
- There are no reserves.
- Producers plan their future production based on current prices without regard for the effect of their own decisions.

- Market prices are determined by the amount supplied with immediate adaptation.

These assumptions are clearly not fulfilled in every case but, at the aggregate level, the prerequisites appear to be acceptable for several agricultural products (potatoes, seeds, etc.) which exhibit regular shifts from large production and low prices to small production with high prices.

Cobweb theory is thus based on the assumption that output in year t, S_t, is a function of the price of the relevant product in the previous period, P_{t-1},

$$St = f(P_{t-1})$$

Since cobweb theory assumes that the future size of production is determined by the market price at the current time, a high selling price must be followed by an increase in production, as a certain lag between the two movements will always occur. This correlation is clearly illustrated in Figure 1.8, which shows the annual percentage change in production and the change in the corresponding prices.

Figure 1.8 clearly shows the existence of time series with mutually contradictory functions: when the supply increases, prices decrease and vice versa.

The cobweb phenomenon is also seen in potato production, and the classic example of supply and demand in the potato market is often used to illustrate the contrasting fluctuations. The relationship is not completely unambiguous, because supply not only depends on the price in the previous year, but climate, pests, etc. also play a significant role and these can contribute to the disruption of the cobweb pattern.

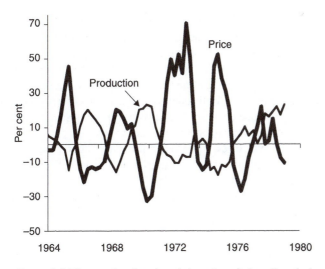

Figure 1.8 The supply of pork and the price of pigs, Canada (percentage change in relation to previous years).

Source: Larry (1981).

Box 1.3 **King's law**

'Gregory King's law' or 'King-Davenant's law' was drafted by the English statistician, Gregory King (1648–1712). Gregory King studied, in particular, how much a decreasing supply of corn would cause the price of corn to rise. He concluded that a reduction in supply of 10 per cent would result in a price increase of 30 per cent. King's law says, therefore, that, with a low supply, the price increases more and thus the value of production increases. King's law thereby questions the wisdom of introducing price-stabilising measures for the benefit of farmers.

In many cases, a drop in production in a local area, because of, e.g., a poor harvest, leads to substantial price increases. The price increases will often be large in relation to the decline in production. In these cases, it can be concluded that King's law applies (see Box 1.3).

The tie to the land

The fundamental basis for agricultural production is agricultural land, water and sunlight. Since agricultural land is naturally dispersed geographically, agricultural production is similarly dispersed geographically.

Agricultural production's tie to the land, and thereby geographical distribution, means that it is not possible to specialise and exploit economies of scale as in other industries.

Agricultural production is therefore different from, e.g., industry, where one can, to a greater extent, move production facilities from one country to another, or where the input factors (capital and labour) can, to a greater extent, replace each other in relation to the countries' resources. For example, cars are produced in many different countries. In this case, the high knowledge and technology-based part of production will take place in the richest industrialised countries, while production will be gradually moved to the less developed countries in line with increasing standardisation, decreasing technological content and greater economies of scale.

In this way, different trade theories, e.g. product life-cycle theory, explain how production can take place in many different countries, but under different conditions and with different resources in each country.

In agriculture, many of the input factors, of which agricultural land is the central factor, are immobile, and therefore no equalisation can occur between the countries.

Agricultural land is a scarce resource

Agricultural land is an inherently scarce resource, which cannot be increased significantly, and which is under pressure due to urbanisation, a demand for nature areas, etc., particularly in the economically advanced countries.

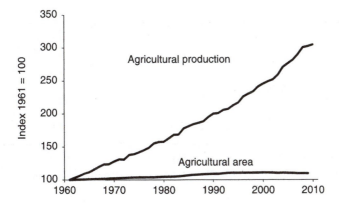

Figure 1.9 Development in total global agricultural area and agricultural production.

Source: Author's calculations based on FAO (2012).

Globally, it is still possible to increase the area of agricultural land. The net increase is, however, relatively small, which also should be seen in light of the fact that a certain amount of farmland is abandoned each year as it can no longer be used for production due to erosion, the accumulation of salt, desertification, etc.

From the early 1960s until 2009, the world's total agricultural area only increased by about 10 per cent, whereas the world's total agricultural production increased by 180 per cent (see Figure 1.9).

The figure illustrates that an increase in productivity, and not an increase in agricultural area, is the main source of increased agricultural production.

High potential for increasing efficiency

In a market economy, the food sector is exposed to persistent productivity pressure just like other manufacturing industries. Competitive pressure from other industries and from agriculture abroad forces companies to introduce new technology, etc. to improve effectiveness. This helps to limit cost increases, because products can be produced with fewer resources and, in this way, income is maintained. The new technique, however, also means that production increases and that prices consequently fall in the longer term.

The potential to improve efficiency in agriculture through increased productivity is significant compared to other industries. Over a longer period there is thus an almost constant additional productivity development in agriculture compared to other manufacturing sectors. A weighted average for OECD countries shows that the annual productivity development in agriculture is 1 percentage point higher than the development in other industries (see OECD (1995)).

Another analysis (Martin and Mitra, 2000) also shows that the productivity increases are larger in agriculture than in industry, but that the gap is greatest in developing countries (see Table 1.1).

Table 1.1 Annual percentage change in total productivity in agriculture and industry in various country groupings

Income group	Industry	Agriculture	Agriculture minus Industry
Low	0.61	1.74	1.13
Medium	0.88	2.20	1.32
Developing	0.81	2.06	1.25
Developed	2.67	3.40	0.73
Average	1.55	2.52	0.97

Source: Author's calculations based on Martin and Mitra (2000).

Note: Data for 50 countries for the period 1967–92; total productivity is the average of data from three calculation methods.

As seen from the table, the increases in productivity are greatest in the rich countries, which applies to both agriculture and industry.

An analysis of the underlying figures for the 50 countries shows a clear tendency for the productivity difference in agriculture to reduce over time compared to the development in industry. The relatively rapid convergence in agriculture's productivity among the countries implies a relatively rapid transfer of new knowledge in agriculture. It also means that a large agricultural sector in a country need not be a disadvantage with regard to growth in the society: quite the contrary.

The potential for efficiency improvements in agriculture has several important consequences. First, it means that potential will always be exploited somewhere, possibly by competing agricultural sectors abroad. This puts constant pressure on farms which have not yet exploited potential, and the result is thus increasing competition.

The efficiency potential also means that resources can be continuously released from agriculture, particularly labour, for use in other sectors. The large efficiency gains also mean that there is the potential for sustained increases in production, as long as there is sufficient demand.

Food is a basic necessity good

Food is a basic necessity good, at the bottom of the hierarchy of needs. This position in the hierarchy of needs also means that demand for food is relatively income inelastic, i.e. the consumption of food does not increase much, even if the population's income increases. Other products are generally more income elastic, which means that economic growth and increasing prosperity in a society will increase demand for these products significantly.

More and more goods are moving upwards in the hierarchy of needs, and companies will often strategically position themselves in market and product segments where demand increases significantly with increasing wealth, and where growth is considerable. Food's status as a basic necessity good also means that the total consumption of agricultural and food products does not change much over time. The increase in real income has therefore resulted in food accounting for an ever decreasing share of total consumption.

Because of demand conditions and low population growth in the most developed countries, total food consumption is increasing very weakly. Within total consumption, however, there are certain product groups for which demand is increasing sharply including, e.g., highly processed foods of high quality.

Conditions in the food sector vary considerably from country to country

Agricultural production depends on the natural conditions, including the agricultural area and value. There are, at the same time, also significant differences in agriculture's structure, effectiveness, importance, etc. among both developed and developing countries.

As a certain amount of domestic production is desirable for historical, political, trade-related and security reasons, significant differences in the conditions from country to country will emerge.

The area of cultivated farmland per capita is thus very different in countries and regions such as China, the EU, the USA and Argentina (see Figure 1.10). Since

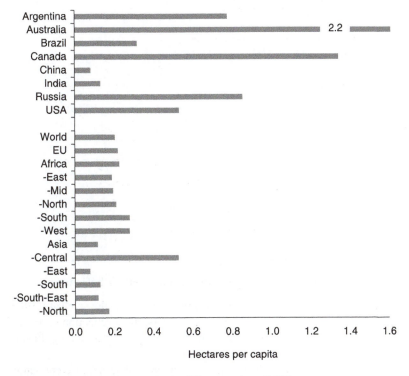

Figure 1.10 Farmland per capita in different regions (2009).

Source: FAO (2012) and author's calculations.

soil is the foundation of all agricultural production, and hence also the vast majority of food production, it is a vital resource and a comparative advantage. Precisely the relationship between agricultural land and the size of the population indicates the extent to which agricultural production can be expected to exceed domestic consumption.

The different natural conditions are also expressed in large differences in agricultural productivity among countries. Partial productivity measures in the form of harvest yields show that there is a wide spread (see Figure 1.11).

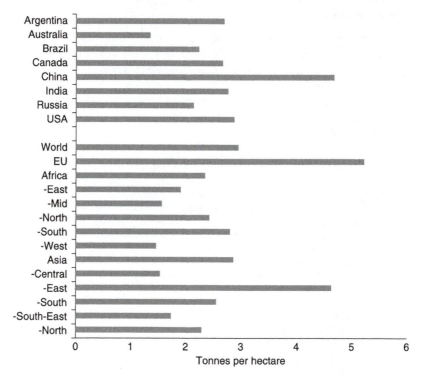

Figure 1.11 Wheat yield per ha (average of 2006–10).

Source: FAO (2012) and author's calculations.

Box 1.4 **Examples of differences in the food sector's basic terms**

The differences in wheat yields say something about the intensity differences between the countries and are not necessarily a reflection of an economic or competitive advantage. A high wheat yield can be an indication of many input factors and many costs.

The differences in productivity, however, show that the different natural conditions vary greatly from place to place.

Agricultural production vs nature and the environment

Agricultural production occurs by exploiting nature and the biological processes. At the same time, agriculture must be located in or close to nature. In many cases, e.g. crop production, the agricultural activity is a direct alternative to nature. Therefore, all forms of agricultural production will, to a greater or lesser extent, affect nature and the environment.

Other industries can function, to a much greater extent, separate from nature. Production can be concentrated in smaller units and need not be located and scattered across the landscape. Therefore, it is not surprising that agriculture and nature are often on a collision course. Other industries have far more scope for avoiding conflicts with respect to nature and the environment.

Structural conditions

Agriculture's structure is special

Agriculture consists of many individually owned farms where the family performs most of the work. At the same time, the units are relatively small compared to other manufacturing industries. The relatively small units in comparison with other industries are thus a defining feature of agriculture.

Agriculture's structure, with many relatively small units, means that many tasks must be solved jointly as the individual business does not have the practical or economic resources to conduct, e.g., research and development. The many small units also affect the farmers' market power in the value chain and opportunities to exploit economies of scale, etc.

The structure of the food industry is distinctive

Ownership forms in the food industry are distinctive in that cooperative ownership is relatively widespread compared to ownership forms in other industries. This is especially true in the parts of the food sector that are most dependent on local agricultural produce, which are close to the agricultural sector in the value chain.

The widespread cooperative ownership in the agri and food industry also affects the sector's overall economic development. Cooperative ownership means, in most cases, that the cooperative members have delivery rights and obligations, which implies that the members often act as an economic buffer during times of fluctuating earnings. If the cooperative's earnings during a period come under pressure, it is possible, to a greater or lesser extent, to adjust the farmers' selling prices and thus the cooperative's costs. A characteristic of cooperatives is that their earnings vary much less than the earnings of their members, especially in the case of long-term contract periods. The cooperatives' financial results are therefore relatively stable from year to year.

Cooperative ownership in the food industry is discussed in greater detail in Chapter 10.

Significant need for capital and investment in agriculture

Agricultural production often requires significant investment in fixed production resources such as buildings, machinery, labour and land.

It is also generally the case that net investments in agriculture are relatively large in relation to the net value added which is created. Several authors have shown that the rate of turnover is greater in industry than in agriculture (see Ritson, 1977).

The relatively large investments measured against the value added therefore mean that the time horizon for investments becomes greater and that flexibility and adaptation in the face of new economic and political conditions deteriorate. Therefore, the provision of advice and training are key strategies for remedying this shortcoming.

Competition and pricing in the agricultural sector are distinctive

Agriculture consists of many small units compared to its processing and retail links, which means that the individual producer does not have the opportunity to influence the price of his or her products by changing the amount supplied. Thus, the market equilibrium and competitive situation are distorted because farmers' bargaining power is weak compared to the fewer and larger suppliers and buyers.

The cooperative ownership form in the supply and processing links, however, significantly increases farmers' market power, while at the same time ensuring that the profit from further processing and sales is channelled back to the producers, i.e. the farmers.

The vertical supply chain from the farmer to the consumer involves several links, with many or few actors in each link. Basically, one can say that there are many players at the beginning and at the end of the value chain in that there are relatively many farmers and consumers. However, between these two links the 'funnel' in the value chain narrows considerably and there are relatively few, but powerful, actors in the central retail link in the middle of the chain. Figure 1.12 illustrates this funnel between the farmers / producers and consumers.

The figure shows the links in the value chain from the farmer to consumer in Europe, together with the number of actors in each link. As can be seen, the number of actors changes considerably in the field-to-fork chain. Retail buying alliances in particular result in a highly concentrated supply funnel, where relatively few actors account for a very large share of the European food trade. Farmers' special position in the value chain and the supply funnel means that they are faced with special challenges regarding maximising their influence and market position.

Vertical integration

Vertical integration – coordination of links in the value chain – also plays a relatively important role in the food sector and in the value chain between producer

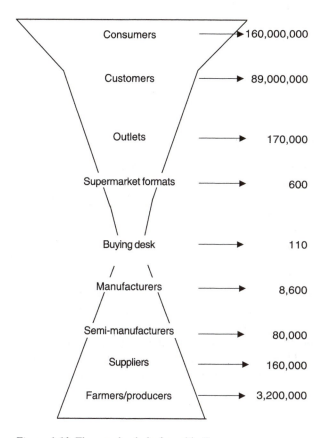

Consumers	160,000,000
Customers	89,000,000
Outlets	170,000
Supermarket formats	600
Buying desk	110
Manufacturers	8,600
Semi-manufacturers	80,000
Suppliers	160,000
Farmers/producers	3,200,000

Figure 1.12 The supply chain funnel in Europe.
Source: Grievink (2003).

and consumer. The starting point is that there is substantial mutual dependence between, on the one hand, agriculture and, on the other hand, the food industry.

Regarding agriculture, it is important to have an efficient market for products. For example, it is essential for milk producers that their daily production of fresh milk is sold effectively.

With regard to the food industry, which to a large extent obtains produce from local farmers, it is important that the supply of produce is stable. A slaughterhouse or a dairy, for example, cannot function without daily deliveries of agricultural products. Even increasing globalisation, with access to many new commodity markets, cannot eliminate the dependence on local agricultural production.

There is therefore a mutual dependency, the like of which does not exist in many other sectors. Increasing specialisation and dependence help to develop vertical integration in the entire food chain, from field to fork.

In addition, factors such as:

- traceability as a selling point;
- genetic engineering;
- product differentiation based on produce diversity;
- minimisation of transaction costs; and
- increased productivity via contractual trade

further help to promote vertical integration.

Market and economic conditions

The food sector is also subject to specific market and economic conditions that are generally not found to the same extent in other industries. These distinct market and economic conditions are also partly linked to the biological and structural conditions, or may be a consequence of them.

These conditions are further discussed below.

Prices are unstable and fluctuate over time

The price of agricultural commodities varies considerably over time. In countries and regions with developed market agreements for agricultural products, these fluctuations are balanced to some extent by adjustments in imports and exports and by domestic support prices. However, these measures can themselves increase the instability on world markets. Nevertheless, even under very free and liberal conditions, price instability will be significant due to climate-induced changes in supply.

Price volatility can vary significantly depending on:

- the product
- the markets and regions; world market prices are often the most unstable
- the presence or otherwise of market agreements, price stabilisation measures, etc.
- whether we are dealing with spot or contract prices
- whether we are dealing with raw products or more processed goods.

The goal of agricultural policy, particularly in developed countries, is to stabilise domestic markets, and here price stability is an important element. In a historical perspective, the EU has a long tradition of stabilising and limiting price fluctuations. In the periods with almost unlimited opportunities for intervention, import tariffs and export subsidies, it was easy to stabilise prices on the EU's internal market.

This is illustrated in part in Figure 1.13, which shows the development in the EU's institutional prices and world market prices for a number of products.

The figure also shows that World Trade Organization (WTO) liberalisation, reforms and the increasing market orientation of the EU's agriculture policy

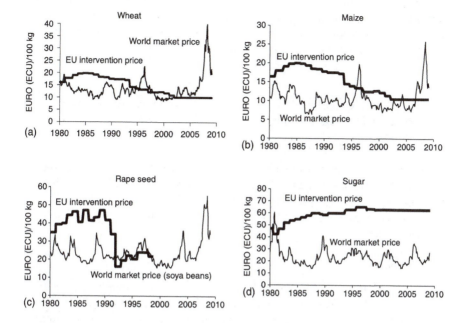

Figure 1.13 EU prices and world market prices on selected agricultural products.

Source: Author's presentation based on European Commission (several years) and market data.

have helped to reduce price support, and that the world market price, to an increasing extent, is the price that farmers have to produce their produce for. Thus, large parts of the existing stabilisation apparatus in the EU's market agreements have also been removed. A reduction in price and market support for the agricultural sector has occurred in most industrialised countries since the early 1990s.

Fluctuating and low incomes

The issue of earnings in the first link of the food value chain, i.e. agriculture, has occupied economists for many years.

From a rational economic perspective, it is illogical if a sector persistently fails to achieve an income which is equivalent to the level in other comparable sectors. Resources are expected to go to where the returns are greatest. It would be expected that the resources in the food sector, i.e. capital and labour, would go to other sectors until earnings reach the average in other sectors. Persistently low incomes in a sector must therefore be due to special conditions.

There is a general consensus that agricultural incomes are more volatile and lower in the long term than for other income groups. A comparison of incomes in agriculture with incomes outside the agricultural industry is not easy to conduct and one inevitably encounters major problems (see Box 1.5).

Box 1.5 The agricultural income problem: special features of the calculation and comparisons

Who should one compare with?

It is necessary to compare with a group of people outside agriculture, who share the same level of education, age, etc. However, it will be impossible to find a basis for comparison which can be used in all cases. Farmers' education, competences, etc. cannot be compared with individuals working in other sectors.

Work hours

In general, farmers work longer hours than individuals employed in other industries. A comparison of annual income will therefore not provide an accurate picture of the actual relative remuneration of labour. A comparison of pay per hour would instead take the different work effort per year into account.

Other earned income

Farmers often earn an income outside agriculture. This is especially due to the increasing number of part-time farmers, but even among full-time farmers, income from outside agriculture represents a substantial share of total income. With increasing income from outside the sector, agriculture's total income will approach the level outside the industry. This development is the result of higher earnings outside the sector and not because the remuneration of farm labour is approaching the levels elsewhere. In all cases, the increasing income from outside agriculture makes it difficult to quantify and compare the actual remuneration of labour in agriculture.

Return on invested capital

Farmers often have substantial equity tied up in the farm. However, this capital does not explicitly yield interest when one calculates the farm's income. An alternative use of the farmer's capital would have provided a continuous market return. Therefore, it may be appropriate to subtract this missing income, or alternative return, from the farmer's income in order to give a realistic picture of returns from all the resources used on the farm.

Capital gains

Over time, capital gains and losses occur. Changed market conditions will naturally affect the value of agricultural assets. Therefore, the capital gains and losses far exceed actual net income. It is, however, important to note that, in the long term, the sum of the capital gains and losses is close to zero.

Risk and uncertainty

Over time, incomes vary in agriculture far more than in other sectors. This significantly greater risk and uncertainty should be remunerated, since a stable and predictable income, *ceteris paribus*, is advantageous and desirable. A fluctuating income should therefore, in the long run, be a little higher to compensate for the greater uncertainty.

Average figures

Furthermore, comparing average figures can involve uncertainty or is at least imprecise. The spread of income between farmers and between agricultural activities is significant, and these significant differences are not visible when using averages. It is likely that the greatest income problem in agriculture is the large income spread, whereby the weakest 25 per cent of farmers have very low or negative incomes.

The larger the comparison group, the lower the instability

The larger the group which is analysed, the lower the instability. A comparison of the instability among some pig farmers in relation to, e.g., the economy or industry's overall instability therefore does not make sense. The economy is normally relatively stable, which of course is due to the fact that, e.g., fluctuations among the individual industries more or less balance each other.

Additional factors

Finally, there are a number of additional factors which can complicate the income comparison, e.g. calculating the consumption of own products, amenity value and housing.

Fixed assets – adaptability

As previously discussed, the need for capital and investment in agriculture is considerable. In addition, the resources in agriculture, i.e. investment in plant and machinery, knowledge, labour, organisation, etc. are often very specific. The resources often have little alternative value when used in other sectors.

This relationship, often described as fixed assets, is specific to the agricultural sector. Also there is probably a tendency that agriculture industrialises and thereby increasingly uses the same factors, methods and competences as other sectors. In this way, agriculture's resources become less specific and more mobile, and thus their alternative value in other sectors increases.

The agricultural treadmill

Agriculture's significant tied-up capital, its fixed assets and great potential for productivity and technology exploitation together lead to what is often termed 'the agricultural treadmill'. Figure 1.14 is a schematic illustration of the process in a typical treadmill.

The treadmill begins with the application of technological advances, which leads to increased productivity and hence better earnings among the progressive and innovative farmers, who first apply the new technology. This results in a gradual increase in supply.

Gradually, as the 'average' farmers also start to use the new technology, supply increases further, while prices fall accordingly. Eventually, the laggard farmers are forced to introduce the new technology simply to maintain their income in the face of the decreasing prices. When new technology is once again introduced, the treadmill continues to turn.

Figure 1.14 The agricultural treadmill.

Source: Author's presentation based on Cochrane (1958).

One of the 'problems' with the treadmill is that the farmers are often locked into the sector and do not move into other industries when incomes are threatened by a persistent fall in prices created by the exploitation of technology.

Agriculture's terms of trade deteriorate over time

As a consequence of both the development in productivity and the treadmill, agriculture's sales prices increase on average more slowly than those of other goods in the economy. The prices of both agricultural and food products increase less than inflation in the long term, and the terms of trade, the relation between agriculture's sales and factor prices, will deteriorate.

Deteriorating terms of trade is something that agriculture in almost all countries experiences, almost regardless of what country we are talking about. As can be seen in Figure 1.15, deteriorating agricultural terms of trade occur in countries as diverse as the USA, Australia and Denmark.

The deteriorating terms of trade over time is a phenomenon that is particularly true for agriculture, which in general does not exist to the same extent in other industries.

Agriculture becomes less important with economic growth

It is a distinct phenomenon that agriculture's economic importance diminishes as a country grows economically, while the importance of other industrial sectors reduces less, and some sectors become more important. The sector's relative decline in importance may have a number of economic, market-related and policy implications:

- In a low-growth sector, it can be difficult to exploit productivity benefits because the potential for increasing production is less.
- In a low-growth sector, excess capacity can occur more easily, which can push down earnings.
- The pressure for mergers and consolidation will increase as the companies' potential for growth through organic market growth is less, and therefore growth through mergers and acquisitions becomes a more appropriate option.
- The opportunities for attracting capital to companies in low-growth sectors are often limited.
- The political attention on the sector diminishes as its economic contribution reduces.

Demand depends on income

Demand's low reliance on income is specific to agricultural and food products. The total consumption of agricultural and food products does not change significantly over time. Even if a family's income increases, they will not eat many more food products. This means that demand is relatively independent of increases in income, or in other words that food is relatively income inelastic.

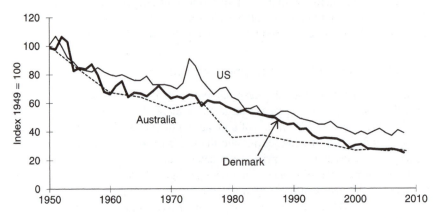

Figure 1.15 Development in agriculture's terms of trade in Australia, the USA and Denmark.

Source: Author's calculations based on Dansk Landbrug (several years), RIRDC (1997), USDA (several years) and ABARE (2008).

Because of the demand conditions and the low population growth in the traditional market regions, total food consumption increases very slowly. However, there are certain groups of products within total consumption whose demand increases sharply, e.g. highly processed foods of high quality, organic products, food service and convenience items.

Trade policy restrictions and subsidy schemes

In practice, all developed countries support their agricultural sector. All developed countries have specific agricultural policy objectives whereby society has set different goals and desires for agriculture, and a number of schemes have been implemented to achieve these objectives.

The extent of the total support and protection for agricultural products in developed countries equates to on average approximately 20 per cent of the production value. This is calculated according to the OECD's total support concept, Producer Support Estimate (PSE), which expresses the proportion of agriculture's production value that can be attributed to support and protection schemes (see Chapter 8).

A study (Hertel and Martin, 2000) of the trade barriers in the agricultural and industrial goods sectors also shows that agricultural commodities in general receive a higher level of protection on the international markets (see Table 1.2).

As can be seen from the table, trade barriers are two–ten times greater on agricultural markets than on industry markets.

Several other conditions are also noteworthy. First, import barriers are generally greater in developing countries than in developed countries. There is thus greater free trade in developed countries than in developing countries.

Table 1.2 Protectionism (trade barriers) for industrial and agricultural goods in developed and developing countries (1995)

	Developed	Developing
Industrial goods	1.5	11.5
Agricultural goods	15.6	20.1

Source: Hertel and Martin (2000).

Second, developed countries have very low import protection against the exports of other developed countries, while import protection is four times greater when it comes to imports from developing countries. The reverse is true when it comes to agricultural products combined: here, developing countries have greater access to developed countries' markets than the developed countries themselves.

Trade policy restrictions and support in general are special features of the agricultural sector.

World trade in agricultural and food products is small and grows slowly

International trade in agricultural products is relatively small in relation to production and trade on domestic markets (see also Chapter 5).

The small world trade in agricultural and food products, together with the slow growth in the market and consumption, is a significant barrier for expanding food businesses. International trade in agricultural and food products is not just small, but growth is also relatively weak.

When international trade becomes increasingly important, a further division of labour or specialisation between countries occurs. Each country specialises in the areas it is best at and abandons the areas where it cannot compete internationally. This process, however, seems to be delayed in the agricultural and food sectors.

Questions and assignments

1.1 Describe briefly how food markets can be unique compared to other markets.
1.2 How may the uniqueness influence:

- the behaviour of food companies?
- food policy?
- the world food situation?
- the economics of companies in the food value chain?

1.3 In general: is uniqueness a positive or negative feature for companies in the food chain? Why and how?
1.4 How can you change the uniqueness of food markets – if desirable?
1.5 Will food markets become more or less unique in future? Why?

2 Food crises

During the last couple of decades, there have been several serious global food crises, with severe economic, political and market-related consequences. Most recently, during 2007–08 and again in 2010–11, crises occurred with rapidly increasing food prices. It is important to shed light on the content, form, causes and consequences of food crises in order to be better able to predict and prevent future food crises. The most recent food crises share many common features, and it was largely the same mechanisms which were at work. With increasing pressure on agricultural and food markets and future changes in market structures, it is likely that food crises will be a recurring phenomenon.

What is a food crisis?

There are several different types of food crisis and one often distinguishes between the local and the global. Local food crises typically occur in developing countries where it is impossible to obtain adequate food due to crop failures and poor supplies. Normally the food crisis is limited to the area affected by the crop failure.

Global food crises mean that international prices and market conditions are also affected. With increasing globalisation, international trade, to a certain extent, compensates for any local shortages which may arise, provided there is sufficient purchasing power. On the other hand, globalisation also means that price changes in one part of the world immediately spread – to a greater or lesser degree – to the rest of the world.

The global food crises have a number of characteristics and consequences which have occurred in recent decades:

- price increases for grain and other important agricultural products;
- large fluctuations and volatility in prices;
- increasing food costs, which is especially a large burden for the poorest members of the population in developing countries;
- deteriorating supply of food and increasing hunger and famine;
- political and social unrest in several places in the world as a result of more expensive food or a pronounced food shortage;

• intervention through agricultural and trade policies in order to ensure domestic food supply and limit domestic food price increases.

Food crises in a historical perspective

Food crises, in the form of rapid price increases for agricultural and food products, are not a new phenomenon. The development of, e.g., the large international grain exchanges shows that international grain prices have been unstable for a long period. However, the development which has occurred over the past few decades has been more pronounced than the changes which occurred during the entire twentieth century (see Figure 2.1).

Figure 2.1 shows the price of wheat, which is one of the most important agricultural products for international production and international trade. According to the figure, there have been four–five dramatic increases in prices, or food crises, during the last century. Until now, these price increases have been relatively short term, often a maximum of 1–2 years, after which the markets have stabilised, so a sustained change in the level of prices has not occurred. Thus, one can, with good reason, describe the previous food crises as price bubbles.

If corrected for inflation, we see that there has been a real decrease in the price of wheat over the whole period. In the long term, the price of grain – as well as other agricultural products – will increase less than other goods in society. This is a clear global trend, which should be borne in mind during periods of soaring grain prices.

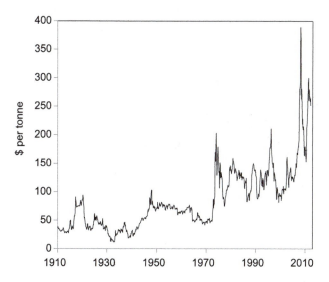

Figure 2.1 Wheat prices in the USA.

Source: Author's calculations based on USDA (2012b).

Note: Weighted averages for all kinds of wheat; shown as monthly averages in current prices, up to and including February 2012.

Figure 2.2 illustrates the international development in real prices (deflated price development) for agricultural products during the period 1948–2012.

The graph in Figure 2.2 thus shows the development in prices of a representative selection of agricultural products, corrected for inflation, on the international markets.

When considering the food crises, one should also take into account the fact that the problems can be very different from country to country and from product to product over time. The differences in the development of prices between the individual agricultural products (here grain products) during recent food crises is illustrated in Figure 2.3.

Figure 2.3 shows that the price development for all eight grain types largely follows the same pattern: the food crisis in 1973–74 and again in 2007–08 resulted in a significant price increase for all grains.

Grain types which are typically grown in temperate climates, including wheat, corn, barley, rye and oats, exhibit a very uniform price development during the entire period. This should be considered in light of the fact that both supply and demand have significant substitution possibilities. If, for instance, the price of wheat increases, it is countered, to a certain extent, by an increasing supply of, and decreasing demand for, wheat, while other grain types substitute wheat.

The typical tropical and sub-tropical grain types, such as rice, millet and durra, cannot be substituted by, e.g., wheat and corn to the same extent. Therefore, it can be expected that the prices of these grain types will be more volatile and will not follow the same patterns as, e.g., wheat and corn.

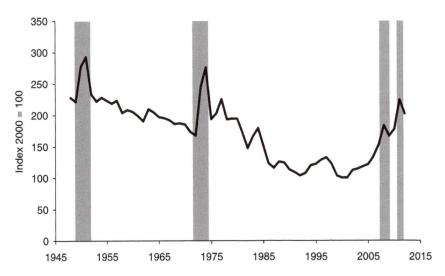

Figure 2.2 International development in real prices for agricultural products.

Source: Author's calculations based on World Bank (2012a, 2012b).

Note: 2012 = February 2012.
The shaded areas indicate the food crises of 1951–52, 1972–74, 2007–08 and 2010–11.

It is also significant that the price increases are large and they occur quickly and within a short period. There are no lengthy periods with high prices. Price increases are thus relatively quickly followed by a decrease in prices, although the decreases often occur more slowly than the subsequent increases.

Based on the previous figures, one can conclude that the four latest food crises have largely followed a uniform pattern and that there has been a relatively consistent price development for all grain types.

Seen from a historic perspective, it is thought-provoking that, in spite of improved economic and technological development, we have been unable to control or stabilise international agricultural and food markets. Even at the beginning of the twenty-first century, it has not been possible to achieve sufficient production, supply or distribution of food. This is a problem and a challenge which has particularly manifested itself in the food crises which we have experienced during the last century.

The food crisis of 1950–51

The first serious global food crisis of modern times took place in 1950–51 and it was closely connected to the Korean War, which started in 1950. The Korean War influenced the international food markets in several ways.

At first, the war created uncertainty and fear of food shortages. The experiences from the Second World War, which had ended just five years earlier, showed that food shortages could become critical during periods of war. Food, therefore, became a strategically important product, and this meant an increased focus on food and increasing prices – also on the international markets. The war and the fear of a prolonged conflict also resulted in a certain speculative pressure on international agricultural and food prices. At the same time, several countries built up significant strategic food reserves, which led to an increase in demand and thereby also in price. The USA's wheat reserve increased from being equivalent to 33 per cent of wheat produced in 1951, to more than 110 per cent in 1954 (see Figure 2.4).

The food crisis and the high food prices began to fade at the end of 1952 when it became clear that the Korean War would not develop into a worldwide conflict. At the same time, significantly lower economic growth also contributed to pushing the prices down.

The food crisis of 1972–74

After many years with very stable international prices for agricultural products and relative market stability, a serious food crisis emerged in 1972–74. There were three essential reasons for the food crisis in 1972–74:

- shock regarding the supply and demand for grain;
- an energy crisis (increasing oil prices); and
- declining reserves as well as prolonged and structural pressure on the international agricultural markets.

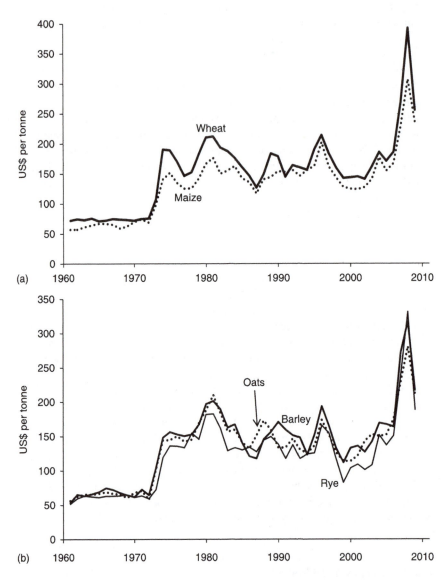

Figure 2.3 International prices of cereal.

Source: Author's own presentation based on FAO (2012).

The development in the price of wheat at the time of the food crisis in 1972–74, as well as significant events and effects, are shown in Figure 2.5.

The USA and the then Soviet Union both had an important influence on the emergence and development of the food crisis. For a long period of time prior to the food crisis in 1972–74, the USA and Canada had been the dominant producers on the international grain markets. At the beginning of the 1960s, the USA and

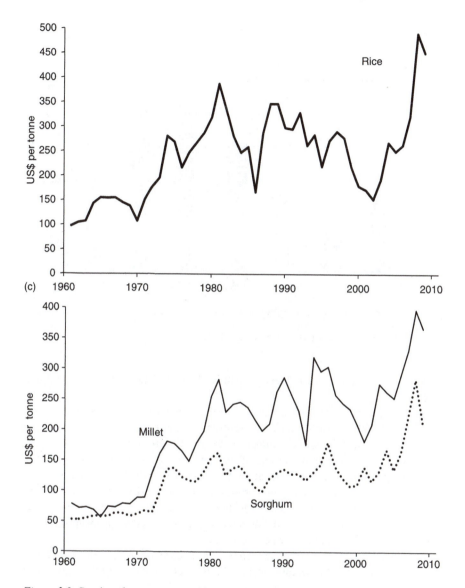

Figure 2.3 Continued

Canada accounted for 60–70 per cent of all wheat exports and more than 50 per cent of global grain exports. At the same time, the Soviet Union and Asia became significant net importers of grain.

What was also very important was the fact that the USA, in particular, had large grain reserves, which, to a large extent, contributed to stabilising the international grain markets. During the years 1960–71, the price of wheat was kept within the range of US $59–65 for 11 out of 12 years. In the years leading up to the price

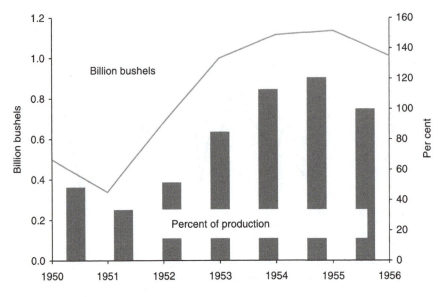

Figure 2.4 US wheat reserve, 1950–56: in total and as a percentage of production.

Source: Author's calculations based on USDA (2012b).

increase in the autumn of 1972, even monthly variations in the price were minimal (see Figure 2.1).

US wheat reserves peaked in around 1960, at which time the USA had approximately half of the world's total wheat reserves. The large reserves, which were to a large extent a result of overproduction created by agricultural subsidies, were cause for growing concern because of the high costs which are connected with building up reserves. The US Department of Agriculture had strived to limit US grain reserves in the 1960s, which resulted in a marked decrease during that decade. At the beginning of the 1970s, the USA and the two other large wheat producing countries, Canada and Australia, took steps to reduce wheat production and thereby also international wheat reserves.

The USA's wheat reserves were thereby significantly reduced in the first half of the 1970s, so that they comprised only 11 per cent of the world's total wheat reserves by 1973, when the food crisis peaked (see Figure 2.6).

With the historically low wheat reserves in 1972–74, it was no longer possible for the USA to use the reserves to stabilise international grain prices. Therefore, the grain markets became much more exposed to shocks and market influences, which can always occur, but which cannot necessarily be controlled.

One such shock came in June 1971, when the Nixon Administration decided to liberalise exports to China and the Soviet Union. The result was, among other things, that the Soviet Union, in November 1971, bought 3 million tonnes of grain feed, which further reduced the USA's grain reserves.

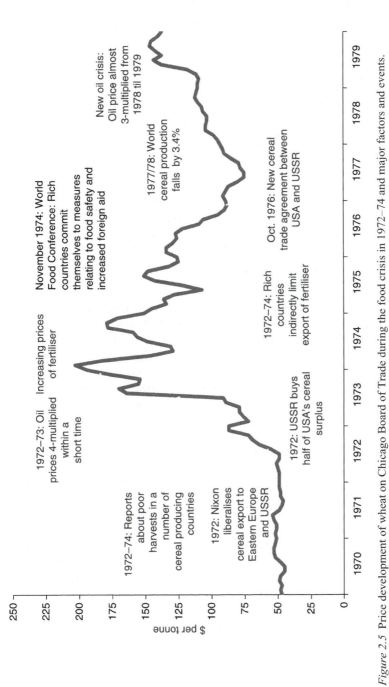

Figure 2.5 Price development of wheat on Chicago Board of Trade during the food crisis in 1972–74 and major factors and events.

Source: Heady and Fan (2010) and author's own presentation.

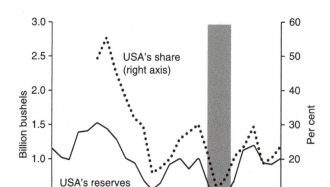

Figure 2.6 US wheat reserves in total and as a percentage of the world's total wheat reserves.

Source: Author's calculations based on USDA (2012b).

The diminished grain reserves, the growing international demand and limits to production in the large wheat-producing countries meant that grain prices rose. From July to August 1972, the price of wheat increased from US $62 to $88 per tonne.

In July 1972, the USA and the Soviet Union entered into a three-year agreement, whereby the Soviet Union committed itself to purchasing more grain from the USA. The grain was sold with export subsidies which were paid by American taxpayers. Furthermore, the Soviet Union bought a considerable amount of grain from other countries.

All in all, international food prices rose by 50 per cent during the first half of 1973, and, after a slight fall at the beginning of the year, a new price bubble developed in 1974. The Nixon Administration tried to limit domestic price increases by introducing limitations on the export of soya beans, but this resulted in considerable criticism from abroad.

The Soviet Union's large grain purchase from the USA and other grain-producing countries can be interpreted as an external shock on the demand side, which helped to create the food crisis in 1972–74. However, there were also shocks on the supply side. Bad weather (cold winters and droughts, among other things) in several of the large grain-producing countries caused a decline of 2 per cent and 3 per cent in the world's total grain production in 1972 and 1974, respectively. This decrease in production, together with a significant increase in demand, which was partly created by increasing imports to the Soviet Union and partly by a general increase in purchasing power and the population, along with historically low grain reserves, caused the price increases of the food crisis in 1972–74.

Therefore, it was hardly the decrease in production alone which created the food crisis. There have been earlier examples of similar decreases in production without the same price increases. On the contrary, it was the combination of a decline in supply and an increase in demand during a period with very low reserves which was decisive.

The oil crisis also had a significant influence on the emergence and course of the food crisis. The background is that agricultural production, especially in the large industrialised countries with significant agricultural production, is relatively energy intensive. The price of input factors such as fertiliser and plant protection products follows, to a large extent, the price of energy. Higher energy prices will, in the short or long run, result in higher prices for agricultural products.

Fertiliser not only became more expensive, but also access to fertilisers became limited and, in several cases, restrictions were placed on the export of fertilisers. This especially hit the developing countries, which had placed their money and trust in the high-yielding grain types which required relatively large amounts of fertiliser (see Box 2.1).

Box 2.1 The green revolution in relation to the food crisis of 1972–74

The green revolution refers to the significant increase in food production, particularly in South America, Africa and Asia, from the mid-1960s thanks to the introduction of new crop varieties and new production methods. The green revolution was initiated by the FAO, among others, and the new types of crops were wheat, rice and corn.

The new varieties required, among other things, the greater use of chemical pesticides and sometimes irrigation in order to achieve the desired yield increases. One of the new rice varieties could achieve a yield which was three times higher than the original varieties. Moreover, the rice matured in just four months, so that each year farmers could grow three crops instead of the previous one or two. As seen in Figure 2.7, India's rice crop yields have increased markedly since the mid-1960s – by a factor of 2.5.

The green revolution increased food production dramatically, and it therefore became possible to feed a much larger population. Thus, the green revolution played a crucial role in the food security situation in both developed and developing countries over a long period – and also for the subsequent food crises.

Cultivation methods, however, were criticised for promoting social inequality because they often required the purchase of seed, fertiliser, pesticides and sometimes machinery and equipment, which only the wealthiest farmers could afford. In addition, the green revolution also led to the increased use of pesticides, water resources and fertilisers, which has unavoidably adversely affected the environmental and ecological balance.

Therefore, there are many very different opinions about the green revolution and its consequences.

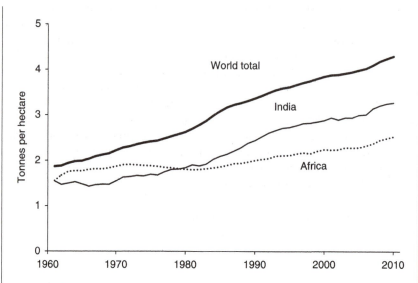

Figure 2.7 Development in yields of rice.

Source: Author's presentation based on FAO (2012).

The green revolution – advantages and disadvantages

Overall, the green revolution was very advantageous for many developing countries, as it improved their food supply considerably. The green revolution also lifted a large number of poor people out of poverty and ensured that many more escaped regressing into poverty and hunger, which would otherwise have occurred.

In many cases, inequality increased between, on the one hand, the countries which were part of the green revolution and, on the other hand, the countries that were not involved. At the same time, the green revolution had many negative environmental consequences, which have still not been satisfactorily resolved (IFPRI, 2002).

Shortages in fertiliser and a decrease in demand for fertiliser as a result of the high prices were the primary causes of, e.g., a very poor wheat harvest in India in 1974. Thus, the green revolution, on the one hand, was instrumental in increasing the supply of grain, which had a stabilising effect on the price development. On the other hand, the significant dependency on fertiliser and pesticides resulted in greater vulnerability during periods of rapidly increasing energy prices.

The food crisis of 2007–08

The entire world experienced a serious food crisis in 2007–08 when the price of important agricultural and food products increased dramatically, followed by a

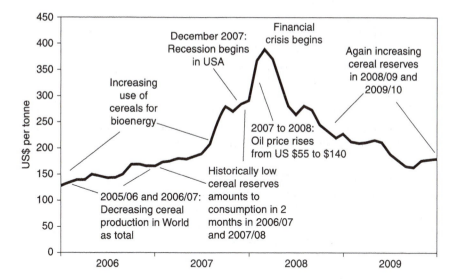

Figure 2.8 Price development of wheat on Chicago Board of Trade during the food crisis in 2007–08 and major factors and events.

Source: Author's own presentation.

subsequent fall in price. The food crisis of 2007–08 is one of the most recent and most studied food crises. This is why the causes and consequences of this particular food crisis are discussed below.

The development in the price of wheat at the time of the food crisis of 2007–08 together with significant events and influences are illustrated in Figure 2.8.

As can be seen in Figure 2.8, there were a number of factors which either directly or indirectly influenced the price of grain.

Some of these influences were temporary or random, while their effect was relatively short-lived. Other causes were somewhat longer term and structural and it was these that were instrumental in increasing the grain prices in the long term. The main causes, divided into temporary/random and structural/long term, are listed below.

Temporary/random causes

A number of temporary or random factors influenced the international grain markets in the years leading up to the beginning of the food crisis:

First, the grain harvest was significantly below average in several places. In 2006/07, the grain harvest in Australia was 50 per cent below the average for a normal year, while the USA and EU also witnessed a significant decline in production. Overall, consumption was higher than production over a number of years.

Second, several years of poor grain harvests resulted in a decline in the world's grain reserves which gradually became critically low. Low reserves always result in higher prices, whereas large reserves lead to low prices.

Third, a financial boom in many countries, including middle-income countries, resulted in an increase in food demand, especially for animal products. This increase in demand influenced the consumption of feed and thus grain prices.

Fourth, speculation exacerbated the development. As a result of a declining property market in the USA, commodities, including grain, became increasing and alternative objects for speculation, thereby increasing both demand and prices.

Finally, hoarding and panic buying exacerbated the food crisis. The significant media attention on increasing food prices increased the pressure on the market. A number of developing and middle-income countries experienced, e.g., consumers buying large amounts of rice, which was stored at home. This caused increased pressure on prices.

Structural/long-term causes

There were also a number of fundamental, structural and long-term causes of the 2007–08 food crisis. One significant cause was the increasing production of bioenergy, which was based on agricultural raw materials, including grain.

The sustained growth and increase in consumption in, among others, Asia and Central and Eastern Europe also played a role. In spite of the generally low income elasticity for food, the better living standards led to increased demand for food, including animal products in particular. An increase in animal production increases the need for grain relatively significantly, as grain is often included in the feed mix for livestock.

Another relationship was that the higher energy prices also pushed agricultural prices upward in several ways. The higher energy and fertiliser prices resulted in higher costs in agriculture, which pushed the sales price up, while the higher energy prices also meant that it became even more advantageous to produce bioenergy, which increased demand for, among other things, grain. The price of energy and grain thus became more closely connected.

Agricultural and trade policies also affected, in several areas, the global market price of agricultural and food products, and thereby also the food crisis. The previous years' liberalisation of agricultural policy in large parts of the world had contributed to increasing world market prices. Production and trade-dependent agricultural support was reduced, while supply was reduced simultaneously, which led to higher prices on the world market. At the same time, the dumping of agricultural surpluses on world markets was reduced, which also resulted in increasing world market prices. Modelling predicts, in general, significant price increases on the world market as a result of the liberalisation of agricultural policy.

During the food crisis, agricultural policy played a new role, which also affected the price level. A number of countries sought to curb domestic food prices by imposing export bans. This increased domestic supply, while the effect on the world market was that prices increased even more.

There are, therefore, many different explanations for the food crisis of 2007–08. It is clearly a complex picture in which many factors played a part. At the same time, some of the factors were interdependent. For example, a poor harvest resulted in lower reserves, and high energy prices increased the grain prices through more expensive fertiliser and through increased bioenergy production.

There was also a certain element of 'convergence of several random unfortunate events' all at once. For example, the prioritisation of bioenergy came exactly at a time when grain reserves were already low. The main causes of the food crisis are analysed in greater detail in the next section.

The importance of reserves

Although the picture is complex, it is nevertheless striking that the mere size of reserves is a very important explanation for the development in the price of grain. One can, to a large extent, explain and partially predict the future of grain prices based on current and future reserves.

Over the past 25 years, there has been a clear correlation between, on the one side, the size of grain reserves and, on the other, international grain prices (see Figure 2.9).

As can be seen in Figure 2.9, during the food crisis, grain reserves were very low (dashed line) and only amounted to approximately 17 per cent of world

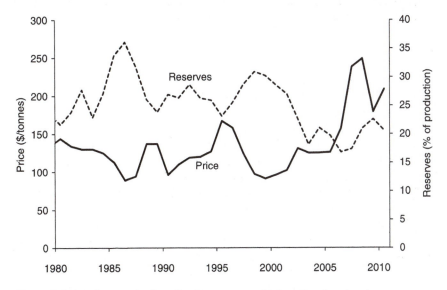

Figure 2.9 Development in size of grain reserves and international grain prices.

Source: Author's calculations based on USDA (2012a, 2012b).

Note: The reserves are the world's total grain reserves as a percentage of production; the price is a weighted average for the USA.

production, which is equivalent to approximately two months' consumption. The grain price is typically high when stocks are low, as they were during the 2007–08 food crisis, as well as during a period in the mid-1990s. It is also noteworthy that a slight reduction in reserves is not as crucial if the reserves are already high. In contrast, a reduction in already low reserves drives prices up.

Reserves thus act as an effective buffer, which helps to stabilise the market. When the reserves are sufficiently large, years with significant fluctuations in production will not cause the same fluctuations in prices, which results in more predictable markets and the avoidance of 'shocks' that dramatic increases in grain prices give to the entire value chain.

Figure 2.9 also illustrates how even a slight increase in grain reserves is apparently enough to drive prices down to normal levels.

Against this background, reserves should not necessarily be considered as 'surplus' or 'overproduction': themes which characterised the public debate some years ago. Reserves of a certain size are effective buffers that benefit the market and provide better stability. What is important is that reserves should be used as a tool to stabilise the market and they should not be a result of an artificially high and subsidised price arising from agricultural subsidies.

The size of the grain reserves is partly dependent on production and partly on consumption. If there is a year with a particularly good harvest, and thus high production, reserves will typically increase. The consumption of grain is relatively stable from year to year, as there is an almost constant yearly increase. Therefore, it is especially production and fluctuations in production from year to year which contributes to changes in the size of reserves.

Bioenergy

Bioenergy was one of the major reasons for the increases in grain price during the 2007–08 food crisis. Bioenergy may also contribute to continued relatively high grain prices in the future.

Bioenergy, or biofuels, which primarily consist of ethanol and biodiesel, can be divided into first- and second-generation biofuels. First-generation biofuels are typically based on sugar cane or corn and biodiesel, while second-generation biofuels are typically made of cellulose, hemi-cellulose or lignin.

Biofuels use, to a greater or lesser extent, agricultural products as raw materials or compete, at least, with agricultural products for agricultural land. Therefore, there is a close interaction between biofuels, grain prices and food crises.

On the one hand, there has been a strong focus on bioenergy and other CO_2-neutral energy sources in recent years. From 2000 to 2010, the production of biofuels therefore increased more than sixfold (see Figure 2.10).

The USA and Brazil are still the largest producers of biofuels. While Brazil uses sugar cane as a raw material for ethanol production, the USA mainly uses corn.

As can be seen in Figure 2.10, leading up to the 2007–08 food crisis there was a dramatic growth in the total world production of biofuels. Subsequently, growth has slowed, but there is still a yearly increase in production.

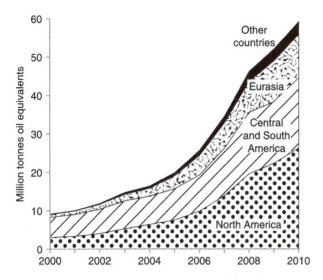

Figure 2.10 World production of biofuels by continent.

Source: BP (2012).

It is expected that the increase in the total global production of biofuels will continue into the future. Even though uncertain factors such as oil, energy and grain prices have a major influence on the profitability of bioenergy production, and despite many political agendas, there is general agreement that bioenergy will continue to have a role in the overall energy supply.

The OECD-FAO (Organisation for Economic Co-operation and Development in collaboration with the UN's Food and Agricultural Organization) expects that total world production of biofuels will increase by approximately 50 per cent by 2020 (see Figure 2.11).

The growth in bioenergy production should be seen against the background of a desire to limit the consumption of fossil fuels including CO_2 emissions. In addition, many countries have a strong desire to become less dependent on imports of oil from 'insecure regimes'. Therefore, there is strong political pressure to promote bioenergy development.

On the other hand, it is certain that, with rising grain prices, it becomes less and less advantageous to produce bioenergy. Some bioenergy plants will therefore have to be abandoned. At the same time, the need for further public funding to make plants economically viable also increases. Finally, doubts will be continually raised about the environmental value of ethanol production.

All in all, it can be concluded that there are political, supplier, environmental and agricultural interests at stake when it comes to the future development of bioenergy production. The advantages and disadvantages change continuously in line with the development of new technologies, fluctuating prices for grain and energy, and the international economic and political situation.

Regardless of all these uncertainties, there is no doubt that bioenergy production will put increasing pressure on grain prices in the short and long term. Today, bioenergy production takes up almost 5 per cent of total world grain production. Given the size of the reserves and the sensitivity of the global grain market to changes in supply and demand, bioenergy remains a significant influence on prices. There is considerable disagreement about the extent to which bioenergy actually influences grain prices. Different analyses reach the conclusion that bioenergy can explain anywhere between 20 per cent and 70 per cent of the increase in grain prices in 2007/08 (see, e.g., World Bank, 2008 and Box 2.2).

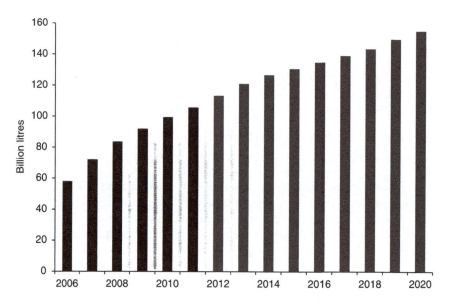

Figure 2.11 World production of ethanol.

Source: OECD-FAO (2011).

***Box 2.2* Various assessments of the impact of bioenergy on grain prices**

> The rapid expansion (of biofuel production) over the past decade contributed to the 2008/09 jump in food prices, though findings from different studies provide a broad range of estimates for the exact impact.
>
> World Bank (2010)

> Significant growth in ethanol production is important in explaining corn price determination.
>
> Fortenberry and Park (2008), University of Wisconsin

The use of corn to make ethanol in the USA is helping to lift the grain price worldwide . . . FAO has been raising its voice against using food to produce bio energy.

> Jose Graziano da Silva, director of FAO (2012)

A number of studies . . . have attributed a sizable proportion (up to one third or more) of increases in international market prices of cereals and oils to the strong growth in crop-based biofuels programs.

> IFPRI (2012)

Speculation

It is generally agreed that speculation, to a greater or lesser extent, helped to reinforce the increase in prices during the food crisis in 2007–08. At the same time as the value of real estate fell in the USA, investors shifted focus from the real estate market to new areas with the potential for increasing value. Thus, the commodities market, including the grain market, received greater attention.

Financial institutions, which usually have no direct interest in traded goods, bought large quantities of grain futures in anticipation of future price increases. The growing interest in investing on the major international grain exchanges thus helped to exacerbate development in this period through sharp price increases. The extent of the speculation is impossible to quantify exactly. This is partly because hedging, which is not speculative but is rather an attempt to predict future prices, also spread to a degree.

As Box 2.3 indicates, there is considerable disagreement regarding the extent to which speculation was a cause for the price increases during the 2007–08 food crisis.

Box 2.3 Assessment of the effect of speculation on the food crisis and price increases

Food price fluctuation driven by financial speculation – UN report

Both the surging food prices from 2007 to 2008 and their subsequent drop in some areas are a result of large-scale speculation.

> UN News Center (2009)

Based on new data and empirical analysis, the study finds that index funds did *not* cause a bubble in commodity futures prices.

> Irwin and Sanders (2010)

Financial speculation likely played no or only a small role in the increase in rice prices.

Timmer (2009)

World set for new food crisis in 2010, UN warns

It was a crisis linked to the evolution of prices on the international market, set by speculation. It was a financial phenomenon primarily and it was not linked to insufficient food being produced.

Olivier De Schutter, the UN's special rapporteur on the right to food
(26 November 2009)

Financial speculation and the food crisis

Financial speculation in basic food commodities played a key role in the 2007–08 food price crisis which pushed millions of people deeper into hunger, says economic historian Peter Timmer.

World Food Programme (6 February 2009)

The drastic increase of food prices in the period 2006–8 spurred fears of global food insecurity. Apart from actual changes in supply and demand of some commodities, the upward swing might also have been amplified by speculation in organized futures markets. However, limiting or banning speculative trading might do more harm than good.

FAO, Policy Brief 9 (June 2010c)

Grain and other agricultural products are traded, for the most part, on international commodity exchanges in the form of futures, i.e. contracts which specify delivery of a given quantity of grain at a certain place at a future date, which is often several months in the future.

However, there are clear signs that there was a surge in interest in investing in grain exchanges prior to the food crisis. In a normal year, trade and transactions on the futures market for wheat on the Chicago grain exchange constitute the equivalent of 20 times the USA's annual wheat harvest. In 2007–08, this increased to more than 80 times the USA's annual wheat harvest (see IFPRI, 2008). It is also noteworthy that the number of outstanding futures and options contracts on the commodity markets worldwide was relatively stable for several years up till 2006, after which it increased significantly (see Figure 2.12).

As can be seen in Figure 2.12, the number of outstanding futures and option contracts on the commodities market rose significantly in 2006. Immediately after, there was a large increase in prices on several commodity markets, including the grain market. This almost parallel increase is an indication that speculation helped push grain prices up and is thus one of the causes of the food crisis. Prices can increase simply because everyone expects them to increase.

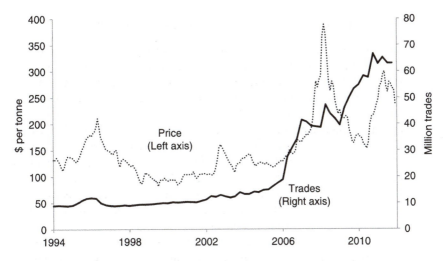

Figure 2.12 Number of outstanding futures and options contracts on commodity markets (millions) globally and international wheat prices.

Source: BIS (several years) and USDA (2012b).

Box 2.4 Speculation: market influence or just betting?

On the one hand, speculation in financial contracts can have a significant effect on the market price – at least in the short term. In particular, a relatively large number of buyers on the market can increase demand and hence the price. This was exactly what happened at the start of the food crisis, when investors fled the property market and sought new investment areas, including the commodity and grain markets. In these circumstances, it is no longer just the relationship between supply and demand in the real market that determines the price.

On the other hand, one can say that speculation represents financial betting on the future, which does not affect the price in the long term, because, at the end of the day, the price is determined by supply and demand. Betting takes place because some actors have a particular expectation regarding the future price development, but the bets themselves do not change with market conditions. Betting or speculation does not bring more or less grain or other commodities to the market. The speculators are therefore just 'messengers' or 'signallers', who think long term and are the first to evaluate and predict market developments and have the resources to make good market analyses.

Box 2.5 **How does speculation in commodities take place?**

Investment and speculation in food products typically takes place through so-called futures contracts. Futures were previously a tool for, among others, grain traders so that they could protect themselves against future price fluctuations by making contracts about the future delivery of specified amounts of grain at predetermined prices.

Gradually, futures contracts have become a standardised form of bonds, which now can also be used by other investors, including pension funds, investment companies and other large funds. Furthermore, many banks have now developed investment certificates, which can be relatively easily used by private investors. Thus it has become significantly easier for many more investors, large and small, to get access to commodities markets and to speculate on future price development.

The entrance of these new actors on the market has resulted in the volume of the commodities market increasing significantly in the last few years. However, on average, an actual trade in goods only takes place in approximately 10 per cent of cases – in all the other cases there is only talk of rights and obligations to buy and sell, which never become actualised.

The world's largest futures market for agricultural produce is located in Chicago (CME Group Inc.). Here the price of, e.g., corn, wheat and soya beans is established, which often guides the global market price.

Conversely, we do not see quite the same parallel development with decreasing prices and the food crisis's gradual end in 2008. The correlation between futures and option contracts and the price development of wheat is therefore not entirely clear.

Analyses from the European Commission (2008) also confirm that the number of financial investors on the corn, wheat and soya bean markets more than doubled after 2005 and in March 2008 represented nearly half of all trade on the Chicago Board of Trade.

UNCTAD (2009) concludes that the price bubble in the food sector in 2007–08 was partly due to widespread speculation and that there is a need for greater control and regulation in this area in order to avoid similar price fluctuations in the future.

A study by the Farm Foundation (2009) examined more than 20 reports and scientific articles and concluded that speculation probably played a crucial role, but that it was not the primary cause of price fluctuations in recent years.

IFPRI (2009) conducted a statistical analysis and concluded that the degree of speculation in agricultural commodities was on the increase leading up to the food crisis; that the difference between spot and futures prices increased; and that speculation may have affected prices, although this cannot be proven.

IATP (2008) considers that speculation was a major cause of price volatility during the food crisis.

Irwin and Sanders (2010) analysed, on behalf of the OECD, the importance of the special index funds. Index funds are a new special investment tool, which makes it possible for both large and small investors to invest in commodity markets, whereby various commodities are typically pooled into one index. The conclusion of the analysis was that these index funds did not cause the food crisis or the price bubble for commodities in 2007–08.

There is, however, general agreement that the precise significance of the speculation is far from being determined and that there is a need for further analyses. In several places it has also been argued, from the political side, that a framework for speculation on agricultural and commodity markets needs to be defined in order to reduce the harmful effects that speculation can have on market stability.

Thus, the exact significance of the speculation has not been determined. There are, however, clear indications that the real estate market collapse led to many investors moving into the commodities market in 2007 and that this large interest from buyers helped increase grain prices in the short term.

However, speculation in itself will not change the supply and demand of grain. Speculation is rather a kind of messenger or signal, which indicates the expectations for the future market.

Finally, there is general agreement that the food crisis and the increasing prices in 2007–08 were caused by a complex interaction of several factors. The size of reserves, however, does seem to be a very important explanation for the price increase. Low or declining reserves result in price increases, while large or increasing reserves push the price down. Speculators can often spot the development in reserves in time and, in many cases, are ahead of the market, and are therefore able to counteract an extreme development in the market.

Consequences of the food crisis

The food crisis in 2007–08 had several different consequences, even though it was relatively brief. In some areas, the situation quickly returned to normal, but in other areas there were long-term consequences. Some of the main consequences are discussed in the following sections.

Increased hunger and malnutrition in the poorest developing countries

The food crisis led to a serious increase in famine in several developing countries. Nearly a billion people went hungry every day and the food crisis increased the number of starving people by more than 100 million.

Millions of people spend more than 80 per cent of their income on food, and there is a clear correlation between, on the one hand, a country's economic development and welfare and, on the other hand, a country's consumption of food in relation to its total consumption. This illustrates how food crises particularly affect the poorest developing countries, for which a doubling of food prices has serious consequences.

On the other hand, more expensive food generally does not affect the rich, industrialised countries significantly. Although, even within the richer countries, there are population groups which spend a relatively large proportion of their income on food.

Changes in agricultural policy and support

The legitimacy and development of agricultural support also came into focus following the food crisis. On the one hand, it was argued that the food crisis illustrated the need for sustained agricultural policy in order to control the markets.

For example, the French Minister of Agriculture commented on the food crisis and the volatile agricultural prices in April 2008: 'We are now witnessing the consequences of too much free trade liberalism' (see *Financial Times*, 2008). At the same time, he recommended that other countries adopt the same trade barriers that existed in the EU's agricultural policy.

There were also a number of cases where several countries imposed export bans or export taxes to ensure adequate domestic supplies at a reasonable price. The number of restrictions on exports increased significantly as a consequence of the food crisis (see, e.g. OECD-FAO, 2009 and WTO, 2009).

On the other hand, others believed that the increasing prices rendered farmer support superfluous, and that it was thus a good time to remove the last remnants of agricultural subsidies.

Box 2.6 Different types of crisis after 2007

The latest food crises have taken place in periods with other significant crises. These other crises, including in particular the financial crisis and the subsequent recession, have both influenced and, to a certain extent, obscured the effect of the food crises. The financial crisis resulted in reduced demand and curbed grain prices in 2008. Conversely, the financial crisis also exacerbated the turmoil and market uncertainty which emerged in the aftermath of the food crisis. Figure 2.13 shows a schematic representation of the latest crises.

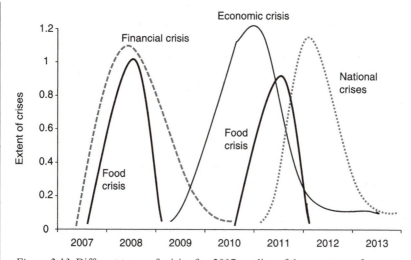

Figure 2.13 Different types of crisis after 2007: outline of the sequence of events.
Source: Author's presentation.

Generally, the following are examples of adjustments in agricultural policy as a result of the food crisis (see, e.g., OECD-FAO, 2009):

- Import duties were reduced or suspended.
- Export barriers were introduced.
- Public reserves of grain, etc. were reduced.
- Domestic production was supported.
- Set-aside and quotas and other supply-limiting measures were reduced or removed.
- Price controls were introduced.
- Bioenergy based on agricultural commodities was assigned a lower priority.

Most of these approaches were subsequently reversed as the food crisis came to an end.

Agricultural markets recover

The market mechanism and farmers' response to the higher prices fully or partially solved the food crisis. The price increases subsequently influenced international grain production: larger areas of land were sown with grain, and the demand for fertilisers, pesticides and other agricultural chemical aids increased in spite of increasing prices. Thus, grain production increased to its highest level ever.

This development showed that agricultural markets, and not least the supply of grain, helped to restore a new balance after the dramatic price increases.

The conclusion is, therefore, that temporary, high grain prices have historically resulted in intensified production. The result, therefore, is increasing supply and thus declining prices after a short period. A world market price which is substantially above the equilibrium price (which was the case during the food crisis) is therefore unsustainable in the long term.

Price instability leads to increased profits

When considerable price fluctuations occur on the market and when the market becomes unpredictable and perhaps obscure for a period, one often finds that there is a good opportunity to increase profit margins in the various links of the food production chain. When the market and prices are stable, competition works better, but when there is turmoil, it is easier to hide or justify exceptional price increases.

More expensive agricultural commodities should not necessarily result in significantly more expensive food. Agricultural products, such as raw materials for the food industry, represent a relatively limited and declining share of the finished products which are sold to consumers. This also means that increasing prices for agricultural commodities do not materialise to the same degree in the retail link nor are they passed on to the consumer (see also Chapter 12).

Changes in food consumption

During the 2007–08 food crisis, increasing food prices had a direct negative impact on consumers as their purchasing power was reduced. In general, food consumption is relatively inelastic in relation to both prices and income, but changes in consumption due to price increases did occur. The composition of food consumption was changed as both discount and private labels (retail chains' own brands) achieved a greater market share.

The impact of the food crisis is, however, difficult to determine precisely, as the financial crisis also affected the economic situation and consumption at the same time.

Political instability

The food crisis led to political and social upheaval in several places in the world. Egypt and Haiti are good examples of the desperation and disorder that arose in the wake of the increasing food prices. In some areas, the food crisis and the more expensive food was not necessarily the decisive cause, but was rather a triggering factor.

In April 2008, the World Bank estimated that 33 countries risked social unrest as a direct consequence of the high food and energy prices (World Bank, 2008).

Economic turmoil in the entire food sector

The food crisis had both winners and losers. The winners were typically farmers with large crop or milk production, who experienced large increases in their prices. The losers were typically pork and poultry producers who had to pay much more for their feed, but did not receive sufficient price increases for their products to offset the additional costs.

Furthermore, a number of farmers, more or less randomly, were squeezed financially because they entered into long-term agreements to purchase feed at an unfortunate time.

There were also significant repercussions in the food industry. Pig slaughter-houses received far fewer pigs, and thus a significant overcapacity arose. Several feed and agribusinesses also got into serious financial difficulties due to the dramatically fluctuating grain prices. Dairy and sugar factories were also pressured into increasing their prices for agricultural commodities, which led to increasing costs.

The food crisis of 2010–11

The most recent food crisis started in July 2010, when international grain prices rose sharply. From early July to early August, the international wheat price rose by approximately 60 per cent (see Figure 2.14). Thus began a new global food crisis, albeit relatively short lived and minor.

The reason for the crisis was that heat waves, drought, crop failures and fires in Russia, Ukraine and Kazakhstan ('RUK countries') caused the international grain exchanges to react dramatically. The wheat harvest in these three countries

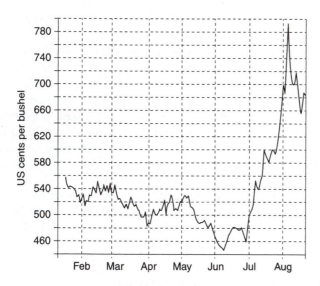

Figure 2.14 Development in international wheat prices (2010).

Source: CME Group (2012).

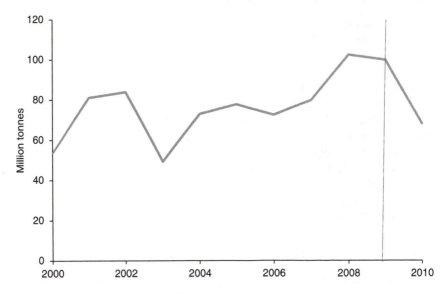

Figure 2.15 Wheat production in RUK countries.

Source: FAO (2012).

Note: RUK countries = Russia, the Ukraine and Kazakhstan.

decreased by more than 30 per cent in 2010 and it became the worst harvest since 2003 (see Figure 2.15).

The drought in Russia was the worst in the country for 130 years. Harvest forecasts for the three countries were continually downgraded during the summer as the drought continued. At the same time, wheat prices on the international grain exchanges increased. The price of grain rose dramatically, as it was predicted that grain exports from Russia, Ukraine and Kazakhstan would fall significantly.

In August 2010, the Russian Prime Minister, Vladimir Putin, announced that Russia would impose a ban on the export of grain for the remainder of the year. Such export bans reduce the supply of grain on the world market considerably. Russia's ban on grain exports caused further fear of a wheat shortage on the international grain markets, as it would significantly reduce the supply of grain, which caused international prices to increase even further.

Figure 2.16 illustrates the development in the price of wheat on the world market as well as the significant events and influences at the time of the 2010–11 food crisis. As can be seen, there were a number of different factors in Russia, which directly or indirectly affected the price of grain.

Russia and the future of the international grain market

The Soviet Union and Russia had a major impact on the food crisis of 1973–74 and 2010–11 respectively. In 1973–74, the Soviet Union was a large consumer of

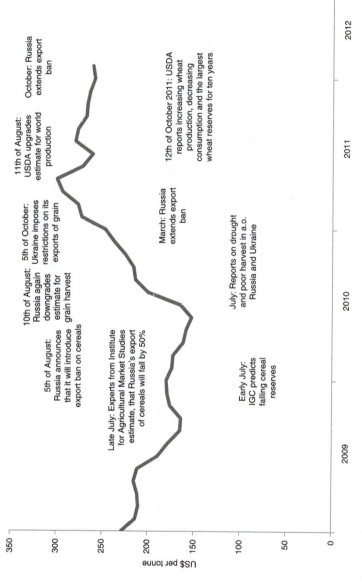

Figure 2.16 Price development of wheat on Chicago Board of Trade during the food crisis in 2010–11 and major factors and events.

Source: Author's own presentation.

wheat on the international market, while in 2010–11 Russia's supply of wheat to the international market was far less than expected.

In addition, Russia and the Soviet Union's role in the international grain markets has changed fundamentally – and repeatedly – over the past 50–60 years. There are also signs that Russia is about to regain its former position as one of the world's largest grain exporters: a development which will probably continue in the coming years. In any case, this development may have significant consequences for future agricultural and food markets.

Against this background, it is important to shed light on Russia and the Soviet Union's previous position on the international grain markets, the reasons for the development and change, and future trends.

In a historical perspective, it is interesting that the former Soviet Union (USSR) was one of the most important producers and exporters of wheat in the 1960s. Subsequently, wheat production decreased, and it was not until around 2000 that the situation began to reverse (see Figure 2.17).

As shown in Figure 2.17, the USSR accounted for 25–30 per cent of world wheat production in the early 1960s, yet only accounted for 7 per cent of the world's population. The USSR's share of world's total wheat production had declined to about 10 per cent by the year 2000, after which it began to rise again.

Wheat export has developed in a similar fashion. In the 1960s, the USSR was a major exporter of wheat, but its importance diminished and by 1990 exports were insignificant. After 1990, exports increased again, dramatically. This development meant that the USSR went from being a major net exporter of wheat to being

Figure 2.17 Share of total global wheat production for the USSR and specifically Russia.

Source: Author's calculations based on FAO (2012).

Note: Rolling 5-year average.

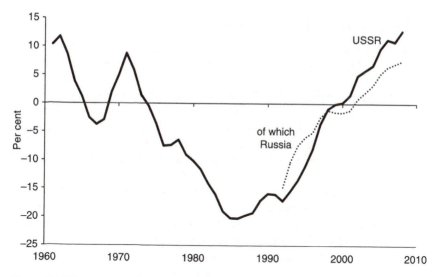

Figure 2.18 Net exports of wheat from the USSR, specifically Russia.

Source: Author's calculations based on FAO (2012).

Note: Rolling 5-year average.

an even larger net importer. In the 1980s, the USSR was the world's largest importer of wheat.

At the end of the 1970s and the start of the 1980s, the USA entered into agreements with the USSR regarding large consignments of grain, the so-called 'Grain Agreements', and significant political interests were at stake during the negotiations for these agreements. After the fall of communism, Russia and the former Soviet republics, now as one, once again became major net exporters of wheat (see Figure 2.18).

There are several explanations as to why there has been a dramatic increase in wheat production and export in the RUK countries since the early 1990s:

First, the abolition of the communist planned economy and the introduction of a market economy had a positive effect. Prices were determined based on supply and demand, which stimulated both production and trade.

Second, crop yields started to increase again. The market economy, together with better access especially to chemical fertilisers, resulted in significant increases in yields.

Third, livestock production decreased significantly after the collapse of the Soviet Union and thus also domestic demand for grain and other feed. Livestock and meat production was nearly halved during this period, while in Russia the decrease was even greater. With the decline in livestock production and thereby the reduced demand for feed, grain became available for other uses, which helped to increase grain exports.

Box 2.7 Ukraine – Europe's bread basket

Ukraine has some of the best agricultural land in Europe. The whole of central and southern Ukraine lies within the so-called black-soil belt, with particularly fertile soils.

Ukraine was Europe's bread basket from the middle of the 1800s to the revolution in 1917. Increasing grain exports from, among others, Ukraine around 1870 resulted in a significant drop in world market prices for grain and it was one of the primary reasons for a reorganisation of agricultural production in several countries in the direction of greater livestock production.

Forced collectivisation after the revolution in 1917 started a temporary decline in Ukrainian agricultural production. It was not until 1968 that Ukraine achieved the same level of agricultural production as in 1913 – the year before the First World War. In the years that followed, the huge potential of Ukrainian agriculture was not exploited.

Future expectations

The US Department of Agriculture, USDA, expects that wheat exports from the RUK countries will have increased by 50 per cent by 2019. Thus, these three countries collectively will become the world's most important wheat exporter. Russia and Ukraine will thus return to their historical role as major exporters of wheat, which they were particularly at the start of the twentieth century.

Similarly, the USA will lose its position as the world's largest wheat exporter. Right up to the mid-1980s, the USA accounted for up to 40 per cent of total world wheat exports. Since then, the USA's share of the world's total wheat exports has fallen so that, today, the USA only accounts for approximately 20 per cent, which corresponds approximately to Russia, Ukraine and Kazakhstan's combined share. The USA's share is expected to decline further in the coming years. Wheat export shares for these countries from 1991 to 2008 and USDA's projections to 2019 are shown in Figure 2.19.

The RUK countries' notable entry onto the international grain markets could also lead to greater market instability for a number of reasons. First, the climate in the three countries is relatively unstable. Both temperature and precipitation vary widely, which results in significant fluctuations in grain production from year to year, which is exactly what occurred in 2010.

Second, the three countries also seem willing to use drastic trade policy measures to ensure domestic grain supplies. During the food crisis of 2007–08, all three countries tried to restrict or even ban grain exports in order to ensure abundant and affordable domestic grain.

This somewhat controversial trade policy should also be seen in the light of the fact that neither Russia nor Kazakhstan were members of the WTO, while Ukraine

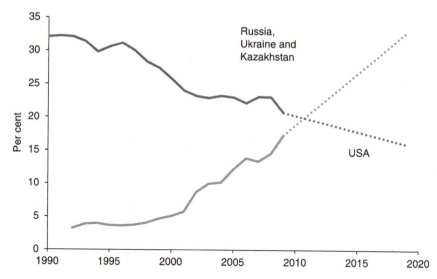

Figure 2.19 Wheat exports from RUK countries and from the USA, including USDA's projections.

Source: Author's presentation based on FAO (2012) and USDA (2010b).

Note: 5-year rolling average.

did not become a member until 2008. Overall, only eight of the original 15 Soviet republics were members of the WTO in 2012. This is important because the introduction of significant export restrictions or bans is directly against the agreements of the WTO.

Lessons learnt from the food crises

The most recent three–four food crises have shown that food supply, food markets and food companies are vulnerable when external influences create the significant price increases that characterise food crises. It is therefore important to learn from the lessons of past food crises so that future food crises can be avoided or their effects reduced.

A consistent feature of the recent food crises is that the *USA* and *Russia/USSR* have played an important role, on both the supply and demand side. Bearing in mind the expectations that the RUK-countries' share of the international trade in grain will increase, this role will probably not change in the future.

It is also noteworthy that *energy* has played an important role. In 1972–74, increases in the price of oil helped to drive grain prices up, while in 2007–08, increased demand for grain for bioenergy production helped to drive up prices. Oil and grain prices seem to increasingly develop concurrently. As illustrated in Figure 2.20, the prices of oil and wheat have developed in much the same direction during the past decade.

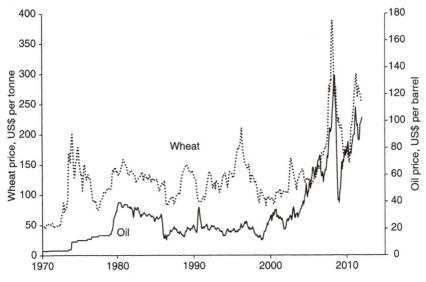

Figure 2.20 Development in prices for crude oil and wheat.

Source: Federal Reserve Economic Data (2012) and USDA (2012b).

Note: Monthly data.

There are several explanations for the correlation between oil and grain prices, and why the correlation has become stronger in recent years. First, agriculture's dependence on energy increases as the sector becomes more industrialised and increasingly efficient. Large-scale production, structural development, crop improvements, increasing productivity, etc. increase the demand for energy. This is either directly through mechanisation or indirectly through pesticide use. When energy prices rise, the cost of grain production also rises, which eventually results in increasing grain prices.

Second, grain is being increasingly used for energy, which means that increasing energy prices make it more advantageous to produce bioenergy based on, e.g., grain. The demand for, and thus also the price of, grain therefore increases when the energy price increases.

The size of reserves has played a significant role in all three food crises. This was particularly the case during the first two food crises, which occurred when the total wheat reserves were at their lowest (see Figure 2.21).

During the most recent food crisis of 2010–11, wheat stocks were relatively high, but at the same time, the world's total corn reserves were relatively low.

Another characteristic of the three food crises is that *trade and agricultural policy* has played a role. It has been possible to identify interventions in the market economy in the form of export subsidies, export bans, export tariffs, state trading,

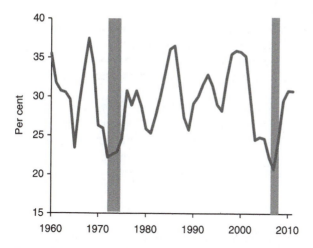

Figure 2.21 Total world wheat stocks, as a percentage of production.

Source: Author's calculations based on USDA (2012b).

Note: Shading indicates the food crises of 1972–74 and 2007–08.

the build up of domestic reserves, etc. (see Nomura, 2010). A further general characteristic is that trade and agricultural policy interventions have primarily been introduced to stabilise domestic markets, but these interventions, in many cases, have upset the stability of the international market.

All three food crises have been affected by, and have more or less created, *supply and demand shocks*. The demand shock came when the Soviet Union purchased large quantities of grain from the USA during the 1972–74 crisis, together with increasing demand for grain for bioenergy production up to the 2007–08 and 2010–11 crises.

Finally, significant economic growth and increasing purchasing power in Asia, especially in China, has led to increased demand, which was also a contributing factor to the recent food crises.

Supply shocks – in the form of declining supply due to crop failures, drought, etc. – have also been decisive in all three food crises. A further common characteristic is that all previous food crises have been relatively *brief and temporary*. All started with significant and rapid price increases and ended with equivalent price reductions.

Finally, food crises have often been influenced by other crises. The food crisis in 1951–52 was a direct result of the Korean War; the food crisis of 1972–74 coincided with the first oil crisis; and the food crisis of 2007–08 occurred at almost the same time as the start of the financial crisis. The only food crisis which was not directly influenced by, or was a consequence of, other major crises, is the food crisis of 2010–11.

Food crisis perspectives

The food crises have proved to be relatively short lived. Dramatic price increases followed by a significant fall occurred in less than one year, from mid-2007 to mid-2008. The food crisis in 2010 started with price increases of more than 50 per cent in one month, but the year after, prices had already begun to decrease.

Food crises have also illustrated that abundant amounts of food at continually declining real prices are not a matter of course. The worsening famine in a number of developing countries also changed the perception that the international food situation will improve continuously. Therefore, the food crises have affected the public debate, and new perspectives are now on the agenda.

How can a new food crisis be avoided?

Even though food crises are short-lived and are often resolved by the market mechanism, they still have serious consequences. At the same time, we can expect a future with relatively low reserves, demand pressures from the bioenergy sector and a constantly growing world population to feed.

A new food crisis can thus quickly arise again. Food crises will therefore continue to be on the agenda – especially in order to analyse how we can avoid another serious crisis.

Does the market work?

The food crises have created a debate over whether the market actually works, whether unrestricted free market forces are sufficient to prevent future food crises and whether there is a need for intervention in the form of reserve-building, regulation of speculation, support for local agricultural production, etc.

Limiting speculation may seem difficult, as there is always a grey area between speculation and normal hedging. Increased reserves, controlled by a supernational body, could stabilise prices and eliminate much of the incentive to speculate. Building and controlling international grain reserves as buffers against dramatic price fluctuations could be extremely effective, but it requires substantial political support from the most significant grain-producing countries.

Supply has proved to respond quickly to price increases, and the market adapts relatively quickly to a new equilibrium. Yet turmoil broke out in the short period of adjustment, resulting in many serious and adverse effects. Therefore, the task involves avoiding new food crises and limiting the most serious effects as much as possible.

The emergence of dilemmas

A series of political and moral dilemmas and questions have emerged in the aftermath of the food crises:

- 'Fuel vs food': Can we allow ourselves to use food for energy when there is a lack of food, and people are dying of starvation?
- 'Land – for nature or for food?': Should we cultivate nature areas to ensure a more stable food supply?
- 'Food and new technology': Should we allow genetically modified organisms (GMOs) in order to produce more food and create a more stable food supply?
- 'Food policy and environmental policy': How should one balance the environment and food in a world of food shortages?

Will globalisation stop?

The food crises illustrated that the world is still vulnerable and that the stable and affordable supply of food is not a given – not even for the economically advanced countries. Countries that are heavily dependent on food imports are hit hard, both economically and politically, when food prices increase dramatically. Therefore, it is not without reason that some fear that food crises can halt or delay globalisation. There is widespread agreement that food is still such an essential necessity good for the population that countries cannot afford to be overly dependent on food imports.

Access to stable food supplies must be guaranteed through buffer reserves, increased domestic production, strategic trade agreements and the like. The specific measures in the form of stricter trade barriers and support for domestic production have already been established. Therefore, food crises might prove to be an obstacle or a brake on the current wave of globalisation and liberalisation.

Unstable markets are inevitable in the future

In many countries, agricultural policy has ensured higher and more stable prices on domestic markets than on the world market for many years – more for some products than others. This will soon be history because, with the liberalisation of agricultural subsidies in most countries, it will no longer be possible to regulate the market to the same degree.

One can no longer enter the market and reduce price fluctuations through building up reserves or releasing reserves, or through the control of imports and exports. Therefore, we will in all likelihood experience considerable price fluctuations in the coming years. Against this background, new measures to stabilise the markets are essential. Insurance schemes, due date trading, futures, etc. will be some of the instruments that farmers will have to consider in the future. These new schemes will probably be offered with help from the government, the EU, the food industry, the financial sector or similar. However, it is most likely that the EU will only contribute by establishing and organising the systems, but will not provide subsidies or other forms of financial support.

Agricultural development in developing countries

The developing countries were, for the most part, hit the hardest by the food crises. A large proportion of poor people's income is spent on food, so they are hit hard when prices increase. At the same time, local governments were not financially able to remedy the worsening famine. In addition, many farmers did not benefit from the higher market prices because they did not have sufficient access to a well-functioning market, or because others in the chain took advantage of the price increase.

Therefore, there is now growing recognition that improving agricultural development in developing countries is one of the keys to limiting the damage from a future food crisis. In the long term, developing countries must produce more food; otherwise they will be too sensitive to future price increases.

In particular, developed countries must increase aid in order to develop agriculture, agricultural production, agricultural markets, and technology and efficiency in the agricultural sector. The potential for increasing food production in developing countries is significant. Increasing earnings and production in agriculture will have a significant spillover effect on the overall economy of developing countries.

Are high world food prices positive or negative?

Especially before the 2007–08 food crisis, low world prices for agricultural products were considered damaging to the food situation in developing countries. Low food prices hamper agricultural production in developing countries, and thus local food supply becomes unstable. When developed countries, through import tariffs and export subsidies, etc. push world prices down, it reduces the incentive for developing countries to produce their own food. During the food crises, however, high world market prices undermined the food situation in developing countries as more expensive food, or a lack of food, naturally creates hunger and famine.

The explanation for the two different assessments is the time horizon. In the short term, low food prices benefit consumers, while more expensive food in the longer term can develop local agricultural production, which benefits the supply of food in the area.

Malthus again

The food crisis has also meant that Malthus is once more on the agenda. Thomas Robert Malthus (1766–1834) was an English economist who is best known for his pessimistic view of the relationship between population growth and food supply.

According to Malthus, the quantity of food determines population growth. It was Malthus's assumption that food production increases linearly, while population grows exponentially when food is not a limiting factor (see Figure 2.22).

Have we reached the limit, where food production can no longer keep up with population growth? The food crises have meant that this question has become relevant once more.

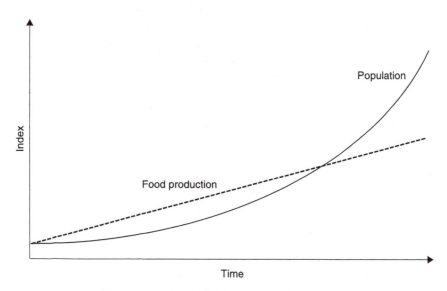

Figure 2.22 Malthus's assumption regarding the development in food production and population.

Source: Author's presentation.

Malthus did not, however, take into account the significant efficiency gains that have occurred in agriculture all over the world, which have the potential to continue for many years to come. Chemical fertilisers, pesticides, crop improvements, large-scale production, agricultural advice, education, etc. will continue to be significant drivers of increased production.

It is likely that Malthus was not completely right, but it requires a sustained effort to find and develop effective and sustainable technologies that can increase the world's total agricultural and food production.

Box 2.8 Malthus's theory: reasons for its lack of explanatory power

First and foremost, population growth is not exponential, as there is a connection between economic growth and population growth. In the short term, increased welfare leads to accelerated population growth, as a result of improved disease control and thereby reduced mortality. However, in the longer term, increased welfare results in a decreased birth rate, which results in a significant fall in the population growth.

Another factor which Malthus did not consider is technological advancements, which have made significant increases in agricultural productivity possible. When Malthus was alive, an individual could obtain enough food from an area of approximately 20,000 m^2. However, today, 2,000 m^2 is enough (Evans, 1998), which nicely illustrates the technological advancements in agriculture during this period. The improved food situation during recent decades was, to a large degree, created by increased productivity. Since 1960, the world's total wheat production has increased by 150 per cent. Over the same period, the land area used to produce wheat has increased by only 8 per cent. This means that productivity has increased (measured by production per unit area) by 130 per cent.

Questions and assignments

2.1 Describe briefly the main elements of a food crisis.

2.2 Describe the different kinds of problems that a food crisis creates.

2.3 How may food crises influence companies in the food chain? How can the companies protect themselves from the negative impact of food crises?

2.4 Who are winners and losers from food crises? Why?

2.5 Food crises seem to be more and more frequent. Why?

2.6. Are frequent food crises evidence of imperfect food markets? Why/why not?

2.7 Should we try to limit the risks of future food crises? Why/why not? How?

3 The food sector during economic development

The food sector and food markets change significantly when society undergoes economic development. This includes changes in agriculture, the food industry, the food production chain, food consumption and many other conditions. The development is often very predictable and there are some clear global tendencies.

The changes in the food sector are created by a series of different internal and external conditions. Some of these conditions are given in advance, while others can be influenced by the individual countries. An understanding of the conditions is very important in order to analyse and create the desired changes in the food sector.

Changes during economic development

When a country undergoes economic development, all sectors, businesses, markets and structures change in the country. This also includes the food sector (which includes food markets, the food production chain and the entire food cluster), which shows some pronounced changes in line with increasing welfare.

One of the general traits is that the food sector becomes less significant during economic development. This development is found in nearly all countries, and the pattern can be seen both by comparing countries with different levels of development and by looking at the development of a single country over time. This is illustrated in Box 3.1.

Box 3.1 **Examples of changes in the food sector and on food markets during economic development**

Figures 3.1 and 3.2 illustrate which role food products and the entire food production chain have in the long term. This is shown both globally and with Denmark as an example of a country which has, for more than 100 years, developed from being a distinctly agricultural country to now being among the most developed countries in the world.

Both figures show very clear developmental trends: food production becomes relatively less significant over time. This development is nearly constant, and it is only short-term food crises and their associated price bubbles that cause international trade with agricultural and food products to increase.

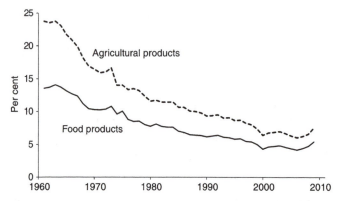

Figure 3.1 Agricultural and food products: share of international trade.

Source: Author's own calculations based on FAO (2012).

Figure 3.2 The significance of agricultural and food markets in the long term for a country during economic development – Denmark as an example.

Source: Author's calculations based on Hansen (1983), Statistics Denmark (2012), Landbrugs raadet (several years) and Henriksen and Ølgaard (1969).

Note: The figure shows food consumption as a percentage of total consumption; agricultural exports include sugar, furs and processed agricultural products.

There are several explanations for this development, with the relationship between supply and demand playing an important role: relatively large productivity increases remove resources from the sector, while relatively small increases in consumption limit market expansion.

The changes during economic development can be seen in the entire value chain. The primary sector, agriculture, becomes more effective and efficient, thereby freeing up the labour force, and thus the employment effect is reduced.

In addition, an increasing labour division between agriculture and the food industry takes place, where the food industry takes over a portion of the processing which was previously a part of agriculture. Thereby the changes created by economic development vary significantly depending on where one is in the value chain.

The food industry will also increase the degree of food processing and refinement in line with economic development. As welfare increases, demand for more prepared foods also increases, which naturally affects food companies' production.

Moreover, the food production chain also changes all the way to the consumer link during economic development, and small, local shops are, to a large extent, replaced by larger supermarkets.

Finally, the changing consumption pattern during economic development also means that consumers will, to a greater extent, demand 'more meals and fewer foods'. Food service, eating out and convenience comes more into focus, which means that new chains and business areas in the value chain and in the entire food product group develop.

Changes in the food sector created by economic development

The changes in the food sector during economic development can be seen in several areas. In the following section, some of the concrete areas where the food sector changes along with increasing economic development are analysed.

Production and value creation in primary agriculture

The international pattern of agriculture's declining share of production and value creation with increasing economic welfare is seen clearly in Figure 3.3.

Figure 3.3 shows, for each individual country, the connection between the country's level of economic development (GDP/capita shown on a logarithmic scale) and agriculture's gross factor income in relation to the countries' total gross factor income. Every point represents one country. As can be seen, despite large differences in the countries' resources, etc. there is a clear tendency for agriculture to become less important as economic development increases.

However, it is noteworthy that population migration occurs so rapidly that the added value in relation to the remaining agricultural workforce increases sharply in line with economic development. This correlation between added value per work force unit and the level of economic development is shown in Figure 3.4.

The figure shows that added value per labour force unit increases significantly as welfare increases. This form of labour productivity, which is what we are really

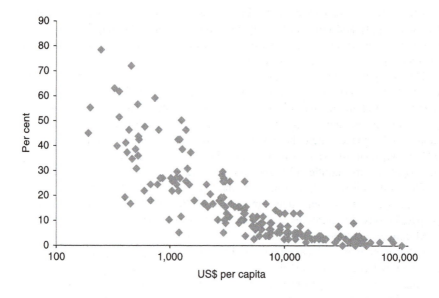

Figure 3.3 Agriculture's share of countries' gross factor income as a function of GDP per capita (2011).

Source: Author's presentation based on World Bank (2012b).

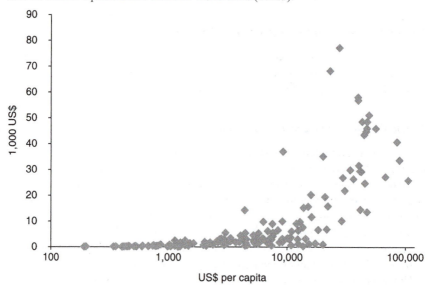

Figure 3.4 Added value per agricultural work force unit under economic development.

Source: Author's calculations based on data from World Bank (2012b).

Note: Added value, in fixed 2000 US $, is calculated for 2011 or for the last year with available data; GDP per capita is for 2011.

Box 3.2 Use of cross-sectional data to describe the food sector during economic development

Cross-sectional data are snapshots of, e.g., the conditions in many countries in a given year. If one assumes that these factors change in line with economic development, one can use cross-sectional data to describe dynamic development. If one analyses cross-sectional data on the connection between a country's level of economic development and the food sector's economic importance, it is possible to get a picture of global development. Such a dynamic interpretation of cross-sectional data should naturally be conducted with caution as factors other than just economic development also help to explain the food sector's development. A comparison of Figures 3.1 and 3.2 with Figures 3.5 and 3.9 shows, however, that there is a good correlation and that the food sector's exports and employment decrease with time *and* in line with economic development.

Therefore, it is possible to conclude that the food sector's employment, value creation, exports, processing industry, etc. can largely be explained and predicted by analysing a country's level of development.

Cross-sectional data in this chapter are illustrated by figures for the food sector as a function of the countries' economic development level (GDP per capita), where the x-axis is logarithmised to get a more uniform distribution of the displayed plots.

---

dealing with, is also evidence of increasing farm sizes in line with economic development. This very clear correlation is remarkable, as there are many factors other than just economic development that explain labour productivity, added value and structural development in agriculture (see for example Huffman and Evenson 2001).

Moreover, it is worth noting that added value per labour force unit is also influenced by the size of agricultural subsidies. Countries with a high subsidy rate (for example, Japan, Switzerland, Iceland and Norway) also have a relatively high value added per farmer.

Exports

Because exports are derived from production, the significance of agricultural and food exports also declines with increasing economic development. There is a definite pattern in that the poorest countries generally are very dependent on agricultural exports, but this dependency lessens as welfare increases (see Figure 3.5).

The pattern is obscured somewhat by the fact that among the poorest developing countries are countries which export very little due to overpopulation and food shortages. Similarly, there are poor countries that export relatively large amounts of raw materials such as metals, oil, etc. and which therefore export

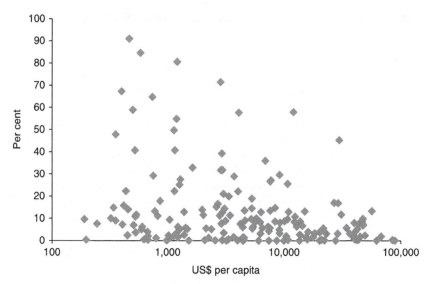

Figure 3.5 Food export percentage of total export during economic development (2010).

Source: Author's calculations based on FAO (2012) and World Bank (2012b).

relatively small amounts of agricultural products. There are also atypical countries, e.g. Denmark and New Zealand, which have a very large agricultural export despite being highly developed countries.

The relatively good correlation between per capita GDP and the relative importance of agricultural exports is remarkable considering that there are parameters other than just economic development that affect the size of food exports. A country's basic comparative advantage, agricultural policy measures, etc. will also, to a large degree, affect the size of food exports.

On the other hand, one can also see that economic development apparently creates new competitive strengths outside the food sector, thus reducing the agricultural sector's role in trade.

The decreasing importance of food exports with increasing economic development is only relative in relation to total exports. Thus, total food exports per capita increase in line with economic development (see Figure 3.6).

As can be seen in Figure 3.6, food exports increase as countries become more affluent. This happens despite the fact that agricultural and food production become less important over the same period.

Imports

Food imports' share of total imports does not vary to the same extent as was the case with agricultural exports. There are, for example, very few countries where food imports comprise more than 30 per cent of total imports.

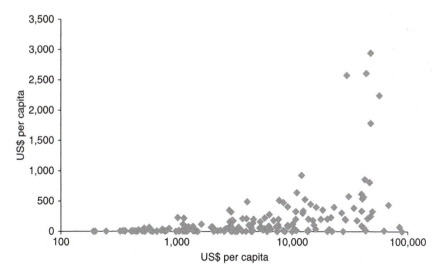

Figure 3.6 Per capita food export during economic development (2010).

Source: Author's calculations based on FAO (2012) and World Bank (2012b).

This can be explained by two relationships. First, all countries have the basic resources necessary for domestic agricultural production. Therefore, agricultural production is a dominant industry in technologically poorly developed countries, and thus food imports are small.

Second, many countries do not want to be dependent on food imports due to agricultural and political security concerns, which also reduces the size and importance of food imports.

The relationship between countries' economic development and the relative importance of food imports can be seen in Figure 3.7.

However, if one looks at the absolute growth in food imports, one sees a clearer pattern. The fact that countries' agricultural imports increase in line with increasing economic growth is a characteristic of the development process. The same picture applies to agricultural exports.

Net exports

When looking at the trend in net exports (exports minus imports) of agricultural products in the economic development process, it should be emphasised that there is no clear picture. As can be seen in Figure 3.8, net exports do not clearly decrease or increase with increasing GDP.

As shown in Figure 3.8, most developing countries have a very small net export or net import of food. However, countries will increasingly become either net exporters or net importers of food products as their economy grows. Thus, greater

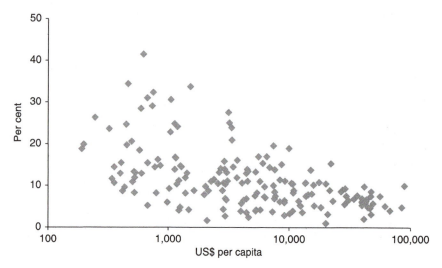

Figure 3.7 Food import's share of total imports during economic development (2010).

Source: Author's calculations based on FAO (2012) and World Bank (2012b).

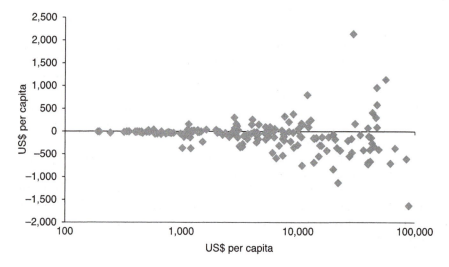

Figure 3.8 Per capita net export during economic development (2010).

Source: Author's calculations based on FAO (2012) and World Bank (2012b).

international specialisation occurs, where countries adjust to a division of labour in relation to their comparative advantage.

The clear-cut correlation between economic development and international food trade emphasises two relationships. First, economic assistance to under-developed countries will, *ceteris paribus*, create new producers and consumers on the global market. Second, it seems that economic development is a necessary precondition for participation in international food trade and specialisation.

Employment

Employment in the food sector depends on the country and the specific part of the value chain. The first link of the value chain is agriculture, the importance of which regarding employment varies greatly from country to country. Once again, there is a relatively homogeneous pattern, where agriculture's importance decreases with economic and industrial growth.

The relatively decreasing importance for employment can be explained by several relationships:

- The relatively weak growth in agricultural production will also result, *ceteris paribus*, in relatively weak growth in employment.
- Labour productivity is high in agriculture because of technological development. In the long term, this results in labour being pushed out of agriculture (push effect).
- The division of labour between agriculture and industry means that a larger portion of processing, supply, distribution, etc. moves from primary agriculture to industry, which means that the diverted employment increases relatively. This more rational division of labour does not in itself mean that agriculture's employment effect becomes less, but rather that a portion of the labour force in agricultural production changes occupation.
- Economic development is, as a rule, characterised by industrialisation, which results in increasing demand for labour in industrial occupations as a side effect. Therefore, labour is pulled from agriculture into the industrial sector (pull effect).

As shown in Figure 3.9, there is a very clear correlation between economic welfare and agriculture's significance for employment.

As can be seen in Figure 3.9, the percentage of the workforce employed in agriculture decreases with economic growth. The correlation presented in Figure 3.9 is in line with the development in most countries during the last century, in that the percentage of the population involved in agriculture has fallen.

When one considers the rural population, which to a large extent is correlated with the agricultural population, there is also a clear decrease in the percentage of the population living in rural areas. Currently, over half of the world's population now live in cities, whereas the rural population is decreasing relatively on all continents. According to the FAO, this development is expected to continue in the coming years (see Figure 3.10).

As the urban population increases, employment in agriculture falls. However, at the same time, the sales potential of food increase because the urban population purchases all their food products.

Thus, moving to the cities has an impact on both employment in agriculture as well as the market situation in the entire value chain.

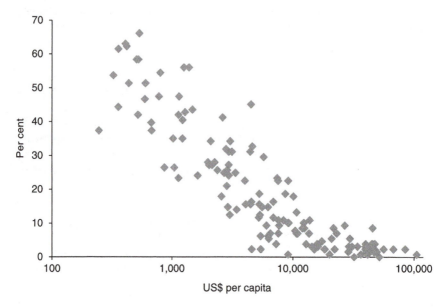

Figure 3.9 Employment in agriculture (as a percentage of total employment) during economic development (2009).

Source: Author's calculations based on World Bank (2012b).

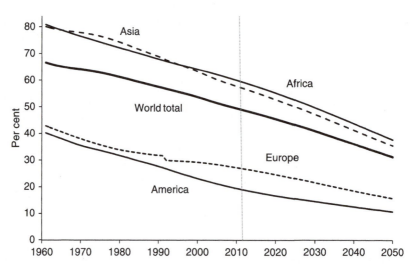

Figure 3.10 Percentage of the population living in rural areas (projected to 2050).

Source: FAO (2012).

Note: The projection to 2050 is conducted by UN/FAO.

Structural development

Economic development not only promotes, but is often a crucial precondition for structural development. Therefore, it is also typical that the entire food production chain is most developed in the wealthiest countries and that structural development occurs continuously in line with economic development.

Structural development, especially companies' size and number, is generally most advanced in the most developed countries. This is the case for all links in the food production chain.

In the agricultural sector, there is a clear tendency for farms, measured in area of cultivated farmland in production per economically active individual in agriculture, to become larger and larger during economic development (see Figure 3.11).

Figure 3.11 uses a slightly simplified size measure, the area of cultivated agricultural land per economically active person in agriculture, as the quality of agricultural land can vary significantly around the world and because other relationships, such as livestock, are also size parameters. However, in order to obtain comparable data from the greatest possible number of countries, it is necessary to use a relatively simple and accessible size measure.

In spite of this simplification, a clear correlation can be seen (Figure 3.11), which indicates a strengthened structure during economic development. Also, when it concerns the other links in the food production chain, the food industry, wholesalers and food retailers, there is a clear tendency for businesses to become larger and larger in line with economic development.

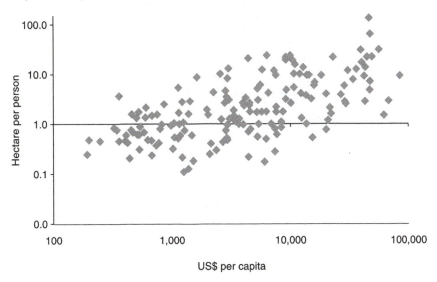

Figure 3.11 Structural development in agriculture during economic development.

Source: Author's presentation based on FAO (2012) and World Bank (2012b).

Note: Size is measured as area of cultivated farmland in production per economically active person in agriculture; the x and y axes are logarithmic.

The food industry

Although the food industry takes over a proportion of the employment and value added from primary agriculture during economic development, it nevertheless seems that the food industry also becomes less important as economic welfare increases (see, e.g., Hansen, 1997). The reason for this is that the increased processing in the food industry cannot compensate for the negative effect of the low growth in demand, etc.

The relationship between economic development and the significance of the food industry can be seen in Figure 3.12, which shows that food typically comprises 20–60 per cent of the total value added in the industry in the poorest developing countries, while it typically comprises 5–25 per cent in the wealthier countries.

There is, therefore, a relative and pronounced decline. If one looks at the food industry's revenue per capita, there is a clear global tendency for revenue to increase in line with increased economic development.

The decreasing importance of the food industry is mainly caused by a low growth in demand along with a dependency on local and national markets. For a long time, the food industry's raw materials and consumers have been preferentially local. In line with increasing liberalisation and globalisation, the food industry is becoming less reliant on local raw materials, so the connection with national agriculture can be expected to be weakened in the future. At the same time, more international sales will also mean that the food industry will no longer be so limited by low growth in demand, as growth can be achieved on the international markets.

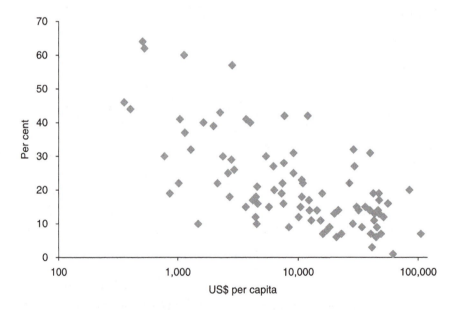

Figure 3.12 The food industry's share of total value added during economic development.

Source: Author's calculations based on World Bank (2012b).

Finally, it is also significant that raw materials from agriculture are playing an increasingly minor role in the food industry's production and value creation. Innovation, processing, refinement, marketing, logistics, etc. comprise an increasing portion of costs compared to the cost of raw goods. Therefore, the food industry is becoming less dependent on agricultural production.

When it comes to the food industry's importance in relation to agriculture, increasing specialisation in the agro-industrial sector occurs in line with economic development in a society. In a developing country, a significant portion of the supply and processing activity occurs in primary agriculture. In line with economic development, a larger division of labour occurs, so that supply and processing industries take over a significant portion of both household and agricultural food processing.

As can be seen in Figure 3.13, there is a clear tendency for the food industry to take over a greater and greater percentage of the value added in the agro-industrial complex.

This development will, therefore, also help to reduce primary agriculture's direct importance as a result of economic development. It should be noted that the importance of primary agriculture, to an increasing extent, is a result of a secondary effect from adjacent sectors.

The food industry's development is therefore affected by, on the one hand, generally weak growth in demand for food and, on the other hand, an increase in food processing.

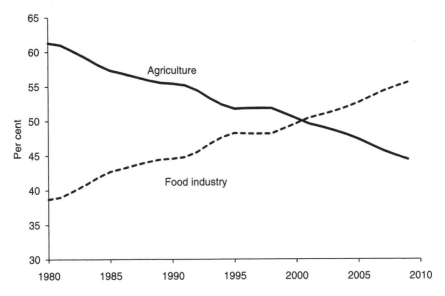

Figure 3.13 Distribution of value added in parts of the food sector in OECD countries.

Source: Author's calculations based on OECD (2012a) and World Bank (2012b).

Note: Weighted average of 29 OECD countries.

Food retail

Retail is the furthest link in the food production chain and is closest to the consumers, and changes also occur here during economic development. Three significant relationships should be mentioned.

First, there is a tendency for fewer and fewer speciality food shops, such as butchers, bakers, fishmongers, etc. Since 1980, the number of speciality shops in several European countries has fallen by 75 per cent.

Second, supermarkets have taken over a significant part of the speciality shops' market share. Super- and hypermarkets have grown rapidly and they now account for approximately 70 per cent of the total sale of staple goods in Western Europe.

Third, supermarkets are being put under pressure by the expanding food service sector. In the USA, which has often been a trendsetter in this area, it has been predicted that a significant number of supermarkets will disappear in the near future. This development is driven by consumers' increasing demand for prepared food (full meals) and decreasing demand for unprocessed food for preparation in the home. It is likely that this trend will also spread to Europe at some point. This development is illustrated in Figure 3.14.

Supermarkets are attempting to gain a share of the food service market. Supermarkets which offer prepared food are widespread but, even with these measures, supermarkets' share of the total food market in several countries has fallen.

Opportunities for improved efficiency and lower costs are among the most important reasons for mergers and acquisitions in the retail sector and thereby structural development and increasing concentration. It is assumed that marketing, distribution and procurement costs can be reduced by increasing the size of firms.

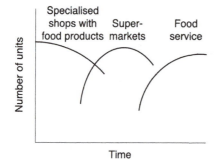

Figure 3.14 Schematic diagram of the structural development in retail trade during economic development.

Source: Author's presentation.

Market power in the food production chain

Market power and bargaining strength in the entire value chain changes dramatically in line with economic development in society. Structural development, logistics, economies of scale, international marketing, etc. create different preconditions for the balance of power.

The power relations in the entire value chain are illustrated in Figure 3.15, which shows the power distribution and its development in four different stages.

> In the *first stage*, the wholesaler has the most power, because the wholesaler controls the information on consumers' demand and their qualitative and quantitative needs, and controls the grocery suppliers' logistical activity. Retail consists of a long succession of small, independent shops that are typically poorly organised. Retail's role is primarily to distribute the manufacturer's goods, which contain very few branded goods.
>
> In the *second stage*, the food industry takes over the wholesaler's role as direct distributer to the shops. By being more effective in marketing, the food industry can bypass the price-raising wholesaler. At the same time, the food industry is able to build consumer preferences through the increased demand for processed products.
>
> In the *third stage*, the balance of power shifts to the retailer's advantage. The retailer's close proximity to the consumer, the strengths of introducing private labels and the advantages of information technology, as well as increasing concentration and internationalisation, mean that the retailer is now a dominant link in the field-to-fork chain. In particular, information on

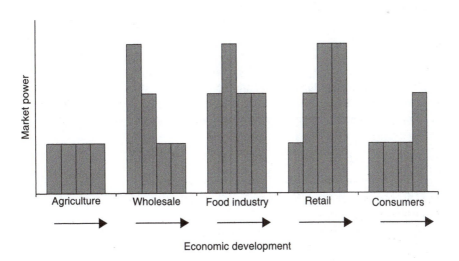

Figure 3.15 Schematic diagram illustrating the power structure in the food sector in four stages during economic development.

Source: Author's representation.

customers and the market, which retailers have via their position in the value chain, is considered to be a significant source of market power (see, e.g. Dekker, 2003).

In the *fourth stage*, the political consumer becomes increasingly important and consumers obtain a stronger position in the food production chain due to high-profile incidents and stronger consumer organisations, and via mass communication and social media.

Agriculture and farmers have relatively little market power in all four stages. This is especially because they are many small suppliers, who organise and coordinate their sales to the far fewer, but larger, buyers, be they wholesalers or food companies, to a limited extent.

Explanation

The food sector changes in several different ways during economic development and there are also different causes and explanations for this. The causes vary from link to link in the value chain, and some can have different effects on different links of the value chain.

Several economists have studied the decreasing importance of agriculture and the food sector during economic development. Anderson (1987) refers to earlier studies (Schultz, 1945; Kuznets, 1966; and Johnson, 1973), which explain that the decreasing importance is partly due to low growth in demand and partly due to new technology and thereby increases in productivity. Besides this, there are additional causes, such as decreasing prices for agricultural goods, which are strengthened even further by political measures.

Other significant factors also play a role. The limited international division of labour also limits the food sector's utilisation of comparative advantages. At the same time, the increased division of labour between primary agriculture and the food industry also affects the single link's position in the value chain.

Often, it is precisely the special conditions within the food sector that provide the explanations for the changes during economic development. The following section outlines and substantiates the most significant causes and explanations.

Low income elasticity

Food generally has low income elasticity, which means that the consumption of food increases less than the consumption of other products during economic growth and development.

When income elasticity is greater than one, the products in question are 'luxury goods', whereby an increase in demand is greater than an increase in income. In these cases, demand increases, both absolutely and relatively, concurrently with economic development. In other words, demand is income elastic. When income elasticity is less than one, but is still positive, demand increases with increasing income, but the increase in demand is less than the increase in income. This is termed income inelastic demand, which is typical for food products (see also Chapter 7).

Therefore, food generally has a low income elasticity, which means that food consumption increases less than other products during economic development and growth. Consumers in the more economically developed countries will not demand significantly more food products, despite an increase in income, as there is simply a limit to how much an individual can eat.

Generally, income elasticity decreases with increasing income (see Figure 3.16).

Figure 3.16 clearly shows the negative correlation between the two variables, while there is also a clear difference between the three product groups.

Therefore, there are two ways in which increasing income contributes to food consumption having a decreasing share of total consumption. First, income elasticity for food is low (and food products therefore become less important as income increases) and, second, the income elasticity for food decreases even further with an increase in income.

Weak price development

The price of agricultural and food products normally increases less than inflation in society. This price effect results in, *ceteris paribus*, a decline in the value of agricultural and food production.

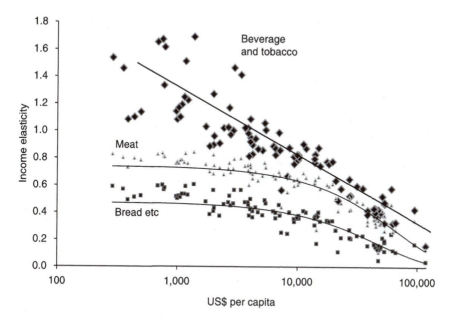

Figure 3.16 Income elasticity as a function of income.

Source: Author's presentation based on USDA (2011c) and World Bank (2012b).

Note: Plot and trend lines are from data from approximately 100 countries.

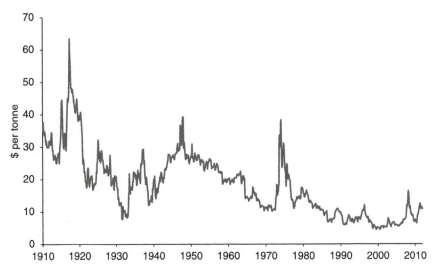

Figure 3.17 Development in the real price of wheat in the USA.

Source: Author's calculations based on USDA (2012a).

Note: Deflated with the development in consumer prices.

The most important source of the real price reduction in food comes from agriculture itself, where improvements in productivity and advantages from economies of scale reduce the costs required to produce agricultural products. Grain, which is directly or indirectly a very important raw ingredient in many food products, has, over a long period, shown a significant fall in real prices (see Figure 3.17).

Figure 3.17 shows a clear decreasing trend in the real price of wheat. Between 1910 and 2010, the real price of wheat decreased by 70 per cent, which is equal to an average yearly decrease of 1 per cent.

The real price decrease contributes to cheaper food, both directly for grain-based products (flour, cereals, etc.) and indirectly in that cheaper grain, to a greater or lesser extent, reduces the cost of livestock production.

All in all, the decreasing real price of agricultural goods means that the costs of food production become relatively cheaper, that the price of food therefore also becomes relatively cheaper and that food's share of overall consumption becomes less.

Significant increases in productivity

With a significant increase in productivity, particularly labour productivity, it will be possible to reduce agriculture's input factor, while production continues to match demand. To the extent that labour is reduced as a result, it will result in more labour leaving agriculture, which will reduce the sector's share of total employment.

Infrastructure

Infrastructure is a significant precondition, and explanation, for development in the food sector during economic growth. Access to markets, raw materials and resources are important preconditions for the development of necessary special-isation in the food sector's value chain.

Countries will develop infrastructure in the form of roads, ports, control systems, market places, educational institutions, communication systems, etc. concurrently with economic development. Subsequently, it will be possible to increase mass production and large-scale operations, which will help create the observed changes in the food sector.

Limited international specialisation

Limitations in transport and export opportunities will hinder normal production development. It is often difficult to transport agricultural goods over large distances. In addition, trade barriers make it difficult to sell a larger part of produc-tion on international markets.

When international trade becomes more important, a type of labour division or specialisation develops between countries. The individual countries begin to specialise in areas where they can best compete and abandon areas where they can no longer compete internationally. Therefore, in a normal situation, it is important that a business maintains its socio-economic position during economic develop-ment by expanding via international trade.

Here, however, it is significant that the development in international specialisa-tion has been relatively weak within food production. As discussed in Chapter 5, international specialisation, measured here as development in international trade and production, has been much stronger for industrial products than agricultural products over the last few decades.

Limited knowledge and technology content

Agricultural and food production does not necessarily demand high technology or knowledge. All countries have the necessary resources to produce agricultural goods, and therefore it is natural that agricultural production becomes relatively less significant for a country's development as technology becomes more and more advanced.

A highly developed country has a comparative advantage within high tech-nological production, and even though a lot of technology is incorporated in food production in many industrialised countries due to efficiency improve-ments, other industries have greater comparative advantages than agriculture. The inevitable result is that the socio-economic significance of the food sector declines.

Questions and assignments

3.1 What are the major changes in the food sector during economic development?

3.2 What are the major drivers behind changes in the food sector during economic development?

3.3 Select a country of your own choice. How will the country develop during the next 10–20 years according to the developments described in this chapter?

3.4 Which factors may interfere with the normal pattern of development in this case (3.3)?

3.5 Some developing countries want to transform from an agri-based country to an industrial country as fast as possible. Why may this motive be widespread? Can they succeed? Why / why not?

4   Food clusters

Clusters, which are groups of companies, suppliers, research institutions and public authorities, have proved to be successful. Companies in well developed clusters grow faster and are more innovative than companies which are not part of dynamic clusters. Several types of cluster exist and they can develop in many different ways. In general, the USA is relatively advanced when it comes to the development of strong clusters. In more recent years, there has been a greater focus on the value of clusters and many countries now support and are attempting to establish clusters.

Introduction

Clusters of interrelated companies, suppliers, customers, public and research institutions, etc. have been in existence for many years. Silicon Valley in California is considered to be the world's largest cluster and the one which has been best described in the literature.

Clusters have often proven to be successful because they create a range of common advantages, which result in increased growth, profit, value creation and employment. It is therefore important to understand the formation, development and significance of clusters so that their continued development can be supported, and new clusters can be created.

Companies form the core of a cluster. They produce related goods or trade intensively with each other. Furthermore, clusters contain a range of institutions, organisations and partners that surround the companies and affect their activities.

Companies which are in a cluster achieve common synergies by being close to each other. In many cases, they have historically had common good and cheap access to raw materials and inputs. The companies have benefited from being able to trade with each other, exchange knowledge and experiences and share a common pool of competent manpower.

Physical proximity between companies makes it advantageous to create improved conditions in the form of, e.g., places of education, logistics or an infrastructure, which provides easy access to raw materials and customers. This close proximity has made cluster companies stronger than the competition for a number of reasons.

In many cases it appears that countries strategically align their industrial policy in order to support existing clusters or to create new ones. Clusters are thus an essential instrument of industrial policy.

In many areas, food products and the food sector are subject to special conditions that require special initiatives or considerations where food clusters need to be supported, developed or created. In other words, one cannot just transfer the experiences and results from other company clusters to the food sector. Conditions such as widespread vertical integration, cooperative ownership, specific market conditions and food safety mean that a food cluster will often have to operate under special conditions in order to succeed fully.

Clusters: definition and content

Groups of companies, as described above, are known as clusters, but they are also referred to by the following terms which, more or less, cover the same content: industry cluster, business cluster, competitive cluster, competence cluster, professional cluster and resource area.

The term cluster was first introduced into the field of strategic management by the American economist, Michael Porter, in his well-known book from 1990: *The Competitive Advantage of Nations* (1990). He described clusters in the following manner:

> A geographically proximate group of interconnected companies and associated institutions in a particular field, linked by commonalities and complementarities. The geographic scope of a cluster can range from a single city or state to a country or even to a group of neighbouring countries.

Bergman and Feser (2007) define clusters as:

> A group of companies and non-profit organisations for which membership of the group is an important element in the competitiveness of each individual company.

McDonald and Vertova (2002) define clusters as:

> Geographical concentrations of companies and supporting institutions which produce identical or nearly identical products, but which are supported by a strong network which distributes the advantages to all the members of the cluster.

On the basis of these definitions, one can conclude that some specific conditions must be fulfilled before one can define a group of companies as a cluster.

First, there must be a formal or informal *cluster structure or organisation*. The companies and institutions in the cluster must directly or indirectly structure themselves so as to ensure cohesion and thereby derive the cluster benefits.

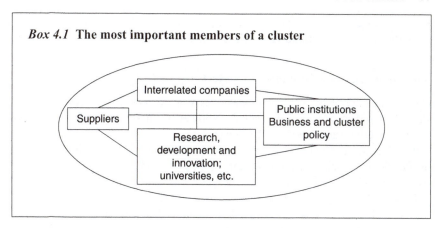

Box 4.1 The most important members of a cluster

Companies are the key participants in a cluster and they cooperate and compete often at the same time, but for mutual benefit. The research and development (R & D) part, which often comprises universities and other research institutions, delivers unique competences that result in innovation and knowledge dissemination. The public sector can contribute to the cluster's development through targeted industrial and cluster policy to establish infrastructure, etc.

The clusters have to develop *competences* that go beyond what the individual companies could develop in isolation. Such competences can relate to the supply chain, marketing, logistics, technology, traceability or knowledge transfer, etc.

The clusters must also be able to attain a certain level of *performance* depending on the desired and strategic goals of the companies. What matters is that the competences lead to results in the form of measurably better performance when compared to similar companies operating outside the cluster. Performance can be measured in market share, profit, etc.

The major participants in a cluster and their interaction are outlined in Box 4.1.

Types of cluster

There is general consensus that there are four different types of cluster:

- *Geographical* (regional) clusters – clusters which are concentrated according to purely geographical conditions.
- *Sector* clusters – a group or cluster of companies that cooperate within the same economic sector.
- *Horizontal* clusters – cooperation between companies on the same level in the value chain. Often there may be cooperation between companies that are formally competitors. Such cooperation could be in the form of, e.g., collaboration on research and development. Examples of formal and informal cooperation can be observed regarding labour movement, research and development, experience groups and social networks.

- *Vertical* clusters – cooperation at various stages of the value chain. The co-operative is an example of a vertical cluster.

The historical development of clusters

Clusters of interrelated companies have been in existence worldwide since the start of the industrial revolution including flowers (tulips) from Holland, watches from Switzerland and steel from Sweden.

The Silicon Valley cluster was established in 1950 and was initially involved in the development and production of semiconductors, and later the development of the entire computer industry.

First, the Silicon Valley cluster is based in a highly innovative environment and draws on the military research which takes place in the area. Second, a number of companies have chosen to locate themselves there: originally Hewlett Packard (HP) and subsequently IT companies such as Apple, Google and YouTube. Third, Stanford University contributes to the cluster.

Knowledge dissemination, a work culture based on cooperation, development, entrepreneurship, and close cooperation between companies and academia were significant drivers of the development of this cluster (see for example Saxenian, 1994).

Clusters can be partly closely related and partly overlap each other. Figure 4.1 shows examples of clusters and their mutual groupings. For specific food areas, the figure shows how a food cluster may include all or parts of other clusters.

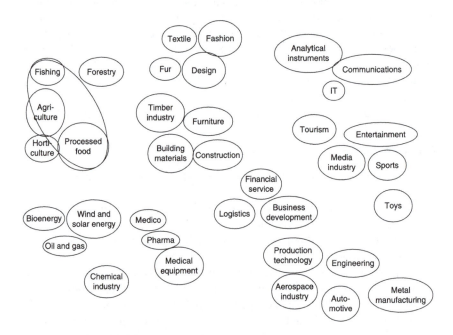

Figure 4.1 Examples of clusters and their mutual groupings.
Source: Author's own presentation.

The renaissance of clusters

The significance of clusters for competitiveness, growth and the economy has received significantly increased attention in recent years. It has also been proven that companies in developed industry clusters grow faster and are more innovative than firms outside dynamic clusters.

According to the OECD (2007), the support of existing clusters and the development of new ones through proactive cluster policy has undergone a renaissance in a number of countries. Cluster policy is a direct means of improving the international competitiveness of companies amid increasingly tough global competition.

Thus, there is evidence of a paradigm shift towards a greater focus on clusters. In clusters, companies compete and cooperate at the same time, and the results include increased innovation, knowledge transfer and increased productivity, which are clear socio-economic gains. There is also recognition that the creation of clusters limits the off-shoring of companies. In fact, clusters help to attract valuable manpower and entrepreneurs from abroad.

Size and significance of the food cluster

The definition and delimitation of food clusters is not always unambiguous, as there is always a grey area regarding where a cluster begins or ends. The following examples illustrate this.

- Companies in, e.g., the pharmaceutical sector, in many cases, started in the agricultural and food sector. However, as the companies evolved, their links to the agricultural and food sector became partly or fully cut.
- An increasing proportion of the raw materials supplied to the food clusters comes from imports, which is in line with increasing globalisation. Companies which produce confectionery, soft drinks, etc. are, in many cases, mainly supplied by foreign suppliers. Seen from a local food production chain perspective, such suppliers are less important in the food cluster.
- Significant parts of the machinery industry arose from provision to the agro-food industry. However, gradually, their exports increased and new business areas were developed, which reduced their direct dependence on the agro-food industry. One of the world's largest wind turbine companies, Vestas, originally started as an agricultural machinery company.
- Finally, delimitation also plays an important role. Sectors such as bioenergy, the fur industry and flower production are not usually considered as food products, but they are often included in the food cluster.

Figure 4.2 illustrates how the food cluster can overlap with other clusters.

The general definition of a food cluster includes a group of interrelated companies, suppliers, companies in related sectors and associated institutions (universities, trade associations, public authorities, etc.), which compete and/or cooperate, and which are linked together by common and complementary factors.

A food cluster can be very complex, with many actors and many interconnections. The vertical chain (food production chain) and the field-to-fork integration often play a central role in the food cluster. In addition, a number of both horizontal and vertical links are also present. The food cluster changes over time, and some actors or links are lost, while new ones join.

Figure 4.3 illustrates the complex structure of a typical food cluster, including the major actors and their interconnections.

As seen from the figure, the cluster is horizontally and vertically integrated.

Integration in the value chain, 'from field to fork', is very developed through cooperative ownership and outsourcing. Vertical integration is essential in most food clusters. Horizontal integration mainly occurs through mergers and acquisitions, which create consolidation and a strong connection across the value chain.

The horizontal integration between the different branches of production is much less significant. The utilisation of the food cluster via the establishment of conglomerates and cross-sector companies is relatively rare. One explanation is that there are insufficient synergies between the different companies. Another explanation is that cooperative organisation typically occurs within the individual branches of production (milk, pigs, farm supplies, fur, etc.). Dairy farmers organise themselves into cooperative dairies, pig farmers into cooperative pig

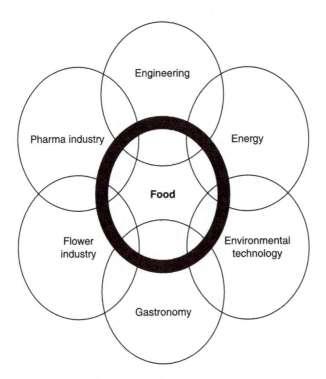

Figure 4.2 The food cluster – major actors and interconnections.
Source: Author's own presentation.

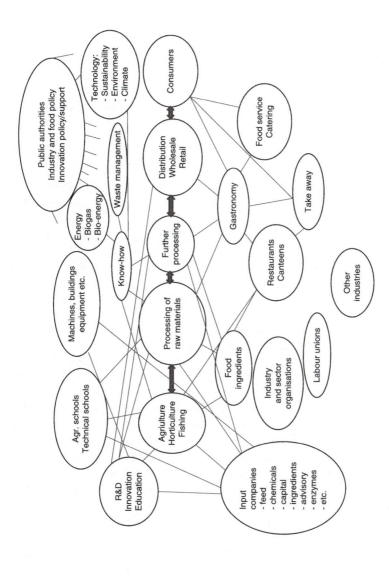

Figure 4.3 The food cluster and its possible interfaces with other clusters.

Source: Author's own presentation.

slaughterhouses, while the main activity of the cooperatives is to ensure the sale of their members' produce.

Cross-sector cooperatives can be difficult to fit into this system. Therefore, integration has primarily been within the specific branch of production, as well as vertically in the food production chain. In addition, during the course of a couple of decades, strategic business development has focused on specialisation and core business, while diversification and conglomerates have been given a lower priority.

Food clusters in a global perspective

Food clusters can be found in all parts of the world. In developing countries, they are typically concentrated in areas with good access to resources or markets, while in developed countries they are often attracted by access to knowledge, innovation and raw materials.

A number of surveys of the world's food clusters have been conducted, but no unambiguous picture has emerged. This is especially because there are several different ways to define, identify and measure food clusters. The mere task of geographically delimiting a cluster can be problematic as there can easily be a number of food clusters in the same country and in the same area, but in some cases this is interpreted as one regional food cluster.

European Cluster Observatory (2012) identified more than 150 European food clusters in a study based on figures from 2006. FORA (2010) base their studies on the Monitor Group's Global Cluster Database. In one such study, FORA mapped all the agricultural and food clusters in the developed countries. Figure 4.4 presents the largest agricultural and food clusters.

As can be seen in Figure 4.4, the world's five largest agricultural and food clusters are in Japan. Japanese agriculture and food production mainly supplies the domestic market, while Japan plays a modest role on the export markets. Indeed, Japan only accounts for 0.3 per cent of the world's total food exports. Conversely, Japan is the world's fifth largest food importer, with a world market share of nearly 5 per cent.

Japanese agricultural and food clusters thus do not play a big role in the international food sector. The main food clusters are located in Western Europe and North America (see Figure 4.5).

Of the ten largest agricultural and food clusters in North America, Europe and Australia, six are located in Europe, three in Canada and one in Australia. The world's largest agricultural and food cluster is in Bretagne, France with nearly 200,000 employees, which is closely followed by a cluster in Ontario, Canada with approximately 190,000 employees. The Danish agricultural and food cluster is the third largest and employs approximately 175,000.

Germany is home to three major agricultural and food clusters in Nordrhein-Westfalen, Bayern and Niedersachsen. Holland also produces significant amounts of agricultural and food products, but the country is divided into four regions in the official statistics. If Holland was considered as one single region, it would be the largest agricultural and food cluster in Europe with well over 200,000 employees.

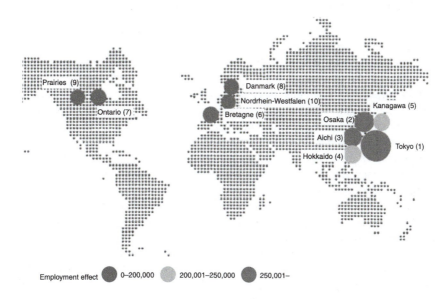

Figure 4.4 The ten largest agricultural and food clusters in Europe, North America and Oceania (2006), measured by employment effect.

Source: FORA (2010) based on Monitor Group's Global Cluster Database.

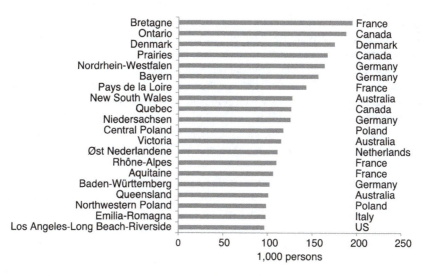

Figure 4.5 The 20 largest agricultural and food clusters in Europe, North America and Oceania (2006), measured by employment effect.

Source: FORA (2010) based on Monitor Group's Global Cluster Database.

Food clusters and cooperative organisation

In many cases, food clusters are based on cooperative organisation as a vertical cluster, with farmers owning the entire field-to-fork food production chain or parts of it, which creates the foundation for optimal coordination and knowledge sharing, and strengthened cooperation in the chain.

It has often been stated that the cooperative movement has been able to build up competence in line with the competence cluster philosophy. The shareholders basically have the same goals and they view each other more as colleagues than competitors and gladly share experience with each other.

Cooperative ownership ensures vertical integration via joint ownership of the links in the value chain. Furthermore, horizontal integration has been strengthened in recent years due to widespread mergers, in particular between cooperatives, which has created a few very large food companies. Close cooperation on research, marketing and the development of new production technologies has also been built up between cooperatives through industry associations and interest organisations.

Cooperative organisation can create vertical integration in some parts of the value chain and consolidation and horizontal integration in other parts of the value chain through mergers and acquisitions. The link to public organisations, research and development is not part of traditional cooperative organisation. Therefore, it can be said that cooperative organisation is fundamentally an important part of a food cluster, but it cannot replace the cluster.

Advantages of food clusters

Clusters can have a number of advantages, the nature of which depends on the type of cluster, be it regional, industrial, horizontal or vertical.

In addition, the driving force behind each individual case can vary and it is this that determines the advantages in each case. For example, natural conditions, the cooperative movement or government regulation and demand can be driving forces behind the creation of clusters. There are thus a variety of drivers and thereby fundamental advantages to clusters, which come into play in each individual case.

However, it is still possible to outline a number of generally applicable advantages (see, e.g., Porter, 1990; ebst, 2003; Kompetenznetze Deutschland, 2008; Persson *et al.* (2007); zu Köcker, 2008; and Ylä-Anttila, 2008):

- Significant advantages can be realised through improved access to customised supplies, knowledge and information. Utilities will focus on clusters and will strive to become a partner and preferred supplier.
- Innovation becomes more important as the need for improvements in the production process comes into focus; these can be fulfilled by companies working in close cooperation in a cluster.
- Knowledge is disseminated through increased job mobility. Employees will be faced with a wide range of potential employers within reasonable commuting distance, while companies will attempt to attract the best employees. In this

way, the individual employees' competences and knowledge, especially tacit knowledge which is difficult to document, will benefit more companies.

- Technological spillovers result from cooperation on research and development. Research results and new knowledge is spread faster in a cluster which is aware of this possibility. Companies can also learn in a more indirect manner by looking at what others are doing.
- Once a cluster has been established, it grows and develops as new businesses and suppliers are attracted. Therefore, a self-reinforcing process occurs.
- The formation of a cluster will naturally attract additional resources in the form of capital, manpower, research and development, etc. once the cluster has proven its legitimacy and its relative strength.
- Internal competition between the companies in the cluster stimulates innovation.
- Experience has shown that the internationalisation of companies can be stimulated and promoted when they participate in network and cluster cooperation.
- Transaction costs are lower.
- Infrastructure is optimal.
- There is high technological development as a result of intense competition.
- There is a high degree of trust between the members of the cluster.
- The geographical distance to suppliers and customers can be small.

The advantages of clusters can be divided into the following four groups:

- micro-economic advantages
- macro-economic advantages
- social-scientific advantages
- economic-geographical advantages.

The advantages of competence clusters are:

Micro-economic advantages

- increased interaction between companies
- supporting companies
- reduced infrastructure expenses
- economies of scale
- competition/rivalry
- logistics
- access to specialised manpower
- forced innovation.

Macro-economic advantages

- knowledge spillover
- dissemination of knowledge
- labour market pool

- customer-supplier relationship via joint technology
- standardisation
- cooperation
- technological development
- joint strategies and goals.

Social-scientific advantages

- access to resources
- reduced transaction costs
- networking
- trust
- technology sharing
- stability
- knowledge transfer
- reduced uncertainty.

Economic-geographical advantages

- technological development
- increased learning
- social-cultural environment.

Source: Persson, *et al.* (2007)

Therefore, there are a number of advantages to participating in a cluster, but it also involves risks, disadvantages and difficulties. Basically, there are a number of economic and market forces that pull in the direction of increased independence and reduced integration.

Disadvantages of clusters

Among the most important possible disadvantages are the following:

- The distance to customers becomes greater when the geographical location is primarily decided by the location of competitors/business partners. A cluster's location can be a disadvantage particularly if customers are very scattered, or if close contact with customers is important.
- The distance to suppliers becomes greater when the geographical location is primarily decided by other conditions. The daily delivery of raw materials is often important for a food cluster and this aspect can limit the advantages of being in a geographical cluster.
- Technological shifts or new trends, etc. which occur outside the cluster may be overlooked. Work within a cluster can become too inward looking and there may not be sufficient contact with companies, institutions and customers outside the cluster.

- Too much focus on cooperation within the cluster can result in a lack of competition in supply and demand. Therefore, in this way, a cluster can actually restrict the market and market forces. What is crucial in this context is whether the advantages of closer cooperation outweigh the disadvantages of reduced cooperation with trade partners outside the cluster.
- If a cluster becomes large, it can be both expensive and difficult to get it to function in practice. The networks can become too extensive and the structures too opaque, which can limit the benefits of cooperating in a cluster.
- A lack of credibility and trust. Empirical studies show that a lack of reciprocal trust is a significant barrier to the spread of clusters, especially internationally (zu Köcker, 2008).
- The participants in a cluster can be colleagues, partners and competitors at the same time. However, the competitive aspect can be so dominant that a conflict of interests emerges which can be a significant barrier to continued cooperation.

Food clusters: development over time

Clusters do not necessarily endure forever. New clusters can form, while others can more or less vanish. The development over time can be due to, e.g., a change in the institutional framework (industrial policy, etc.), a change in demand or a technological shift in production, based on new resources (e.g. the English textile industry and the German coal industry).

Clusters can also change character or emphasis over time. In vertical clusters, the emphasis can, e.g., move forward in the value chain. Other clusters may become more focused and specialised over time as the surrounding competitive conditions change.

New clusters which are based on the food cluster may also emerge. For example, agriculture has to some extent been the driving force behind the development of enzymes for feed, food products and bioenergy production, which has created new business areas. Several biotechnology companies have developed or have started in connection with agriculture and food clusters.

In additon, a number of new businesses have been created in the fractures between agriculture and energy production, where several institutions, companies and investors in and outside the agri-industrial sector have cooperated to solve technological and economic problems in this area. And finally, other countries can strategically align their industrial policy in order to create clusters in competition with existing clusters. In this way competition can emerge between existing and emerging clusters.

In this context, it is important that these new potential and competitiveness-based clusters are developed and supported. This is a task for all 'stakeholders' involved with the competence cluster topic, i.e. manufacturers, suppliers, academia, consultants, financial institutions, etc. Here it is especially important that not only public, but also private, companies become involved in the development (Porter, 2008).

It is also essential that the potential clusters are identified on the basis of fundamental competences; that they reflect relevant and attractive market conditions; and that they are not determined by artificial and unsustainable motives. Some clusters become specifically emphasised for being well founded in historic and natural competences and not to the same extent as a result of political lobbying (IFC, 2004), and it is important to continue to avoid gambling on artificial or defensive clusters.

Cluster policy

In order to support and further develop food clusters, targeted industrial policy initiatives are necessary in the form of a cluster policy. Today, many countries have a formal cluster policy as part of their industrial development strategy, but the area is relatively new and underdeveloped, and the content, tools and focus are very different from country to country (Oxford Research, 2008). However, it is possible to name a number of elements that can be part of a cluster policy:

- *Innovation* is a key driver for the establishment, support and further development of food clusters. In a European perspective, there is a clear correlation between innovation and cluster formation (see, e.g., Sölvell, 2008). Innovation must be developed and disseminated to all parties in the cluster, which is an essential part of cluster policy. In addition, several studies have shown the need to support and promote cooperation between companies and knowledge institutions in the food sector. The establishment of a knowledge and innovation centre to support innovation, networking and cooperation in the food sector has been described by several authors (see, e.g., ReD Associates, 2008).
- It is also essential that cluster policy ensures good *infrastructure* (communication, proximity, opportunity for knowledge sharing, low transaction costs, etc.) within the cluster.
- Cluster policy must also help to ensure that there is a *well-functioning market* where knowledge, products, know-how, employees, etc. have free movement and where competition is perfect.
- The cluster policy must give participants in the cluster a *competitive advantage* – a unique competence or the like – in terms of increased productivity, a technology boost, etc.
- The cluster policy, as an independent initiative, can also help *foster entrepreneurship*. New ideas, projects or businesses are often not realised because a potential entrepreneur does not receive the necessary support. Clusters are often based on many large and small companies, new products and new methods, and it is in the interests of society to support this development in order to move forward from the concept phase.
- Finally, the cluster policy should be so attractive and have so much potential that *private companies* become fully engaged in the area. Companies are central to food clusters and they should be the focal point of any future development.

Food clusters and globalisation

Globalisation can in many ways change existing clusters. One can immediately ask how a company's physical location can have such a significant influence when labour, technology, money and research can now move around freely in the globalised world via, e.g., the Internet. Does localisation still play an important role?

It also seems that the more globalised and liberalised the world becomes, the more specialised the individual local areas. The international division of labour increases, and each area or segment increasingly focuses on its specific strengths and comparative advantages. According to international economic theory, an increase in international specialisation will occur as a result of a more open and globalised international economy, which has now be observed in the food sector.

The same phenomenon can be seen with regard to clusters which also become more specialised (Porter, 2006). There are several examples of parts of the production in one cluster being outsourced to low-wage countries in Eastern Europe or the Far East, while development, technology, design and marketing is focused upon in the original cluster.

The question is whether a national food cluster, which has developed from the national network, national owners, primarily domestic supplies, etc. can cope in a time when all the links in the value chain are becoming increasingly global: global strategic supplies, global outsourcing, global sourcing, global owners, etc. are now very much in focus, and these global approaches are seen as vital in efforts to strengthen the international competitiveness of companies. It is remarkable that in a period of strong globalisation companies search for and find competitive advantages by positioning themselves geographically close to each other.

Situations arise whereby nationally contingent parts of clusters (interaction with the public system, vertical integration in the value chain, etc.) come into conflict with globalisation or cannot be fully utilised in a more open and global world. Here, there are two options: one must either attempt to further develop the clusters so that they have a global character or one must develop new and different competences to partially or totally replace the previous benefits of the cluster.

An obvious question is whether cooperative organisation, which has until now been largely nationally based with regard to management, commodity supply and ownership, is geared for the future globalised world. Immediately, there are indications that the cooperatively based food sector is able to develop based on the cluster elements in globalisation: some elements become globalised (the supply of raw materials, alliance partners, sales, investment), while other parts retain their national basis (management, ownership, etc.).

Problems can arise when vertical integration is an absolute key factor for large parts of the food sector. Clearly, the food sector cannot easily transfer the field-to-fork chain abroad and expect foreign farmers to make the same contribution as the farmers who developed and supported the food cluster in the native country. The unique cooperative competence is, on the one hand, a strong competitive parameter but, on the other hand, the competence is immobile and cannot be actively transferred to foreign countries and used for international expansion.

The conflict between national clusters and globalisation can also be seen in other sectors and in areas where cooperative ownership does not necessarily exist. Thus, one can in general see a tendency for national clusters to be no longer 'protected' by distance, and there is, therefore, a fear that they will gradually fall apart and disappear. However, it seems that clusters actually seem to be important in the new global economy, even though some will naturally disappear. Knowledge will be the determining factor for value creation.

Success criteria for food clusters

Michael Porter has created a model that illustrates the various types of advantage that arise in a cluster environment. The model, which is known as the Diamond Model or 'National Diamond', shows the four essential pillars which are required to achieve an effective cluster. It illustrates how the framework conditions such as skilled labour and advanced demand create clusters of related and competitive companies across the traditional industrial sectors.

The Diamond Model is illustrated in Figure 4.6.

In the Diamond Model, *Factor conditions* include the supply of critical and unique resources of which there are two groups: natural resources and more sophisticated resources like skilled labour, infrastructure and R & D.

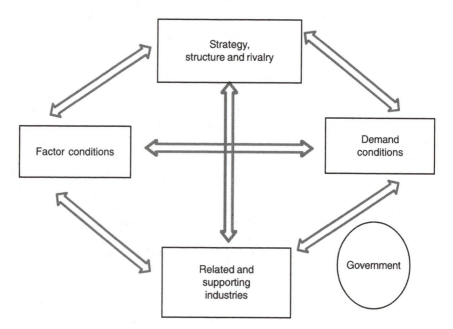

Figure 4.6 Porter's Diamond Model.
Source: Porter (1990).

Company strategy, structure and rivalry are the positive effects that internal rivalries and competition can result in.

Demand conditions involve, among other things, critical and demanding customers who pressurise companies to be innovative and competitive in order to meet their needs.

Related and supporting industries include those in the vertical and horizontal connection which are located close to one another. Close contact with suppliers, customers, competitors and colleagues ensures the effective development of competences and competitiveness.

The government's role through industrial and cluster policy is to ensure adequate infrastructure, so that the market is well functioning. It is also the government's responsibility to ensure public R & D, innovation, education, and so on and to support the areas where society has special interests, but where the market itself is unable to produce the necessary resources, etc.

The Diamond Model can be developed further by, e.g., incorporating elements from other theories so that it gives a more complete and up-to-date picture of the advantages of clusters.

Questions and assignments

4.1 Describe the elements in a cluster.
4.2 Why does innovation often play an important role in a cluster?
4.3 How may globalisation influence the role of clusters in future?
4.4 Select a random cluster of your own choice. Describe the content, context, synergies and benefits of the cluster.
4.5 How may cluster policy support and further develop the food cluster mentioned above?

5   Globalisation and food markets

Globalisation, i.e. increasing international economic integration through trade, foreign investment, migration, global alliances, etc., is a major strategic challenge for virtually all businesses in the agro and food sector. The driving forces behind globalisation seem to be stable, and the globalisation trends in the form of increasing international trade, more foreign direct investment (FDI) and cross-border mergers and acquisitions seem to be set to continue.

Alongside globalisation, more and more regional trade agreements (RTAs) are being established, and a significant and increasing proportion of international trade in agricultural and food products is now taking place between countries within the same regional trading bloc. Trading blocs can either be a substitute for more multilateral liberalisation, or they may be a step towards a more globally oriented economy.

The setting of prices on the international agricultural and food markets is both important and complex. A variety of factors closely interact and affect international prices. Knowledge of the connections and influences makes it increasingly possible to predict price development.

The international agricultural and food markets are also characterised by significant and increasing instability and volatility. This uncertainty naturally spreads to food companies and, therefore, is an important external environment factor.

Definition

Globalisation in the context of company and market development can be defined as follows:

> Globalisation is the continued development of a company's international involvement in relation to geographic markets, products, management, resources (labour, raw produce, etc.) in order to optimise in the face of the opportunities and threats on the international market.

Globalisation is not just about selling to foreign customers. It also involves recognising the international competition and adjusting production, resources, investment and organisation in line with these conditions.

Box 5.1 **Different definitions of globalisation**

For some people, globalisation means to expand the company's presence abroad, for others it means standardising a product and selling it to the world, for yet others it denotes an approach to management in which decision-making is centralised at corporate headquarters.

Lasserre (2003)

Globalization is an elimination of barriers to trade, communication, and cultural exchange.

About.com (2012)

Globalization refers to the growing economic interdependence of countries worldwide through increasing volume and variety of cross-border transactions in goods and services and of international capital flows, and also through the more rapid and widespread diffusion of technology.

IMF (1997)

In our opinion, and based on our knowledge of globalization as it is understood today, we propose the following definition:
'Globalization is a process that encompasses the causes, course, and consequences of transnational and transcultural integration of human and non-human activities.'

GCSP (2006)

Globalization may be thought of initially as the widening, deepening and speeding up of worldwide interconnectedness in all aspects of contemporary social life, from the cultural to the criminal, the financial to the spiritual.

Held *et al.* (1999)

What does 'neoliberal globalization' mean?
This concept implies complete opening of all national markets with almost no restrictions with regard to social, democratic and ecological control and regulations.

Attac (2012)

Globalisation is far from being an unambiguous concept. Globalisation is defined differently in many places, as discussed in Box 5.1.

Globalisation and internationalisation are often used interchangeably. Globalisation, however, is usually regarded as something more than internationalisation.

The first step in a company's international development – sporadic exports to neighbouring markets, export via an agent and intermediary, etc. – is usually regarded as internationalisation, while a company's establishment of overseas production, distribution of production across the world in relation to competitive conditions, etc. is usually considered as globalisation.

'Internationalisation', directly translated, means 'between nations', that is, increased international interaction. 'Globalisation' goes further in that there is a degradation and transformation of the national aspect, e.g. control and regulation within national borders, which we have become accustomed to. This distinction between internationalisation and globalisation in relation to a company's international involvement is, however, far from common.

As the literature review has shown, the terms 'internationalisation', 'globalisation', 'international diversification' and 'multinationality' are often used interchangeably. However, the way we define these theoretical constructs has dramatic consequences for how we measure them, and for what purpose. Globalisation seems to be a stronger word than internationalisation and should therefore be defined as a higher-order construct (Asmussen *et al.*, 2005).

The term, globalisation, can also have multiple dimensions and applications. Often scientists distinguish between different interpretations of globalisation, e.g.

* the liberal economic
* the technological
* the radical
* the military-strategic
* the ecological
* the sociological
* the liberal political.

The measurement of globalisation

The question is, how does one define internationalisation and globalisation? And another question is, how does one quantitatively and empirically measure globalisation? Clearly, when the definition of globalisation varies so much, its measurement will also vary in scale.

There are two different methods for quantifying globalisation. The traditional unidimensional method and the more advanced, multidimensional one. The differences between the two methods, their subcategories, etc. are presented in Box 5.2.

The unidimensional method compares a company's 'activity' on the international markets with its corresponding 'activity' on the domestic market. Thus, one can compare the following activities on the international and domestic markets (see, e.g., Asmussen, *et al.*, 2005):

* sales
* assets
* earnings

Box 5.2 Grouping of methods for measuring companies' internationalisation

	Unidimensional			Multidimensional
Category	Dichotomy	Spreading	Competence	
Concept	Home market versus export market	Dissemination of international activities	Global competence among leaders, employees and board	Several different methods used
Parameter	Turnover, employment number of subsidiaries, assets, etc.	Export markets, international investments; measured by Entropy, Gini or the like	Professional experience from working in foreign and culturally removed companies	Combination and weighting together of unidimensionel parameters

Source: Author's own presentation based on Asmussen *et al.* (2005)

- employment
- value added
- shareholders / owners.

It is possible to examine several factors which can then be weighed together. UNCTAD uses, e.g., a weighted index of assets, sales and employment on international markets and the domestic market to calculate a Transnationality Index (TNI) (UNCTAD, 2005b). Table 5.1 presents parts of UNCTAD's surveys of the TNI values for the world's largest multinational corporations.

The list includes the five most globally oriented multinational companies in the world in terms of asset distribution abroad and domestically. The table also specifically includes the nine food companies which are on the list of the 100 most globally oriented companies in the world.

The TNI values of the four most globally oriented companies lie between 43 and 82 per cent. These measurements of globalisation are relatively easy to calculate, since most data are often found in financial statements or annual reports. However, there are three major weaknesses:

First, companies in geographically small countries will, *ceteris paribus*, have a small domestic market and therefore their globalisation index value will be relatively large. Similarly, small countries have relatively significant foreign trade compared to large countries. This means that comparisons across national borders, in particular, should be treated with caution.

Second, these measurements do not account for the geographical distribution of international activities. Exports to, e.g., a large local market are ascribed the same importance as exports to many different export markets which are strategically distributed in many and distant countries. The degree of international involvement will often be very different in the two cases.

Third, the measurements do not account for whether a company follows a clear multinational strategy, or whether it is involved in more sporadic exports. With a multinational strategy, a company is seeking to achieve an optimal international division of labour and resources. Coordination of production, labour and know-how between countries is required but, conversely, the opportunities for achieving economic benefits also increase. Less strategic globalisation may occur in the form of sporadic export or a multidomestic market strategy. With a multidomestic market strategy, a company copies the set-up and concept that exists on the domestic market, and establishes it in the same form on the foreign markets.

A multidomestic market strategy facilitates significant growth and exploitation of economies of scale. However, the potential with regard to the exploitation of an international division of labour is more limited.

The comparison between activities on the domestic and export markets does not, as previously mentioned, take account of the distance to the export markets and their dispersion. Therefore, different dispersion estimates have been made, which can be

Table 5.1 The world's top five non-financial transnational corporations and the top nine food, beverage and tobacco corporations, ranked by foreign assets (2010)

		Assets		*Sales*		*Employment*		*TNI*
	Rank Company	*Foreign*	*Total*	*Foreign*	*Total*	*Foreign*	*Total*	*%*
1	General Electric	552	751	80	150	154	287	60
2	Royal Dutch Shell	272	333	231	368	82	97	77
3	BP	244	273	234	297	66	80	84
4	Vodafone	161	210	200	254	78	96	79
5	Toyota Motor	221	360	140	222	118	318	53
	Food, beverage and tobacco							
17	Nestlé	114	119	103	105	272	281	97
18	Anheuser-Busch InBev	108	114	32	36	104	114	92
46	Kraft Foods	55	95	28	49	90	127	62
54	Unilever*	50	55	54	59	136	165	88
62	British American Tobacco	43	44	23	23	46	92	83
70	SABMiller	39	39	23	28	55	70	86
90	The Coca-Cola Company	32	73	21	35	69	140	51
92	Japan Tobacco	31	43	31	72	24	48	55
97	Pernod-Richard	31	33	9	10	16	18	90

Source: UNCTAD (2012).

* Unilever is normally catagorised as a diversified company but is here included in food, beverage and tobacco.

Note: Assets and sales in US $ billion; employment in 1,000.

TNI = Transnationality Index.

very different in structure, content and complexity. Some contain simple statements of the number of countries in which companies have subsidiaries. Other methods use Gini coefficients, the Herfindahl–Hirschman Index (HHI) or the Entropy Index to calculate the concentration of export markets. At the same time, the assumption is that the more spread the export markets, and the more there are, the more a company is able to take advantage of the international division of labour.

A random distribution of export markets regardless of their size and potential can, however, give an inaccurate picture of the market dispersion. Large or small exports, e.g. to the USA, should not be attributed the same value. Therefore, a company's market dispersion can be compared with the equivalent purchasing power or welfare on the basis of the GDP of the relevant countries. This method is, however, far from perfect, as the market's size and potential is far from being reflected in, e.g., the countries' total GDP.

There are several multidimensional methods. 'Sullivan's Degree of Internation-alisation' is one example which is widely used. The method includes five variables (see Sullivan, 1994):

- foreign sales as a percentage of total sales
- foreign subsidiaries as a percentage of total subsidiaries
- foreign assets as a percentage of total assets
- cultural dispersion of international activities
- top management's international experience.

Sullivan's method includes the following three types of reference standards: domestic vs international markets, market dispersion and management's interna-tional orientation. All the indicators are calibrated from zero to one, are attributed the same weight and are added together, which results in the DOI (Degree of Internationalisation), which ranges from zero to five.

Another multidimensional index was developed by Ietto-Gillies (1998), which is also an attempt to move beyond the traditional domestic-versus-foreign market comparison. The method includes the dispersion of international activities, which are multiplied by the usual index, i.e. assets, turnover and employees on domestic and foreign markets.

The spread estimate is called the Network Spread Index (NSI), which is obtained by dividing the number of countries in which the company has subsidiaries (n), with the maximum number of countries which a company can have subsidiaries in (n*). A random distribution in many export countries is not in itself an unambiguous expres-sion of significant internationalisation. A very internationally oriented company will probably disperse sales according to its size and economic importance.

This aspect is the foundation for the 'Degree of Globalisation', as developed by Fisch and Osterle (2003), whereby, among other things, a company's global spread is compared with the spread in the world economy. The starting point is that both the geographical spread of the company's international activities and the cultural spread and diversity in the countries in which the company is involved, are included in the internationalisation index.

The Degree of Globalisation (dog) is defined as:

$$dog = \sqrt{gs^2 + cd^2}$$
$$gs = (1 - g_{MNC}) / (1 - g_{GNP})$$

g_{MNC} = geographical spread of all economic activity in the world calculated as Gini coefficient

g_{GNP} = the spread of the company's international activities calculated as Gini coefficient

cd = cultural diversity (as defined by Hofstede, 1993).

The Degree of Globalisation is more complex and far-reaching than the traditional internationalisation index. The advantage is that the method is multidimensional, but the drawback is data availability.

The use of multidimensional indices gives, on the one hand, a fuller and more comprehensive picture of a company's internationalisation / globalisation. Participation in the international division of labour is described better when multiple dimensions of a company's international involvement are analysed. On the other hand, weighing together several completely different indices which apply completely different methods and content to reach a single figure is problematic. Therefore, it will always be possible to question the comparability and weighting. It may, e.g., appear unscientific to take the average of 'the management's international experience' and 'the relationship between assets at home and abroad'.

The importance of globalisation

Globalisation as we have witnessed it in recent years is very important for socio-economic development.

The *positive* approach, which is generally dominant in international business, is that globalisation in the form of greater international trade and cooperation, investment and the movement of capital across national borders, etc. gives better resource allocation and increased economic welfare. Increasing international competition also benefits consumers by way of lower prices. Companies can take advantage of the freer market to expand globally in the areas where they have a competitive position.

This results in an increased division of labour and international specialisation, which ensures that goods are produced where production is cheapest, including in environmental and resources terms. If there are environmental costs, they can simply be passed on to the consumer or the use of resources can be controlled, even during globalisation.

This problem is particularly relevant for the agricultural and food sector, as a very locally based agricultural market can result in significant environmental problems. Without participation in globalisation, Japan, for example, would be self-sufficient in agricultural products. Japan is able to feed its own population, but this would demand a very intensive and resource-demanding agricultural sector.

The *critical and negative* attitude to globalisation can be found in several places. The international grassroots movement, Attac, is a significant opponent of globalisation in its current form. Attac is an international organisation which is involved in the alter-globalisation movement. Attac opposes neoliberal globalisation and develops social, ecological and democratic alternatives which aim to guarantee fundamental rights for all. Specifically, Attac fights for the regulation of financial markets, the closure of tax havens, the introduction of global taxes to finance global public goods, the cancellation of the debt of developing countries, fair trade, and the implementation of limits to free trade and capital flows (see Attac, 2012).

There are other anti-globalisation positions and movements which work against further globalisation and instead focus more on the local. Hines (2002) is an interesting exponent of this position. In essence, Hines turns things upside down and argues for increased protectionism, increased self-sufficiency, less international trade and fewer foreign investments, areas in which the trend is in exactly the opposite direction.

Hines is attempting to create a change in attitudes away from the automatic acceptance of globalisation as inevitable development. He instead argues for development that protects and rebuilds local economies worldwide. The starting point is: everything that can be produced within a country or a region is produced within that country or region. Therefore, countries, or geographical regions, only import goods which they cannot produce.

According to Hines (2002), greater localisation and less globalisation should also apply to developing countries. Agriculture in developing countries should not produce for export, but rather mainly for the very local markets. This is a somewhat controversial suggestion, which goes very much against the flow. Today, many developing countries want access to markets in particular and not support (Trade not Aid).

Many have pointed out that the environment is best protected under localisation and is damaged by globalisation. In particular, transport costs involved in a global market are being used as an argument that the environment is better protected by a local market.

The drivers behind globalisation

When globalisation is mentioned as one of the greatest challenges, and when globalisation is an implicit or explicit precondition in many companies' strategic action plan, it becomes relevant to ask oneself whether the extent and duration of globalisation is consistent. Is globalisation merely a transient phenomenon, a wave which will soon subside, die out, to be replaced by a second wave with completely different content? Can external conditions such as international terrorism, new serious energy crises, etc. force back the tide of globalisation?

Or is globalisation really a permanent leap which changes the conditions for citizens, nations and companies, and which will result in borders becoming superfluous and eventually disappearing? Is a paradigm shift occurring, which necessitates, e.g., the reformulation of the theoretical foundation of international business economics, trade theory and the welfare state? Has globalisation gained so much momentum that it cannot be stopped?

The future will probably be somewhere in between. Globalisation does not come by itself, but is due to a number of underlying 'drivers' which are consistent and stable and which will probably promote globalisation in the future. These conditions are set out in Box 5.3.

Yip (1992) and later a number of other authors, including Lasserre (2003), emphasise that globalisation became more and more widespread in the early 1970s because of a series of political, technological, social and competitive factors.

Box 5.3 Driving forces behind globalisation

Political and macro-economic factors

- trade and capital liberalisation
- market economy reforms in many developing countries
- the failure of communism and the planned economy
- the spread of emerging economies
- private equity funds
- privatisation of state-owned companies
- development of internal markets and trade blocs
- public business and export promotion
- international trade organisations, etc.

Technological factors

- faster and cheaper transport options
- international communication
- developmental pressure and shorter product life-cycles.

Social factors

- organisations across borders
- international tourism
- the human desire to explore
- language and other cultural barriers become less significant.

Competitive factors

- International comparative advantages
- global marketing is possible and advantageous
- the exploitation of first-mover effect
- need to match global players
- focus on core activities and outsourcing.

Source: Author's presentation based on Yip (1992),
Lasserre (2003) and UNCTAD (2005b, 2006)

The *political* factors included the ongoing liberalisation of international trade and investments. The WTO can be highlighted as a significant example of a political authority which has helped to promote liberalisation.

The *technological* factors include transportation, communications and economies of scale. The technological factors have reduced the cost of, e.g., air and sea transport. At the same time, technological developments such as satellite and the Internet have greatly improved and reduced the cost of global communication. Technological development has also enabled new industrial economies of scale that can be exploited via an international division of labour and specialisation.

The *social* factors include the fact that lifestyles, consumer preferences, tourism, etc. are becoming increasingly international. The same brands are in demand worldwide, and fashion, music and lifestyle spread rapidly throughout the world.

The *competitive* factors include the fact that some companies strategically choose a global approach when it comes to the supply of raw produce, production, marketing, etc. In a more free-trade-based world, these companies gain a competitive advantage, which puts pressure on other companies to adopt the same strategy.

There is a complex relationship among the individual driving forces. Some stimulate globalisation and are in turn stimulated by globalisation itself. Some conditions can be driving forces and effects at the same time, thereby resulting in a self-reinforcing effect. Thus, it can be difficult to distinguish between, e.g., the content of globalisation and its effects.

Globalisation: international trade and investments

The globalisation of companies and business sectors has changed significantly in recent years. Generally, globalisation in the form of international trade, foreign investments and mergers across borders is increasing. The trend is clear, although international recession, the economic downturn and a significant fall in share prices slows the development for shorter or longer periods.

Globalisation in the form of increasing international trade is very apparent. An increasing share of trade occurs across national borders, and international trade is increasing much more than the world's total production (see Figure 5.1).

The figure shows that growth in international trade has been much greater than the growth in the world's total production.

In order to illustrate increasing globalisation, Figure 5.2 presents world trade in relation to the world's total GDP, and foreign investments in relation to total investments.

There is a clear increasing trend for both international trade and international investments. International investments increased most during the period, but they were also the most sensitive to economic cycles.

When one considers FDI stock, it is worth noting that, following a significant increase during recent decades, it now equals the world's total international trade per year (see Figure 5.3).

As is evident from the figure, international trade and FDI increased significantly more than the world's total GDP during the period. It is especially worth

Figure 5.1 Development in total international trade and total production.

Source: Author's calculation based on WTO (2012a).

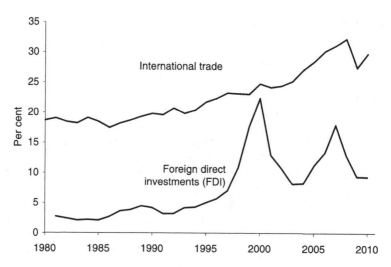

Figure 5.2 The relationship between world trade and the world's total GDP, and between the world's total foreign investment and total investments.

Source: WTO (2012a).

noting that FDI stock has risen dramatically since the mid-1990s. This emphasises that globalisation via FDI is becoming increasingly important, while globalisation through international trade is becoming relatively less important.

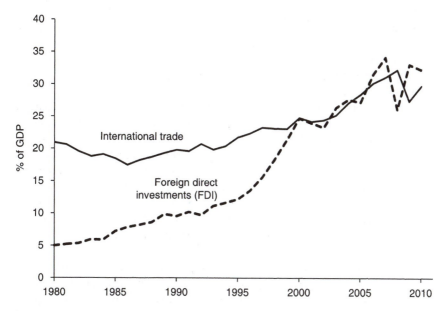

Figure 5.3 International trade and FDI stock as a percentage of world GDP.

Source: World Bank (2012b), WTO (2012b) and author's calculations.

This sensitivity to international cycles is particularly evident when one considers the FDI flows, which are compiled on an annual basis. It is noteworthy that these FDI flows vary significantly over time and develop very much in line with the development in the state of the market (see Figure 5.4).

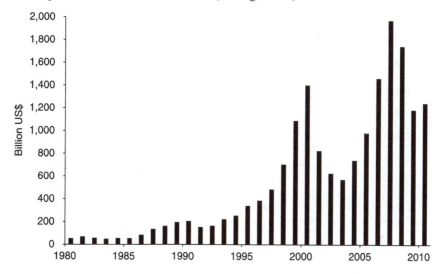

Figure 5.4 FDI flows.

Source: UNCTAD (2012).

When one looks at the world's total FDI, there has been a marked increase in recent decades. However, the development has not been uniform across all sectors, and the food industry is one of the sectors where the increase in foreign investment has been relatively weak. The world's total foreign investments in the food industry therefore represent a decreasing share of the corresponding investments in the overall industry.

In recent years, the service sector in particular has gained an increasing share of foreign investment. Despite this relative decline, there has been a significant increase in foreign investment in the food industry over the last 10–20 years.

During the past decade, globalisation, in the form of international mergers, has become increasingly significant – to some extent at the expense of domestic mergers. From 1995 to 2000, the annual value of acquired or merged international businesses increased from US $185 billion to $1,150 billion, which corresponds to approximately 3.5 per cent of the world's total GDP. Subsequently, the significance of mergers and acquisitions, both national and international, has reduced (see Figure 5.5).

The figure shows the total annual value of international mergers in relation to the world's total GDP. Historically, international mergers and acquisitions primarily took place between a number of industrialised countries. However, during the last few years, the development has spread to the third world. Mergers in the food industry develop in much the same way as in industry as a whole (see Figure 5.6).

As the figure shows, the food industry and total manufacturing follow a similar development over time.

When viewed over a longer perspective, several global and/or national merger waves are apparent. The latest merger wave was predominantly generated by the

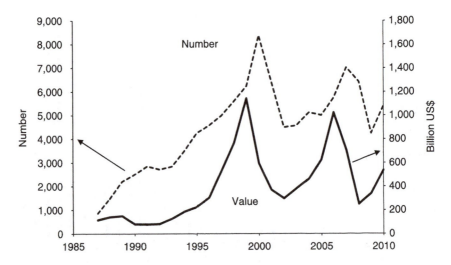

Figure 5.5 Total number of international mergers.

Source: UN (2012).

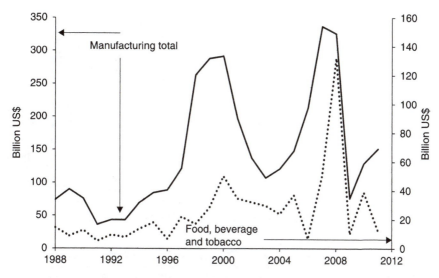

Figure 5.6 Number of global mergers and acquisitions in the food industry (food, beverages and tobacco) and in total.

Source: UNCTAD (2012).

globalisation wave, which in turn was generated, in part, by the fall of the Berlin Wall and increasing economic and political liberalisation. Globalisation has created new and larger markets, which promote international integration. Also, technological development, economic growth, share price increases and deregulation have contributed to the recent merger waves.

Similarly, the merger waves of the 1930s were based on vertical integration, while around the 1970s, they were rooted in the creation of several large conglomerates see (Figure 5.7).

As can be seen in Figure 5.7, the recurring merger waves appear to be systematic to a degree. In each case, the 'wave crests' can be explained by external factors that created fertile ground for increased merger activity.

Mergers and acquisitions result in a number of subsidiaries abroad. These subsidiaries provide far greater sales than the 'traditional' exports, i.e. actual exports of goods from the home country. Mergers and acquisitions abroad are a greater source of globalisation than exports (see Figure 5.8).

As shown in the figure, significant growth in sales through foreign subsidiaries has occurred since the mid-1990s, while internationalisation through exports has increased only slightly.

A similar pattern can be seen in, e.g., the US food processing industry. Here, sales through foreign subsidiaries, etc. have been three–four times as important as direct exports from the USA (see Handy *et al.* 1996). Sales through foreign subsidiaries, created by mergers and investments outside the country, have thus become a very important instrument in a company's strategic development and globalisation.

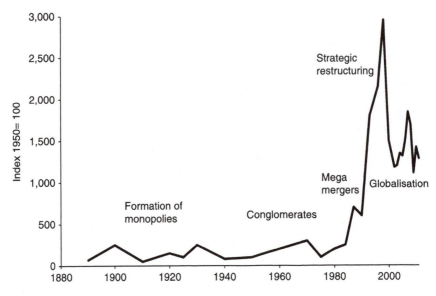

Figure 5.7 Global merger waves: 1880 to the present.

Source: Author's presentation based on Bayrak (2002), Sisodiya (2004), Yago (1999) and UNCTAD (2012).

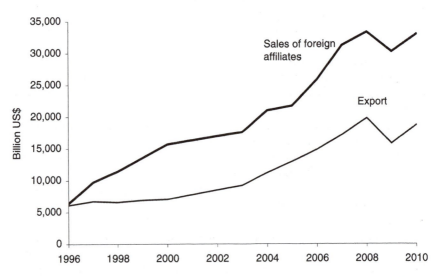

Figure 5.8 Development in the world's total exports and sales through foreign subsidiaries.

Source: UNCTAD (several years).

Globalisation of the food industry and markets

Globalisation affects all markets and sectors. However, some areas are more exposed than others and therefore the effect is different between the various markets and sectors. Globalisation has, therefore, a general and a specific influence on food companies and markets.

When it comes to development in international trade, it is typical that trade with agricultural and food products across borders is relatively small in relation to trade on the domestic markets.

The world market's limited importance can be seen as being the result of agricultural and trade policy, although other factors also play a role. In general, one can say that the modest global trade is due to the following conditions:

- A short shelf-life makes long-distance transportation difficult and expensive.
- All countries can achieve a certain degree of self-production, which limits the need for imports.
- The desire to achieve a certain degree of self-sufficiency created through import barriers limits trade opportunities.
- Other trade and agricultural policy conditions are present.
- Fixed resources and general low adaptability in agriculture are limiting factors.

Even though there are political and economic obstacles to the internationalisation of agricultural markets, there has been significant growth in international trade in agricultural products. The international trade as a percentage of total production has increased significantly for most of the important agricultural products (see Figure 5.9).

When international trade becomes increasingly important, a further division of labour or specialisation occurs between countries. Each country specialises in the areas which it is best at and abandons the areas in which it cannot compete internationally.

Here, however it is also valid that the development in international specialisation has hitherto been relatively weak regarding agricultural products. As can be seen in Figure 5.10, international specialisation, here measured as the development in international trade and production, has been much stronger for industrial goods than for agricultural products in the past few decades.

The figure shows the development in international trade in relation to the development in the world's total production. As can be seen, in general, international trade has increased more than production, but the development has been much stronger for industrial goods than for agricultural products.

Within the category of agricultural goods, there are also considerable differences regarding the degree of globalisation. The general trend is that international trade in processed agricultural products increases much faster than trade in semi-processed or unprocessed agricultural products.

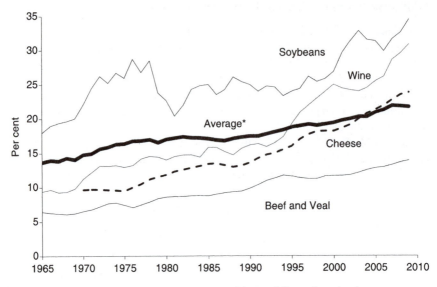

Figure 5.9 International trade as a percentage of the world's total production.

Source: Author's calculations based on FAO (2012).

* Weighted average of 14 major agricultural goods.

Note: 3-year moving average.

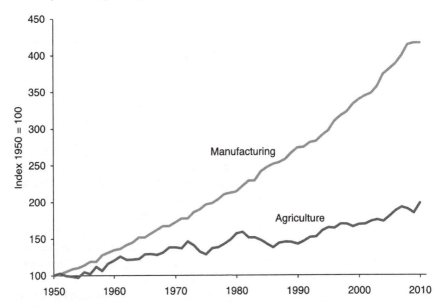

Figure 5.10 Development in the international specialisation of agricultural and industrial products.

Source: WTO (2011) and author's calculations.

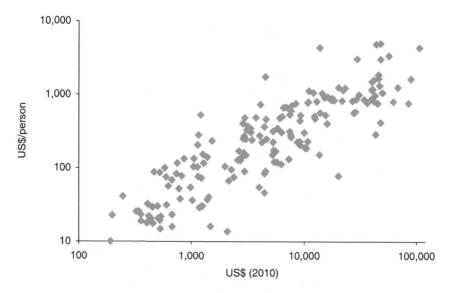

Figure 5.11 Total international food trade per capita as a function of countries' GDP per capita.

Source: Author's calculations based on FAO (2012) and World Bank (2012b).

Increasing globalisation in the food sector is not just development over time, as internationalisation is also a function of economic development. It is noteworthy that most developing countries have very small net exports or net imports regarding agricultural commodities, but these countries become increasingly either net exporters or net importers in line with economic growth. Therefore, greater and greater international specialisation occurs whereby countries adapt to a division of labour in relation to their comparative advantages.

The large international trade and specialisation in the agricultural sector in line with economic development is emphasised by Figure 5.11, which shows countries' total international agricultural trade per capita.

The very clear connection between economic development and international trade, as shown in Figure 5.11, suggests that economic development is a prerequisite for participation in international trade and specialisation in the food area.

Regional trade agreements (RTAs) – trade blocs

RTAs, free trade agreements, customs unions and the like between different countries are becoming increasingly important. Some 30–40 per cent of international trade today is conducted under RTAs, of which there are over 200 active agreements. On average, a country is involved in three–four different RTAs. Globalisation and regionalisation thus occur in parallel.

RTAs can, on the one hand, be a substitute for further WTO liberalisation. On the other hand, they can be a first step towards a more general opening up of countries' trade and economy to the outside world. Therefore, it is not possible to say anything unequivocal about the pros and cons, as RTAs can both promote and distort international trade. However, there are striking examples of distortion due to RTAs.

RTAs also have a major influence on international food markets – although food products often have a special status in these agreements.

Trade agreements: concept and content

RTAs, trading blocs and the regionalisation of international trade are concepts which cover several types of cooperation. One form of cooperation exists in a free trade area where there is in principle free movement of goods across borders. In relation to third countries, countries in free trade areas can maintain their individual trade barriers.

In a customs union, economic integration is greater, as a common external tariff is maintained with the rest of the world. Once again, goods have free movement across the internal borders. However, trade distortions and thereby a sub-optimal resource allocation will not be avoided on this basis, as the individual member countries' economic policy, industrial policy, legislation, etc. may favour domestic production. If the target is perfect competition with equal economic conditions in all member states, coordination of the economic and political conditions will be necessary. Thus, we are now dealing with economic and political union, which is the closest form of integration between independent nations (see Box 5.4).

When studying the incidence of economic trading blocs, the whole spectrum of different forms of integration can be observed. In the EU, the process is well advanced, as the original customs union is now moving towards economic and political union. In the EFTA, the development has not gone beyond a free trade area, from which even agricultural products are excluded.

Over 80 per cent of the RTAs which are notified by the WTO are free trade agreements and they are, when measured in number, still the most widespread form of cooperation.

Despite the different levels of integration, we are dealing with the same fundamental meaning: internal trade must be free, so that the member countries receive preferential treatment. In contrast, the countries which are outside the agreement are discriminated against.

RTAs represent a complex and highly heterogeneous system. First, as shown in Box 5.4, the different contractual forms represent different degrees and types of integration. Second, the content and scope can be very different from agreement to agreement.

The following conditions are normally included in a trade agreement, depending on the nature of the agreement, political negotiations, etc.:

- the size of the duty (internally and externally)
- goods and/or sectors excluded from the agreements
- transition rules and duration

Box 5.4 Regional trade and cooperative agreements: types and content

	No customs, import quota or non-trade barriers among participating countries	Common external trade policy with common external tariffs quota and non-trade barriers to third countries	Free movement of capital and labour	Harmonisation and coordination of economic and social policy in order to ensure free movement	Common and harmonised monetary policy	Harmonisation and coordination of the political system in order to control the economic and monetary union
Free trade area	■					
Customs union	■	■				
Common market	■	■	■			
Economic union	■	■	■	■		
Economic and monetary union	■	■	■	■	■	
Political union	■	■	■	■	■	■

Increasing integration, complexity and commitment →

- rules concerning country of origin
- non-tariff restrictions
- exemptions for the sake of the environment, protection of health, etc.
- safeguards which countries can rely on in emergency situations, with balance of payments problems, agricultural problems, etc.
- rules concerning anti-dumping and retaliatory measures
- rules concerning admission of new countries in the agreements.

As can be seen, many factors must be determined in each individual case. Therefore, the scope and the variation in trade agreements is also great.

RTAs can be divided up in ways other than via the degree of integration. RTAs can also be either mutual or unilateral, and they can favour a small or a large and unrestricted group of countries. This division should be seen in light of the fact that a growing number of RTAs are unilaterally favourable in that developed countries favour developing countries.

In some cases, these agreements are not defined as being part of the official regional trade agreements, while, in other cases, they carry equal weight. Box 5.5 presents a schematic breakdown with examples of each type of trade agreement.

Development

In recent years, RTAs have become increasingly important. The number of RTAs is increasing, and a growing share of world trade takes place under special conditions under RTAs (Crawford and Fiorentino, 2005). Especially from the beginning of this century, there has been a significant increase (see Figure 5.12). Since the establishment of GATT (the General Agreement on Tariffs and Trade) in 1948, almost 300 RTAs have been created, of which approximately 200 are active today.

Box 5.5 **Trade agreements by form and beneficiary (World Bank, 2005)**

| | *Form* | |
Target group / beneficiary **Reciprocal**		**Unilateral**
Selected countries	NAFTA, EU COMESA, etc.	GSP, AGOA EBA, Cotonou
All countries	GATT/WTO Multilateral agreements	Autonomic liberalisation*

* There are several examples of countries which have unilaterally reduced their trade protection to all countries.

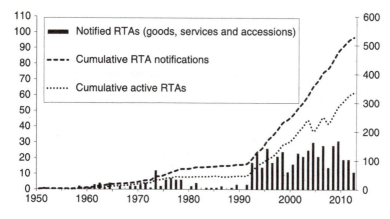

Figure 5.12 RTAs notified by the GATT / WTO, including inactive RTAs.
Source: Author's presentation based on WTO (2012b).

The figure shows the new agreements, while the accumulated number of RTAs which were concluded in the period, but which are no longer active, have been removed. Unilaterally favourable trade agreements between developed and developing countries are not included in the figure.

Development trends in recent years have been:

- RTAs are being increasingly used by countries which otherwise prefer and rely on general and global trade liberalisation measures. RTAs thereby have the same priority as, e.g., WTO negotiations.
- RTAs are becoming increasingly complex and thus opaque.
- Agreements between two or more trade groups are being increasingly concluded.
- Factors other than just access to trade are being included in the agreements. Foreign direct investment, cooperation on economic development, etc. are more often part of the contractual basis.

Several authors (e.g. OECD, 2001; CEPII, 2004) talk about how the development in regional trade cooperation has occurred in waves – even if one does not completely agree about the waves' position and content. However, three significant processes and 'epochs' can be identified – as shown in Figure 5.13.

The first wave was created in connection with the establishment of the two European regional trade agreements, the EC and EFTA. Thus European integration began in earnest as a result, among other things, of the end of the Second World War.

The second wave came in the mid-1980s with the EC's internal market and free trade agreements between the USA and Canada, and later also with Mexico. The establishment of the internal market in the European Community developed free internal competition even further.

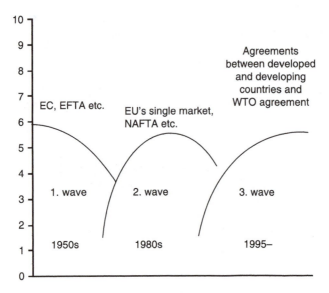

Figure 5.13 Previous waves in regional trade cooperation.

Source: Author's presentation based on OECD (2001), CEPII (2004) and WTO (2011).

The third wave came in the late 1990s and early twenty-first century. Several new agreements between developed and developing countries were concluded, which were to stimulate economic development and welfare in the developing countries through trade and by improving developing countries' conditions regarding international trade and investments. Finally, the establishment of the WTO and the progress during the recent rounds of negotiations, have created a new generation of free trade agreements.

Scope

Almost all countries in the world today have signed up to an RTA. The EU has the greatest concentration of RTAs and has had more than 20 active regional trade agreements with other countries and areas. As the EU enlarges, many of the agreements that the EU had with candidate countries no longer apply.

The importance of exports to regional trading blocs as a share of total exports and the total export of agricultural products for different countries is presented in Table 5.2.

The table shows that the dependence on exports in an RTA varies considerably from country to country and from product to product.

Previous analyses (WTO, 2002) show that 60–80 per cent of imports to Europe come from countries with which the importing country has entered into an RTA. Canada has 70 per cent of its imports coming from countries with which the

Table 5.2 Exports within regional trade agreements (2009)

Country	RTA	Total export %	Agr. export %
Mexico	NAFTA	84	79
Canada	NAFTA	76	54
US	NAFTA	32	29
NAFTA	NAFTA	48	40
Brazil	Mercosur	13	4
Argentina	Mercosur	27	12
Mercosur	Mercosur	14	9
Russia	CIS	16	23
Ukraine	CIS	35	27
CIS	CIS	19	33
Germany	EU (15)	52	67
Italy	EU (15)	48	62
Netherlands	EU (15)	69	74
EU (15)	EU (15)	57	70

Source: WTO (2011).

country has entered into an RTA, while Mexico's figure is as high as 80 per cent. Also African countries like Uganda and Namibia have 80 per cent, while the proportion is significantly lower in Asia.

According to two different studies (OECD, 2005 and WTO, 2011), the share of total trade which can be attributed to RTAs has increased significantly since the early 1980s (see Figure 5.14).

As the figure shows, there has been a sharp increase in the proportion of world trade covered by RTAs in recent decades.

However, it should be borne in mind that significant liberalisation of international trade also occurred in the period. The average tariff rate in developed countries fell below 40 per cent of the level in 1980 and market price support for agricultural products fell by 80 per cent in the period 1986–2010.

A large proportion of world trade is now traded without any duties. For example, import duty was 3 per cent or less in 45 per cent of US and EU customs tariffs. This means that countries do not achieve any significant advantage by entering into trade agreements for these goods. If one takes into account this 'dilution' of the value of entering into an RTA, a somewhat different picture emerges. Conversely, one should also consider the value encompassed by the fact that RTAs can be the impetus for further multinational liberalisation. In this way, RTAs can render themselves superfluous.

Motives for establishing trade blocs

From a socio-economic and business-economic perspective, RTAs are only a 'second best' solution. It will always be more optimal, financially speaking, to

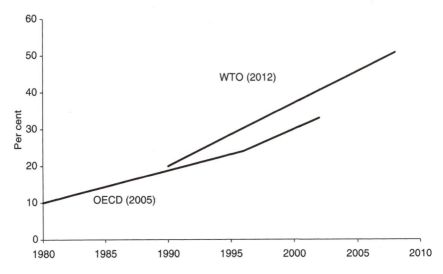

Figure 5.14 Share of world trade which is covered by RTAs (excluding unilateral contracts which favour developing countries).

Source: WTO (2011) and World Bank (2005).

create free trade between all trading partners than between a group of countries. The question is, therefore, what are the motives behind the recent significant growth in the number of free trade agreements?

In the following section, the most important motives for the establishment of RTAs in recent years are discussed:

Lack of results for global liberalisation

There have been several examples of RTAs which have emerged as substitutes for WTO agreements, but which have not or have only partly been successful. The mere prospect of a WTO round of negotiations failing to achieve the desired results has been the motive for the establishment of RTAs. For example, the step backwards in negotiations during the Doha Round in Cancún in 2003, explains the subsequent growing interest in establishing RTAs (Crawford and Fiorentino, 2005).

More than trade cooperation

RTAs can also be interpreted as attempts to go one step further in the globalisation process. In particular, the highly integrated forms of cooperation such as economic and monetary unions, political unions, etc. go far beyond what can easily be agreed by the WTO in the form of multilateral agreements, etc. The EU is an example of an RTA that has been expanded from being a customs union to being an economic and monetary union, and in some areas also a political union.

Quick and easy to adopt

Trade agreements between a few countries (two or more) frequently occur, which is often because such agreements are easy to adopt and implement. Large multilateral agreements under the auspices of the WTO, which are also significant in scope and importance for subsequent trade liberalisation, have to be negotiated for several years before they can be adopted, see Table 5.3.

When there are only a few countries involved in the trade negotiations, it is usually easier and faster to reach an agreement. This is an important aspect for both politicians and the business community.

Discriminatory liberalisation

Countries with political aspirations to protect vulnerable business sectors (ship-building, the textile industry, agriculture, etc.) can establish free trade agreements with selected countries that do not have a significant competitive industry in these areas. In this way, gains from free trade within the trading bloc can be achieved, albeit partially.

Experience building

For countries which have previously had a planned economy and state trade, entering directly into a global or far-reaching trade agreement can be a big and uncertain step to take. A limited bilateral agreement with a neighbouring country which is perhaps facing the same challenges may be a first step. At the same time, experience can be built which can be exploited in subsequent more far-reaching agreements.

Political motives

There may be other motives and initiatives than just trade political ones in an RTA. Trade agreements, for example, have become an integral part of EU foreign policy, especially in relation to the Eastern and Central European countries after the collapse of the Berlin Wall.

Table 5.3 Recent trade rounds in GATT / WTO and their duration

Round of negotiation	Start	Duration (years)
The Kennedy round	1964	3
The Tokyo round	1973	6
The Uruguay round	1986	7½
The Doha round	2001	

Source: WTO (2012b).

Developing country policy

Developed countries have, in many cases, established regional trade agreements with developing countries as a tool for assisting developing countries. There are many examples of developed countries entering into framework agreements with developing countries, which include bilateral free trade, support and funding. Financial help is thus an incentive to become involved in more open free trade cooperation. With regard to the EU, the Cotonou Agreement can be mentioned, which is the successor to the former Lomé Agreement and which contains a series of measures in the form of economic aid, trade cooperation, political initiatives, etc. EBA (Everything but arms) is also an EU initiative which gives the 49 poorest countries free access to EU markets (see also Box 5.7).

Trade agreements and the WTO

A fundamental rule of both GATT and WTO is that trade between countries must be conducted without discrimination. In other words, all trading partners must be treated equally when exporting or importing.

However, permission to set up regional trade agreements is granted in three areas: Article 24 of the WTO, a special exception regarding developing countries (enabling clause) and Article 5 of the WTO's General Agreement on Trade in Services (GATS).

The WTO's Article 24 allows regional trade agreements as an exception to the general regulations. However, there are special preconditions attached to this exemption. It is particularly essential that RTAs make trade between participating countries freer, while, at the same time, barriers to countries outside the agreement must not be tightened. Countries outside the agreement must not experience trade barriers becoming tighter with the establishment or expansion of the agreement. This means that RTAs should complement, not undermine, the general WTO regulations and aims, the main principle being non-discrimination.

Article 24 also states that if a free trade area or a customs union is created, all customs duties and other trade barriers in all trade areas in the region must be reduced or removed. Thus, a free trade area which only covers a few selected products or sectors cannot be established. There are thus three conditions:

- freer internal trade
- no tightening of trade barriers to third countries
- all product categories in the internal trade must be covered.

In particular, the last condition is not always satisfied in all cases. It appears that agricultural products are often partially or totally left out of free trade agreements.

The second exception rule relates to 'differentiated and more favourable treatment, reciprocity and participation of developing countries (enabling clause)'. This exemption facilitates the creation of specific and advantageous trade agreements with developing countries without other countries being able to claim the same advantages (GATT, 1979).

Finally, Article 5 of the GATS (an agreement under the WTO, the aim of which is to include services, etc. in the same manner as the WTO covers trade in actual goods (see WTO, 2012b)) allows member states to enter into regional agreements to liberalise trade in services. The overall goal is to support trade between participating countries. It is also the case here that the agreements must not lead to tighter trade barriers to third countries.

Figure 5.15 shows that almost 60 per cent of all RTAs are based on the exemption clauses listed in GATT / WTO, Article 25. Approximately 30 per cent are based on GATS, Article 5 and 10 per cent are based on the exemption clause regarding developing countries (enabling clause). The calculation thus covers all the 336 agreements that were in force in 2012.

Generally it turns out to be difficult to estimate whether the exemption clauses and the conditions are satisfied in each individual case. It is, however, relatively easy to calculate the amount of duty before and after establishment, while it is much harder to visualise and quantify the other trade limitations. It is especially difficult to assess the consequences when the agreements are complex and include exemptions and interim arrangements, etc. In addition, the contractual basis of the

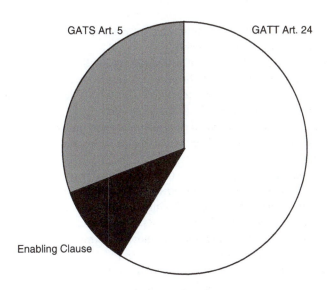

Figure 5.15 Background for establishment of regional trade agreements (2012).

Source: Author's presentation based on WTO (2011).

WTO is not very precisely formulated in certain key areas, which opens it up for individual interpretation.

Economic effects

The establishment of regional trade blocs affects the economies of both participating countries and third countries in several ways. Relative prices are changed, thereby affecting the competitive situation in the whole area. Resource allocation, welfare economics, international trade and economic transfers between different sectors of society are some of the factors which are influenced to a greater or lesser extent. Lipsey (1960) provided the first fundamental analysis of the consequences of regional trade blocs.

The establishment of a regional trade bloc can have a negative or positive effect on a country's economic welfare. On the one hand, it may be that the removal of internal tariffs means that consumers can buy goods more cheaply in one of the other countries instead of more expensive domestically produced goods which they were previously forced to buy. Thus, more goods are produced and traded which have been produced at lower costs. This positive effect is generally known as *trade creation* (see, e.g. Viner, 1950).

On the other hand, it is possible that consumers have previously demanded cheap goods from a third country, but that this possibility is removed because of the trade bloc protection from the outside world. Instead, the demand is directed towards one of the trading countries, where production costs are higher, but where free trade selectively favours internal trade. The result is that internal trade increases, but with higher costs for consumers. This negative effect is called *trade diversion*.

The establishment of a trading bloc will thus have a positive welfare economic effect if *trade creation* exceeds *trade diversion*.

In the longer term, the establishment of a trading bloc will lead to changed terms of trade and increasing income, both of which can be beneficial to third countries. The creation of free internal markets will lead to a considerable increase in welfare among member countries. This increased growth will also greatly benefit third countries. This effect is called external trade creation (OECD 1992). It is therefore too narrow to assess trade creation and trade diversion through an assessment of the trade bloc's consequences.

Quantitative assessments of the importance of trading blocs are obviously difficult to conduct. Even in the short term, many price relationships are affected, and these new relationships have to be compared with the previous conditions or in relation to a situation with free trade. These considerations alone, *ceteris paribus*, result in significant uncertainty. In addition, the more dynamic and long-range effects are even more difficult to estimate.

Numerous analyses have been conducted into the effects of RTAs. Many studies conclude, however, that nothing definite can be said about the economic consequences, but that it depends on the structure and content of the trade agreement as well as the alternative to the trade agreement.

An optimal trade bloc

A series of preconditions can be mentioned which must be met to ensure that trade agreements have an important and positive effect on the international economy:

- WTO rules must be respected. This implies, in particular, that all major product groups and sectors are covered and that protection against third countries is not increased.
- Protection within the trade bloc is too much before, but small (or zero) after the establishment of the trading bloc.
- There are significant differences in the comparative advantages between countries which are part of a trading bloc. Two similar countries with similar comparative advantages and possibly the same resources will not have the same specialisation and economic welfare benefits as two very different countries.
- The trade bloc includes many countries and large economies.
- The trade agreement results in diverted liberalisation. The internal trade liberalisation in a trading bloc often results in a spillover effect in the form of liberalisation in other areas. It may well be the case that, in the long run, it can be difficult to exclude some product areas or sectors from a trade agreement because the interface between protected and unprotected products gradually makes separation impossible. Also, pressure for the liberalisation of capital markets, the harmonisation of standards, etc. can be a beneficial consequence of an RTA.
- Internally in a free trade area, there will usually be special rules regarding the country of origin. When there is no common external tariff, a country may have very low tariffs for third countries and can thus act as a 'transit country'. Therefore, there will, in reality, be virtually free access to the entire free trade area with the low tariff, which can undermine the entire agreement. Therefore, it is normal that the internal free trade only applies to products which originate in the countries which are part of the agreement. For instance, it can be difficult to precisely determine the origin of processed products and, therefore, this regulation can be of greater or lesser importance. The fewer constraints within rules regarding the country of origin, the more free trade with third countries, and the more economically optimal the free trade areas.
- In addition to the fact that trade barriers against third countries should be as small as possible, they must also distort trade as little as possible. For example, the import duty should be fixed and not variable to create the least possible artificial upheaval in world markets.

RTAs in relation to agricultural and food products

Agricultural and food products are, in many ways, afforded special status by the WTO. For several decades, there have been exemptions for agricultural products, while there is also a generally higher level of protection for agricultural goods than for all the other products combined.

Agricultural and food products, however, are treated very differently in the individual RTAs. On the one hand, we have the EU, where agriculture is fully integrated, and where decoupled schemes as well as veterinary and phyto-sanitary schemes are more or less harmonised and thus common. On the other hand, we have the actual and specific free trade agreements, which are often targeted on specific areas.

In addition, an increasing proportion of agricultural policy and support is now administered through non-trade instruments. Thus, an increasing share of agriculture will, *ceteris paribus*, be outside the range of normal trade agreements.

Therefore, even though agriculture has received more attention in recent trade rounds, and although agricultural subsidies have been reduced significantly, agriculture is still often subject to specific exemptions in RTAs.

According to Lee (1995), agriculture is one of the sectors which is most often subject to exemptions and exclusions in free trade agreements. This takes the form of long transitional regulations and special security exemptions. The WTO (2002) also note that most RTAs exclude certain sectors, e.g. agriculture. The OECD (2005) also confirms that the sectors that are difficult to include in multinational trade liberalisation within the WTO, are similarly difficult to integrate and liberalise in RTAs. It should be noted, however, that it is a very complex and diverse area which makes it difficult to conclude very much in general about the position of agricultural products in RTAs.

Damuri (2009) shows that in several bilateral agreements a number of products are excluded either temporarily or permanently. These products are mainly within the agricultural or food sectors.

Examples of RTAs

The significant growth in the number of RTAs in recent years has meant that many contracts overlap each other to a greater or lesser extent. This has made the picture very complex, which has been described as the 'spaghetti bowl' effect. As an example, Figure 5.16 illustrates a 'spaghetti bowl' based on RTAs in the USA and the Asia-Pacific region.

As can be seen in Figure 5.16, there are many examples of RTAs which overlap each other, and all countries are on average in four RTAs.

The World Bank (2005) also warns that the myriad agreements will result in a large bureaucracy, and will therefore also result in significant administrative costs. The overlapping agreements with different content, processes and conditions result in a number of complications:

First, the country of origin must be specified, but the criteria for this often conflict, which necessitates a series of administrative measures.

Second, the membership of several RTAs can result in import duties, etc. varying from product to product and from country to country, which makes it very opaque and difficult to administer, especially for developing countries.

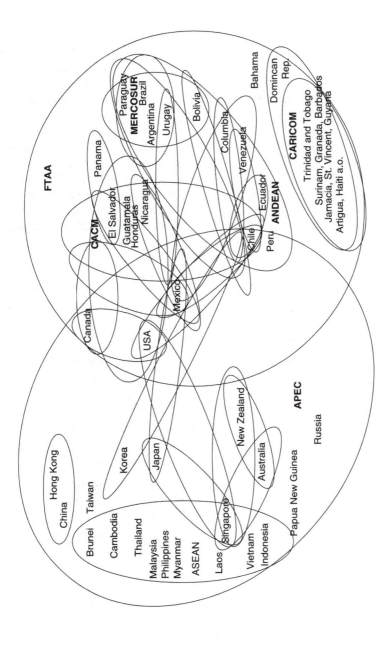

Figure 5.16 RTAs in the USA and the Asia-Pacific region (spaghetti bowl).

Source: Author's presentation based on Devlin and Estevadeordal (2004).

Third, there is a risk that too much emphasis on negotiating and exploiting RTAs will mean that the optimal multinational negotiations under the WTO on global trade agreements will receive less attention and will thus be given less priority.

However, there are also examples of fewer overlapping trade agreements and examples of agreements being consolidated into larger agreements. This was the case in relation to EU enlargement in 2004 when a series of trade agreements between the former candidate countries and EU countries became superfluous with full membership of the EU. This also explains why the number of active RTAs in 2004 fell for the first time. Box 5.6 lists some of the most important RTAs.

Box 5.7 contains a somewhat fuller description of an example of an RTA with unilateral preferential treatment. The agreement, Everything But Arms (EBA), was signed by the EU and some of the poorest developing countries. The agreement gives the developing countries, among other things, free access to the EU market for sugar. Thus, the agreement may be a catalyst for further changes in the EU's agricultural policy and thereby also greatly influence globalisation and the international division of labour in the area.

Box 5.6 Examples of regional trade areas (RTAs)

RTA	Complete name	Members
Andean	Andean Community	Bolivia, Columbia, Eucador, Peru
AFTA / ASEAN	ASEAN Free Trade Area	Brunei, Myanmar, Cambodia, Indonesia, Lao People's Democratic Republic, Malaysia, Philippines, Singapore, Viet Nam, Thailand
APTA	Asia Pacific Trade Agreement	Bangladesh, China, India, Republic of Korea, Laos, Sri Lanka
CAFTA	Central American Free Trade Area	USA, Costa Rica, El Salvador, Guatamala, Honduras, Nicaragua, Dom. Republic
CER (ANZERTA)	Closer Economic Relations Trade Agreement	Australia and New Zealand
CIS	Commonwealth of Independent States	Armenia, Azerbaijan, Belarus, Georgia, Kazakhstan, Kyrgyz Republic, Moldova, Russian Federation, Tajikistan, Turkmenistan, Ukraine, Uzbekistan

COMESA	Common Market for Eastern and Southern Africa	Burundi, Comoros, Democratic Republic of the Congo, Djibouti, Egypt, Eritrea, Ethiopia, Kenya, Libya, Madagascar, Malawi, Mauritius, Rwanda, Seychelles, Sudan, Swaziland, Uganda, Zambia, Zimbabwe
EAC	East African Community	Burundi, Kenya, Rwanda, Tanzania, Uganda
ECOWAS	Economic Community of West African States	Benin, Burkina Faso, Cape Verde, Côte d'Ivoire, Gambia, Ghana, Guinea, Guinea Bissau, Liberia, Mali, Niger, Nigeria, Senegal, Sierra Leone, Togo
EEA	European Economic Area	EU, Iceland, Lichtenstein, Norway
EFTA	European Free Trade Association	Iceland, Lichtenstein, Norway, Switzerland
EU	European Union	Austria, Belgium, Bulgaria, Cyprus, Czech Republic, Denmark, Estonia, Finland, France, Germany, Greece, Hungary, Ireland, Italy, Latvia, Lithuania, Luxembourg, Malta, Netherlands, Poland, Portugal, Romania, Slovak, Republic, Slovenia, Spain, Sweden, United Kingdom
Mercosur	Southern Common Market	Argentina, Brazil, Paraguay, Uruguay
NAFTA	North American Free Trade Agreement	Canada, Mexico, USA

Source: WTO (2012b)

Box 5.7 'Everything but arms' – an example of an RTA with unilateral preferential treatment

Everything But Arms (EBA) is an RTA which the EU entered into with some of the poorest developing countries in 2001. The agreement gives these developing countries free access to the EU. Transitional arrangements were agreed for bananas, sugar and rice, which would terminate in January 2006, July 2009 and September 2009, respectively. Hereafter, all these developing countries' products – except weapons – have had tariff-free access to the EU market. This means that developing countries' agricultural products can be sold on the EU market at prices which are, in several cases, significantly above the world market price due to the EU's agricultural policy.

The overall objective of the EBA agreement was to support the poorest countries' economic development. The basis for the EBA goes back many years:

- Back in 1968, the United Nations (UNCTAD) recommended a system that favoured developing countries' market access to developed countries. The system, 'Generalised System of Tariff Preferences', or just GSP, should therefore be a model for RTAs between developed and developing countries.
- The reason was that developing countries were often unable to compete with developed countries, while some developing countries could not compete against other developing countries either. Therefore, there was a need for a system that gave the poorest countries special benefits in the form of free access to developed countries.
- The EU was the first to implement a GSP agreement back in 1971. Since then, a number of other countries have signed GSP agreements with poor developing countries – with different content.

The EBA agreement from 2001 is one of five specific measures under the GSP.

There have been several quantitative analyses of the consequences of EBA (see, e.g., Wusheng and Jensen, 2005; UNCTAD, 2005c; Adenäuer, 2005). The main message is that the EBA promotes the developing countries' exports and economy.

The following developing countries are in the EBA agreement:

- Afghanistan
- Angola
- Bangladesh
- Benin
- Bhutan
- Burkina Faso
- Burundi
- Cambodia
- Central African Rep.
- Chad
- Comoros
- Congo (Dem. Rep.)
- Djibouti
- Equatorial Guinea
- Eritrea

- Ethiopa
- Gambia
- Guinea
- Guinea Bissau
- Haiti
- Kiribati
- Laos
- Lesotho
- Liberia
- Madagascar
- Malawi
- Maldives
- Mali
- Mauritania
- Mozambique

- Nepal
- Niger
- Rwanda
- Samoa
- São Tomé e Príncipe
- Senegal
- Sierra Leone
- Solomon Islands
- Somalia
- Sudan
- Tanzania
- Timor-Leste
- Togo
- Tuvalu
- Uganda
- Vanuatu
- Yemen
- Zambia.

Source: WTO (2012b)

Regionalisation and globalisation?

An expected result of the increasing scope of RTAs is that trade between agreement countries increases relatively more, thereby becoming increasingly important for the countries' trade pattern. Given that RTAs favour internal trade at the expense of trade outside the region, it is natural that internal trade increases to a greater or lesser extent. This means that international trade becomes partly regionalised, and development, thus, exhibits both globalisation and regionalisation at the same time. Table 5.4 and Figure 5.17 show that there is a trend for increased internal trade within the regional trade agreement countries in several cases.

The figure shows the development in the significance of internal trade (trade between countries in the same RTA) relative to the level in 1995. For the EU, however, it is for 1999, and the calculation is made with the EU-25 for the entire period to eliminate the effect of enlargement.

The figure shows examples of both increasing and decreasing internal trade. This suggests that the effects of trade cooperation can be very different from area

Table 5.4 Key ratios for selected RTAs

2010								
	Population	*GDP*	*Export*	*Food export*	*Internal trade as a % of total trade*			
	– as a % of the world's total				*1980*	*1995*	*2000*	*2005*	*2010*
EU-25	7.3	25.7	35.0	43	—	—	66	67	64
NAFTA	6.6	27.2	13.9	17	34	42	48	45	41
ASEAN	8.6	2.8	6.6	19	18	22	24	25	25
Mercosur	3.6	4.0	1.8	9	9	19	20	16	16
Andean	1.9	1.4	1.2	1	—	8	8	10	9

Kilde: World Bank (2005, 2012b), WTO (2012a) and FAO (2012).

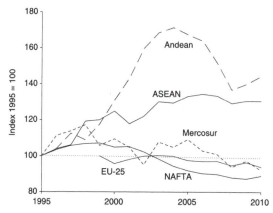

Figure 5.17 The significance of internal trade on selected regional trade areas.

Source: Author's calculation based on WTO (2012a).

Note: EU-25: 1999 = 100.

to area. To this should be added that many other factors can affect trade flows. Moreover, intra-regional trade increased significantly even before the agreements were concluded in several cases, including NAFTA (North American Free Trade Agreement), Mercosur (Mercado Común del Sur), Sapta (South Asian Association for Regional Cooperation (SAARC) Preferential Trading Arrangement) and SADC (Southern African Development Community), which was established in 1990).

Several studies have analysed whether international trade becomes increasingly regionalised in RTAs. A study by the OECD (1992) analysed the development in

---

Box 5.8 Unasur – Union of South American Nations

Unasur is an intergovernmental union which integrates two existing customs unions: Mercosur and the Andean Community (CAN), as part of a continuing process of South American integration.

There are 12 member states in Unasur: Argentina, Bolivia, Brazil, Chile, Columbia, Ecuador, Guyana, Paraguay, Peru, Suriname, Uruguay and Venezuela, while Mexico and Panama are observer states.

Unasur is modelled on the European Union. One of the goals of Unasur is to create a single market, where tariffs on non-sensitive and later on sensitive products are gradually eliminated. Defence policy, infrastructure cooperation, immigration policy, etc. are also part of the Unasur cooperation.

Unasur is a major step towards greater political and institutional cooperation in Latin America.

internal trade within the EU, EFTA and the free trade areas in the USA/Canada and Australia/New Zealand. It was concluded that, with the exception of agricultural products, the increasing regionalisation has not led to increasing internal trade at the expense of trade outside the region.

The analysis also concluded that the reason why the trading bloc accounted for an increasing share of world trade was that the blocs had been expanded and that the participating countries had become increasingly important for world trade. With regard to the product group 'food' in the EC and New Zealand/Australia, there was evidence of significantly increasing internal trade created by the trade bloc.

In an analysis of RTAs, the World Bank (2005) concludes that there are several examples of internal trade increasing significantly. An analysis conducted by the US department of Agriculture (USDA, 1998) examines the effects of six RTAs on agricultural trade: AFTA (ASEAN Free Trade Area), APEC (Asia-Pacific Economic Cooperation), CER (Closer Economic Relations), CUSTA (Canada-United States Free Trade Agreement) and Mercosur. The study concludes that internal trade in agricultural products, in general, is increasing in these areas and that entry into trade agreements could be the cause. Most trade agreements have, however, stimulated increased economic welfare. With regard to the EU, there are signs of 'trade diversion'.

A study by CEPII (2004) also examines the regionalisation and its possible causes. It is concluded that the EU, EFTA and Mercosur greatly promote internal trade, but they also create increased trade (trade creation) to third countries, although not when it comes to the EU and its primary products, including agricultural goods. Here the EU's agricultural policy is an explanation for the negative effects on trade.

In an analysis of the South African free trade agreement, SACU, Sandrey (2006) concludes that 'trade diversion', as a result of entry into RTAs, particularly occurs in Africa and results in significant costs.

Prospects for the future

The tendency to enter into RTAs has been significant and, especially in recent years, there has been a considerable increase in the number of new trade agreements. This will probably form the basis for the future trend.

On the one hand, strong regionalisation of the world economy into trading blocs is occurring and we are experiencing a new form of protectionism, only now with slightly larger units and groups of countries, but also with political resistance. States choose trade partners themselves based on political motives, and this comes at the expense of the overall global desire for increased free trade.

At the same time, temporary and limited RTAs are not so politically binding, and they are therefore not as valuable when the economy worsens. On the other hand, one can say that the trend towards more and more RTAs is a step in the right direction. The starting point is that an RTA should increase internal free trade and must not increase protection against third countries. Thus, the overall result must be greater global free trade. Furthermore, RTAs can be the first step in a process whereby countries gain experience through gradual liberalisation.

Three conditions are very significant for the world economy, globalisation and international economic welfare:

> First it is important that the RTAs stay within the WTO's framework and intentions with regard to contributing to further liberalisation.

> Second, RTAs must be considered a part of a learning process that results in the RTAs hopefully being gradually replaced by multinational trade agreements.

> Third, it is important that the establishment of RTAs does not take undue focus away from multinational negotiations in the WTO. RTAs should not be seen as a permanent replacement for agreements in the WTO.

Pricing on international agricultural and food markets

Introduction

It is often difficult to explain and especially predict the international prices of agricultural commodities. This is not least due to the fact that setting prices on the world market is very complex and that many different factors affect prices.

In addition, many random and totally unpredictable conditions come into play. For example, the weather is an important factor. The high grain prices in mid-2010 were largely caused by drought and fires in Russia and Ukraine, which resulted in a smaller harvest and thereby decreasing exports.

The size of reserves plays an important role in grain prices. Low grain stocks almost always lead to higher prices. Also, the use of grain for the production of bioenergy, the increasing purchasing power of middle-income countries, speculation, etc. have a greater or lesser effect on the price of grain.

It is thus a complex interplay involving many different factors. Based on this complex interaction, it is possible to develop a model with five different groups of drivers behind global price development. Some drivers have a direct influence on supply and demand, while other conditions seem to be self-reinforcing. Other drivers help to restore balance on the markets. Finally, there is a group of drivers that can be described as uncertainties.

It is certain that there will be a delicate balance between supply and demand on the agricultural markets in the future. If supply is not able to keep up, we will quickly experience soaring prices. Developments in recent years have also shown that agricultural markets function: that farmers worldwide increase both production and productivity and that consumption stagnates or falls when the price rises. Thus, changes in the supply of agricultural products will ensure that we will continually approach a market equilibrium and prices which are in balance. Farmers and food producers will help to ensure that we do not experience permanently high prices for agricultural and food products, as long as the right technology and market conditions are present.

In order to better understand the complexity in price formation, it is possible to group the conditions which influence the long-term price development into the following five categories: demand, supply, uncertainty, automatic stabilisation and self-reinforcing conditions (see Figure 5.18).

Demand

Increasing demand, *ceteris paribus*, also causes prices to rise. It is, in this connection, significant where and how the increase in demand comes. Agricultural and food goods are generally relatively income inelastic, which means that demand for these goods does not rise as much as it does for other more luxurious goods. In the richest countries in the world, demand for food only increases marginally with an increase in income, and it is to a greater extent the value of the food products and the degree of processing which increase.

The significant economic growth and rising prosperity in countries like China and India in particular has led to growing demand for agricultural and food products. IFPRI (2008) estimates, e.g., that rising incomes can explain half of the price increases during the food crisis in 2007/08. Bioenergy could explain 30 per cent of the increases, while the remaining 20 per cent was due to weather conditions.

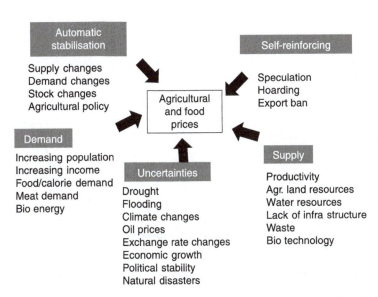

Figure 5.18 Drivers behind the development of international agricultural and food prices.

Source: Author's presentation.

In low- and middle-income countries, increasing demand which is due to increasing incomes will have a relatively large influence on agricultural and food markets. There will be an overall demand for more food products, and more animal products in particular, such as meat and dairy products. It should be noted that a growing population does not in itself lead to increased demand, as purchasing power is also necessary.

Therefore, it is remarkable that population growth in particular is taking place in relatively poor areas with limited purchasing power. Demand for grain for bioenergy production has increased substantially in recent years and therefore bioenergy has also affected the price of grain and other agricultural products.

As can be seen in Figure 5.19, corn which is used for bioenergy represents a significant and growing share of the total corn and grain production in the USA.

Bioenergy production results in a valuable by-product that can be used, among other things, as pig feed. This by-product can partially replace or supplement the production of feed grains, and hence the full effect on grain prices does not occur. However, there is considerable disagreement about how significant bioenergy actually is regarding grain price increases (see Chapter 2).

Supply

On the supply side, factors such as productivity increases and the size of agricultural areas are important. Agricultural areas are unlikely to grow much in the

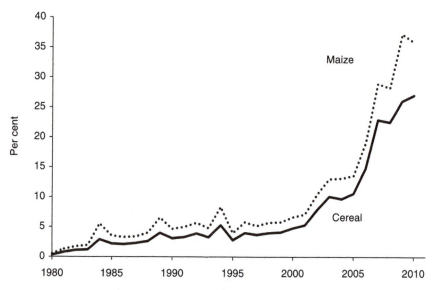

Figure 5.19 Corn used for bioenergy: proportion of total corn and grain production in the USA.

Source: EPI (2011) and author's calculations.

coming decades. Urban development, afforestation, nature restoration, land as storage for carbon and, not least, the erosion and destruction of agricultural land will mean that the necessary increase in agricultural production will have to occur on a nearly constant agricultural area. This, by its very nature, puts great demands on future increases in productivity by way of greater crop yields, etc. Finally, it is worth noting that increased irrigation over several decades has been an important precondition for increased productivity. However, water is becoming an increasingly scarce resource, in line with population growth, climate change and increasing demand for nature conservation. Increasing productivity through increased irrigation is therefore becoming more difficult, both at the national and global level.

Uncertainty

There a number of risks and uncertainties which can affect the international agricultural markets and, hence, prices. It is often difficult to account for these factors, and therefore it is inevitable that they also lead to fluctuating prices. These uncertainties were especially emphasised in 2010. The weather phenomenon El Niño is a good example of an uncertainty that has significant consequences for international agricultural and food markets; it is difficult to predict and is unpreventable (see Box 5.9).

Automatic stabilisation

In a market economy, there are a number of automatic stabilisers, which ensure that the market automatically tries to reach an equilibrium or market balance. For

---

Box 5.9 The weather phenomenon El Niño

El Niño is a recurring natural disturbance of the normal weather patterns in the Pacific region. The phenomenon occurs every three to eight years and it has several consequences.

Southeast Asia receives less rain, and droughts occur in several countries in the region. In Australia, droughts typically occur, especially in the south-east (Queensland), while more rain than usual falls in the north-west. Latin America receives more rain and higher temperatures, which often results in flooding. Also, the weather conditions in North America, Africa and Europe are affected – mostly in a negative direction for agriculture and food production.

The last time a particularly powerful version of El Niño occurred was in 1997–98. El Niño killed 21,700 people, caused more than US $33 trillion damage, left nearly 5 million people homeless and set back development in many countries.

example, if there is a lack of grain, prices will increase, which will encourage farmers to increase production, through more intensive farming, cultivating larger areas, etc. At the same time, demand will decrease due to the higher prices, and thus the supply and demand response will help to ensure a new equilibrium in the market, until the emergence of a new external influence. This automatic stabilisation is illustrated in Figure 5.20.

The outer shock in this case can be drought, bioenergy, speculation, etc., all of which cause prices to rise. There will then be a reaction in the form of increasing supply and decreasing demand, which sooner or later will cause prices to fall again.

It can also be seen in practice that the market automatically stabilises. It turns out that the increases in the price of grain in recent years influenced international grain production in many ways: more and more land produced grain, and the demand for fertilisers, pesticides and other inputs increased, despite increasing prices. Thus, grain production increased to its highest level ever.

Farmers thus adjust the amount of land which will produce grain in relation to the actual market price. The connection between grain prices and the total area producing grain is clearly presented in Figure 5.21.

As the figure shows, increasing grain prices leads to increasing amounts of land producing grain, with approximately one year's delay. It is also clear that the land adapts to both rising and falling prices.

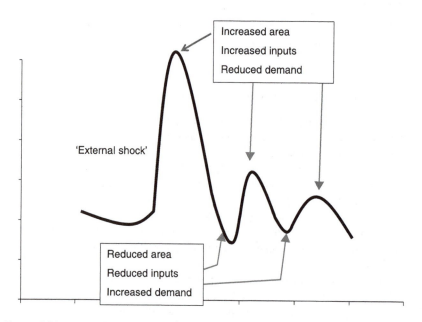

Figure 5.20 Automatic market stabilisation after an external shock.

Source: Author's presentation.

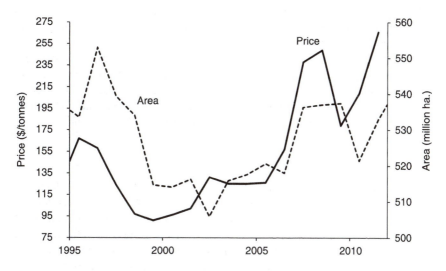

Figure 5.21 Development in grain prices and area.

Source: Author's presentation based on USDA (2012a, 2012b).

Note: The figures for 2010/11 are preliminary or estimated.

There are also examples of stabilising food markets through agricultural policy measures such as the suspension of set-aside and quota systems during periods of low supply. These agricultural policy adjustments often prove to be too slow to have any significant and structural influence on market stability.

Reserves play a significant role in the setting of prices for agricultural produce. Reserves act as a buffer that can reduce fluctuations in both supply and demand. Reserves can also contribute to greater security and reduce market risks. Reserves are therefore both an effect of the driving forces, as shown in Figure 2.9, and a solution to a large part of the price uncertainty that exists on the international agricultural and food markets. If reserves are of sufficient size, neither too large nor too small, the market is calm, and speculators will not be attracted to a market where there is no prospect of imbalance.

Self-reinforcing conditions

However, there are also some conditions which are counterproductive to automatic stabilisation. There are some self-reinforcing conditions which make things worse and which can push the market into a vicious circle.

For example, the start of price increases along with uneasiness on the market and rumours of further price increases can incite buyers and consumers to hoard out of a fear of shortages of basic foods. Increasing prices can thus, in the short term, increase demand. This kind of panic is thus self-reinforcing.

Similarly, the start of price increases can prompt speculators to take action in the belief that it is merely the beginning of a price increase. This kind of speculation can be self-reinforcing.

Finally, there are also examples of countries panicking over rising food prices and introducing export bans to keep domestic prices down. However, the export ban makes world prices increase even more, and thus we are again in a vicious circle. Russia imposed a ban on exports of grain after the harvest in 2010, which quickly led to an increase in international wheat prices of 7–8 per cent.

Complex interaction

The pricing of agricultural products occurs as a result of the complex interaction of many different factors. With the international liberalisation of agricultural policy and increasing globalisation, market forces have become more important and it has become more difficult for individual countries to control the trend. At the same time, pressure on agricultural production to meet rising global demand increases, whether it be for food, feed, energy or environmental benefits.

Market and price volatility

The agricultural and food markets, particularly the international ones, are characterised by considerable instability and volatility. In step with increasing globalisation and liberalisation of food markets, companies are becoming more and more exposed to this instability. Continued increasing demand for agricultural and food products is expected, while the potential for further increases in supply and productivity is limited, which will put further pressure on markets. This market pressure can increase market and price instability in the future.

Especially after the food crisis in 2007–08 there was considerable focus on food markets and their stability throughout the world. The large price increases and subsequent price drop caused significant turbulence, and many areas that were directly or indirectly dependent on the agricultural and food sectors were affected.

Security of supply with regard to food, that is continuous access to food at a stable and reasonable price, suddenly became important again. Several decades of development in actual price decreases, declining terms of trade and price stability was broken.

Food security also became a highly political issue in the UN and the G8 and G-20 meetings. In the EU, the price volatility on agricultural markets was analysed, and measures were implemented to create a more efficient food market.

The high, unstable and less predictable agricultural and food product prices has led to a debate about whether an actual shift in market conditions and trends has occurred and whether the development can be expected to continue in the future. If significant price volatility is expected in the future, it will place new demands on both farmers and companies' risk management. Also international food supply will come under increased pressure.

Methods and principles

Unstable markets and prices are often measured by calculating so-called volatility. Volatility can, in principle be measured in two different ways:

Historical (realised) volatility is calculated based on observed (realised) data from a historical period. Historical volatility therefore shows how stability has been in the past. Historical volatility is thus a picture of the past price and market conditions.

Implicit volatility describes the market's expectations regarding the future development in price. It is thus a picture of the expected future price development, as market actors perceive the situation. Implicit volatility can be calculated based on futures prices, which are continuously determined on the commodity markets. Two different horizons are therefore used in the two methods – the backward and the forward / expected.

There are also differences in the specific ways in which volatility is calculated. The Europe Commission (2009a) calculates volatility as the standard deviation of the logarithm of (price t/price t-1), whereby price changes from month to month are investigated, i.e. the standard deviation of the monthly growth without seasonal levelling.

The FAO *et al.* (2011) calculate volatility as the standard deviation of the logarithmic changes in monthly prices calculated on an annual basis, which involves seasonal levelling.

The OECD-FAO (2010) asserts that it is customary to cleanse price development of fluctuations which can be predicted, including, e.g., seasonal fluctuations, before price volatility can be calculated. Thus, volatility is more or less the random residual which results from a model calculation. The different methods mean that the results are not directly comparable.

In addition, volatility analyses can be based on prices from day to day, from week to week, from month to month or from year to year, while there may also be differences in the intervals when volatility is measured. Furthermore, there are significant differences in the price series which form the basis of the volatility calculations. One can be dealing with international, national, local or deflated prices in several places in the value chain.

Is price volatility something new?

Agriculture and agricultural production are characterised by a significant degree of market instability and variations over time, also in comparison with other industries. The fundamental fact is that the size of agricultural production in each year is affected by many factors, which farmers cannot fully control, such as the weather, pests and diseases. The result is large annual swings in production, primarily in crop production. Even though drought rarely occurs in all agricultural countries at the same time, there is also significant instability in total global production.

***Box 5.10* Volatility, variation, instability**

Volatility is an expression of the variation in some conditions (sales and purchase prices, profits, etc.) over time. Often the variation in the price of grains, seeds and pork will be in focus in particular. Volatility is thus an expression of the price uncertainty on the market.

In addition, supply often reacts more slowly than demand. Therefore, changes in supply cause prices to change relatively significantly. Furthermore, demand for many food products is relatively income inelastic, with relatively few substitutes, which can further create price volatility.

This means that price volatility is a fundamental framework condition that can be expected to occur persistently. This is also emphasised by the fact that price volatility on the international grain market is not a new phenomenon, but has been around at least as far back as the beginning of the 1900s (see Figure 5.22).

The figure shows that price volatility over the past decade has been the highest since the early 1970s and also that, during the last 100 years, price volatility has

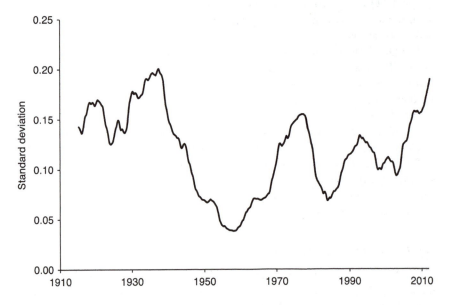

Figure 5.22 Development in price volatility of wheat on the Chicago grain exchange.

Source: Author's calculations based on USDA (2012a).

Note: Price volatility is measured as the standard deviation over 12 months in ln (price t/price t-12), where ln = natural logarithm = $\log_e$; and t = the monthly average; 10-year running average.

been relatively high. Conversely, price volatility was even higher in the first decades of the 1900s.

Trends in price volatility

A number of different analyses of both short- and long-term price volatility in agricultural products have been conducted. Since methods, data and time periods vary, one cannot expect a completely clear picture.

An analysis by the European Commission (2009a) examines the historical volatility of a number of agricultural commodities on the Chicago commodities exchange (CBOT – Chicago Board of Trade). The study goes back to 1980, and the calculated price volatility is presented in Figure 5.23.

The volatility in Figure 5.23 is shown for the period from 1980 to 2011, and there appears to be an increasing tendency. The period is divided into four intervals:

- 1980–90: decreasing volatility
- 1990–2000: increasing volatility
- 2001–06: constant volatility
- after May 2006: soaring volatility.

Volatility reached two peaks, one in 1998 and one in 1996, and in both cases it was due to the prospect of a poor harvest and a decline in production. After the

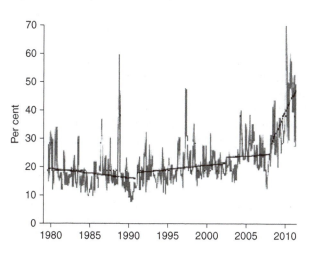

Figure 5.23 The historical price volatility of wheat (per cent).

Source: European Commission (2009a).

Note: Monthly prices are calculated on a yearly basis; data from the Chicago grain exchange.

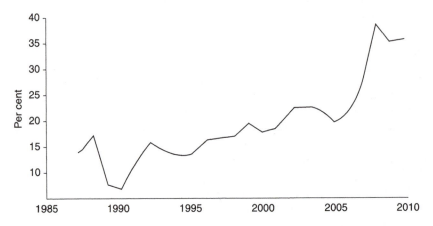

Figure 5.24 Implicit price volatility for wheat (per cent) on the world market.

Note: Volatility is calculated as the market's expectation regarding how much the price of a good will fluctuate in the future.

Source: FAO (2010c).

food crisis in 2007–08, the FAO has been further involved in price volatility on the agricultural markets. In an analysis from 2010, the implicit volatility is calculated over a longer period, see Figure 5.24.

The figure shows that the implicit price volatility on the world market for grain has increased markedly during recent decades. In an analysis by FAO *et al.* (2011), the more long-term trends in the price volatility of agricultural commodities are analysed. It is concluded, among other things, that there is no, or only small signs of, increasing volatility in international agricultural prices when analysing with the usual statistical methods. However, volatility in the period 2000–10 was higher than in the previous two decades. On the basis of these analyses of the long-term price trends, it is also concluded that periods of high price volatility are often followed by long periods of stable and low prices. Finally, it is also concluded that the agricultural markets are generally characterised by greater price volatility than other markets.

Other studies compare the price volatility on domestic and international markets (see, e.g., FAO *et al.* (2010)). The general conclusion is that volatility is lower on the national markets, and particularly on the most protected markets. This must be seen against the background that many countries in fact seek to maintain stable domestic prices through trade regulation.

Why are unstable prices a disadvantage?

Unstable, fluctuating and very unpredictable prices and market conditions are generally a significant drawback for several reasons:

First, fluctuating prices make it difficult to plan production optimally. There can be many months or even years between planning and sale, and very volatile prices can significantly change the conditions of the planned production.

Price variations, which are not a result of changing market conditions, will therefore lead to increased uncertainty, which increases the risk of suboptimal decisions among producers, intermediaries, consumers and public authorities.

Second, unstable prices also mean that farmers and companies have to spread their risk, and hence also their activities, across several different areas. If prices fall in one area, one can hope for increasing prices in other areas, and thus risk can be spread. It also means, however, that full specialisation and economies of scale cannot be achieved.

Third, volatile prices may also mean that companies do not secure their commodity positions adequately, which may also result in intentional or unintentional speculation. There were several examples of this in the wake of the food crisis of 2007–08.

Fourth, fluctuating prices can create food shortages, famine and political unrest in poorer countries where food represents a large share of total consumption.

Fluctuating prices can be an advantage

Unstable or changing prices are not necessarily a drawback. Price changes can be a reflection of changes in demand, and thus the changing prices are a signal to suppliers to change production.

Fluctuating prices may also be an advantage in other cases. If supply is low due to poor harvests, etc., the result, according to cobweb theory, will be that the prices in the relatively short term will adjust to a higher level. Thus, gross income, supply times price, will stabilise. The opposite reaction will occur with a large supply. The result will again be income stabilisation.

In these cases, fluctuating prices will be an advantage. It can therefore be the case that a poor harvest may actually be an advantage, because prices increase more than supply decreases. These benefits occur only if all farmers experience the same reduction or increase in supply.

It may also be an advantage for, e.g. pig producers, if pork and feed prices fluctuate in parallel. This will ensure more constant terms of trade, which can stabilise earnings.

Price volatility: causes and drivers

Several attempts have been made to explain the causes and drivers of price volatility in the agricultural sector (see, e.g., Balcombe, 2009; Tangermann, 2011; FAO *et al.*, 2011). As price volatility often refers to price fluctuation that cannot be explained, it can be inherently difficult to find and calculate all the driving forces behind price volatility.

When it comes to price volatility on the global market, which is generally more unstable than domestic markets, special conditions apply. The world market for agricultural products has long been affected by dumping, import restrictions, export subsidies, etc. This has meant that the setting of prices has not functioned optimally and that the world market's significance has been very limited. Therefore, there were also large price fluctuations from year to year.

Recent years' liberalisation and greater free trade have contributed to greater stability on the world market, *ceteris paribus*. Conversely, many national markets have become more volatile.

Even though we are in a period of generally increasing liberalisation and free trade, there have also been new political interventions and protectionism with the aim of stabilising the national agricultural and food markets. In the period 2006–08, approximately 70 per cent of developing countries introduced trade policy interventions as a result of the food crisis and high food prices (see Tangermann, 2011). The interventions were the reduction of import barriers and / or restrictions and bans with regard to exports. These interventions can stabilise domestic prices, but they exacerbate volatility on the world market. Also, Russia's ban on grain exports due to their poor harvest in 2010 meant a sharp increase in world prices and thus increasing volatility.

Finally, the natural conditions in agriculture represent an important driving force behind fluctuating prices. Supply changes due to the weather, productivity, etc. quickly affect the market and thus also change prices.

The significance of reserves

It is worth noting that reserves of agricultural and food products play a vital role in market development. In particular, prices are sensitive to the size of reserves and this applies to both the price level and price volatility.

As previously discussed, the development in the international price of grain is closely correlated with the change in the size of reserves: small reserves lead to high grain prices and large reserves lead to low prices. The explanation is that small reserves may be a sign of reduced supply in the future, which, *ceteris paribus*, pushes the price up.

In almost the same way, it can be expected that small reserves will lead to greater price volatility. Small reserves can cause uncertainty about future supply, as the necessary buffer is not present to stabilise the market if there is a decline in production. This uncertainty can result in increased price volatility. The relationship between the size of reserves and price volatility can be seen in Figure 5.25.

Figure 5.25 shows total world grain reserves as a percentage of production. The price is a weighted average price in the USA. As the figure shows, grain reserves were very low during the food crisis. Grain reserves amounted to approximately 17 per cent of total global output, equivalent to approximately two months' consumption. The figure also shows price volatility.

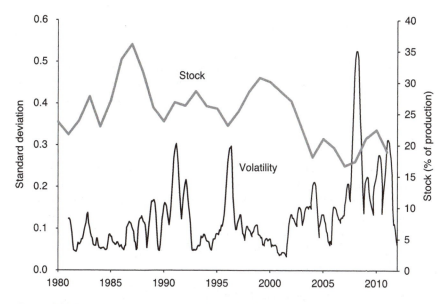

Figure 5.25 Development in price volatility and wheat reserves.

Source: Author's calculations based on USDA (2011a, 2011b).

Note: Price volatility is measured as the standard deviation over 12 months on ln (price t/price t-12), where ln = natural logarithm = $\log_e$; and t = monthly average.

As can be seen, price volatility is typically high when reserves are low, as they were a couple of years ago, and as they were during a period in the early and mid-1990s. It is also noteworthy that a small decline in reserves is not as significant if the reserves are already high. In contrast, a decline in reserves which are already low increases price volatility significantly.

The relationship between the size of reserves and price volatility is discussed by several authors (see, e.g., Balcombe, 2009 and OECD-FAO, 2010).

Will volatility remain high in the future?

This is a very important question to answer – can we expect persistently high or even increasing price volatility on agricultural markets in the future? In the light of the previous serious economic and human consequences of price volatility, it is important to get an idea of the future challenges in this area.

The FAO *et al.* (2010) concluded in its analysis of long-term price trends 'that periods of high price volatility are often followed by long periods of stable and low prices.' The question is, therefore, whether we can expect that this will happen again, or whether structural changes or influences have occurred, which will mean that agricultural markets will respond differently in the future.

Box 5.11 Volatility will remain elevated

Due to several structural changes in both the futures markets and the underlying agricultural commodities markets, prices and volatility levels will probably remain elevated for the foreseeable future.

FAO (2010a) p. 66

The development in recent years, however, has in many ways been special: abnormally low world grain reserves; high grain prices in both 2007/08 and 2010; significant and increasing use of grain for bio-energy; extreme weather events; and increasing food consumption in many high-growth economies. To the extent that these conditions can be expected to continue in the future, it will likely lead to a sustained high price volatility (see also Box 5.11).

A number of factors point to high price volatility in the future:

- *Climate change* and more extreme weather will result in more unstable and varying crop production around the world as well as greater price volatility.
- *Increasing demand* for agricultural commodities for food, feed and energy purposes will mean increasing pressure on the market, which can lead to situations of undersupply and thus price fluctuations. The increasing demand pressure will also mean that more marginal agricultural resources will be used and thereby crop security and subsequently also price stability will be reduced.
- *Water resources* are becoming increasingly scarce, which increases the risk of crop failure due to drought, and this limits the area of farmland that can be irrigated, while it can also lead to poorer crop security.
- Continued *trade liberalisation* will, in many cases, mean that countries will not be able to implement sufficient market stabilisation measures, which will mean that it will not be possible to remove price volatility from the internal market, but also that price volatility on the world market will be reduced.

Other conditions point towards decreasing price volatility in the future: increasing focus on *crop improvements*, greater *dissemination of knowledge*, improved *infrastructure* and *increased international trade* can contribute to increasing price stability. Finally, the considerable *political attention* on the problem, and the concrete policy measures in this area, could also help to reduce price volatility in the future.

What can be done to reduce price volatility?

It is possible to reduce and / or manage price volatility, and it can be done through economic and political measures:

> *Trade liberalisation* has to continue, and measures like export taxes and export bans, which have been practised especially during periods with unstable and high prices, must be prevented.
>
> Building up *buffer reserves* of the most important agricultural products can reduce both prices and price volatility.
>
> The better protection of *infrastructure*, trade routes and local markets in developing countries will reduce bottlenecks and thereby undersupply and price fluctuations in a number of areas.
>
> Better *monitoring and warning* of potential problems in the global food supply are needed. Price fluctuations are partly caused by panic buying, hoarding and speculation, and here greater market transparency can reduce instability.
>
> Price volatility can also be reduced with the help of more technological measures, which can *increase production and productivity*, help to improve the security of supply and thereby also price stability.
>
> There is a need for increased *research and development* and increased knowledge dissemination to areas where price volatility is most harmful. The poorest developing countries are most vulnerable to price fluctuations, which is why the focus should be on these areas.

Although it is economically, politically and technologically possible to reduce price volatility on agricultural and food markets in the future, it is certain that, in the future, there is a need for better tools to handle the volatility that will always be present. With an ever increasing population, increasing demand, scarce resources and the increasing impacts of climate change, volatility will continue to be an important framework condition that must be handled well.

Questions and assignments

5.1 What is globalisation and what makes globalisation grow?

5.2 Is globalisation a 'bubble' or a long-term trend? Why?

5.3 Why is international trade of agricultural and food products growing rather slowly?

5.4 Globalisation and regional trade agreements: can they co-exist? Why / Why not? What are the advantages / disadvantages of regional trade agreements?

5.5 Select a regional trade agreement of your own choice. Describe the content, size and type of agreement. What is the potential influence on the inter-national food market?

5.6 What kind of factor will influence the pricing on international agricultural and food markets? Select three factors and describe the impact.

5.7 What is meant by market and price volatility?

What are the trends?
Why is it important?

5.8 How are companies in the food value chain influenced by the factors mentioned above?

6 Newly industrialised countries, developing countries and food markets

International food markets are important because they allow international specialisation and a division of labour. The significance of international food markets varies widely, however, from country to country and from country group to country group. The least developed countries are highly dependent on agricultural production and exports, but their share of total world exports of agricultural and food products has been declining. The economic and political role of the newly industrialised countries (NICs), and especially the BRIC countries (Brazil, Russia, India, China), has been increasing in importance, but their influence on the international food markets has not increased correspondingly.

There is a great need to develop and internationalise the agricultural and food sector in many developing countries, especially in Africa. Over the past few decades there have been interesting examples of African countries having managed to develop significant exports of specific areas within their food and agri business where they have competitive advantages.

Newly industrialised countries

Thirty to 40 years ago, the NICs were still developing but, since then, they have experienced significant growth and development and have now, more or less, caught up with the developed countries.

An NIC is, therefore, one which was traditionally considered as a developing country, but which no longer exhibits the typical characteristics. In this way, the NICs set themselves apart from the ranks of developing countries.

The term emerged in the 1970s, when it was used to refer to the so-called, Asian 'tiger states', which had very high growth rates. Occasionally, these countries are also referred to as 'take-off countries' because they have overcome the typical structural problems present in developing countries. An NIC is thus moving in the direction of industrialisation, if one measures it against economic development factors (see Chapter 3).

The NICs are characterised by extensive development and change in economic structures, moving them away from an agricultural-based economy towards industrialisation. In this process of change, altered power structures, the redistribution of wealth among the population and strong growth can create economic and political instability.

The term NIC is not unambiguous, and therefore the countries comprising the NIC group is also not well defined. This is partly because there are no clear definitions of when a country is 'newly industrialised' and partly because the countries are constantly developing and changing.

Table 6.1 shows the different key performance indicators for the countries which are most frequently considered to be NICs.

As the table shows, the NIC group consists of nine countries (South Africa, Mexico, Brazil, China, India, Malaysia, the Philippines, Thailand and Turkey). However, the following four additional countries are sometimes considered to be on the periphery of the NIC group, depending on the defining criteria used: Russia, Argentina, Egypt and Indonesia. The term 'NIC +' therefore covers all 13 countries.

The table also shows that the NICs have a much lower average GDP per capita than the OECD countries: approximately 15 per cent of the OECD average. Conversely, economic growth in the NICs is approximately three times as high as in the OECD countries when looking at the average for 2005–10. This means that the difference in economic welfare between the NIC and OECD countries is gradually reducing.

The NICs are a heterogeneous group when it comes to food. The NIC group consists of both major food exporters (Brazil) and large food importers (China), measured in a global perspective. Some countries are still large exporters of food, while in others food represents a significant portion of imports. These countries are typically net importers of food. It also shows that the NIC countries can have very different industrialisation processes, and that some of the countries are more advanced in the process than others. It is, however, noteworthy that countries which are regarded as newly industrialised are net exporters as a group.

Although almost half the world population lives in NICs, these countries only account for around 20 per cent of total world GDP. However, if one corrects GDP for the fact that purchasing power, and hence the real value of GDP, can vary widely between countries, the NICs have a larger share of total world production. GDP, PPP (Purchasing power parity) in the NICs amounts to 25–30 per cent of the corresponding figure for the whole world (see Table 6.1 and Box 6.1).

Box 6.1 Purchasing power parity (PPP)

Purchasing power parities (PPPs) are indicators of price level differences across countries. PPPs can be used as currency conversion rates to convert expenditures expressed in national currencies into an artificial common currency, thus eliminating the effect of price level differences across countries. In particular, PPP can be used to compare the gross domestic product (GDP) of different countries without the figures being distorted by different price levels in the countries.

Table 6.1 NICs and selected economic and trade indicators (2005–10)

	GDP per capita US $	GDP growth, annual %	Food export of total export %	Food import of total import %	Share of world:					
					GDP %	GDP, PPP %	Population %	Food export %	Food import %	FDI, inflow %
South Africa	5,881	3.5	8.1	5.3	0.5	0.7	0.7	0.5	0.4	0.3
Mexico	8,865	2.0	5.8	6.6	1.8	2.2	1.6	1.7	2.3	1.4
Brazil	7,554	4.2	28.3	4.7	2.6	2.8	2.8	5.3	0.7	1.6
China	3,007	11.2	2.8	4.1	7.2	11.4	19.7	3.2	5.1	8.1
India	1,031	8.5	8.8	3.5	2.2	4.9	17.7	1.3	1.1	1.6
Malaysia	6,909	4.7	9.7	6.6	0.3	0.5	0.4	2.0	1.0	0.3
Philippines	1,699	4.9	6.7	9.1	0.3	0.5	1.3	0.4	0.6	0.1
Thailand	3,634	3.8	12.7	4.6	0.4	0.8	1.0	1.8	0.5	0.5
Turkey	8,828	4.2	9.7	3.6	1.1	1.4	1.1	1.2	0.6	0.9
NIC	4,651	7.6	9.1	4.5	16.4	25.2	46.4	17.4	12.3	14.9
Russia	8,698	4.1	2.1	14.2	2.2	3.6	2.1	0.8	2.8	2.5
Argentina	6,977	7.2	49.6	3.3	0.5	0.8	0.6	3.0	0.2	0.4
Egypt	1,913	5.9	11.4	18.8	0.3	0.6	1.2	0.3	0.8	0.5
Indonesia	2,016	5.7	14.9	8.7	0.9	1.3	3.5	2.0	0.9	0.4
NIC+	5,005	7.1	9.6	5.9	20.3	31.4	53.8	23.4	16.9	18.6
OECD	33,262	1.2	7.3	7.0	72.8	57.9	18.2	68.1	65.9	67.1
World	8,287	2.5	7.4	7.0	100	100	100	100	100	100

Source: Author's calculations based on World Bank (2012b) and FAO (2012).

Note: Average for 2005–10.

The figures in Table 6.1 also show that the NICs are decidedly low-cost countries in relation to the OECD countries.

Despite the NICs' definition as high-growth, low-cost countries, foreign interest in direct investment in the NIC countries is relatively low. The inflow of FDI is relatively insignificant compared to the NIC countries' total GDP.

BRICS

The BRICS countries (Brazil, Russia, India, China and South Africa) have formally established an association. The BRICS countries have a number of common features, of which high economic growth is the most significant. Furthermore, they are also experiencing a transition from being a developing country to becoming a more developed industrialised country. In addition, the countries, on an individual basis but especially together, have significant economic and political power.

As a result of the considerable growth in China in particular, global attention has been focused on China's development for periods, while the other BRICS countries have played a secondary role.

The very high growth rate in the BRICS countries since the early 1990s has meant that the group has gained a strong foothold in the international economy. Indeed, in 2000, their combined purchasing power-adjusted GDP overtook both the Eurozone and North America (see Figure 6.1).

Since the early 1990s, the BRICS countries' share of total world GDP (PPP) has increased from approximately 15 per cent to approximately 25 per cent (see Figure 6.2). The figure emphasises that the BRICS countries will become more and more significant in relation to the world economy because of their high growth rates.

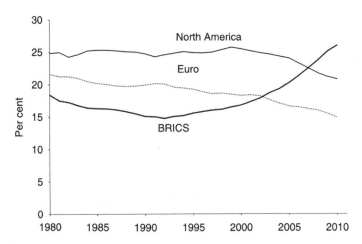

Figure 6.1 Share of total GDP (PPP) for BRICS, Eurozone and North America.

Source: Author's own calculations based on FAO (2012).

Note: Until 1992: USSR = Russia.

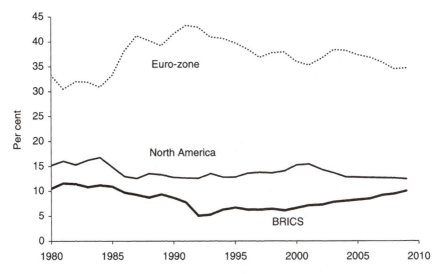

Figure 6.2 Share of total international food trade for BRICS, Eurozone and North America.

Source: Author's own calculations based on FAO (2012).

Note: International food trade = food import + food export. Until 1992: USSR = Russia.

As approximately half of the world's population lives in the BRIC countries, they also account for a large proportion of the world's agricultural and food production. China and India, as well as Brazil, have a dominant role in the global production of food products, including staple crops such as wheat, maize, and rice. China and India are the world's largest producers of rice (30 and 18 per cent of world production in 2010, respectively). The BRICS countries produce nearly 40 per cent of the world's wheat and 30 per cent of the world's corn.

An important explanation is that China is still a relatively closed country in terms of the import and export of food. China's degree of self-sufficiency is generally close to 100, so only a very small proportion of production and consumption is connected to the international markets.

It is also noteworthy that Brazil, despite its status as a newly industrialised and BRICS country, is still relatively dependent on exports of agricultural and food products. In 2009, agriculture and food accounted for 35 and 26 per cent of Brazil's total exports, respectively (see Figure 6.3).

As the figure shows, agricultural and food products play an important role in Brazil's exports, despite the process of industrialisation and high growth rates. Furthermore, since the early 1990s, agricultural and food products have accounted for an increasing share of the country's total exports. In this way, Brazil's development differs greatly from the normal pattern of development (see also Chapter 3).

One explanation is that Brazil's agricultural and food sector is highly industrialised in several areas. The agricultural sector is comprised of many large efficient

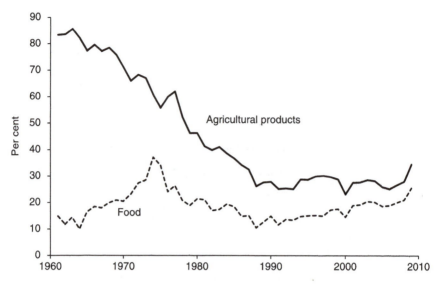

Figure 6.3 Brazil: food and agricultural products as a percentage of total exports.

Source: Author's calculations based on FAO (2012).

units, while, in the food industry, there are companies which, through internationalisation, growth and large-scale production have become extremely competitive internationally.

Another explanation is that Brazil, but also other countries in South America, has favourable natural conditions for agriculture and food production. Therefore, Brazil has a viable basis for maintaining strong agricultural and food sectors during industrialisation.

A third explanation is that the composition of agricultural and food exports has changed. Food in particular is becoming increasingly important, and especially meat exports have increased. Furthermore, the processing of agricultural commodities and value added are also increasing. In general, however, exporting countries' ability to increase processing and value added is limited by the tariff structure which is found in many countries. Import restrictions are often stricter for processed goods, while they are more relaxed when it comes to raw produce. In this way, countries can support the domestic value added and employment (see also Box 6.2). Figure 6.4 highlights the extent of tariff rate escalation in some important areas.

Finally, it is also important that international agricultural and food prices were generally undergoing positive development in the early 1990s. Food crises, the liberalisation of agricultural policy, the spread of bioenergy, increasing population growth and purchasing power forced international prices upwards. Since Brazil has relatively relaxed trade protection regarding agriculture and the food sector, the country has been directly dependent on international prices, and therefore the increasing world market prices have had a positive effect on the value of its agricultural and food exports.

Box 6.2 **Tariff escalation**

Tariff escalation refers to a progressive increase in import duties. For raw produce, import duties are low, but these escalate and are higher for intermediate and semi-finished goods, while they reach their highest level for final and finished goods.

Tariff escalation is systematically practised in many countries. While, for example, wheat trade has become less distorted, tariff escalation is still high. Tariffs on flour are well above those on wheat, while tariffs on bakery and pasta products are even higher. Consequently, trade in wheat products is largely confined to free-trade areas such as the European Union and NAFTA (Aksoy, 2005).

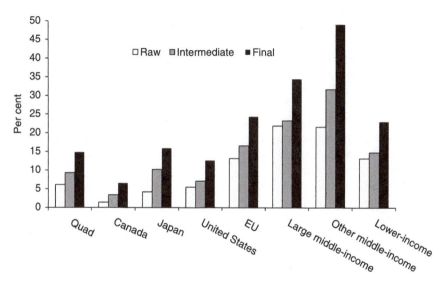

Figure 6.4 Tariff rate escalation in agriculture; selected country groups and years.
Source: Aksoy (2005).

As discussed in Chapter 3, countries' international trade in food increases significantly in line with their economic growth and it is therefore expected that the BRICS countries will undergo the same process.

Developing countries

The group, developing countries, is rather ill-defined. There is no established definition for the designation of 'developed' and 'developing' countries or areas in, e.g., the United Nation's system. In most cases, GDP per capita is an important indicator of a country's level of economic development.

Developing countries are mainly agricultural countries in that a large proportion of production, value added and exports occur in the agriculture and food sector. In several developing countries, over half of employment and exports originate in the agricultural sector, while approximately 75 per cent of poor people worldwide live in rural areas, with the majority of them being dependent on agriculture. The rural poverty rate exceeds the urban rate by a large margin in almost all developing countries (World Bank, 2007c).

Some conditions suggest that exports of agricultural and food products from developing countries will rise, while others suggest the opposite. On the one hand, a relative decline in exports of agricultural and food products can be the result of developing countries seeking to promote the industrialisation process. Developing countries' desire to promote industrialisation at the expense of agricultural and food production can be due to limited access to exports, negative development in terms of trade, etc. Developing countries can thus in several ways move resources (labour, capital, research, etc.) from the agricultural and food sectors to industrial sectors, thereby limiting agricultural and food production.

Developing countries' limited export potential is also, to a large extent, a consequence of their agricultural policy. A relative decline in agricultural and food exports may also be the result of an increase in domestic demand due to increasing prosperity and purchasing power.

On the other hand, there are conditions which suggest that developing countries ought to increase their agricultural production and exports. Agricultural and food production is often one of the few comparative advantages that a developing country possesses. To ensure maximum international competitiveness, it is necessary to focus on those sectors where the comparative advantages are greatest. A developing country also needs to develop exports to obtain foreign currency for the imports, which are needed.

On the basis of these different considerations, it is conspicuous that developing countries' share of world food exports has been declining over a long period (see Figure 6.5).

The figure shows that, in general, the developing countries' market share has declined when it comes to food exports. This is especially the case for the least developed countries, for which exports have almost entirely ceased. From the early 1960s to the early 1990s, the developing countries' total market share fell by more than 50 per cent, from 22 per cent to 10 per cent. Subsequently, their market share increased, which may have been the outcome of WTO negotiations regarding the liberalisation of trade in the agricultural and food sector.

Africa in particular has experienced a decline in its share of the world market for food. In the early 1960s, Africa and Asia each accounted for approximately 10–12 per cent of the world's total food exports. However, since then their development has gone in opposite directions: Asia has increased its market share, while Africa's market share has declined significantly (see Figure 6.6).

At the same time as Asia has increased its share of the world's total food exports, the continent has also increased the average food supply per capita. This has also occurred in Africa, but the development has been slower (see Figure 6.7).

There is no simple explanation for the two continents' different development trends, which is rather the result of the complex interplay of a number of factors.

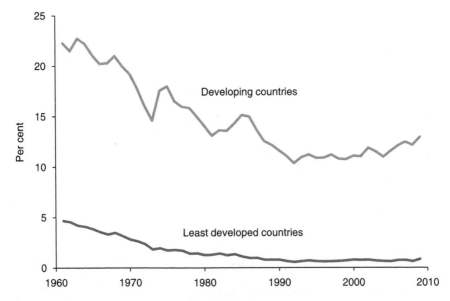

Figure 6.5 Developing countries' share of total food export.

Source: Author's calculations based on FAO (2012).

Note: FAO's definitions have been applied.

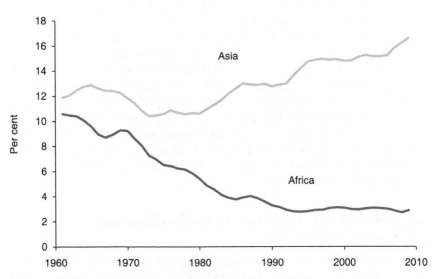

Figure 6.6 Export of food: share of total food export.

Source: Author's calculations based on FAO (2012).

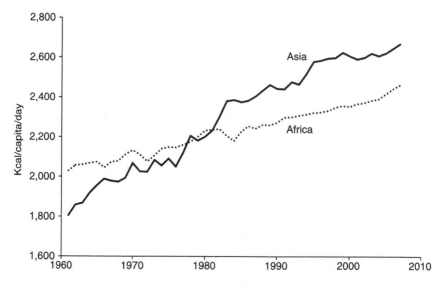

Figure 6.7 Average food supply in Africa and Asia.

Source: Author's calculations based on FAO (2012).

However, it is clear that the significant economic growth and development in Asia has also stimulated the agricultural and food sector's international competitiveness. Economic development is in most cases a prerequisite for the agricultural and food sector being able to operate on the international markets.

Developing countries have relatively little foreign trade, which applies to agricultural and food products as well as other goods. The least developed countries in particular have a low rate of participation in the international division of labour via foreign trade. However, imports and exports increase with economic growth.

Developing countries' relatively insignificant international trade should be seen in the light of the fact that exports require infrastructure, organisation and efficient companies. Markets must be effective and allow suppliers and consumers to meet, but this is not always the case in the least developed countries. Conversely, there are also examples of targeted foreign direct investment successfully developing parts of the agricultural and food sector, resulting in a significant increase in exports and a significant international market share. The following section discusses some of these examples.

Africa's position in the international trade of agricultural and food products – Kenya as a case

Africa has so far had a relatively limited role in international trade. This applies to international trade in general and also specifically to international trade in agricultural and food products. Apart from tropical products such as coffee, tea, cacao and bananas, Africa's collective export, but also that of individual countries, has been very modest. The African continent as a whole is also a net importer of agricultural and food products.

Compared to both the population base and production potential, Africa's external trade in agricultural and food products is relatively minor in a global perspective. For example, Africa accounts for 20 per cent of the world's total population employed in agriculture, 24 per cent of farmland, but only 3.7 per cent of total world exports of agricultural and food products. Figure 6.8 shows Africa's share of total world trade, resources, etc.

The figure shows that Africa has a significant share of total world agricultural resources (land, farmers and value creation), but its share of total world exports of agricultural products is far more modest. The limited international trade may, to some extent, be explained by the countries' low level of economic development, as participation in international trade normally increases in parallel with economic growth. International trade can help to generate economic growth and prosperity through major international specialisation and a division of labour. Therefore, greater international trade is both a prerequisite for, and a result of, economic development.

Over the past few decades, there have been interesting examples of African countries which have managed to develop a significant export in specific areas where they have competitive advantages. These examples are of interest since they may illustrate how comparative advantages and competitive strengths can be exploited through international trade in Africa, while they may also highlight

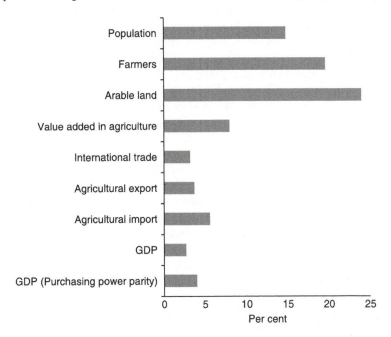

Figure 6.8 Africa's share of world resources and international trade – selected examples (2010).

Source: Author's calculations based on World Bank (2012b) and FAO (2012).

some of the key drivers and preconditions that must be present for international trade to succeed. Finally, the examples also illustrate some of the consequences, positive and negative, of growing international trade and specialisation.

Kenya's vegetable sector – focusing on green beans

Kenya has significant exports of agricultural and horticultural products. For many years, coffee and tea have been important export products for Kenya, and the country is today the world's second largest exporter of tea and one of the world's major coffee exporters. Coffee and tea now account for more than 25 per cent of Kenya's total exports.

In total, Kenya exports more than 80 different kinds of vegetable and ten different kinds of fruit, which includes packaged and prepared products (HCDA, 2012). Of these exports, fresh green beans (French beans) are one of the most important products.

A total of 70 per cent of these green beans are exported to the UK (UN, 2012), where supermarket chains such as Marks and Spencer, Tesco and Sainsbury's are among the major buyers. The UK is the world's second largest importer of green beans, and approximately 70 per cent of its imports come from Kenya.

The value chain for fresh beans produced in Kenya and sold in Europe can be relatively long, despite beans being a natural product which does not undergo processing or value added before it reaches the consumers. As can be seen from Figure 6.9, there may be several links between farmers and consumers.

The first part of the value chain, farmers, may consist of three different types:

- farmers who work in producer groups;
- individual farmers who do not participate in producer groups and who primarily sell to local buyers or at a local outlet;
- farms owned by an exporting firm further down the value chain.

The local market either takes the form of a spot market or sales to local buyers. These local purchasers may be restaurants, etc., but they may also be traders who then sell their products on local fruit and vegetable markets.

Produce for the European market is air freighted from the airport in Kenya's capital city, Nairobi. An efficient infrastructure with packaging, refrigeration, distribution, etc., has been established which makes transportation to Europe relatively inexpensive.

As can be seen in Figures 6.10 and 6.11, Kenya is currently the world's third largest exporter of green beans, and there has been a significant increase over recent decades.

It is notable that, among the major exporters, there are European countries, which produce for their own domestic markets, as well as African countries, which almost exclusively export the produce to Europe.

Kenya's strong position among the largest exporters in the world should be seen against the background of a high demand for fresh fruit and vegetable products from European supermarket chains and a well-established and strong export

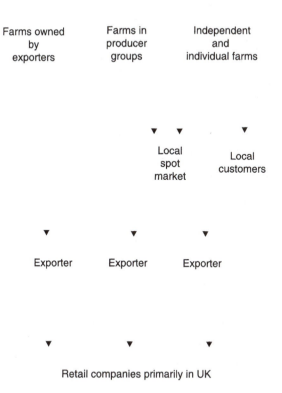

Figure 6.9 The value chain for fresh green beans produced in Kenya.

Source: Author's presentation based on field research.

cluster. Several large export companies have substantial market power over the suppliers in the agricultural sector.

The value chain is largely controlled by European retail chains, which set the quality standards and regularly check the quality of the products in all links of the value chain. The size and market share of the retail chains in relation to their suppliers in the value chain also shows that market power is indeed concentrated in the retail chains.

The long value chain and the strong export companies also affect the price transmission from farmer to consumer. Only a very small share of consumer prices at the retail level can be traced back to the farmers in Kenya. As can be seen in Box 6.1, the payment to farmers equates to only 7–8 per cent of the final selling price.

Box 6.3 presents the real prices of green beans in the value chain.

As can be seen, the 'food dollar', i.e. the farmer's share of the retail food price, is relatively modest. Farmers are paid approximately US $0.5 per kg of beans if they meet the quality requirements of the European supermarket chains. The final

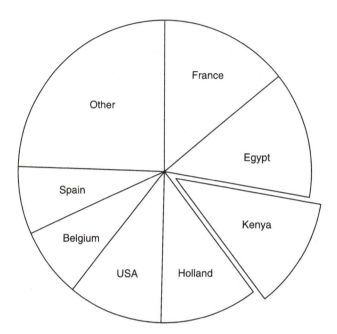

Figure 6.10 World's most important exporters of fresh green beans.

Source: Author's calculations based on UN (2012).

Note: Beans, shelled or unshelled, fresh or chilled.

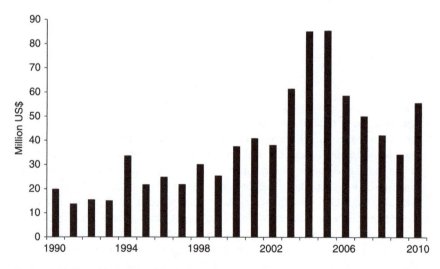

Figure 6.11 Kenya's export of fresh green beans.

Source: Author's calculations based on UN (2012) and FAO (2012).

Note: Beans, shelled or unshelled, fresh or chilled.

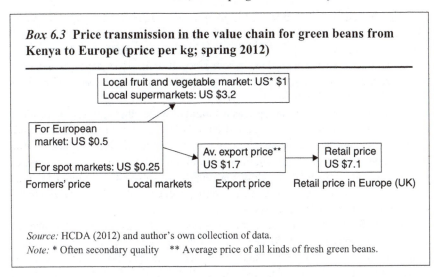

Box 6.3 **Price transmission in the value chain for green beans from Kenya to Europe (price per kg; spring 2012)**

Local fruit and vegetable market: US* $1
Local supermarkets: US $3.2

For European market: US $0.5

For spot markets: US $0.25

Av. export price** US $1.7

Retail price US $7.1

Formers' price   Local markets   Export price   Retail price in Europe (UK)

Source: HCDA (2012) and author's own collection of data.
Note: * Often secondary quality   ** Average price of all kinds of fresh green beans.

retail price in the UK is approximately $7.1. This of course involves distribution costs, including airfreight from Kenya to Europe, but there are no significant processing, preserving or packaging costs.

The farmers' share of the retail food price has probably reduced in recent years, as farmers' average selling price has fallen by more than 40 per cent since 2006

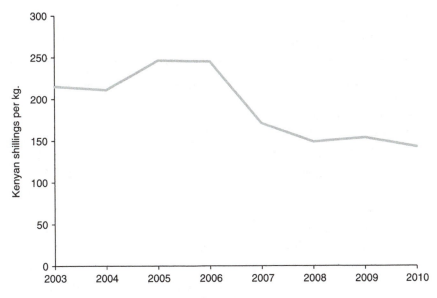

Figure 6.12 Producer prices for green beans in Kenya.
Source: Author's calculations based on HCDA (2012).
Note: Yearly average of all kinds of fresh green bean.

when calculated at current prices in local currency. Figure 6.12 presents farmers' average selling price for fresh beans sold for export. As can be seen in Figure 6.12, there has been a negative trend in prices, especially since 2006.

The decline in farmers' producer prices since 2006 is also a major explanation for the reduction in Kenya's exports of green beans during the same period, as previously shown in Figure 6.11.

With regard to the decreasing prices it should be added that agricultural productivity increased during the same period with the production of beans per hectare increasing which may, to some extent, compensate for the falling prices. In the period 2008–10, the average yield in bean production in Kenya was 6.3 tonnes per year per hectare (FAO, 2012). However, yields are substantially higher in areas with intensive production where farmers only produce for the British retail chains and where beans are harvested six times a year.

The box shows that Kenya, in many ways, has features which characterise developing countries: low GDP per capita, a major role for agriculture, low food supply, high unemployment and significant income inequalities. Kenya's international competitiveness is ranked as number 102 out of 146 countries. Kenya is rather competitive regarding innovation, education and efficiency on the labour market, while instability and uncertainty in the country weakens its international competitiveness.

Kenya is – due to the capital, Nairobi – included in the Emerging Markets Index (by MasterCard), which is a ranking of the 65 most influential cities in emerging economies.

Box 6.4 Facts about Kenya

	Kenya	OECD	World
GDP per capita (US $)	775	34,631	9,228
Value added in agriculture (% of GDP)	19.4	1.5	3.2
Value added in agriculture per labour input (US $)	334	14,951	1,053
Arable land (ha per person)	0.14	0.33	0.21
Food supply (kcal/capita/day)	2,089	3,466	2,798
Food export (% of all export)	47.9	7.9	8.2
Tariff rate, average of all products (%)	12.1	3.2	6.9
Unemployment (% of total labour force)	40	8.1	6.2
Income share held by highest 10%	38	26	—
Corruption (rank among 182 countries)	154	20*	—
International competitiveness (rank among 146 countries)	102	11*	—

Source: (Transparency International, 2012; World Bank, 2012b; FAO, 2012; CIA, 2012).
Note: * Weighted average rank.

Kenya's flower industry

Kenya is a good example of a country which has improved its competitiveness through foreign investment in the flower sector. Kenya has some of the largest flower gardens in the world, where up to 10,000 people are employed.

Kenya's flower industry is the oldest and largest in Africa and the commercial production of flowers dates back to 1969 (de Groot, 1998). Danish investors were the first to enter the Kenyan flower sector, followed by the Dutch. Kenya has since grown to become the largest exporter of roses and carnations in the world. In 2010, Kenya exported cut flowers to the value of US $396 million (of which $277 million were fresh cut flowers), which accounted for almost 8 per cent of Kenya's total export revenue. Exports of cut flowers have increased significantly in recent decades (see Figure 6.13).

Decades ago, Kenya had limited opportunities to export flowers due to a lack of knowledge, technology and especially access to foreign markets with affluent consumers. Thus, Kenyan capacity to develop this sector was inadequate. However, Kenya has significant comparative advantages regarding floriculture due to a favourable climate and low wages, which is a particularly significant advantage as flower production is very labour intensive. Despite Kenya having a good climate for floriculture, most flowers are produced in greenhouses to protect them from the elements.

Besides a favourable climate and low labour costs, Kenya had the advantage of significant tourism to the country which meant that there were many air flights to and from the western hemisphere.

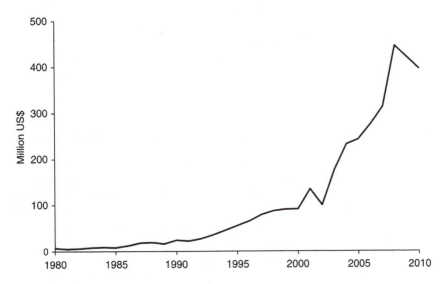

Figure 6.13 Kenya's total exports of cut flowers.

Source: Author's presentation based on UN (2012) and UNCTAD/DITE (2008).

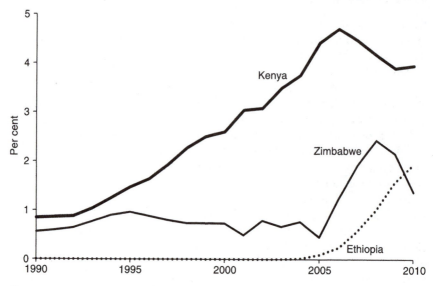

Figure 6.14 Exports of fresh cut flowers: the most important exporting countries in Africa.
Source: Author's presentation based on UN (2012) and UNCTAD/DITE (2008).

Kenya's comparative advantage in the production of cut flowers has resulted in a rapidly increasing market share. While Kenya in the early 1990s accounted for approximately 1 per cent of the world market for fresh cut flowers, the proportion subsequently increased to 4–5 per cent (see Figure 6.14).

As the figure shows, exports from the two other major African exporters, Zimbabwe and Ethiopia, were much lower.

The figure shows a classic example of new international specialisation, whereby production, to a greater or lesser extent, moves to regions with the lowest costs.

Box 6.5 A new world order within flower production and trade

In recent decades, Western countries' share of the world market for flower production has declined so that, today, an increasing share of world production and export of cut flowers comes from non-Western countries, where production costs are lower and the climate is more favourable. This development has also been facilitated by globalisation and improved and cheaper air travel. However, European growers and investors are behind the growing flower production, particularly in Africa.

The reason for this is that global flower production is constantly changing, partly as a result of globalisation. Before 1970, most of the world's flower production was sold on domestic markets and flower trade was primarily local and based on local markets. Today, the markets are becoming much more international and some of the largest exporting countries are located in Africa, South America and Asia, where the climate is favourable and labour costs are low.

This is indeed the case for cut flowers, which now has a substantial trade across borders. Here the international trade often takes place over great distances, as cut flowers are now increasingly produced in Africa and South and Central America and then transported by air to the West.

The increasing international trade is the result of the exploitation of comparative advantages, whereby production is continually relocated to areas with comparative advantages in order to remain competitive on the international markets.

At the same time, a significant proportion of Western horticultural production is being relocated to a number of tropical and sub-tropical countries. In many cases, investors in the traditional horticultural countries own and operate the production plants. Thus, it is clear that more and more developing countries or less developed countries in Africa and South America and Asia are experiencing rapid growth in horticultural exports, especially when it comes to cut flowers.

Some 20–25 years ago, Western countries accounted for approximately 90 per cent of the international trade in cut flowers, whereas today this share has declined to below 70 per cent (see Figure 6.15).

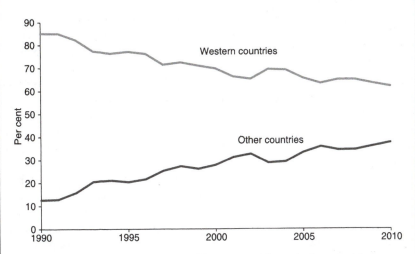

Figure 6.15 Exports of cut flowers by Western countries and other countries.

Source: Author's calculations and estimates based on UN (2012).

Foreign investment in Kenya's flower sector

Foreign investment in the Kenyan horticultural sector has played a significant role in its growth. Indeed, the World Bank estimates that direct foreign investment has been instrumental in the success of many development projects in the horticultural sector in Africa, and it still plays an important role (World Bank, 2007b).

About 80 per cent of total income in the horticultural sector in Kenya comes from 10 leading companies, all of which are foreign owned, while approximately two-thirds of flower nurseries are run by foreign companies. Large foreign companies plus white Kenyan producers own almost 90 per cent of all flower gardens (see Learning Africa, 2010). It is estimated that the flower industry in Kenya creates direct employment for approximately 55,000 people.

Foreign investment in Kenya's flower industry mainly comes from countries which are competing in the flower sector, especially the Netherlands, Israel and the UK (see World Bank, 2007b).

In recent years, a significant feature of the development in Kenya's flower industry is investment in seedling production. A significant and increasing proportion of the cuttings used in the production of potted plants in northern Europe is now produced in Africa, and especially in Kenya.

Consequences of FDI

Kenya's government is trying to attract foreign investment as this can increase output, employment and exports.

Basically, attracting foreign direct investment is a win-win situation in that both the local producers in Kenya and the multinational corporations and retail chains benefit from the collaboration. There is general consensus that transnational corporations have helped to increase the value of developing countries' agricultural exports. Developing countries have thus been better able to exploit their comparative advantages, especially the climate and low labour costs.

Meanwhile, the foreign-owned flower companies in developing and newly developed countries have also contributed to significant improvements in both production and productivity in several places in the flower sector's value chain (Wee and Arnold, 2009).

In some areas, the cooperation and vertical integration of the value chain, however, has become unbalanced because the large multinational corporations benefit from market power, size relations and access to market intelligence. In the long run, the smaller local producers in Kenya, in particular, will come under pressure from competitors and customers, and they may be far too dependent on their customers. In addition, the small producers hardly have the opportunity to join the collaboration, since they cannot meet the customers' requirements regarding standards and volume.

Producers in Kenya, Zambia and Ghana in particular have, however, successfully established cooperatives, which have ensured them greater critical mass and greater market power over their customers, (see, e.g. Golup and McManus, 2008).

However, there are other, negative consequences of foreign direct investment. Such consequences include adverse environmental effects. For example, the growing flower industry is one of the reasons that the water level in some lakes has declined markedly, and there is a risk that they will completely dry up. There is also some concern about the widespread use of fertilisers and pesticides in flower production, as this may cause the pollution of groundwater and lakes (Learning Africa, 2010).

The increasing flower production in developing countries has led to an increase in the international supply, which is far stronger than the demand. This oversupply has been particularly true for cut flowers, including roses, and has resulted in a sharp decline in market prices.

Increasing competition from new exporting countries, particularly Africa and South America, and the subsequent fall in prices have also had major consequences for the European flower sector, where production has dropped substantially. Many European flower producers have made significant investments in foreign flower production, either as a defensive or a proactive response to the new production potential in foreign countries.

Challenges

Although Kenya has established an impressive flower and vegetable industry oriented to European customers, there are still significant challenges that need to be tackled in order to further develop the potential, to maintain and strengthen international competitiveness, and to ensure that international marketing and specialisation benefit all actors in the value chain equally. Therefore, a number of initiatives are necessary. This is also the case if other countries in the same situation want to copy and learn from the Kenyan experience.

The challenges which need to be overcome in order to increase African exports of horticultural products are significant based on Kenya's experience:

> The requirement to comply with high, and probably ever more stringent, standards and quality demands from European customers will continually put pressure on the entire value chain in the country of production. It may be difficult to monitor and control the value chain at all stages, especially when the first link in the food chain, agriculture, mainly consists of smaller units and some subsistence farming. The challenge thus involves securing the required quality and building the necessary competences.
>
> The structure of African agriculture can also be a major challenge. Farms are generally small and hence output per farm is low, while the infrastructure is often inadequate. This means that an exporter, an industrial company or a purchaser must use considerable resources to ensure the adequate supply of raw materials.
>
> The many small units also carry benefits for exporters, etc. – but disadvantages for farmers and also disadvantages for the whole sector. Market power and bargaining power are unbalanced, as the large number of farmers face a very few large buyers. Market information is not symmetric, which means that the market is imperfect and that there is a market failure.

The field-to-fork value chain is inefficient in several places. Access to the market seems to be a very significant barrier, especially for the smaller farms, which account for a significant portion of Kenya's total agricultural production.

Ensuring better market power and a more equal distribution of bargaining power and market information may be provided by building and developing cooperation in producer groups in agriculture. The establishment of farm-owned cooperatives which are forward integrated in the value chain up to the European customers may be an ideal way of securing an improved market situation.

The establishment of cooperatives would give farmers an alternative outlet, and would also give the farmers a share of the value added downstream in the value chain. However, there seem to be several barriers which prevent farmers from becoming deeply involved in cooperatives.

The small farmers are significantly hampered by poor access to inputs such as seed, crop protection, advice, market intelligence and research. In order to increase exports of vegetables, fruits and flowers to the increasingly demanding retail chains in Europe, public research, development and consultancy in the field need to be strengthened while market access needs to be improved, with the main focus being on small farmers.

Building efficient and large farmer-owned cooperatives in many cases requires a certain level of mutual trust, transparency, accountability and social competence. The question is whether African farmers in general possess these characteristics. In addition, cooperatives in many cases are most successful if they are established 'from below'; if the farmers recognise the advantages and have a strong motivation to start up the cooperative. Among African farmers there is a degree of scepticism regarding cooperatives, as previous attempts at their establishment have been with the State as the initiator and driver.

Finally, it is questionable whether significant changes, an entire paradigm shift, are necessary to achieve a substantial increase in exports of agricultural and food products. Corruption, general distrust of government initiatives, crime, polit-ical instability, poverty and excessive income inequalities are structural and fundamental barriers that may prevent the desired development of agricultural and food exports in developing countries.

Questions and assignments

6.1 Describe the role of NICs, BRICS and developing countries on the international markets for food and agriculture. Describe trends, drivers, etc.

6.2 What are major potentials and barriers for these countries on the international food markets in future?

6.3 What can be learnt from the Kenyan case?

7 Food demand

Demand for agricultural products is an important parameter for agriculture's development and position. First, demand for agricultural and food products is special compared to other products. Second, the extent of the demand, its composition and development is crucial for future agricultural production. Finally, food is an absolutely essential consumer good upon which there is a great deal of focus in developed and developing countries both economically and politically.

Introduction

The total consumption of food depends on the size of the population and per capita consumption. Population development in particular plays a major role and, in this regard, it is noteworthy that population growth is greatest in countries where purchasing power, and hence nutritional status, is the worst.

Demand for food products is determined by a variety of factors (parameters). Therefore, it is possible to formulate a general demand function which combines all the factors that affect market demand:

$$Qd = f(P_p, P_1 \ldots P_n, Y, N, Z, G, e)$$

where

Qd	= the demanded amount during the period.
P_p	= the product's price.
$P_1 \ldots P_n$	= the price of n other complementary or substitutable products.
Y	= the average personal income within the area.
N	= the number of individuals (consumers).
Z	= a variable which represents special preferences or habits in the area.
G	= income distribution.
e	= coincidental residual.

In particular, P_p, $P_1 \ldots P_n$ and Y will be used, as these independent variables are considered to be the most important.

The elasticity concept is used to analyse the three variables' influence on demand for food.

Income elasticity of demand

Income elasticity is a measure of how demand changes in relation to a change in income. It is calculated in the following manner:

Income elasticity of demand (e_I):

$$e_I = \frac{\% \text{ change in quantity demanded}}{\% \text{ change in real income}}$$

In other words, income elasticity is the change in demand divided by the change in income.

It seems natural that the income elasticity of food is small: when a population's income increases, demand for primarily consumer durables increases, while the quantitative consumption of food is hardly affected.

A shift in the consumption pattern usually occurs in favour of quality products, or certain groups of products which are relatively more income elastic. Although the cost of food is therefore likely to increase, it will still constitute a smaller part of total consumption.

In developing countries, income elasticities will be relatively high, as an increase in income will also cause demand for food to increase significantly. As illustrated in Figure 7.1, an increase in income will especially lead to a significant increase in the consumption of basic foodstuffs in the lowest income classes. In the higher income classes, the consumption of purchased food (non-subsistence food products) will increase along with the consumption of services.

In developed countries, income elasticities will generally be low, and they will – *ceteris paribus* – be the lowest in countries which have the highest average income. The differences in income elasticities between developed and developing countries and between different food categories is illustrated in Box 7.1.

Box 7.1 Income elasticities for different countries and different products

Food demand varies from country to country and from product to product. Income is a more important driver in developed countries and for the demand of high price and high quality products. Figures 7.1 and 7.2 illustrate (schematically) how food demand reacts to changing income in different situations.

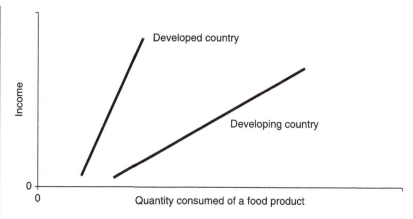

Figure 7.1 Income and food demand in developed and developing countries.
Source: Author's presentation.

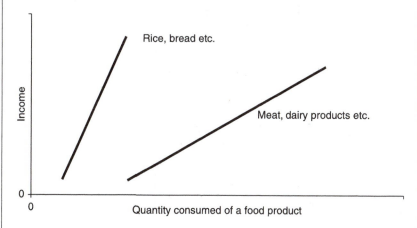

Figure 7.2 Income and food demand for different categories of food product.
Source: Author's presentation.

The figures in Box 7.1 illustrate how food consumption in developing countries is more sensitive to income changes than in industrialised countries. The figures also show that the consumption of basic food products is less sensitive to income changes than more luxurious foods.

The differences in income elasticities between countries and between products has been confirmed by empirical studies (see Table 7.1).

Numerous studies and reports on income elasticities in different countries have been conducted. Broadly speaking, one can observe the same pattern in all the

Table 7.1 Income elasticities of demand for selected food products and countries

	Beverages and tobacco	Cereals	Meat	Fish	Dairy	Oils and fats	Fruit and vegetables	Other food	Food, beverages and tobacco
USA	0.12	0.05	0.10	0.10	0.10	0.03	0.07	0.10	0.09
France	0.41	0.19	0.34	0.36	0.35	0.12	0.26	0.34	0.32
Korea	0.63	0.31	0.50	0.54	0.52	0.24	0.38	0.50	0.47
Poland	0.79	0.40	0.62	0.66	0.64	0.33	0.48	0.62	0.58
Brazil	0.87	0.44	0.66	0.71	0.68	0.37	0.52	0.66	0.62
Peru	0.93	0.47	0.69	0.75	0.72	0.41	0.54	0.69	0.65
Vietnam	1.43	0.59	0.79	0.88	0.83	0.55	0.64	0.79	0.74

Source: Heston et al. (2009).

studies, but the specific coefficients and estimates may vary from analysis to analysis. This is mainly due to the varying data bases and differences between the models. However, several clear conclusions can be drawn from Table 7.1 and from similar analyses:

> There is a pattern in that the income elasticities have different levels depending on the consumer's current income, while the level generally decreases over time with increasing income.
>
> The studies also show that, although the income elasticities are generally low ($e_i < 1$) for food, there are significant differences between the groups. The more expensive and luxurious foods such as fruit, cheese, meat and vegetables have the highest income elasticity, while eggs, oil and fat have very low income elasticities.
>
> The population's eating habits change with increasing income in that demand for expensive and high-quality products increases.
>
> All in all, the analyses support the assumption that the income elasticity of food varies significantly from product to product, although there is a general downward trend over time.
>
> The studies also show that services are much more income elastic than food. An increase in income results in a rapid increase in the demand for services – a trend seen in all countries.
>
> While the volume of food demanded tends to be relatively constant in highly developed countries, a significant increase in value will almost always occur. It is therefore necessary to distinguish between the volume and value effect of an income change. This can be achieved by using quality and value income elasticities. Hence, the two estimates show whether an income change results in a purely quantitative change in demand, or whether, e.g., an increased consumption of quality products occurs within the same product category.

Box 7.2 Engel's law and Engel's curve

Engel's law and Engel's curve are essential in explaining food demand, and major characteristics of food demand can be traced back to Engel's law.

Engel's law states that, as income rises, the proportion of income spent on food falls, even if actual expenditure on food rises. Engel's law was proposed by the German statistician Ernst Engel (1821–96).

This law does not suggest that the amount of money which is spent on food decreases with an increase in income, but that the percentage of income spent on food increases more slowly than the percentage increase in income. In other words, the income elasticity of demand for food is between 0 and 1.

Engel's law can be illustrated by Engel's curve, which shows the relationship between the income level and the food consumption level.

There are two types of Engel's curve. The first describes how the absolute demand for and expenditure on food varies with income. In this case, one expects that demand will increase at a decreasing rate as income rises. The second type describes how the proportion of household income (relative demand) spent on food varies with income. In this case, one expects that demand will decrease as income rises.

Engel's law and Engel's curve can be illustrated in several ways depending on which axis, data and parameters are used. Figures 7.3–7.6 present examples of the correlation between income and food demand using either cross-sectional or time series data.

Figure 7.3 shows that food consumption – measured as daily food supply in calories – tends to increase with increasing income, but at a decreasing rate and is almost constant for high-income countries.

Figure 7.4 demonstrates that food's share of total consumption decreases significantly when income increases. On a logarithmic scale, the trend is very clear and decreasing, using cross-sectional data for almost all countries in the world – developing and developed.

Figure 7.5 shows Engel's law very clearly: as countries start to develop economically, demand for food increases, but food's relative share of total consumption decreases simultaneously.

Figure 7.6 shows that the role of food decreases as income increases – here illustrated by time series data. Countries such as the USA, Canada and Denmark have witnessed a significant and constant decrease in food's share of total consumption over several decades during which massive economic development occurred.

Slight differences over time and from country to country may be caused by data breaks or different applied definitions and methods.

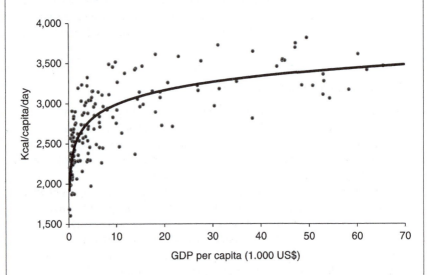

Figure 7.3 Food consumption and level of economic development (2010).

Source: Author's presentation based on World Bank (2012b) and FAO (2012).

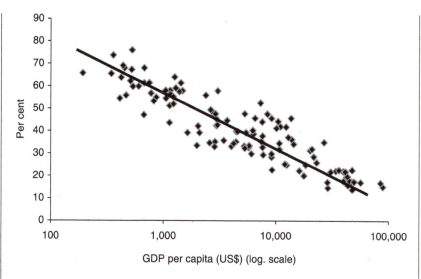

Figure 7.4 Food's share of total consumption and level of economic development (2010 or latest year with available data).

Source: Author's presentation based on World Bank (2012b), Seale and Regmi (2006) and FAO (2012).

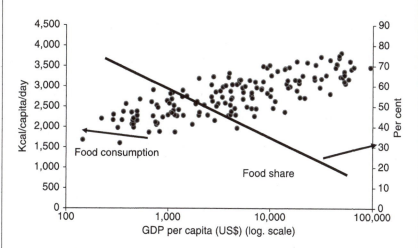

Figure 7.5 Food consumption: absolute and relative to total demand as a function of the level of economic development (2010).

Source: Author's presentation based on World Bank (2012b), Seale and Regmi (2006) and FAO (2012).

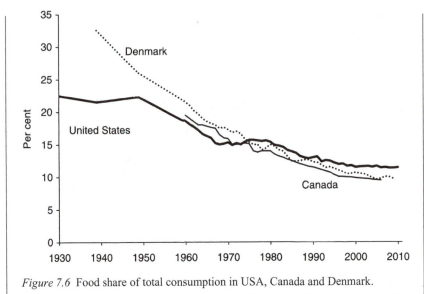

Figure 7.6 Food share of total consumption in USA, Canada and Denmark.

Source: Agriculture and Agri-Food Canada (2012); USDA (2011c); Statistics Denmark (several issues).

Table 7.2 presents three income elasticity concepts which are used for some food groups.

Quality elasticity, which is value minus quantity elasticity, shows the extent to which value increases more than quantity. If value increases relatively significantly, it is probably because the quality of the demanded product has increased.

Table 7.2 Income elasticities (quantity, value and quality) for certain food groups in the UK in 1971

Product	Quantity income elasticity	Value income elasticity	Quality income elasticity
Milk	0.17	0.18	0.01
Cheese	0.24	0.28	0.04
Meat*	0.21	0.27	0.06
Fish	0.04	0.17	0.13
Eggs	0.09	0.12	0.03
Butter	0.18	0.19	0.01
Sugar	−0.09	−0.05	0.04
Potatoes	−0.17	−0.09	0.08
Vegetables	0.34	0.50	0.16
Bread	−0.20	−0.16	0.04
Beverages	0.00	0.10	0.10
All food products	—	0.20	—

Source: MAFF (1974) and author's calculations
Note: *Excluding tinned goods, etc.

All the illustrated foods have low income elasticities. Indeed, bread and potatoes even have negative income elasticities, which means they are inferior goods (see Box 7.3).

Relatively speaking, quality elasticities are small and, in general, the amount contributes more to value increases than does quality. It is also worth noting that the amount of bread and potatoes demanded decreases with increasing income, but an increase in quality means that the decline in value is not very large.

Box 7.3 Inferior goods

Inferior goods are products which have a negative income elasticity of demand. This means that demand falls as income rises. Inferior goods are often products for which there are superior goods available if the consumer has sufficient money to purchase them. Inferior goods include low-processed products, bulk products, staple foods, private label products and discount products.

Food products such as bread, frozen food, rice, etc. are also often inferior goods in highly developed countries. Furthermore, demand for tobacco, e.g. cigarettes, and also sugar often tends to decrease when income rises.

Inferior goods and negative income elasticities usually appear among individuals with high incomes for whom the daily intake of food is sufficient and for whom increasing income is unnecessary to fulfil basic needs.

As Table 7.3 shows, wheat and, to some extent, sugar are inferior goods in highly developed countries.

Table 7.3 Examples of negative income elasticities and inferior goods

	Wheat	*Sugar*
USA	−0.3	0.1
Sweden	−0.3	0.0
France	−0.4	0.3
Australia	−0.1	−0.1
UK	−0.2	0.0
Italy	−0.2	0.4
Spain	−0.3	0.6
Brazil	0.4	0.1
Kenya	0.8	1.0
India	0.5	1.0
Indonesia	1.0	1.4

Source: FAO (1971).

A significant reason that the quality income elasticity of certain products is low is that price and product differentiation is probably small. In particular, milk, butter, sugar, bread, eggs and, to some extent, meat (especially if it has not undergone much processing) belong to fairly homogeneous product groups, where it can be difficult to distinguish the quality that gives a significant price premium.

Price elasticity of demand

Another important parameter which influences demand for food is the price elasticity of demand. This parameter is an expression of the change in the amount demanded for a product divided by the change in the price of the same product.

The price elasticity of demand is calculated as follows:

Price elasticity of demand (e_p):

$$e_p = \frac{\% \text{ change in quantity demanded}}{\% \text{ change in price}}$$

In other words, the price elasticity of demand is the change in demand relative to the change in the price of the product.

Price elasticities of demand will usually be negative for all products – when prices rise, demand falls. Generally, food and other so-called necessity goods have numerically small price elasticities of demand. This is because one needs necessity goods almost regardless of the price. In addition, food – as a group – is impossible to substitute. There is no alternative to food, which makes demand for it even less price sensitive.

In developing countries, purchasing power is lower, so here prices have a greater influence on demand. Even though one is starving, one may not be able to afford to purchase the necessary amount of food. Therefore, the price of food has a significant influence on food demand among the poorest people in developing countries.

The effect of food prices on food demand in developed and developing countries – and for different categories of food – is illustrated in Box 7.4.

Box 7.4 Price elasticities of demand for different countries and different products

The impact of prices on food demand varies from country to country and from product to product. Price is a more important driver in developing countries and for the demand of non-necessity products. Figures 7.7 and 7.8 illustrate (schematically) how food demand reacts to changing prices in different situations.

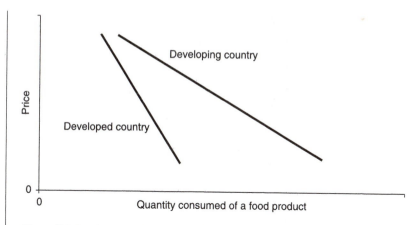

Figure 7.7 Food price and demand in developed and developing countries.
Source: Author's presentation.

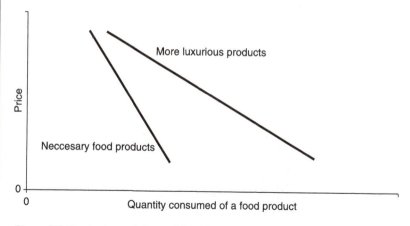

Figure 7.8 Food price and demand for different categories of food product.
Source: Author's presentation.

The differences in price elasticities of demand between countries and between products has been confirmed by empirical studies (see Table 7.4).

Numerous studies and reports on price elasticities of demand have been conducted in different countries. Once again, a consistent pattern can be observed in all the studies, although the estimated elasticities vary due to the varying data bases and model assumptions. However, several clear conclusions can be drawn from Table 7.4 and from other similar analyses.

Table 7.4 Price elasticities of demand for selected food products and countries (2005)

	Beverages and tobacco	Cereals	Meat	Fish	Dairy	Oils and fats	Fruit and vegetables	Other food
USA	-0.31	0.06	-0.25	-0.19	-0.26	0.00	-0.15	-0.32
France	-0.44	-0.01	-0.35	-0.27	-0.37	-0.07	-0.23	-0.46
Korea, Rep.	-0.56	-0.19	-0.44	-0.35	-0.45	-0.21	-0.31	-0.59
Poland	-0.58	-0.15	-0.46	-0.36	-0.47	-0.19	-0.32	-0.61
Brazil	-0.68	-0.27	-0.51	-0.42	-0.53	-0.29	-0.38	-0.72
Peru	-0.69	-0.26	-0.52	-0.43	-0.54	-0.29	-0.39	-0.73
Vietnam	-0.85	-0.39	-0.57	-0.48	-0.59	-0.40	-0.46	-0.99
Kenya	-0.89	-0.41	-0.58	-0.49	-0.60	-0.42	-0.47	-1.07
Ethiopia	-1.09	-0.46	-0.60	-0.52	-0.62	-0.46	-0.50	-1.67

Source: USDA (2011d)

In almost all cases, price elasticities of demand are negative: an increase in price leads to a fall in demand. However, in rare cases, an increase in price results in an increase in demand. Such goods are known as Giffen goods – see Box 7.5.

Box 7.5 Giffen goods

Normally an increase in price will result in a decrease in demand. However, there is an exception: in special cases, demand increases when the price increases. This is called a Giffen paradox or a Giffen good.

A Giffen good – after the English economist Robert Giffen – arose from a classical example: poor Irish peasants' demand for potatoes increased when the price of potatoes increased during the famine of 1845. The explanation for this reverse – perverse – reaction was that, when the potato price rose, the poorest people could not afford to purchase more expensive items such as meat, and so they ate relatively cheaper food, including potatoes.

In general terms, the explanation is that the poor become less able to afford more luxurious goods as they have less purchasing power as a result of the price increase. The result can be that they are forced to buy even more of the basic food, which has risen in price.

In the usual case, the public will react to the increasing price by demanding less of the product. However, in a Giffen paradox situation, the driving force will be the decrease in income (declining purchasing power) which results from the price increase. Here the decline in purchasing power is the dominant factor, and it results in consumers substituting more luxurious goods with other cheaper products, even if the cheaper products have just increased in price. The relationship between price and demand is shown in Figure 7.9.

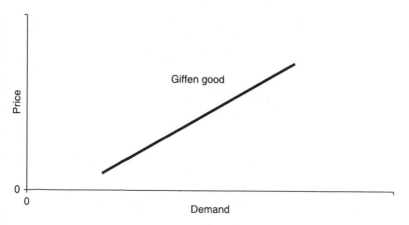

Figure 7.9 Demand for a Giffen good.

Source: Author's presentation

A Giffen good is definitely a special case which does not have much practical significance. However, it can be used to illustrate some of the mechanisms and relationships that exist in food markets.

There are other cases where the price elasticity of demand is positive, but on the basis of other motives.

While a Giffen paradox occurs when people defensively adjust to higher prices, so-called Veblen goods arise when a price increase attracts people.

Veblen goods are primarily bought to demonstrate wealth. Therefore, if the price of a Veblen good decreases, more people will be able to afford it and it thereby becomes less effective as an indicator of wealth, so demand for it falls.

Veblen goods are best described as visible-status goods, which is rarely the case with food products.

There is a pattern in that the price elasticities of demand have different levels depending on the consumer's current income, while the level generally decreases over time with increasing income.

The studies also show that demand elasticities are the smallest (closest to 0) for products which are the most difficult to substitute. For example, bread, potatoes, milk and eggs are well-defined products which are difficult to replace with other goods, and they therefore have low demand elasticities. Therefore, it is clear that the more well-defined and homogeneous the product groups become, the closer to zero the demand elasticities.

However, price elasticity of demand does not only depend on the product aggregation level. Clearly, the quality of the product can also influence the demand response to a price change, although contradictory reactions can occur.

The starting point is that quality products are the most price inelastic. If a product has a strong quality image, then quality will be a significant determinant of demand, whereas the price, which in the majority of cases is the decisive purchasing parameter / demand determinant for homogeneous products, will have less influence. The price elasticity of demand thereby decreases.

Moreover, conscious product differentiation on the basis of the quality parameter will mean that the market will become more heterogeneous, in that the consumer will be able to distinguish the product from similar products and its elasticity will therefore change. The greater the product differentiation, the fewer the substitutes, and thus the less price sensitive the demand function.

A third point is that high-quality products are demanded by consumers with high incomes, and it is reasonable to assume that this population group's consumption is determined by price to a lesser extent.

Cross-elasticity of demand

As is apparent from the preceding sections, substitution opportunities between food products play a crucial role in food demand. The general demand relation also contains the prices of substitutable products as significant independent variables.

One would expect that the possibilities for substitution are relatively large within the food group, as the range of products is large and the supply is almost unlimited. This means that, if a specific food increases in price, consumers can choose alternative foods at a lower price.

An empirical measure of the substitution opportunities can be performed by estimating cross-elasticities, which express the relationship between the price of product A and the demand for product B. Cross-elasticity of demand is calculated in the following manner:

Cross-elasticity of demand (e_{AB}):

$$e_{AB} = \frac{\text{\% change in quantity demanded of product A}}{\text{\% change in price of product B}}$$

If the two products are close substitutes – and the market is transparent – even a small price change of A will result in a change in demand for B. In other words, the higher the cross-price elasticity of two goods, the closer substitutes they are for one another.

Products which belong to a very limited and well-defined group are often the most substitutable (see the example in Figure 7.10).

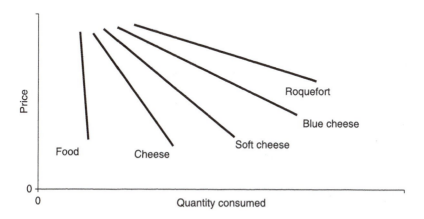

Figure 7.10 Schematic example of different demand curves and elasticities in relation to products' substitutability.

Source: Author's presentation.

Box 7.6 Cross price elasticities of demand for different products

Two products can be dependent on each other in two different ways. In the first case, one of the products can be a substitute for the other. For example, apples can replace bananas. Therefore, if the price of bananas rises, demand for apples will increase. This is a case of substitution. The cross-price elasticity of substitutable goods is positive as a price increase for one product leads to an increase in the quantity demanded of the other product.

In the second case, demand for one product is enhanced by simultaneous demand for the other product. Examples include 'bread and butter', 'bacon and eggs' and 'red wine and steak'. Such products are complementary and they have a negative cross-price elasticity of demand. The explanation is that a price increase for one product leads to a decrease in demand for the second product.

The degree of dependence may vary but, the greater the dependency, the greater the nominal cross-price elasticities of demand. Figures 7.11 and 7.12 illustrate two different cases of cross-price elasticity of demand.

Figure 7.12 illustrates that there are very few substitutes for the product group 'food', but far more opportunities to substitute special cheeses with other very similar cheeses.

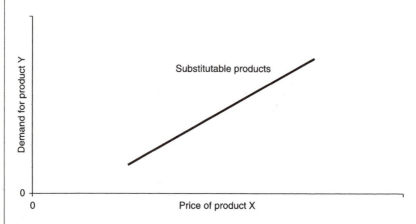

Figure 7.11 Cross-price elasticities of demand: substitutable products.

Source: Author's presentation.

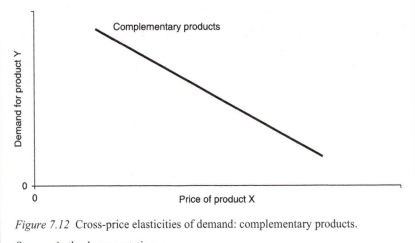

Figure 7.12 Cross-price elasticities of demand: complementary products.

Source: Author's presentation.

When analysing substitution possibilities, it is important to compare products in the same category and to apply specific and homogeneous units. It is therefore of no interest to estimate cross-elasticities or substitution elasticities for completely aggregated studies.

Clearly, the possibility for substitution is an important point with regard to the demand for food, because total consumption – calculated in quantity – is extremely stable. Any increase in sales in the market will mainly be at the expense of competitors' market share. The competing products may be more or less identical, but differentiated on the basis of quality, processing, packaging, etc. Products can also be very different, but still be potential substitutes if the relative price changes significantly.

From the perspective of the food industry, the challenge is therefore to develop products which stand out from the other products on the market and which also give consumers a particular preference. If the preference is high, it creates a unique market from which competitors can be kept out, and where consumers are willing to pay a premium as there are no substitutes or alternatives. In this way, a product is created which is not particularly price sensitive (low price elasticity of demand) and which has few substitutes (low cross-elasticity of demand).

Food demand trends

Food demand is influenced by prices, income and long-term stable development trends. These food demand trends should be viewed against the background that food is a basic necessity, that opportunities for substitution are very limited and that there is relatively little scope for differentiation. These factors contribute to relatively stable food demand and the occurrence of longer-term trends.

The following sections discuss some of the most significant food demand trends.

From a producer to a consumer orientation

For decades, agriculture and food production was based on technical, biological and economic production possibilities. Today, a paradigm shift is occurring from traditional production-driven agriculture towards market and consumer-driven agriculture, so that the value chain 'from field to fork' is increasingly becoming 'from fork to field'.

This change has been reinforced by a power shift in the value chain. Consumers have become more powerful and critical than ever before, while the power shift has been supported by media attention on consumer interests.

Low market growth, together with significant overcapacity in the food sector, has thus meant that the firms closest to the consumer have obtained a more central position. A company can basically focus on its product, its customers, its competitors or the market (see Figure 7.13).

According to Kotler and Armstrong (2010), over the years, companies have made a shift from a product orientation to a customer, a competitor and finally a market orientation, as shown in the figure.

If a company is product oriented it means that the company itself and its production are in focus, while investment in market research and marketing is minimal. The price of a product is determined by the cost of its production and not considerations regarding value or competition. In such a company, the role of the sales team is to sell the goods which the company chooses to produce and, if the customers are not satisfied, the sales team is told to find new customers.

A customer-oriented company has a greater focus on its customers, while a competitor-oriented company focuses on its competitors, including their strategies, strengths and weaknesses.

Finally, a market-oriented company focuses on the market, which consists of products, customers, competitors and distributors. The market is monitored

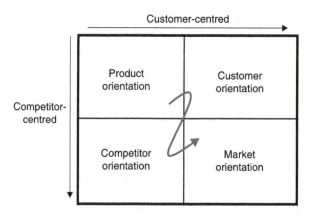

Figure 7.13 Evolving company orientations.

Source: Based on Kotler and Armstrong (2010).

systematically, while the company is simultaneously heavily involved in strategic and market-related planning and creative product planning. The market-oriented company thus makes a balanced consideration of its resources and products, the current and future needs of its customers and the market position and role of its competitors.

Box 7.7 The political consumer – Islamic boycott

The political consumer has special consumer preferences which are not directly related to his / her personal needs, but which go beyond those which normally control the more traditionally conscious consumer. Such a consumer expresses conscious attitudes or values which are socially oriented when choosing between producers or products. Demand is often based on the consumer's political position.

Political consumption was first recognised as a form of political participation in the mid-1990s in connection with the Brent Spar campaign against Shell and the consumer boycott of French goods, especially wine, in protest against French nuclear testing.

Another example of the political consumer on the food market occurred in 2006. In September 2005, the Danish newspaper, *Jyllands Posten*, published 12 cartoons of the Prophet Muhammad. This led to strong reactions within Islamic countries, some of which demanded an official apology from Denmark, which was not forthcoming. Subsequently, a delegation of Danish Muslims travelled to the Middle East and called for the international condemnation of the cartoons.

The situation escalated in mid-January when the condemnations were followed by a boycott in most Arab countries to which Denmark had significant exports of mainly dairy products, but also meat and other products.

The Danish dairy company, Arla Foods, had significant operations in the Middle East in terms of direct exports and production and processing, which corresponded to approximately US \$0.5 billion. In 2006, Arla's sales in the Middle East almost came to a standstill from one day to the next as a result of the Muhammad cartoon crisis. Revenue of nearly US \$0.5 billion was reduced to almost nothing in the space of a few days.

This shows that the foundation of a company's – or a sector's – international activities can be significantly changed very quickly. As the timeline below shows, Arla Foods very quickly lost access to the Arab markets, while the subsequent recovery took much longer.

2006

- 12th January: the Egyptian Grand Mufti Muhammad Said Tantawi issued a fatwa against Denmark.
- 20th January: the Saudi Grand Mufti calls for a boycott.

- 22nd January: SMS messages and e-mails sent calling for a boycott.
- 24th January: Saudi Arabia calls their ambassador in Denmark home.
- 25th January: Saudi Arabia and Kuwait begin to remove Danish products from shelves.
- 26th January: Arla out of 300 stores.
- 28th January: Arla out of 5,000 stores.
- 31st January: Arla out of 50,000 stores in five days – equivalent to 95 per cent of all outlets in the region.
- 1st February: a number of European newspapers also publish caricatures of the Prophet Muhammad.
- 4–6th February: the Danish embassies in Syria, Lebanon and Iran burned or attacked.

2007

- October: Arla Foods' exports of dairy products to the Middle East reach 80 per cent of the pre-cartoon level. In a number of countries such as the UAE, Oman, Qatar, Bahrain and the Lebanon, consumers quickly returned to the Danish products. In contrast, there was much greater inertia in Saudi Arabia, where a more or less permanent boycott of Danish goods was expected.

2008

- January: Arla Foods' exports of dairy products to the Middle East reach 95 per cent of the pre-cartoon level.
- February: a number of Danish newspapers reprint cartoons of the Prophet Muhammad. The reason was that three people were arrested for a murder plot against the cartoonist who had drawn the caricature, and the Danish newspapers wanted to show support for freedom of expression by publishing the cartoons.
- End of February: protests take place in Jordan's capital, Amman. In Sudan, the government initiates a boycott of Danish goods. In the Yemen, the government condemns the reprinting of the Danish cartoons.
- Early February: Arla Foods finds that its sales in Arab countries have been halved as a result of this second cartoon crisis.
- June: the Jordanian society, 'The Prophet Unites Us', starts a new boycott of Danish goods.
- October: Arla Foods announces that they have regained two-thirds of their lost revenue in the region.

2012

- Arla Foods has now grown larger in the Middle East than before the cartoon crisis.

- As Figure 7.14 shows, there was a marked decline in Danish dairy exports to the Arab countries during the two crises in 2006 and 2008. In 2006, exports almost completely disappeared, while they were more than halved in 2008.
- Although Saudi Arabia was one of the most important export countries for Denmark, it was possible to maintain and even increase exports of dairy products during and after the two crises. New Zealand, Australia and Egypt in particular took over the Danish sales (see Figure 7.15).

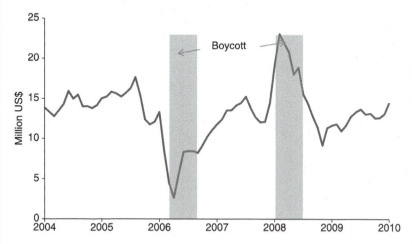

Figure 7.14 Danish export of dairy products to Arab countries: 3-month moving average.
Source: Author's calculation based on Statistics Denmark (2012).

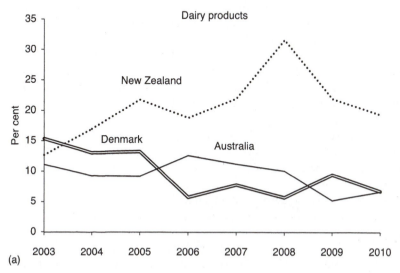

Figure 7.15 Major exporters to Saudi Arabia: share of Saudi Arabia's imports.
Source: Author's calculation based on UN (2012).

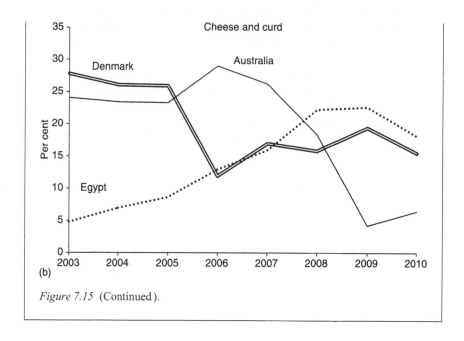

Figure 7.15 (Continued).

A greater focus on qualitative parameters

The consumer of tomorrow will increasingly prioritise qualitative parameters such as animal welfare, cultivation methods, ecology and the environment. Political consumers are here to stay, and, although they represent a minority, they will increasingly influence the agenda.

There are numerous signs that the market for organic products is growing rapidly. Even though the starting point was low, a significant increase in organic agricultural land, production and sales has occurred. During the period 1999–2010, annual global growth rates were approximately 10 per cent (see Table 7.5).

As illustrated in Figure 7.16, the consumption of organic products increases concurrently with a country's economic development. This also means that the consumption of organic products can be expected to increase when there is economic growth.

It also seems that organic consumption mainly occurs in the richest countries. Therefore, demand for organic products can be said to be relatively income elastic.

Organic production is also mainly located in the economically highly developed countries (see Figure 7.17). However, there are also several examples of developing countries with some organic production, which is then sold on affluent export markets.

Table 7.5 Organic agricultural land by region (per cent of total agricultural land)

Continent	1999	2000	2001	2002	2003	2004	2005	2006	2007	2008	2009	2010	Average yearly change, %
Africa	0.00	0.01	0.03	0.03	0.04	0.05	0.05	0.07	0.09	0.08	0.10	0.10	57
Asia	0.00	0.00	0.03	0.03	0.04	0.28	0.20	0.23	0.21	0.24	0.25	0.20	126
Europe	0.79	0.95	1.06	1.14	1.23	1.26	1.34	1.48	1.60	1.70	1.89	2.06	9
Latin America	0.46	0.69	0.80	0.96	0.95	0.83	0.81	0.79	1.03	1.28	1.39	1.36	12
Oceania	1.13	1.10	1.16	1.34	2.48	2.67	2.56	2.76	2.75	2.81	2.82	2.87	11
North America	0.19	0.27	0.33	0.32	0.36	0.44	0.57	0.46	0.59	0.66	0.68	0.68	14
Total	0.30	0.36	0.41	0.47	0.60	0.69	0.67	0.70	0.75	0.81	0.85	0.85	10

Source: Organic World (2012).

Note: Total as based on the reporting countries.

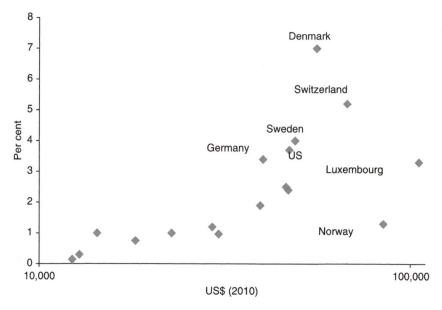

Figure 7.16 Domestic sales of organic products (per cent of total sales) and level of economic development (GDP / capita) (2010).

Source: Own calculations based on Organic World (2012) and World Bank (2012b).

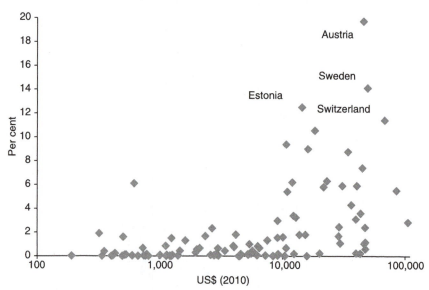

Figure 7.17 Organic agricultural land (per cent of total agricultural land) and level of economic development (GDP / capita) (2010).

Source: Own calculations based on Organic World (2012) and World Bank (2012b).

Different scenarios for future trends regarding the qualitative parameters can be advanced. However, there is no doubt that the qualitative parameters have already had a long-lasting influence. This is confirmed by the change in behaviour that has taken place in agriculture, and the policy interventions that have been introduced to adapt production to the desires of consumers and society in general. There are, therefore, three possible future scenarios regarding the qualitative parameters.

In the first scenario, agriculture will be continually met with new demands regarding production. The qualitative parameters will be continuously tightened, and agriculture will have to adapt.

In the second scenario, agriculture will fulfil the qualitative parameters. Animal welfare, environment and ecology will become an integral part of agricultural production as they will either be legal requirements or consistently demanded by consumers. The consumers' goals will naturally be fulfilled, and thus interest in the area will fall.

In the third scenario, the qualitative parameters will turn out to be public goods which the individual consumer is unable to promote through increased demand. Market demand will therefore be limited, as it will only be possible to achieve the qualitative parameters through legislation. In this case, the qualitative parameters will only be a temporary or limited phenomenon.

No clear trend in the qualitative parameters will occur as, among other reasons, we will be dealing with welfare preferences which will mainly be expressed in countries with very intensive agricultural production and without adequate control and regulation.

Food safety

Food safety, i.e. food which is guaranteed to be free from bacteria, viruses and chemical residues, etc. will become increasingly important regarding global food demand. The various food scandals of recent decades have created a greater awareness of food safety (see Box 7.8). At the same time, the consumer segment which demands food with a high level of food safety will grow and the increased attention to food safety will be promoted by the media's intense interest in the subject.

As previously mentioned, consumer interests often come in waves, and it is therefore likely that food safety will become less important in the long run, because the consumers' demands will be gradually fulfilled. However, based on an overall assessment of the risk for individual cases, the attention given to the subject by the media and overall greater consumer preference, it is likely that food security will continue to be a significant demand parameter.

Food safety also has a veterinary and thus trade policy dimension. Outbreaks of BSE ('Mad Cow Disease'), Foot and Mouth Disease and Swine Fever have had a significant influence on international demand for agricultural commodities.

Although the most developed countries will increasingly be able to take precautionary measures regarding food safety, it is unlikely that it will be possible to prevent similar disease outbreaks in the future. On the contrary, the growth in international trade and the increase in specialisation and concentration may well increase the risk of spreading disease. At the same time, veterinary and health-related requirements will be among the few permitted forms of import control. Therefore, the possibility that highly protected countries will try to maintain import restrictions, albeit now justified by scientifically documented food safety, cannot be ruled out.

Box 7.8 Lack of food security and food scandals – examples

There have been a number of local and international cases of varying significance of food security which has been insufficient. These cases have had dramatic consequences for health and food markets and they are interpreted as food scandals. The cases have ranged from contaminated food to poor hygiene and infectious livestock diseases. Almost all the cases have had a significant impact on international food markets. Four major examples are outlined below.

Chinese milk scandal – melamine

The 2008 Chinese milk scandal was a food safety incident in China, which involved milk and infant formula and other food substances which had become contaminated with melamine. Melamine had been added to milk to make its protein content appear higher. China reported an estimated 300,000 victims, with six infants dying, and a further 860 babies hospitalised.

The issue raised concerns about food safety in China and damaged the reputation of China's food exports, with a number of countries stopping all imports of Chinese dairy products.

BSE 'Mad Cow Disease'

BSE was first detected in cattle in Britain in 1984 and, within a few years, the disease had spread like an epidemic in Britain. BSE subsequently spread to other countries, albeit to a much lesser extent. The foundation was laid for panic reactions among consumers when clear signs that BSE-infected beef could lead to a variant of the incurable and fatal Creutzfeldt-Jakob Disease (CJD) in humans were discovered.

Researchers determined that the disease was spread among cattle through meat and bone meal which was commonly added to cattle feed at the time. The BSE outbreaks had a significant impact on the consumption and trade of beef.

The dioxin scandal

In May 1999, the Belgian government announced that traces of the toxic substance dioxin had been discovered in Belgian chickens and eggs. There had been suspicions that there was something wrong for several months due to the earlier discovery of elevated levels of dioxin in a batch of eggs.

Chicken and eggs were immediately removed from shelves across Europe, while a large number of countries outside the EU decided to ban the import of Belgian chicken and eggs. The USA chose to refuse the import of all European meat and dairy products.

It transpired that the source was dioxin-contaminated animal feed, which meant that the scandal quickly spread to include pork and beef and by-products such as milk, butter, cheese, chocolate and cakes. The neighbouring countries France and Holland were also affected as they had imported Belgian feed.

Austrian wine

In 1985, Austria was hit by a large wine scandal. It was discovered that approximately 70 Austrian wine producers had been systematically adding the harmless, but illegal substance, diethylene glycol (coolant), to their wine to make it more full-bodied for a number of years. The scandal was a significant blow for exports and, in the space of a year, sales shrunk to 20 per cent of pre-scandal levels.

As a result of the scandal, Austria implemented a very tough Wine Law, which led to the disappearance of inferior cheap wine from the market. Together, the Austrian government, sales people, technologists and innovators raised the standard for wine production. Therefore, the wine scandal represented a positive turning point for Austrian wine.

Origin

Some consumers are becoming increasingly interested in the origin of food products, which is in line with the increasing interest in food safety, qualitative parameters, traceability, etc., but is in contrast to the trend towards increased globalisation. In other words, the origin of food has become a demand parameter whereby consumers attempt to determine where a certain product has been produced, often preferring food which has been produced locally or nationally. There may be several reasons for this preference.

First, consumers may believe that locally produced foods are higher quality.

Second, the preference may be due to a counter-reaction against the internationalisation and commercialisation of food sales.

Third, the consumer may be searching for an experience when purchasing food. By buying locally produced food, the consumer can more easily get a sense of the product's journey from field to fork.

The trend towards greater sales through farm shops is a more or less extreme desire to know the origin of food.

Finally, by ascribing special value to products based on their origin it is possible to differentiate. Wine and cheese are obvious examples, but other foods are increasingly differentiated according to their origin.

Health

In general, there is a growing interest in food's effect on health. Products with a low fat and sugar content and with a beneficial effect on cholesterol, etc. are becoming increasingly popular during a time when people are doing less and less physical work.

An increased awareness of the risks of obesity, unhealthy eating habits, etc. has also stimulated interest in healthy foods. In general the consumption of low-fat products is rising. Therefore, this is a high-growth area in relation to total food consumption.

Convenience

Convenience is becoming increasingly important with regard to food demand. In general, there is an increasing desire for more processed goods, which require less preparation in the home. There are several factors which will stimulate this trend which is, therefore, expected to become even more widespread.

First, increasing prosperity will lead directly to an increase in demand, as convenience food is relatively income elastic.

Second, more and more women will enter into paid employment outside the home which will increase the need for convenience.

Third, household size is becoming smaller and smaller in line with economic development. Despite cultural differences, etc. there is a very strong correlation. With increasingly smaller households, demand for convenience on the food market will, *ceteris paribus*, increase.

Eating out

Another clear trend regarding food demand is that an increasing proportion of consumption is taking place outside the home. Eating at the workplace, for example, but also at restaurants, is increasing considerably in line with an increase in participation rates.

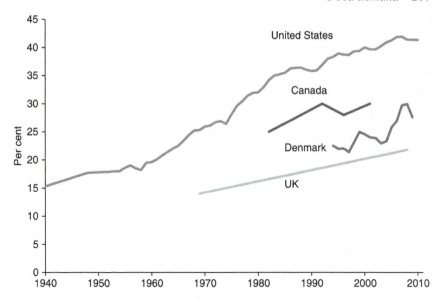

Figure 7.18 Eating out as a percentage of the total.

Source: Author's calculation on the basis of Agriculture and Agri-Food Canada (2012), USDA (2011d), Statistics Denmark (2012) and DEFRA (several issues).

Note: USA: food consumed outside the home as a percentage of total food expenditure. Canada: food purchased from restaurants as a percentage of total food consumption.

UK: eating out as a percentage of total expenditure on food and beverages.

Denmark: consumption in restaurants, canteens, etc. as a percentage of total food and beverage consumption.

Eating out is typically income dependent and is thus sensitive to the state of the economy. Thus, eating out will increase in line with economic development.

Almost half of the food consumed in the USA, which is a trendsetter in this area, is consumed outside the home (see Figure 7.18).

The figure shows the value of eating out as a percentage of total food consumption. As can be seen, there is a clear international trend towards more eating out, which will therefore have increasing importance on food markets.

Functional foods

Functional foods (functional foods, nutraceuticals or pharmafoods) are everyday food products which are developed or altered so that they have a scientifically proven health-promoting or disease-preventing effect. The process, therefore, expands the role of food so that it does not only provide nutrition.

The ability to produce food with beneficial health effects can be traced back thousands of years, with yogurt being a particularly early example of a foodstuff with such properties. The term was originally coined in Japan in the 1980s, and subsequently the development and supply of such goods increased in the USA in the 1990s and thereafter also in Europe.

Functional foods can be said to be the third generation of health foods that have reached Europe:

> The first generation started in the mid-1970s and consisted of healthy and convenient foods such as fruit juice, yogurt and whole grain bread.
>
> The second generation appeared in the mid-1980s and consisted of foods which were low in fat and sugar.
>
> Finally, the third generation can be said to be proper functional foods and these appeared due to technological advances in food science and a consumer desire for health-promoting foods.

One of the advantages of functional foods, from the producers' perspective, is that it is much easier to differentiate products. It is now possible to give a food product completely new and very essential characteristics which make it stand out from the other goods on the market. This makes demand less price elastic, which may increase both revenue and profit of food companies.

The spread of functional foods has been resisted in several areas of the world, while there have also been significant regulatory barriers – particularly in Europe. Today, a significant amount of research and development is underway in the area of functional foods in the expectation that functional foods will constitute a significant portion of the market in the future.

The future spread of functional foods can be stimulated or limited by several factors:

> *Consumer preferences* regarding health, healthy lifestyle, etc. will result in increasing demand for functional foods.
>
> *Food legislation* regarding health could be a significant barrier to growth in the consumption of functional foods. European legislation in particular is restrictive in this area.
>
> *The market* for functional foods is expected to grow significantly in the coming years due to an increase in both supply and demand.
>
> *Research* in the field is extensive, and the more the effects of functional foods can be documented, the greater the demand. Research will also probably lead to the availability of a significantly greater range of functional foods.
>
> *Technology*, including genetic engineering, will mean that it will be possible to adjust the content and composition of production to the necessary specifications of functional foods as far back as the raw material processing stage.

Non-food

The relatively stable demand for agricultural and food products is largely due to the fact that they are basic goods, which are relatively unaffected by economic development and growth. Demand can only be increased significantly if the products can be introduced to a completely different market.

This is an important aspect in the case of the alternative use of agricultural products – especially in the form of non-food use.

On the non-food market, demand is considerably more price elastic, which means significantly greater production of agricultural products is possible, as long as there is a price-based competitive advantage.

To date, non-food has been utilised in the following manner and sectors:

- energy (ethanol)
- paper manufacturing
- textiles
- plastic and rubber manufacturing
- the pharmaceutical industry.

There are also stimulants, such as coffee and tea, which also cannot be characterised as food.

Today, energy production is by far the most important use for non-food, and an increasing amount of agricultural production is used as energy. In the USA, there has been a significant increase in the production of ethanol from corn since 2000, and today more than 40 per cent of total corn production is used for ethanol (see Figure 7.19).

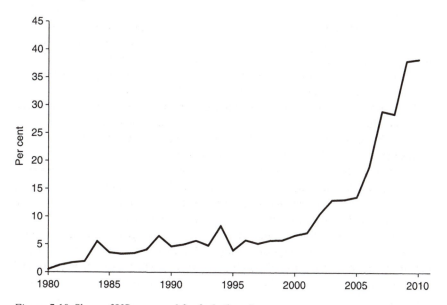

Figure 7.19 Share of US corn used for fuel ethanol.

Source: Author's own calculation based on USDA (2012b).

Although there is increasing pressure on international food markets, it is certain that the future use of agricultural products for energy purposes will lead to increased demand, which will result in further pressure on food markets.

Case: meat demand trends

Meat plays an important role in food markets, food demand and food demand trends.

First, the consumption of meat is increasing considerably in most of the world.

Second, it appears that economic growth and rising prosperity are important drivers of meat demand.

Third, it is expected that the rising demand for meat (and other animal products) will put the international food market under considerable pressure in the coming years. Meat production and consumption requires much more resources than vegetable production, and this will result in increasing demand for basic agricultural commodities in the future.

Meat consumption during economic development

As previously discussed, development in income has an effect on our consumption of meat. As incomes rise, so does meat consumption, although the growth in consumption decreases at the same time and consumption becomes less sensitive to income changes. Meat consumption also becomes less sensitive to price changes when income rises.

Both the level and composition of meat consumption changes concurrently with a country's economic development. In general, the consumption of calories from animal products – of which meat constitutes a significant share – rises in line with a country's economic development. However, the consumption of calories from vegetables remains almost unchanged (see Figure 7.20).

The figure shows that the poorest countries consume very few animal products. As economic growth increases, meat consumption also increases until it reaches 1,000–1,500 calories per capita / day when a country is highly developed. This corresponds to 35–40 per cent of total calorie consumption.

The figure also shows a very clear and unambiguous connection between economic development and consumption of calories from animal products. The extent of vegetable consumption is very scattered, but it does not increase significantly in line with a country's economic development.

The consumption of meat – measured in kg / capita / year – increases significantly when a country undergoes economic development. Cross-sectional data – data for a single year, but for all countries – indicate that an increase in countries' GDP per capita results in an almost unambiguous increase in meat consumption (see Figure 7.21).

The figure shows that, despite cultural, geographical and climatic variations, there is a very clear increase in meat consumption during economic development.

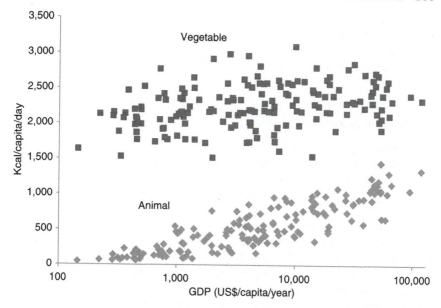

Figure 7.20 Consumption of calories from animal and vegetable products in relation to the level of economic development (2007).

Source: Author's own calculation based on FAO (2012) and World Bank (2012b).

Note: Each dot represents a country.

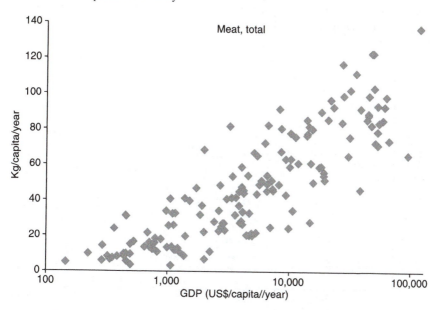

Figure 7.21 Total consumption of meat in relation to individual countries' level of economic development (2007).

Source: Author's own calculation based on FAO (2012) and World Bank (2012b).

Note: Each dot represents a country.

However, there are significant differences between the development of different meat types during economic development. The consumption of lamb and goat meat is almost constant with respect to a country's economic development, while the consumption of poultry and pork increases in line with increasing economic prosperity.

Development in meat consumption

Meat consumption has developed greatly over the past 50 years. From 1961 to 2007, the global average total meat consumption per capita increased from 23 kg to 40 kg. In the same period, the world's population rose from 3.1 billion to 6.7 billion, so total consumption increased by almost 400 per cent.

During the past almost 50 years, poultry meat in particular has had a growing influence on consumption (see Figure 7.22).

As total consumption has increased and its composition has altered, meat consumption in the individual countries has also changed significantly. This is especially the case for the poorer countries where there has been a significant increase in consumption.

A figure of 56 per cent of countries had a rate of meat consumption of less than 20 kg / capita / year in 1961 but, by 2007, this had fallen to 25 per cent. In the same period, the proportion of countries with a level of meat consumption in excess of 100 kg / capita / year only increased from 3.3 per cent to 4.5 per cent. This suggests that the distribution has become much more equal during the past nearly 50 years. Figure 7.23 presents the distribution of countries according to their meat consumption in 1961 and 2007.

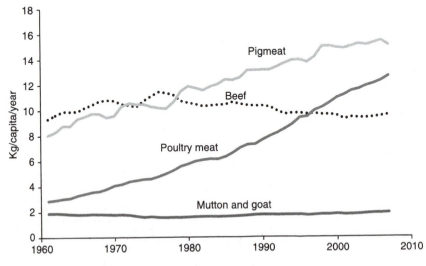

Figure 7.22 The world's total meat consumption per capita – by meat types.

Source: Author's own presentation based on FAO (2012).

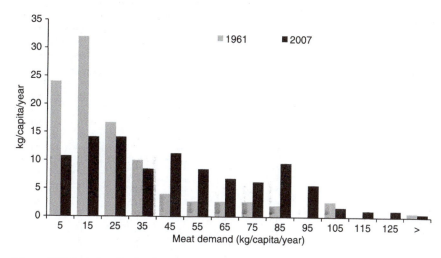

Figure 7.23 Relative distribution of countries according to their meat consumption in 1961 and 2007.

Source: Author's calculations based on FAO (2012).

Meat consumption in individual countries

Meat consumption may be largely explained and almost predicted by a country's level of economic development. Yet, there are differences between countries which have the same level of development – especially when one examines the consumption of specific types of meat (see Table 7.6).

The table shows that pork is the most important in Europe, while beef is the most important in North America. The consumption of lamb and goat meat is especially high in countries where production is also high.

High-growth countries

Table 7.6 also shows that meat consumption in the high-growth countries such as Brazil, Mexico, China and Russia is relatively high. In general, the consumption of animal products is growing relatively significantly in the BRIC countries (Brazil, Russia, India and China) where it constitutes an increasing share of total food consumption (see Figure 7.24).

Meat consumption internationalises

Consumption, production and trade are still very nationally oriented. The norm is that meat is produced, traded and consumed in the same country. This predominantly national basis is because many countries have a self-sufficiency rate of approximately 100 per cent in the case of meat products. This means that

Table 7.6 Meat demand (kg/capita/year) in individual countries (2007)

	Pigmeat	Poultry meat	Bovine meat	Mutton and goat meat	Other meat	Meat total
Selected EU countries						
Austria	66	17	18	1	1	103
Belgium	34	25	19	2	2	82
Bulgaria	18	20	5	2	0	45
Czech Republic	47	25	8	0	6	86
Denmark	50	18	27	1	2	98
Finland	34	17	19	1	2	73
France	32	21	27	3	6	89
Germany	56	16	13	1	3	88
Greece	27	14	18	14	2	76
Hungary	47	28	4	0	1	80
Italy	45	16	24	1	5	92
Latvia	31	21	8	0	0	61
Netherlands	33	15	18	1	4	71
Poland	51	20	5	0	0	77
Portugal	45	25	18	3	1	93
Romania	32	19	8	3	1	63
Spain	62	28	15	5	3	112
Sweden	36	15	24	1	2	79
UK	28	29	22	6	1	86
Other developed countries, etc.						
USA	30	51	41	1	1	123
Canada	27	37	33	1	0	99
Australia	23	40	44	15	1	123
New Zealand	23	35	32	23	4	117
Japan	20	17	9	0	0	46
Saudi Arabia	—	41	6	6	2	54
Developing countries						
Burkina Faso	3	2	8	3	1	17
Bangladesh	0	1	1	1	0	4
High-growth countries						
Mexico	14	29	18	1	1	63
Brazil	11	32	37	1	0	80
China	33	12	5	3	1	53
India	0	1	2	1	0	3
Russia	18	22	18	1	1	61
South Africa	4	25	16	4	0	49
Country groupings						
Low income, food deficit	2	3	4	2	1	11
Africa	1	5	6	2	2	16
America	17	35	31	1	1	85
Asia	14	8	4	2	1	28
Europe	36	20	17	2	2	77
Oceania	22	37	40	15	1	115
World total	15	13	10	2	1	40

Source: FAO (2012).

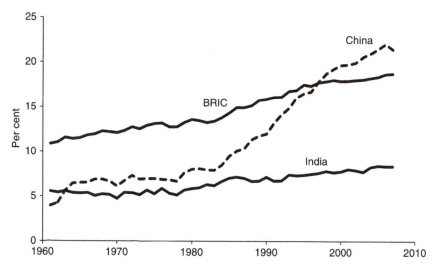

Figure 7.24 The consumption of calories from animal products as a percentage of the total.

Source: Author's calculations up based on FAO (2012).

Note: BRIC = Brazil, Russia, India and China; unweighted average.

domestic consumption almost equals domestic production, and imports and exports are therefore very limited.

Figure 7.25 shows that approximately 35 per cent of countries are almost entirely self-sufficient, i.e. they have a self-sufficiency level in the range 95–105 per cent when it comes to poultry.

Approximately 30 per cent of countries have a self-sufficiency level in the range of 98–102 per cent. In practice, this means that they are actually self-sufficient and do not have to rely on exports or imports.

Only very few countries have a self-sufficiency level which is well over 100. In other words, very few countries have large exports or are highly export-oriented with regard to poultry. The figure also illustrates that very few countries are highly dependent on – or have specialised in – exports of poultry meat. Only 3.5 per cent of countries have a self-sufficiency level which is over 130 per cent.

Worldwide, meat production is adjusted so that it matches consumption very closely. Domestic consumers are by far the most important.

However, although world consumption and production of meat is very nationally oriented, there are clear trends towards greater internationalisation. A steadily increasing share of the world's total meat consumption comes from imports from foreign producers (see Figure 7.26).

Another major trend in food consumption is that a kind of 'standardisation' in consumption is occurring, so that we are moving in the direction of more and more uniform and 'international' eating habits. For example, consumption patterns in Northern and Southern Europe in particular are becoming more uniform,

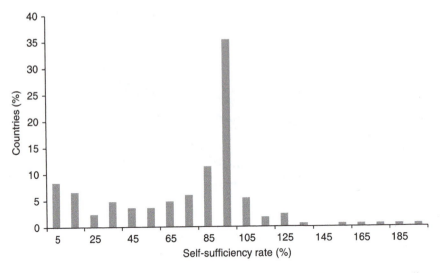

Figure 7.25 Distribution of countries according to level of self-sufficiency regarding poultry (2007).

Source: Author's calculations based on FAO (2012).

Note: Self-sufficiency for 5 = 0–10, 25 = 20–30, etc.

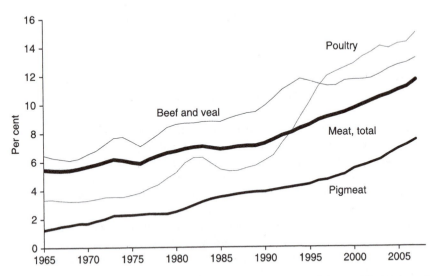

Figure 7.26 The world's total import of meat as a percentage of the world's total meat consumption.

Source: Author's calculation based on FAO (2012).

Note: 3-year average.

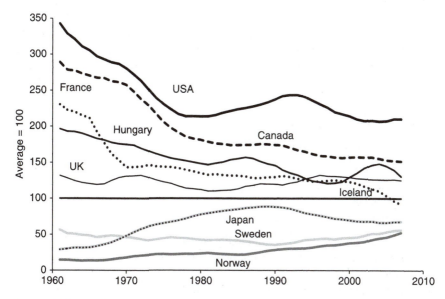

Figure 7.27 Development in the consumption of poultry per capita in various industrialised countries.

Source: Author's calculation based on FAO (2011).

Note: Unweighted average of all OECD countries ('the West') = 100.

although American, European and Asian food habits are also beginning to resemble each other.

Figure 7.27 shows the consumption of meat in some countries in relation to the average in developed countries as an example of the more uniform eating habits.

The figure shows the development in consumption per capita compared to the average. For example, the figure shows that, in the early 1960s, three times as much poultry was consumed in the USA than the average for the Western world. However, subsequently, consumption in the USA has decreased so that today it is 'only' twice as much as the average in the Western world.

As can be seen in the figures, the trend is toward more uniform consumption. The countries are more or less nearing the average level for OECD countries. Consumption of meat is high in the USA, but growth has been highest in countries with low consumption levels. Thus, all countries will come closer to the OECD average.

On an international level, there are several explanations for the more uniform eating habits. Generally, 'communication' between countries and between continents has increased substantially in recent decades. Tourism has witnessed rapid growth and thus consumption habits have also become more well-known and widespread. Moreover, television in particular has helped to spread knowledge regarding ways of living and consumption to other parts of the world.

Finally, many large international companies have expanded their marketing to include many markets at once. Advertising through global media reaches consumer groups worldwide very quickly, which creates an internationalisation of consumer eating habits.

Questions and assignments

7.1   Define the different elasticities presented in the chapter.

7.2   What is:

a Giffen good?
Engel's law?
an inferior good?

7.3   Why is meat an important commodity for the international demand of food?

7.4   Give (other) examples of the political consumer. What are the lessons to be learnt?

7.5   What is the impact of food demand on food companies? How should food companies adapt to food demand conditions, food trends, etc.?

8   Food market policy

Agricultural and food policy has a major influence on both the national and international food markets. In many cases, these political measures are implemented through the regulation and management of markets. The high-price system in particular, which is still used in agricultural policy, affects both supply and demand, and market prices are largely controlled and used as an instrument. The low-price system will also affect markets, depending on the support's coupling to production. In both cases, the support systems can influence market conditions and competitiveness in the entire food value chain. Food market policy is undergoing a process of change at the moment: the support systems are changing, support is being reduced and a general liberalisation of international agricultural and food markets is occurring, which thereby also changes the competition conditions for food businesses.

Introduction

Agricultural and food market policy has a major impact on both national and international food markets, while international competitiveness and business conditions are also significantly influenced by these market interventions. In many cases, agricultural and food market policy is the major factor which determines the competitiveness of a food industry in a given country.

This illustrates that agricultural protection and support are very important elements of agricultural policy in many countries. Agricultural support is basically an instrument to obtain the overall objectives of agricultural policy: objectives which are set by society. There are a great number of instruments and methods of intervention in agricultural policy and they have different functions and consequences. Often, price mechanisms are used as support instruments, while direct income support is used in other cases. The choice of the support system is of major importance and may have far-reaching consequences.

However, the entire agricultural and food policy setup, including protectionism, trade barriers and market interventions, is changing globally. Agricultural policy is gradually changing; support is being reduced and creates less trade distortion. Free markets and international competition are becoming more dominant, and this change and liberalisation may have a severe impact on the global food industry.

In general, the aim of agricultural policy is to provide farmers with economic support and not the food industry. However, as the food industry very often depends on inputs produced by farmers, a direct or indirect spillover effect occurs in the food industry and in the entire food value chain.

Food and agricultural policy objectives

Intervention through agricultural policy is a very important phenomenon in the agricultural and food sector in many countries. Often, intervention takes place through the market, and the aim is to improve or stabilise economic conditions. Intervention itself is not an objective, but is an instrument to achieve the overall objectives and aims set by society.

Before analysing the different instruments, it will be valuable to highlight the underlying factors that legitimise the instruments, including support and price policy, of agricultural policy. There is a close correlation between the objectives and the instruments in agricultural policy.

Basically, society has set up a number of objectives which lay down guidelines and directions for the development of agricultural policy. These objectives, which to a large degree are similar from country to country, explain and set the foundation for the instruments used in agricultural policy.

There are a number of common features in the objectives which are found in agricultural policy in developed countries. In general, agricultural policy in developed countries aims to improve:

- income in agriculture
- income distribution among farmers
- agricultural productivity
- efficiency in the processing and marketing chain
- supply and price stability
- the demographic situation
- the state of the environment
- export, employment, production, added value, etc.

Many different types of instrument can be used to achieve the given objectives and it is a very complicated relationship: some instruments can be used to achieve several different objectives, while other instruments benefit some objectives and limit the achievement of others. Finally, important differences according to financing, impact on production and trade, transparency, etc. can be observed.

The instruments in agricultural policy can be split up into different groups:

Price support
Support in the form of higher market prices than for example on the world market.

Deficiency payments
Transfers from taxpayers to farmers which correspond to production multiplied by the difference between the world market price and a given target price on the domestic market.

Support coupled to input factors

- area premiums
- headage premiums
- financial support
- other support to reduce costs.

Direct support coupled with other factors

- extensification
- protection of landscape
- support to enhance structural change
- economic development in rural areas.

Support fully decoupled from production

- compensation caused by drought, etc.
- income support, lump-sum payments
- early retirement schemes.

A number of additional instruments exist, which should not directly be used to achieve the objectives, but should be used to reduce supply and / or costs related to agricultural policy. Quotas and set-aside are examples of such instruments.

Price support and deficiency payments are the most important instruments in the agricultural policy of industrialised countries.

High- and low-price systems

Market price support and deficiency payments are two very important instruments in agricultural policy. However, they belong to two different support regimes or support systems. Market price support operates in the so-called high-price system and is financed by consumers, while deficiency payments operate in the so-called low-price system and are financed by taxpayers.

In the high-price system, support is mainly provided by means of import regulations, etc. which ensure a relatively high domestic price. In the low-price system, support is provided by means of direct support, while market prices are left undistorted at, or close to, the world market level.

The two different support systems have very different implications for agricultural production, financing, markets, etc. However, there is still an income transfer to agriculture in both systems in the short run.

The balance between market price support and direct payments varies greatly from country to country (see Figure 8.1).

In countries like the USA, Australia and Chile, agricultural support is mainly granted as direct payments financed by taxpayers, while market price policy, which is mainly financed by consumers, is predominant in, e.g., Japan, Korea and China.

Figure 8.1 also shows the total level of agricultural support. Agricultural support includes transfers from consumers and taxpayers to agricultural producers arising from policy measures that support agriculture – Producer Support Estimate (PSE). PSE is here measured as the percentage of gross farm income including support. The figure illustrates that countries like Norway and Switzerland have a high level of agricultural support. On the other hand, countries like New Zealand, South Africa, Australia, Chile and Brazil have almost liberalised agriculture.

During recent decades, agricultural support has changed significantly. The level of support has decreased, while protectionism has been reduced and liberalisation has been strengthened. At the same time, the composition of agricultural support has changed significantly. Consumer-financed market price support has decreased, and taxpayer-financed direct support has increased (see Figure 8.2).

Structure and function

As shown in Figure 8.1, countries like Korea and Japan mainly use the high-price system in agricultural policy. In this system, support to farmers is given through high market prices maintained by different instruments like import tariffs (variable or fixed) or other import restrictions and export subsidies. These instruments ensure an artificially high price level compared to the price level which would result from supply and demand in an undistorted market.

Support in high-price systems is financed by consumers through high consumer prices. Depending on the self-sufficiency rate, public costs and income are also affected. If the country is a net exporter, it will receive revenue from the import tariff. On the contrary, a net exporting country will have to pay export subsidies to ensure the price level on the domestic market.

The low-price system has been the predominant support system in agricultural policy in the USA for decades. As a result of the recent reforms of the Common Agricultural Policy (CAP) in the EU, and as a result of more focus on decoupled support in the WTO negotiations, the EU has moved towards increased low-price support and less high-price support. The low-support system is now the most important support system in the EU.

In low-price systems, market prices are more or less unaffected, and farmers receive prices which in principle correspond to world market prices. Instead, market support payments are given directly to farmers.

These payments can be coupled with production or they can be fully decoupled. Coupled support means that a farmer receives a payment which corresponds to production multiplied by the difference between the world market price and a given target price on the domestic market. In this case there is no major difference between a high- and a low-price system from a farmer's point of view.

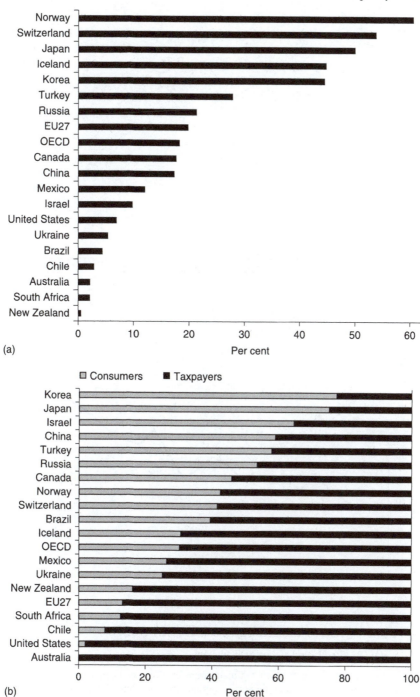

Figure 8.1 Level and composition of agricultural support (2010).

Source: OECD (2012b).

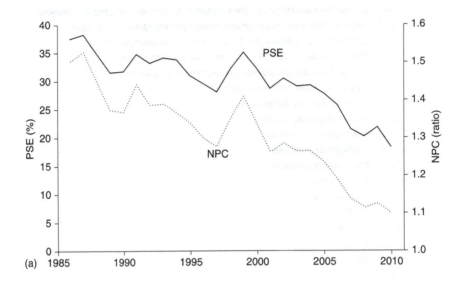

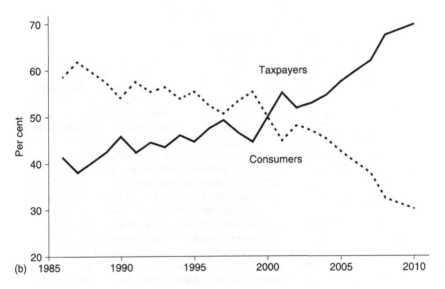

Figure 8.2 Level and composition of agricultural support in OECD.

Source: OECD (2012b) and author's calculations.

Note: PSE (%): Producer Support Estimate: transfers from consumers and taxpayers to producers from policy measures supporting agriculture – as a share of gross farm receipts

NPC: the ratio between the price received by producers (including payments per tonne of current output) and the border price (measured at the farm gate).

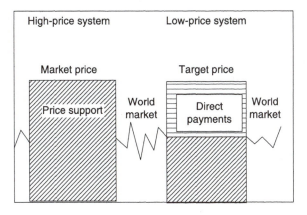

Figure 8.3 General structure of high- and low-price systems.

Source: Author's presentation.

If support is more or less decoupled from production, the economic transfer to farmers may have an element of income or social aid. Support can be coupled with the agricultural area or the number of animals belonging to the farm. In this case, support is still decoupled from production.

Low-price systems are financed by the public budget, which implies that taxpayers ultimately finance this kind of agricultural support.

High- and low-price systems may have different modifications, individual structures, etc. The income transfer can have various nuances, leading to different consequences in each case. However, the general structure of high- and low-price systems is shown in Figure 8.3.

It does not make sense, *a priori*, to determine whether one system is superior to the other. The support level is independent of the support system, and both systems have advantages and disadvantages. Therefore, it is necessary to compare these pros and cons with the objectives of agricultural policy. It is evident that the choice of high- or low-price systems may have profound consequences within and outside the agricultural sector.

Consequences of high- and low-price systems

Conditions and competition in the food (processing) industry

High-price systems necessitate border protection of commodities traded internationally. This means that border protection must encompass processed commodities and not the basic agricultural raw materials. This is the case for, e.g., milk, where border protection must cover processed and traded goods like butter, cheese and condensed milk.

In this way, the high-price system influences a major part of the food industry and not only the primary agricultural sector. This must be seen in relation to the fact that it is normally only the conditions in the primary agricultural sector that should be improved through agricultural policy. Especially if the food industry is very concentrated and has significant market power, farmers may not achieve the intended advantages of the high-price system.

In other fields, a high-price policy can be negative for the food industry. At first, the raw materials of the food industry will become more expensive and, unless this cost increase is fully compensated through other systems, it will lead to deteriorating competitive power.

Such competitive distortions in the food industry do not occur in a low-price system. Here a free world market price exists and is created by supply and demand without market intervention, and the food industry automatically adjusts in accordance with the international comparative advantage of the sector.

Competition conditions in the agricultural sector

Another problem with the high-price system is that it is often difficult to give the same subsidies for all products. It is most difficult to implement a uniform subsidy if it is a question of high- and low-processed products and, also, there is only import protection for some products, while for others there may also be supply restrictions, etc.

Furthermore, a general price increase in all agricultural products of, e.g., 10 per cent will primarily benefit crop production, whereas gains in animal production will be lower. The explanation is that a major part of the production factors in animal farming consists of crop products and, in this way, a general price increase will not have a full impact in these production areas.

For all industrial countries there is a clear negative correlation between the grade of self-sufficiency and agricultural subsidy. This means that the higher the grade of self-sufficiency, the lower the agricultural subsidy.

It is a characteristic of some countries to often reduce the subsidy level for the products where the grade of self-sufficiency increases considerably to over 100 per cent. With increasing net exports, the nationally financed agricultural subsidy increases, and therefore there is a distinct incentive to decrease the subsidy. Apart from this, the self-sufficiency objective encourages in particular protection of products where the grade of self-sufficiency is low.

In both cases, there are signs that the products which agriculture has poor potential to produce are especially protected. On the other hand, the subsidy for the products that have the best natural conditions will be relatively low. It is assumed that a relatively high grade of self-sufficiency all in all is a sign of a comparative advantage.

Seen in a global perspective, support is highest in the countries where the level of self-sufficiency is low, while, in a national perspective, support is relatively high for products where the level of self-sufficiency is relatively low. Both factors are part of a blurring of the comparative advantages, and the result is welfare economic losses.

In the low-price system, it can also be difficult to give the same subsidy to all products, although this is less complicated than in the high-price system. One explanation is that support is given directly and by-passes the processing sector and in this way the real agricultural support in the individual production areas is easier to calculate.

Apart from this, price support for one product does not result in extra costs in another product area in the low-price system.

On the other hand, in a low-price system, it can be very difficult to distribute a 'fair' subsidy among farmers which is independent of production. Historical, structural or social criteria are often necessary, although these are rarely logical and they can be very static and not least very difficult to control.

The composition of consumption

The composition of consumption is also affected by the choice between the high- and low-price systems. In the high-price system, consumers primarily finance agricultural policy through higher food prices. This means that food prices increase compared to other products, and in this way the consumption of food decreases compared to the consumption of other products. The result is that the consumers' purchasing power decreases.

Even though the prices of agricultural products in a high-price system are artificially high, it has a far from full impact on food prices. This is due to the fact that only approximately 25–30 per cent of the consumer price of food in highly developed countries can be traced back to the agricultural sector. The rest of the costs are wages in the processing industry, transport, etc. and these are basically independent of the support level in primary production.

Income distribution in society

The choice between the high- and low-price system also influences income distribution in society.

A high-price system, which causes an increase in food prices, will after all be the largest burden on the lowest income groups in society. People with low incomes use a relatively large part of their earnings on food, which means that a price increase for these products will limit their consumption possibilities relatively significantly. Higher prices for food and other necessary products as a result of political or economic measures will in this way have the same effect as a regressive tax.

On the other hand, the low-price system builds on low prices to producers as well as consumers and that is why this form of protection is the cheapest solution for the part of the population who have the lowest incomes. The financing of public expenses for income support, supplementary payments, etc. is normally done by means of income tax, which in most cases is progressive. Contrary to the high-price system, the costs of agricultural policy in this case are passed on to citizens with higher incomes.

State expenses

High- and low-price systems have a significant impact on public costs and expenses. Market intervention often implies economic support, taxes, levies, etc., which means that public expenses are affected.

For a net-import country, the revenue of the state will initially increase through imposition of a high-price system based on import tax. The state receives customs receipts and, on the domestic market, consumers finance the price subsidy to the agricultural sector.

On the other hand, there can be large costs for state finances with the low-price system, where direct support to farmers is a major instrument.

Finally, any intervention and protection measure will have a negative impact on resource allocation and economic welfare in society. Different measures have different consequences but, in general, coupled price support tends to be the most distorting measure, imposing the highest loss of economic welfare in society.

The change in agricultural policy during recent decades in OECD countries, decreasing support and increasing the role of taxpayer costs, has reduced total cost, but taxpayer costs have increased both in relative and nominal terms.

Direct or indirect subsidy

The choice between the high- and low-price systems can also be of great importance in relation to how direct the subsidy systems are. In a high-price system, the agricultural subsidy is given 'through the market', and therefore the subsidy is more indirect and invisible. In a low-price system, where you, by means of tax collection, directly transfer the money to the agricultural sector, the transfer is much more obvious.

In this way, the low-price system contains a very direct subsidy for the farmer. However, the effect on international trade is more indirect and invisible. Nevertheless, in most cases, the effect is the same for agricultural trade and therefore it is only a pedagogical and comprehension problem.

Still, it is certain that a low-price subsidy is so visible that there will be natural pressure from stakeholders (the taxpayers) to reduce the subsidy.

Production and productivity development

The choice between the high- and low-price system can also be of great importance to agricultural production and productivity. As productivity is a major competitive factor for companies in the entire food value chain, it may have a long-term and strategic impact on the industry.

The high-price system initially gives farmers better sales prices, and thereby better terms of trade, while it undoubtedly stimulates production. The size of the productivity increase depends on the size of supply elasticity.

In general, agricultural production responds relatively weakly to price changes. In the long term, and especially in the case of price increases, it is common for agricultural production to adjust itself to a great extent to changed price relations.

Normally, productivity is improved through structural political instruments, where production is made more rational through research, development, education, advice, etc.

However, the high-price policy can also affect productivity. On the one hand, there is an incentive to increase production in relation to, for instance, the acreage effort. In this way, an increased yield will result, while the yield in livestock production will also increase. This in turn increases productivity.

On the other hand, agricultural policy will also attract input factors which, under normal conditions, would be used in other sectors, or would not be used at all. For instance, poor soil will be cultivated, which will reduce the average yield. This will also be the case for other input factors, e.g. fertiliser, pesticides, capital and labour.

The low-price system has, in principle, the same consequences for production and productivity development, provided that it entails fully production-coupled subsidies.

If, on the other hand, the payments to farmers are partly or fully decoupled from the size of production, the consequences will be crucially different. A totally independent income subsidy means that farmers receive a relatively low price for their products and that they have no incentive to increase production. It is only economically optimal to increase production if marginal earnings are greater than the marginal costs, and this point is reached relatively quickly with the low market prices.

At the same time, the income subsidy is assigned to the farmer regardless of the size of production, which means that production does not increase considerably.

However, it must be expected that even an income subsidy that is decoupled from production in a low-price system can seem encouraging to production. All measures in agricultural policy affect resource allocation in society and in this way an income subsidy maintains resources in the agricultural sector. In this way production is also affected to a greater or lesser extent.

Decoupled income subsidies significantly limit production development in the agricultural sector. Farmers are not sufficiently stimulated (or forced) to introduce new technology or new production methods. At the same time, the more efficient farmers do not benefit sufficiently from the extra effort or risk which they undertake.

The high- and low-price system can, in this way, have different consequences for production and productivity development in the agricultural sector. You cannot in advance say that one consequence is better than the other.

Market price support

Market price support, where the market price is kept higher than the world market price, is still a common subsidy measure in the agricultural policies of several countries (see, e.g., Figure 8.1). Among others, the EU has for decades used market price subsidy as an important instrument in its agricultural policy.

The use of market price support in a high-price system naturally demands the considerable regulation of markets. To secure the high price level, the markets are more or less isolated from the surrounding world, as free import or export would make the system collapse. Further, there may be a need for public buying (intervention) or export support, depending on the grade of self-sufficiency.

There are different types of market price support, but the most important one is a price system where the state in different ways adjusts the market with the aim of ensuring that farmers are able to obtain the desired prices on the market. In a schematic form, this type of market system can be illustrated as shown in Figure 8.4.

The target price is the price that is aimed at for producers to obtain on the market. The intervention price forms a safety net for price formation on the market, as the product can be sold within the internal market at this price.

The actual market price will often be between the target price and the intervention price. If the market price level falls below the intervention price, some suppliers will start to sell to intervention. This will reduce the supply on the market as the purchased products will be stocked. This will normally lead to recovery of the market price. The intervention price and the intervention system are, in other words, a central part of the internal regulation of a high-price market.

However, intervention alone is not enough to secure the price, as imports and exports must also be regulated. When importing, an import duty is collected, which in principle is the difference between the price on the world market and the domestic market price. In principle, it can be both a variable and a firm import duty. If the import duty varies, it can be changed continuously according to the world market price and it therefore increases when the world market price is low and vice versa. In this way, the variable import duty can be a way of securing a constant price level on the internal market.

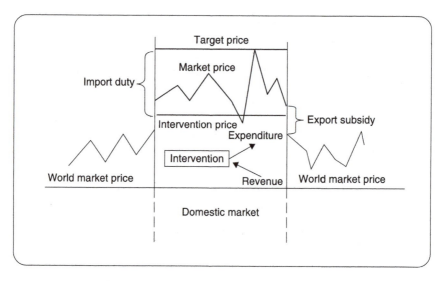

Figure 8.4 Instruments in a market-price system (high-price system).

Source: Author's presentation.

Previously, the variable import duty was often used but, as a result of WTO agreements, a gradual change in tariffs has taken place. This means that import barriers have changed to more fixed tariff rates.

When exporting, an export restitution (subsidy) is paid which, in principle, is the difference between the price on the world market and the domestic market price.

The market price subsidy works in such a way that domestic farmers are secured higher prices than on the world market. This is still the case for some products where reforms have not yet changed the original support system. This is naturally especially true for products where the market price subsidy is the most important measure and where the subsidy level is high.

Future development

Several conditions will influence future development with regard to instruments in agricultural policy. The choice between the high- and low-price system should

---

Box 8.1 WTO, agriculture and food

For several decades agricultural trade has been a topic in international trade negotiations. Agriculture was also included in GATT,* although with several exceptions. The original GATT agreements allowed countries to use some non-tariff measures such as import quotas and export subsidies. Export subsidies would normally not have been allowed for industrial products.

A remarkable change took place when the WTO's Agriculture Agreement was negotiated in the 1986–94 Uruguay Round. It contributed to a gradual reduction in agricultural support, fairer competition and a less distorted agricultural sector. WTO member governments agreed to improve market access and reduce trade-distorting subsidies in agriculture. The agreement did allow governments to support their rural economies, but preferably through policies that would cause less distortion to trade. In general, these commitments were phased in over six years from 1995.

Meanwhile, members also agreed to continue reform after this period. These negotiations were included in the agenda set at the 2001 Ministerial Conference in Doha, The Doha Round.

Developing countries have special treatment in the WTO's Agriculture Agreement. They do not have to cut their subsidies or lower their tariffs as much as developed countries and they are given extra time to complete their obligations. Least-developed countries are completely exempt from these actions.

* GATT, General Agreement on Trade and Tariffs, was signed in 1947 and lasted until 1993, when it was replaced by the World Trade Organization in 1995.

Source: WTO (2012b)

not only be seen from an economic and social point of view. The international negotiations in the WTO are also of great importance (see Box 8.1). The explanation is that the high- and low-price policy influences international trade in different ways.

At first it is important that the consequences for the size of production are different. All influences on the size of production directly influence foreign trade as, e.g., an increase in production leads to decreases in imports or increases in exports. In this way, these trade-influencing and trade distorting instruments become the subject of negotiations in, e.g., the WTO.

As all instruments in agricultural policy influence resource allocation and production, foreign trade is also affected to a greater or lesser extent.

Still, in international trade negotiations one talks of 'non-trade distortion', which are instruments which do not influence trade. This implies that some instruments in agricultural policy have a less harmful influence on international trade and they are thus more or less legitimate to use.

Second, it is important that one is forced to introduce trade barriers in a high-price system, which makes protection very transparent. The trade barriers can of course be of the same magnitude in a low-price system, but here trade protection is less transparent. From a political point of view, relationships with trade partners can therefore favour the low-price system.

The use of import duties, import taxes and especially export subsidies is normally necessary in a high-price system, but these very clearly illustrate that you wish to protect the domestic producers against the surrounding world.

It is certain that the WTO rounds were a set-back for the high-price system and a victory for the low-price system. This should be seen in light of the fact that the low-price system does not necessarily create more free trade or greater economic welfare than the high-price system.

On the other hand, the results of the WTO rounds until now have meant that more countries in the future will be prompted to implement agricultural policy which is based on the low-price system. Also, more experts argue for a gradual change from the high-price system to the low-price system. The arguments include, e.g., that the subsidy rates will be more transparent and sometimes more trade neutral as well. Also, the instruments and the subsidy level are easier to remove gradually in a low-price system and can even be completely replaced by pure social support arrangements.

Third, protection by means of trade barriers becomes harder and harder to maintain in an increasingly globalised world. As foreign direct investment becomes an increasingly important route to globalisation at the expense of international trade, international trade barriers will become more difficult to maintain. High import barriers and trade protectionism cannot prevent foreign companies from establishing themselves, which they will often do if opportunities for trade become too restrictive. The previous trend will probably continue: support conversion from high- to low-cost systems, decoupling and reduced effects on markets, a general reduction in support and freer competition on international agricultural and food markets.

Questions and assignments

8.1 In general, how does agricultural and food policy disturb international markets?

8.2 How can agricultural and food policy be more or less decoupled and trade disturbing?

8.3 How can food companies adapt to agricultural and food policy?

8.4 How may agricultural and food policy develop in the future? Why? What are the consequences for the international markets?

9   The structure of the food industry

The term 'structural development' covers several different conditions, including size, number, concentration and specialisation. Structural conditions are important because they strengthen food companies' international competitiveness. The structure of food businesses varies greatly from country to country, but it is generally the case that structural development follows the economic development of a country. Structural development occurs vertically and horizontally in the value chain.

Structural development in the food industry has been significant in recent years, under the influence of globalisation and liberalisation, which characterises the global food sector. The global poultry industry is an example of a food industry which is developing significantly and which is under the influence of both structural development and globalisation. The global poultry industry and the global market for poultry is changing significantly at the moment in the direction of fewer, larger and more globally oriented companies with increasing market power.

What is structural development?

The food industry's structural development can be defined and described in many different ways. Structural development is more than just the size of the individual company and the number of companies. Factors such as specialisation, concentration, types of ownership, vertical integration and globalisation also help to describe the structure.

With a greater focus on vertical integration, structural development covers all the links in the value chain from research and development, supply and agricultural production to processing, refining, distribution, marketing, retail and consumption. Thus, the entire food system is involved.

In the following sections of this chapter, a number of factors will be used to describe the food industry's structural development:

> *The number of companies* is an important parameter in the food industry's structural development. In recent decades there has been a sharp decline in the number of companies and this is both an expression of, and a result of, structural development. At the same time, there is also an international trend which is very visible to the rest of society.

Company size is also a very visible result of structural development. Although the average conceals a wide spread, and although size can be measured in several different ways, company size is an important yardstick. Seen in relation to both national and international competitive regulations, company size is one of the structural parameters which is regulated.

Specialisation describes the production set-up of individual firms. The spectrum ranges from large conglomerates with diverse activities to the highly specialised and focused businesses which only operate in a specific area. Here we are also dealing with very significant development.

Concentration is also, in general, becoming more widespread. Concentration is understood as large companies securing an increasing share of total production. Concentration also occurs geographically, where production becomes more concentrated in areas that have the greatest comparative advantage.

Form of ownership is central, as it describes the ownership of production facilities. A distinction is made between different types of ownership: limited liability companies, cooperatives, fund ownership, etc.

Vertical integration, including specific contract production, highlights the food industry's connection and dependence on suppliers of raw produce (farmers) and buyers (retail). The entire value chain from research and development right through to the final end user is often involved.

Input factors in the food industry are also rapidly changing and are an essential part of structural development. Input factors in this context cover labour, capital, education, etc.

Globalisation/internationalisation are also sometimes included in the description of structural development. The companies' relative sales on the export markets often increase over time and thus an important structural characteristic of the companies changes. In this connection, the relative importance of direct production, employment or investment in other countries can also be included in the description of structural development.

The number of companies

The number of food industry businesses, and the industry's structural development in general, will significantly depend on market growth. A low growth in turnover will, *ceteris paribus*, exert further pressure for structural development in the form of fewer and fewer companies.

In general, food production increases from year to year in most countries (see Figure 9.1).

As the figure shows, total world food production has increased significantly since the 1960s. Only in Europe is development constant or stagnant.

Despite this general increase in activity in global food production, a decline in the number of food companies from year to year is a widespread phenomenon.

The development in a very long-term perspective shows that technological development, infrastructure and generally increasing prosperity promote consolidation.

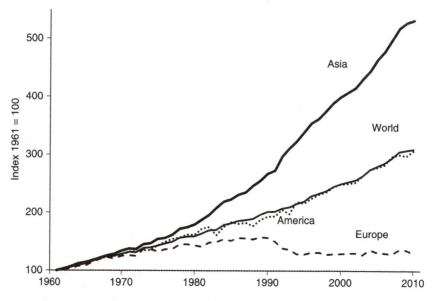

Figure 9.1 Development in food production.

Source: Author's calculation based on FAO (2012).

There is thus a global pattern whereby the structure of the food industry (and other industrial sectors) is most consolidated in the most industrialised and developed countries. Among the most developed countries, consolidation in the food industry began in the 1930s and 1940s as the examples in Figure 9.2 illustrate.

The scope, process and duration of consolidation vary from sector to sector. Sectors which were exposed to competition and which were export-oriented with distinct potential for economies of scale were the first to initiate consolidation.

Also, in the shorter term, there is clear development towards there being fewer companies. During the period 1995–2008, the number of food companies in the OECD area fell by more than 15 per cent, while there was decline or stagnation in most countries (see calculations and estimates based on OECD, 2012a).

In the USA, for example, the number of food companies has decreased on average by approximately 2.5 per cent per year in recent decades. However, this development has been faster in some sectors than in others; the dairy sector in particular has been exposed to significant structural development, while development has been less significant in, e.g., the sugar and flour industries (see Rogers, 2000).

When looking at the total number of food companies in the USA, there has also been a downward trend, although the development seems to be stagnating or even reversing (see Figure 9.3).

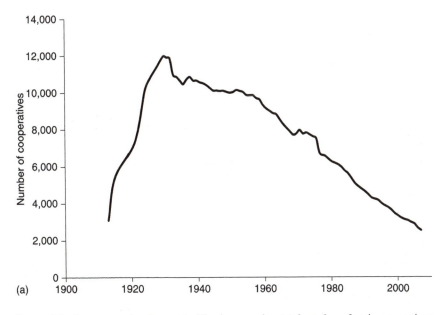

Figure 9.2a Long-term development of food companies: total number of agri-cooperatives in the USA.

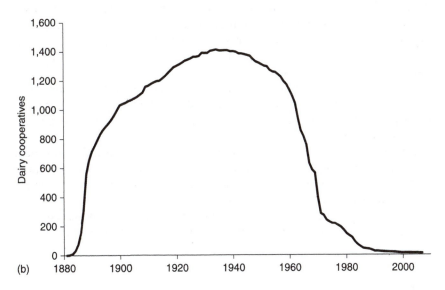

Figure 9.2b Number of dairy cooperatives in Denmark.

Source: USDA (2012c), Statistics Denmark (several issues), Federation of Danish Cooperatives (FDC, several issues a, several issues b), Danish Agriculture and Food Council (2012) and the Danish Dairy Board (1982).

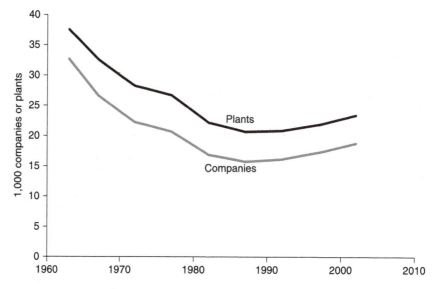

Figure 9.3 Total number of food businesses in the USA.

Source: Martinez (2007).

The increase in the number of manufacturing plants and companies since the early 1990s was mainly due to an influx of new small start-up companies, typically in high-growth niche markets and often only with activities for part of the year. These numerous new small companies have no great significance regarding the overall picture, as they only represent a very small part of the total turnover and activity in the sector.

There are, however, also examples from other countries of new small businesses emerging in the shelter of large and growing groups. New niches are developed, and entrepreneurs start new businesses based on new technology, new markets and the like.

This can thus be interpreted as a sign that the number of companies has a certain lower limit. Large-scale operations and international mergers and acquisitions, along with efficiency improvements, will, above a certain threshold, create a vacuum that will attract new businesses.

At the same time, it is also an indication that structural development and consolidation may well occur simultaneously with the establishment of new businesses.

Company size

During recent decades, food companies around the world have, in general, grown significantly through mergers and acquisitions. First, the large companies in particular have become even larger, so that concentration has increased.

Second, the average size has also increased. Growth has been, and is, a consistent strategic goal for many agro-food businesses. The increasing average size is partly a result of a desire for growth and fewer and fewer companies. As an example of growth, Figure 9.4 shows the development in the average size in the dairy sector, in the USA and Denmark.

The figure shows that the average size of dairies, measured as milk / kg / dairy / year, rose significantly in the period. Average annual growth was approximately 7 per cent in both cases. The same tendency can be seen in a number of other countries and other sectors in the food industry.

Box 9.1 Consolidation and concentration

'Consolidation' is a reduction in the number of firms in a business sector. Consolidation generally implies that firms become larger. 'Concentration' is the process of larger firms increasingly dominating market share.

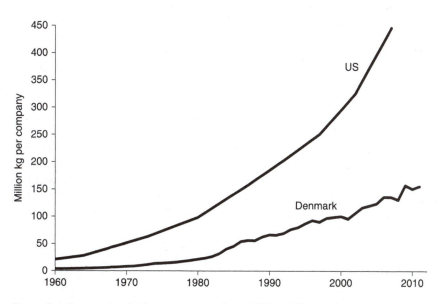

Figure 9.4 Cooperative dairies: average size in the USA and Denmark.

Source: Author's calculation based on the Danish Dairy Board (several years), LF (2012) and USDA (several years).

Note: Calculated as total volume of milk delivered in proportion to the number of dairy companies.

Specialisation

Food businesses can specialise in several ways and this can be horizontal or vertical in relation to the value chain. If the company has a very narrow range of products (e.g. sugar, poultry or dairy products), specialisation is high. Conversely, if the company is engaged in several, more or less independent, areas, specialisation is low and there is high diversification. If the areas are very independent, then we are dealing with conglomerates.

In this context it is possible to distinguish between concentric and conglomerate diversification. Concentric diversification occurs when a company expands its activities into related products or markets. This represents a strategic and deliberate measure, and the rationale is to achieve both growth and synergies at the same time. There must, therefore, be a connection between the existing and new activities which can be exploited in the form of spin-offs, economies of scale, synergies, efficiency improvements, etc.

In the food area, there are many examples of industrial companies achieving a high level of competence and market power with regard to sales to retail chains. This competence can be exploited in other product groups in the grocery market, including, e.g., health and care.

With conglomerate diversification, the connection with existing activities is less or negligible. The aim may be to spread risk by engaging in completely new business areas which have nothing to do with the core activities.

Conglomerate diversification may also be advantageous if the company is in a market which is experiencing low growth, which is often a characteristic of food markets, so that opportunities for organic growth are limited. If, at the same time, there is also a well-consolidated and concentrated structure, it can be difficult for the company to achieve desired growth on the existing market and in the existing product segment.

Finally, conglomerate diversification can also be the solution if the company has good leadership skills, which can be exploited in new business areas.

The extent and importance of specialisation, diversification and the formation of conglomerates varies greatly over time. From the 1950s to the 1970s, many companies followed a conglomerate and diversification strategy. The aim was mainly to spread activities into several areas to reduce risk. This development, which started in the USA after the Second World War and subsequently spread to the rest of the world, can be seen in Figure 9.5.

The figures are based on the 500 largest companies in America.

As can be seen, the number of conglomerates increased in the period, and the 'mild' conglomerates, in particular, with a certain connection between their activities became important. At the end of the 1970s, the trend reversed. Especially among financial investors, conglomerates became unpopular mainly because of their lack of transparency and focus.

Moreover, the growing market-related economies of scale made it necessary for many companies to limit their areas of activity and portfolios in order to maximise market share. In order to achieve a sufficiently large market share

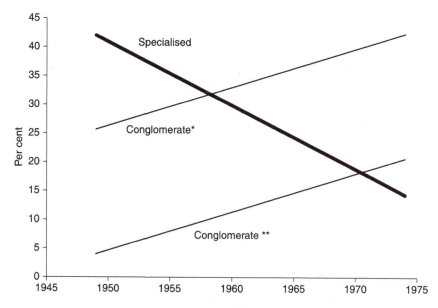

Figure 9.5 Importance of specialised companies and conglomerates with related or unrelated activities, respectively in the USA (1949 and 1974).

Source: Author's presentation based on Rumelt (1982).

* With related activities

** With non-related activities

of a growing global market, it was necessary to focus and specialise on core activities.

Conglomerate mergers are now very rare. The trend is to increasingly focus on core activities, and companies are therefore looking to strengthen their market position on existing markets. This is achieved by seeking merger partners among existing competitors.

Concentration

If one looks at the development of concentration in the industry in general over a long period, a trend becomes apparent. If one focuses on the agri and food industries, it can be generally concluded that there has been a marked increase in concentration in the food industry in the Western world for a prolonged period (see, e.g. Deboo, 2000; Rogers, 2000; MacDonald *et al.*, 2000; see also Table 9.1).

All links in the chain from farm to fork appear to be more concentrated, as the large companies become even larger (Rogers, 2000). In the USA, the 100 largest

Table 9.1 Concentration in the global agri and food industry (the ten largest firms' percentage share of total world production)

	1980	1995	1997	2000	2002	2007	2009
Pharmaceutical sales	20		36	48	53		37
Biotechnology					54		
Animal pharmaceutical sales	30	56	63	60	62		76
Seed companies		37	39			55	64
Agrochemical industry		81	82	84	80		89
Food and beverage industry					37		
Animal feed companies							52

Source: ETC (several years).

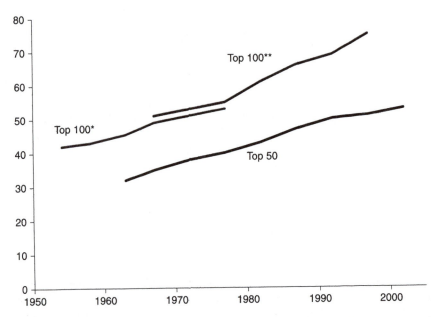

Figure 9.6 Food companies in USA: top 100 share of value added and top 50 share of shipment value.

Source: Rogers (2000) and Martinez (2007).

Note: * including alcohol ** excluding alcohol

food companies have secured a significantly larger share of the total value added in recent decades (see Figure 9.6).

As can be seen in Figure 9.6, the 100 largest food companies account for nearly 80 per cent of the total value added in the sector. Their share has almost doubled since the 1950s.

Data for the 50 largest food companies show the same trend of increasing concentration, whereby the largest companies have grown rapidly at the expense of small ones. Comparisons of concentration tendencies between different countries can be difficult to conduct, since smaller countries, *ceteris paribus*, due to their geographical size, have a higher degree of concentration than large countries (see, e.g., Deboo, 2000).

When looking at the European food market as a whole, it can be concluded that concentration has been increasing in recent years, but this development has been relatively moderate compared to other industrial sectors and retail.

It is also true that there are considerable differences from country to country due to, among other things, countries' size and their level of economic development.

Concentration in the agri and food industries at the global level is also increasing. The ten largest firms' share of total world production has been increasing, especially in the veterinary medicine industry. In the agrochemical industry, concentration development has been relatively constant over the last ten years, but the level is high. For several of the major sectors, the trend at the moment is characterised by increasing concentration (see Table 9.1).

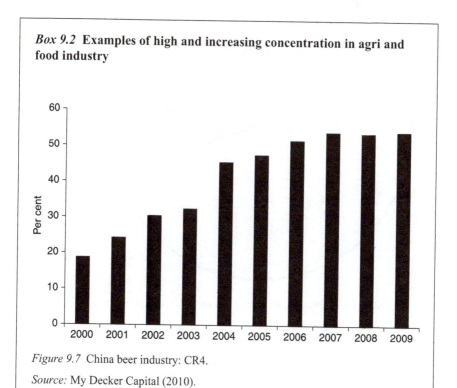

Box 9.2 Examples of high and increasing concentration in agri and food industry

Figure 9.7 China beer industry: CR4.

Source: My Decker Capital (2010).

Table 9.2 Concentration ratios (CR4) for businesses by industry in UK (2004)

Industry	Per cent
Dairy products	32
Grain milling and starch	31
Animal feed	36
Bread, biscuits, etc.	17
Sugar	99
Confectionery	81
Other food products	39
Alcoholic beverages	50
Soft drinks and mineral waters	75
Tobacco products	99

Source: Mahajan (2006).

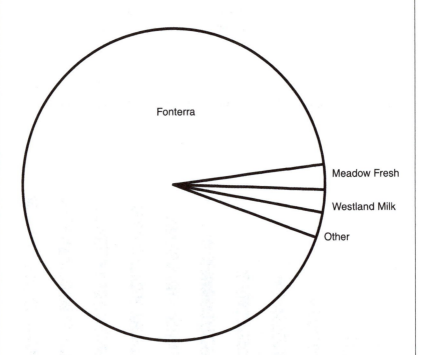

Figure 9.8 Total global turnover of New Zealand-based dairy firms.

Source: Coriolis (2010).

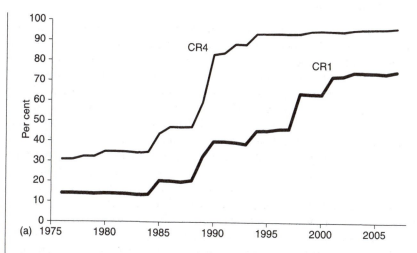

Figure 9.9a Consolidation in Danish food industry: concentration rates for all food industries.

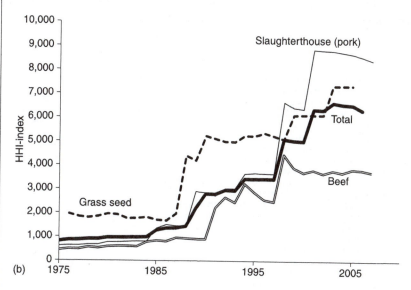

Figure 9.9b HHI – Herfindahl-Hirschmann Index for selected industries in Denmark.

Source: Author's analyses based on annual reports.

Form of ownership

When one talks about ownership as a part of structural development in the food industry, the issue of cooperative form versus limited liability form is important.

As discussed in Chapter 10, there is no clear pattern regarding the importance and development of cooperative organisation in a global perspective. Generally, the cooperative sector in agriculture is most common in northern Europe, while it is considerably less common in the Mediterranean countries. At the same time, its prevalence varies from sector to sector with, in particular, milk, but also meat production, having a relatively high proportion of cooperatives.

As an example, Figure 9.10 shows the prevalence of cooperatives in the dairy sector in several countries. As can be seen, cooperative ownership is significant in many countries, although there are considerable differences between countries.

In connection with larger company takeovers, international mergers and acquisitions, FDIs, etc., private equity funds play a significant role, even when it comes to the non-cooperatively owned food industry. Private equity investments are typically characterised by a group of large investors who invest directly in a number of companies in order to achieve a higher return than they would otherwise by investing in listed shares. The largest share of capital injection comes from institutional investors such as banks, pension funds and insurance companies, but companies, private funds and individuals also invest money in equity funds.

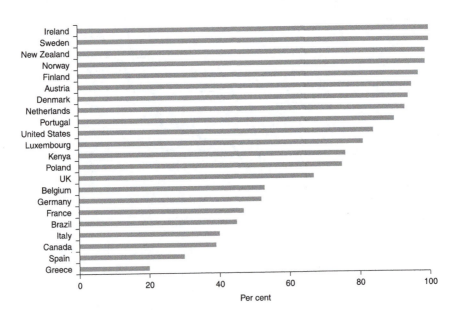

Figure 9.10 Cooperative intake share of total milk supply (per cent of milk supply marketed; various dates 1997–2005).

Source: Coriolis (2010).

When a private equity investment is made, the private equity fund, over a period of typically 3–7 years, will try to further develop the company in order to optimise the return when the company is sold.

Private equity funds provide capital, advice, networking, knowledge, management resources, etc. to the companies they invest in. It is with the help of these resources that a higher return on investment is therefore expected.

Private equity funds have been responsible for 10–30 per cent of all international mergers and acquisitions since the mid-1990s, and the proportion was especially high in the period 2003–08 (see UNCTAD, 2011). About 30 per cent of the companies that receive capital via private equity funds are located in developing countries.

Box 9.3 Measuring concentration

There are several ways of calculating the degree of concentration in an industrial sector. The methods have very different conceptual bases and can lead to very different results, so they should be used with caution in relation to the desired aim.

In the following, several examples of methods to measure the degree of concentration are discussed.

CR – Concentration rate

CR is the simplest method of measuring the concentration trend in a production area. CR is defined as the percentage share of a market held by the largest company or companies. CR is thus a measure of how large a share of a market is held by a specified number of the largest companies.

Several versions of CR can be applied, depending on how many companies are to be included. The most common variant is CR4, which calculates the four largest companies' total percentage share of the market. CR is defined as

$$C_k = s_1 + s_2 + \ldots + s_k = \sum_{i=1}^{N} s_i$$

Where

s_i = is the ith company's market share.
N = is the number of companies.

HHI – The Herfindahl-Hirschmann Index

Another very popular method for calculating the degree of concentration is the Herfindahl-Hirschmann Index (HHI). HHI is expressed by the formula:

$$HHI = s_1^2 + s_2^2 + \ldots s_i^2 = \sum_{i=1}^{N} s_i$$

s_i = is the *i*th company's market share.
N = is the number of companies (see Scherer and Ross, 1990).

Squaring means that companies with a large market share are given more weight in the calculation of the index than companies with a small market share.

When a company has a monopoly on the market, the HHI will be 10,000 (if market share is calculated as a percentage). HHI will always be $\leq$ 10,000. When the number of companies increases, the HHI value falls.

HHI will increase with increasing inequality between companies, since it is the square of the market share that is included in the index. A large market share will thus be attributed relatively more weight than a small share.

The Entropy Index

Another method for calculating the degree of concentration is the Entropy Index (Entropy). Entropy is expressed by the following formula:

$$\text{Entropy} = s_1^* \ln(s_1) + s_2^* \ln(s_2) .. + s_k^* \ln(s_k) = \sum_{i=1}^{N} s_i^* \ln(s_i)$$

Where si is the *i*th company's market share.

The logarithm means that companies with a large market share are given more weight in the calculation of the index than companies with a small market share. When a company has a monopoly on the market, Entropy will be 460 (if the market share is calculated as a percentage). Again, Entropy will increase when the number of firms decreases.

The Gini coefficient

Another measure of the degree of concentration on a market is the Gini coefficient, which is related to the Lorenz curve, which is a measure of variation. The closer the Lorenz curve to the straight line a–b in Figure 9.11, the greater the similarity regarding the size of the companies.

The Gini coefficient is calculated as the area of the space between the Lorenz curve and the equilibrium line as a proportion of the entire area below the equilibrium line.

In Figure 9.11, the Gini coefficient is:

$$\frac{\text{Area } d}{\text{Area } abc}$$

Thus, the Gini coefficient is always a number between 0 and 1, where a value close to 0 indicates a high degree of similarity between the individual companies, i.e. the companies are almost equal in size. The weakness of Gini coefficients is that they tell us nothing about the total number of companies. If, as is the case here, one is examining the degree of concentration in an industry, one does not know whether two or 1,000 companies share the market / production on the basis of a low Gini coefficient. One can also

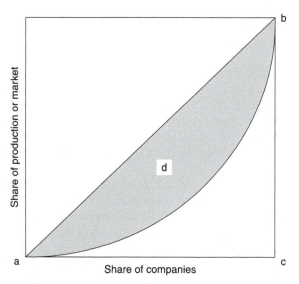

Figure 9.11 The Lorenz curve.

Source: Author's presentation.

point out that the Gini coefficient tells us more about variation than concentration in a sector (see, e.g., Hannah and Kay, 1977).

Vertical integration

Overall, there is a shift in emphasis, concurrently with economic development in a society, from primary agriculture to the supply and processing sectors. A significant part of both households' and agriculture's processing is taken over by the other businesses outside primary agriculture.

On the one hand, an increasing division of labour occurs between agriculture and the agri and food industry. On the other hand, the division of labour also means that the two sectors are becoming increasingly interdependent. For agriculture, it is important to have an efficient market for products. For, e.g., milk producers, it is essential that the daily production of fresh milk is sold effectively.

Also for the food industry, which to a large extent obtains its raw produce from local farmers, it is important that the supply of raw produce is stable. For example, a slaughterhouse or a dairy cannot function without daily deliveries of agricultural products. Ever increasing globalisation with access to many new commodity markets can eliminate dependence on local agricultural production.

There is thus, to a certain extent, a mutual dependency, which is not present in other sectors. Increasing specialisation and dependency help to develop vertical integration. In addition, factors such as:

- traceability as a selling point;
- genetic engineering; and
- product differentiation with a basis in commodity differences

further help to promote vertical integration.

Contract production, as a common example of vertical integration, regulates the relations between, on the one hand, farmers and, on the other, private, cooperatively owned or public companies, so that it replaces the usual spot market. A contract usually includes price, quantity, quality, credit, etc. Development during recent decades has shown a tendency towards more and more contract production (see Figure 9.12).

The figure shows that contracts and packer-owned hogs are the preferred methods of vertical coordination between large packers and producers. In 2006, 70 per cent of all hogs were sold through marketing contracts, while 20 per cent were owned and slaughtered by the same packer. This means that only 10 per cent of hogs are traded on an open market, compared with 87 per cent in 1993.

In the USA, approximately 36 per cent of agricultural production is covered by contract production and sales, and the share has been increasing since 1960 (see Martinez, 2007). In the EU, the significance of contract production has also increased (see Hansen, 2005). Again, the prevalence varies considerably from product to product and from country to country. In general, contract production is most prevalent when it comes to sugar, pea and poultry production. Also outside the EU, contract production varies widely from country to country, and not least from

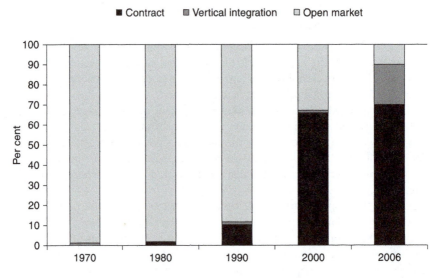

Figure 9.12 Share of hogs delivered to processors via contracts and vertical integration in the USA.

Source: Martinez (1999, 2007).

Box 9.4 **Vertical integration**

Vertical integration means that the links in the process from research and development, and primary production, to processing, refining, distribution and sales are coordinated. Often it is the 'field-to-fork' process which is coordinated.

Integration, coordination or interconnection can be either backward or forward. Backward integration is typically seen when a food industry is involved in the earlier link, including primary production. Forward integration, however, is usually when farmers are involved in processing and marketing.

Vertical ownership with vertical management and control of all or part of the value chain is the ultimate form of vertical coordination. In this case, the production link and the sales link (e.g. agriculture and the food industry) have the same owner.

Ownership can be both forward and backward. This means that farmers can own the agri and food industry companies (typically via cooperative ownership), or the agri and food industry can own all or a proportion of the farms. This latter kind of backward integration is increasing in several places in the world. Some major U.S. agricultural and food companies have as their direct objective the acquisition of agricultural farms to secure raw material supplies.

---

product to product. In a global perspective, direct sales through the market remain dominant (see, e.g., Rehber, 1998) and it is likely that this picture will not change significantly in the foreseeable future, despite increasing contract production.

Input factors

The development in input factors, as an expression of structural development, is viewed in conjunction with the production and value added which is created. The relationship between production and input factors (productivity) broadly develops in line with uniform global trends in the agriculture and food sector.

It is a general characteristic that development in productivity in agriculture is higher than in other industries, including the food industry. An analysis by Martin and Mitra (2000) also shows that increases in productivity are greater in agriculture than in industry, but that the gap is greatest in developing countries. Productivity increases are greatest in the rich countries, and that goes for both agriculture and industry.

Agricultural productivity clearly increases with increasing economic prosperity (see also Chapter 3). When productivity is measured as value added per worker in agriculture, it is also noteworthy that productivity growth is greatest in the most economically developed countries (see Figure 9.13).

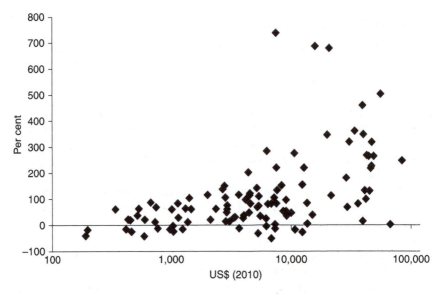

Figure 9.13 Growth in value added per worker in agriculture.

Source: Author's calculations based on World Bank (2012b).

Note: Value creation is calculated for 2010 or for the latest year with available data at constant 2000 dollars in relation to the level in 1980; GDP per capita for 2010.

The figure shows, for each country, the connection between the country's economic development level (GDP / capita, shown on a logarithmic scale) and agriculture's growth (per cent) in value added per worker.

As can be seen in the figure, growth in value created increases sharply per labour unit with increasing welfare. In other words, the differences in labour productivity between developed and developing countries increased during the period. Data for development after 2000, however, shows that the gap in productivity between developed and developing countries has reduced.

When looking specifically at development in the food industry in the USA, as an example of a country with a large agri and food industry, it is noteworthy that employment in the sector falls more or increases less than output. When viewed over a longer period, labour productivity has increased considerably in the American food industry (see Martinez, 2007).

When one looks at all the developments in production in relation to all the input factors, including labour and capital, multifactor productivity can be calculated. Here it turns out that development in the US food industry has been negative and weaker than in other comparable industries see (Table 9.3).

As the table shows, the annual change in multifactor productivity in the food, beverage and tobacco industries fell in the period 1987–2009. In relation to other sectors, development in multifactor productivity in the food industry has been

Table 9.3 Multifactor productivity measures for manufacturing industries in the USA (annual growth rates)

	%
Manufacturing	1.1
Durable manufacturing	1.8
Non-durable manufacturing	0.1
Food, beverage and tobacco	−0.2
Textile mills and textile product mills	1.0
Apparel, leather and allied products	2.1
Paper products	0.1
Printing and related support activities	0.3
Petroleum and coal products	0.8
Chemical products	−0.4
Plastics and rubber products	0.3

Source: USDL (2011)

Note: Multifactor productivity compares output growth to changes in all input requirements.

low. Low investment in research and development in the period is a possible explanation (see Huang, 2003).

Globalisation/internationalisation

The globalisation of the international food industry is also changing dramatically, which influences structural development. Generally, globalisation is increasing, through more international trade, more foreign investment and more international mergers.

There are two relevant aspects of globalisation: first, globalisation is one of the factors which is included in the description of structural development. A company's international orientation, foreign activities and global strategic alliances are thus factors that are included in the actual structure concept.

Second, globalisation is an external influence which affects all industries and also structural development. Globalisation may lead to increasing international competition, which creates new economies of scale, which in turn can promote the development of larger companies. Globalisation can also affect the form of ownership, and in particular ownership structure, in the food industry.

The scope and development of globalisation in relation to the food industry is further discussed in Chapter 5.

Case: Structural development and globalisation in the global poultry industry

The global poultry industry is currently experiencing considerable changes. Structural development and globalisation in this case are two significant, and largely connected, trends. For many years, the global poultry industry has been relatively unregulated, internationally oriented and with a high level of international specialisation – and thus this industry is probably some years ahead of other food industries regarding development. In this way, development in the global poultry industry can be used as a benchmark for future development in other food industries.

The global poultry sector is influenced by globalisation. The liberalisation of international food trade, the exploitation of economies of scale, cost differences, health aspects, integration of the chain from field to fork and many other factors have played a role in this globalisation development.

Trade in poultry meat is becoming more and more international and it has overtaken other meat with regard to the significance of international trade. This has resulted in, among other things, the leading exporting countries exchanging positions regularly and companies in the poultry sector coming under persistent pressure to improve their international competitiveness. This pressure will probably lead to more mergers and acquisitions, both nationally and internationally.

At the same time, significant structural development is occurring towards fewer, larger and more globally oriented poultry slaughterhouses, which strengthens vertical integration, the coordination from field to fork. Vertical integration is increasingly becoming backward, i.e. it is the poultry slaughterhouses which are responsible for coordination, and they have significant influence in relation to poultry producers.

Major trends

The global poultry industry is exposed to significant influences at the moment, which also means that factors such as markets, company structure, specialisation and competition are changing considerably. Development is characterised by the following:

- increasing globalisation in the form of more international trade
- new patterns of trade and international specialisation
- cost differences in poultry production between countries leading to changes in global production
- poultry meat becoming increasingly significant internationally in relation to total meat production, consumption and trade
- countries outside the West securing an increasing share of international trade and production
- increasing liberalisation:

  - declining support
  - more poultry trade between WTO member states

- increasing concentration
- increasing vertical integration
- market power in the value chain shifting in favour of poultry slaughterhouses
- more international investment and foreign ownership.

Poultry meat and international trade

Poultry meat is becoming increasingly important economically in a global perspective. An increasing share of total meat production in the world is poultry meat. Thus, poultry is also a growing component of our total meat consumption.

Globally, poultry is now the second most important meat product, measured in kg, after pork. As can be seen in Figure 9.14, poultry meat's share of total world meat production and of the total international meat trade has generally increased in recent decades.

Poultry's share of the world's total meat production has risen almost constantly since the early 1960s. More than 30 per cent of the world's total meat production, measured in tonnes, is poultry, and the share has more than doubled since the mid-1970s.

Furthermore, poultry meat's share of total world meat trade is also increasing. The share of international trade is increasing faster than the share of total output during the entire period, but development in international trade is far more unstable. This must of course be seen in light of the fact that international trade is far more influenced by trade policy and market prices, as well as veterinary and health conditions, etc.

Although the vast majority of the world's total production of poultry meat is sold on national and very local markets, it is noteworthy that international trade in

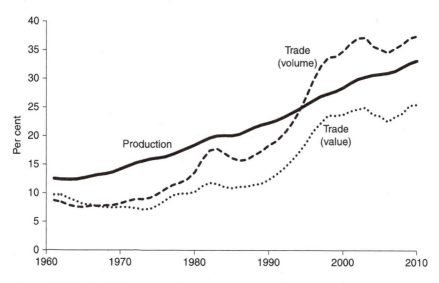

Figure 9.14 Poultry's share of world meat production and of the international meat trade (measured by amount and value respectively).

Source: Author's calculations based on FAO (2012).

poultry products is growing rapidly at the moment and is increasing more than total world production. Thereby, imports and exports are becoming increasingly significant. This also applies to other agricultural products, including other meat products, but the trend is relatively strong when it comes to poultry (see Figure 9.15).

As can be seen in Figure 9.15, approximately 14 per cent of all chicken meat is traded internationally, while the corresponding figure is just under 12 per cent for all other meat combined. Poultry meat has achieved this position as a relatively important product in international trade during the last 20 years.

International trade patterns

The following developments characterise international trade in poultry:

- An increasing share of production is traded internationally.
- The leading exporting countries have exchanged positions regularly (see Box 9.5).
- The concentration in the leading exporting and importing countries has declined.

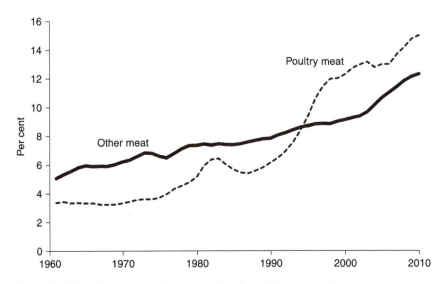

Figure 9.15 The importance of international trade in chicken and other meats.

Source: Author's calculations based on FAO (2012).

Note: Total world exports as a percentage of total world production.

Box 9.5 Development in share of the world market for chicken meat

In the last 30–40 years, the world market for poultry products has changed considerably. The Netherlands accounted for up to 45 per cent of the world market in the early 1970s, whereas, today, the Netherlands' role on the international markets is much less significant and emerging countries such as Brazil, Thailand and China are now important on the world market, although Bird Flu hit the Asian countries hard a few years ago (see Figure 9.16).

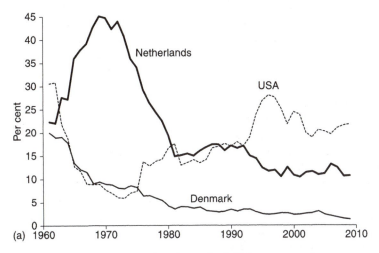

Figure 9.16a World market share (export) of chicken meat: major exporters in the early 1960s.

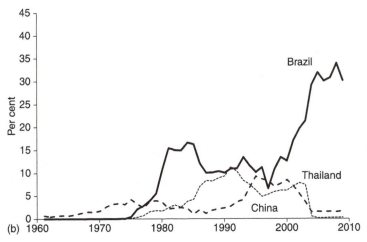

Figure 9.16b World market share (export) of chicken meat: newer and larger exporters.

Source: Author's calculation based on FAO (2012).

In the early 1960s, the USA, the Netherlands and Denmark had almost the entire world market. The international trade in poultry meat has now spread to several large countries in line with growth in the world market and in line with changing competitive conditions. Previously, the four or five largest import and export countries accounted for almost all international trade in poultry meat. However, in recent decades, their share has declined considerably (see Figure 9.17).

As can be seen in the figure, the world's four largest poultry importing and exporting countries accounted for 80 per cent of the world market in the early 1960s, but this share has since declined significantly. The four largest exporting countries today account for less than 60 per cent of the world's total poultry imports. However, the share has increased slightly in recent years as a consequence of, in particular, Thailand's and China's declining exports of poultry meat as a result of Bird Flu.

The share of total world production of the world's largest exporters of poultry meat in 2008 is discussed in Box 9.6.

Globalisation is deemed not in itself to have created concentration between the international trading countries within the poultry sector: more the opposite. Although increasing market dispersion and decreasing concentration has occurred in recent years, the world's total exports of chicken in particular are still distributed in relatively few countries. Whereas the two largest exporting countries account for 40–50 per cent of world trade, this is not the case for the other major animal products (see Figure 9.19).

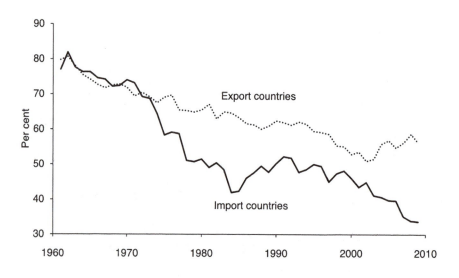

Figure 9.17 The four largest exporting and importing countries' share of total world trade in poultry meat.

Source: Author's calculations based on FAO (2012).

The strong country concentration with regard to the export of poultry meat can be a positive sign that some countries are able to exploit their international competitive strengths and thus achieve significant exports. From an economic perspective, a division of labour is an advantage, as all countries then produce the goods they are relatively best at.

On the other hand, the presence of only a few large exporters increases the world market's vulnerability and instability. For example, the outbreak of Bird Flu in Asia in 2005 resulted in a sharp decline in Thailand's and China's exports, two countries that until then had been relatively large poultry exporting countries.

Despite increasing international trade and specialisation, many countries have a degree of self-sufficiency which is very close to 100 when it comes to poultry.

Box 9.6 The world's largest export countries

Today, Brazil is the largest exporter of chicken meat in the world, followed by the 'traditional' countries such as the USA, the Netherlands and France. As can be seen in Figure 9.18, the five largest exporting countries account for approximately 75 per cent of total international trade in chicken meat.

Figure 9.18 The world's largest exporters of chicken meat by value (2009).

Source: Author's calculations based on FAO (2012).

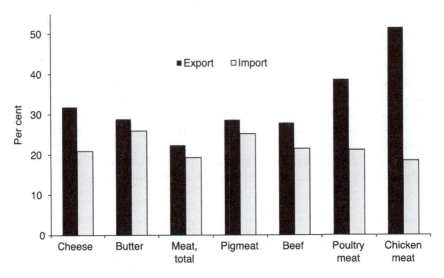

Figure 9.19 The two largest import and export countries' share of total world trade in selected animal products (2009).

Source: Author's calculations based on FAO (2012).

When self-sufficiency is close to 100, it is often an indication that the country prefers domestic products and is trying to become free of imports. As can be seen in Figure 9.20, many countries have a degree of self-sufficiency in chicken meat of approximately 100, while not many countries have a degree of self-sufficiency which is, e.g., over 120.

The figure illustrates that there is a large concentration of countries which have a degree of self-sufficiency in chicken meat in the range 90–110. Nearly half of the countries are in this interval. However, not many countries have a high degree of self-sufficiency.

However, it is most likely that the curve will be less concentrated and more spread in the future in line with increasing globalisation and trade liberalisation.

International specialisation

The location of international poultry production and export is changing. In line with economic and technological development, production moves to those countries where it can be conducted at the lowest cost or at the highest quality. There are many such examples, of which the relocation of the Danish textile industry to Asia is one of the most notable.

Today, more than half of the world's total production of chicken meat is located in non-OECD countries, and the proportion has almost doubled since the early

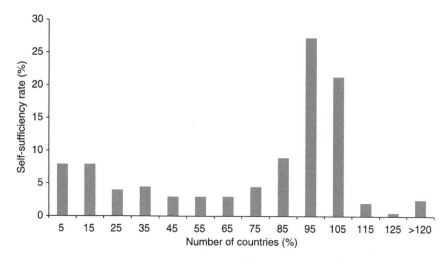

Figure 9.20 The world's countries according to their degree of self-sufficiency regarding chicken (2008).

Source: Author's calculations based on FAO (2012).

Note: The x-axis shows the number of countries in intervals where, e.g., 25 is the range 20–30.

1960s. Also, these countries' share of total world exports in chicken has increased significantly in recent decades (see Figure 9.21).

As can be seen in the figure, non-OECD countries are becoming increasingly important on the international markets for poultry meat.

Non-OECD countries are both developing countries and newly industrialised countries, and it is especially the latter which is interesting in this context. The NICs (newly industrialised countries), e.g. Brazil, China, India, Malaysia, the Philippines, Mexico, Turkey, South Africa and Thailand, now account for approximately 25 per cent of the world's total export of chicken.

There are several explanations for this development and the new 'world order' in poultry:

- Trade liberalisation in agriculture has made it possible for countries which are competitive in this area to expand and increase exports, as international trade restrictions have been reduced.
- Dissemination of knowledge has become more efficient, and technological know-how and innovation in the poultry sector now spreads more rapidly from industrialised countries to the rest of the world.
- The trend is for more and more foreign direct investment, mergers and acquisitions. This means, e.g., that companies in the Western world's poultry

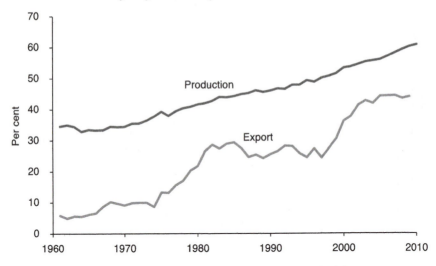

Figure 9.21 Non-OECD countries' share of total world exports of chicken.

Source: Author's calculations based on FAO (2012).

Note: OECD = Organisation for Economic Co-operation and Development. The organisation consists of 34 countries which are among the richest and most developed countries in the world, including the EU, the USA and Japan. The graph includes the countries which were not actual members of the OECD at 1st January 2012.

industry are expanding by investing in, e.g., South America and Asia, which gives the companies access to new growth.

• Limited growth opportunities in several EU countries is also helping to push an increasing proportion of the growth in poultry production and exports to countries with fewer restrictions. Countries with large areas of farmland and fewer environmental regulations, together with access to large grain and feed supplies, will therefore be favoured.

Growth in consumption

In general, the consumption of food does not increase much with increasing income. As economic prosperity and consumption opportunities increase, so does especially the demand for durables, services, holidays, cars, housing, etc. In contrast, the consumption of food remains more constant, as 'one cannot eat until one is full more than once'. A shift towards more processed and expensive foods does however occur, but the actual increase in value is modest. In addition, food prices often increase less than general inflation in society, and thus the value of food consumption declines in relation to total consumption.

Animal products, however, belong to a food group which is relatively income elastic, which means that consumption increases relatively significantly as income rises. Meat and dairy products can be defined as welfare products, where demand is relatively dependent on income. In general, the more expensive a product, the more demand depends on consumers' income.

Although poultry is usually one of the cheaper meats, it can clearly be seen that per capita consumption increases in line with increasing economic welfare in a society (see Figure 9.22).

Countries to the left in the figure are the poorest developing countries with low GDP and a correspondingly low consumption of poultry meat. In these countries, vegetable products account for the bulk of food consumption. As countries become richer, moving to the right in the figure, consumption of poultry meat increases considerably.

Total world consumption of poultry meat therefore depends on total population and its income. Narrod *et al.* (2007) expect the production and consumption of poultry meat in developing countries to increase by 3.6 per cent and 3.5 per cent per year, respectively, by 2030 due to increasing incomes, changing eating habits and market growth.

Differences in competitiveness – agricultural policy and costs

Increasing globalisation of agriculture, and not least the poultry sector, can be largely explained by the liberalisation and reduction in aid which the sector has experienced, and which is still occurring.

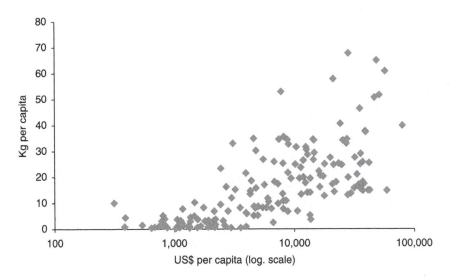

Figure 9.22 Per capita consumption of poultry meat in relation to level of economic development (GDP per capita) (2009).

Source: Author's presentation based on FAO (2012) and World Bank (2012b).

Note: Each point denotes a country; GDP is converted to purchasing power parity (PPP).

Agricultural support, and in particular trade-influenced support, has declined in most countries in recent years as a result of WTO negotiations. As can be seen from Figure 9.23, market price support, which is particularly trade distorting, has been more than halved in the agricultural sector in developed countries since the mid-1980s, when a really serious attempt was made for the first time to reduce agricultural subsidies.

As the figure shows, market price support for all agricultural products declined significantly in the period, while market price support for poultry production developed more constantly, albeit at a relatively low level. The reduction in agricultural subsidies – both historically and in the future – will be especially challenging for most OECD countries. As emphasised in Figure 9.24, agricultural subsidies for poultry production in OECD countries is still high compared to the level in countries like Brazil, China and South Africa.

Figure 9.24 presents the agricultural support for poultry production in several countries. The countries shown account for more than 95 per cent of total world poultry exports.

Figure 9.24 illustrates that poultry support varies considerably from country to country. It is also worth noting that the two largest exporting countries, Brazil and the USA, which account for more than 50 per cent of the world market for poultry, do not provide any support for poultry production.

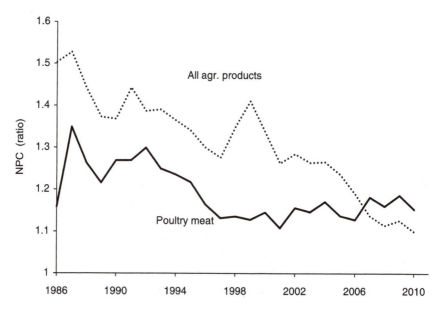

Figure 9.23 Agricultural subsidies for agricultural goods in developed countries (OECD).

Source: OECD (2012b).

Note: NPC = Nominal Protection Coefficient: an expression of market price support; 1.0 = no support.

It is also worth noting that, in the OECD, the support for poultry production is close to the average for all agricultural products.

International trade is conducted on increasingly liberal terms. In general, protectionism and trade protection are in decline, and there are many driving forces that are continually promoting more globalisation (see Chapter 5).

As previously discussed, there is a clear trend towards decreasing agricultural support in the Western world. In addition, more and more countries are now members of the WTO, where the goal is to reduce restrictions on international trade.

In 2012, membership of the WTO reached 155 countries, and an increasing share of international trade is now occurring between countries covered by WTO rules. A total of 99 per cent of world exports of poultry meat comes from WTO countries and approximately 90 per cent of imports go to WTO countries (see Figure 9.25).

The figure also provides important explanations as to why the curve has moved.

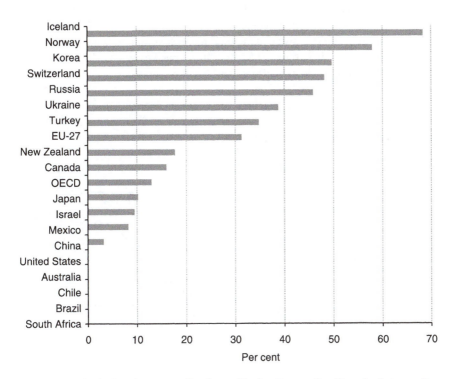

Figure 9.24 Agricultural support (Producer Single Commodity Transfers) to poultry production in different countries (2010).

Source: OECD (2012b).

Note: Transfers as a share of gross receipts.

It is noteworthy that it is especially poultry meat-exporting countries which are included in the GATT / WTO, while imports of poultry meat still, to some extent, go to countries that are outside the WTO.

As can be seen in Figure 9.25, only approximately 50 per cent of poultry imports came from countries outside the GATT in the early 1980s. When international trade increases, production will increasingly move to where it is cheapest or best, which is also a direct result of liberalisation and globalisation. Agricultural policy can no longer, to the same extent, protect areas with low efficiency or high costs.

A number of studies illustrate the significant cost differences that exist between poultry-producing countries. In general, it can be concluded that production costs are substantially higher in Europe than in several other countries, which have great potential for growth in poultry production, and which already produce without any significant agricultural subsidies.

Production costs in Brazil, which is the world's largest exporter of chicken meat, are significantly lower than in the USA (25 per cent lower) or France (40–45 per cent lower). The reason is lower feed costs, lower wages and a currently favourable exchange rate against the euro (Pouch, 2005). Another study concluded that the feed cost per chicken produced in the EU is about €0.9, while the corresponding cost in Brazil is €0.2.

World Poultry (2003) shows that the production cost for chicken is US $0.7 per kg in the EU, while it is only $0.53 and $0.40 per kg in Thailand and Brazil respectively. Clearly such cost differences have consequences:

> First, low-cost countries continue to secure an increase in exports and an increasing share of the world market at the expense of the traditional exporting countries with their higher costs.

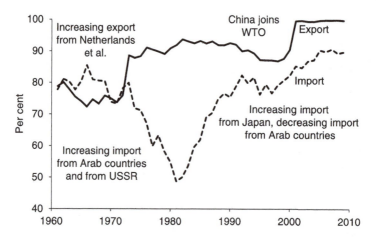

Figure 9.25 Proportion of poultry exports and imports from GATT / WTO countries.

Source: Author's calculations based on FAO (2012) and WTO (2012b).

Second, high-cost countries need to differentiate their products, so they stand out from the products from low-cost countries. Higher quality, food safety and traceability are some of the properties that can compensate for a higher price.

Third, these trends will also put pressure on for further efficiency improvements to be made to compensate for the additional costs in relation to foreign competitors. Increased productivity at all links in the chain can be a necessary consequence of the increased competition.

Low-cost countries also focus on increased efficiency, which increases the pressure on competitors if they want to stay ahead: In the period 1975–2004, the production cycle was reduced from 59 to 36 days in Brazil, while consumption of feed per kg of produced meat was reduced from 2.4 to 1.8kg (Yasushi, 2006).

Fourth, competition and increasing globalisation will lead to further mergers and acquisitions, both nationally and internationally (see, e.g., Manning and Baines, 2004), as it will be necessary to create larger and more international units in order to match the growing retail chains, to exploit economies of scale and to exploit the advantages of globalisation and openings in the international market.

Structural changes in the international poultry industry

In many parts of the world, the agri and food industries have experienced significantly increasing concentration in recent decades. This means that fewer, but larger companies have obtained an increasing share of the total turnover in the sector. The large companies' market share has increased, while the group of medium-sized companies has become smaller.

The degree of concentration is, as previously mentioned, usually smaller on large markets, and one therefore cannot simply compare the concentration across borders.

The development in the degree of concentration, however, follows a uniform international pattern; increasing concentration is therefore an international trend. As can be seen in Figure 9.26, the degree of concentration among poultry slaughterhouses has increased in recent decades in Canada, the USA, Brazil and Denmark.

While nothing definite can be concluded about the level of concentration in the three countries, a clear trend towards increasing concentration in the sector is apparent. In the USA, two companies control 40 per cent of the market (Tyson Foods Inc. and Pilgrim's Pride Corporation).

There are several driving forces behind food companies' growth and increasing concentration, which can be divided into internal company conditions and external market conditions.

- Internal company conditions comprise the exploitation of economies of scale and synergies and the improvement of efficiency. When companies grow through mergers, acquisitions or organic growth, it is often possible to use

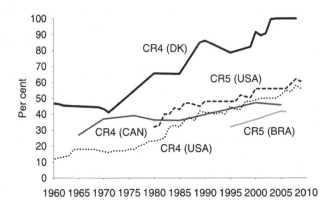

Figure 9.26 Studies of development in concentration in the poultry industry in the USA (two studies), Canada, Brazil and Denmark.

Source: Agriculture and Agri-Food Canada (2007), Watt Poultry USA (2010a, 2010b) and Hansen (2005).

new technology or new methods that make production cheaper and more efficient.

- External market conditions entail the company securing more market and bargaining power in relation to suppliers, customers and competitors. The larger the market share, the more interesting the company is for customers and suppliers, which, *ceteris paribus*, gives the company greater bargaining power. It is certain that these drivers will continue to be applicable in future and they will result in persistent pressure for further structural development, concentration and internationalisation.

Vertical integration

For the agri and food industry, it is important that the supply of raw produce is stable. For example, an abattoir or a dairy cannot function without daily deliveries of agricultural products. Even increasing globalisation, with access to many new commodity markets, cannot eliminate dependence on local agricultural production. Therefore, there is, to a great extent, an interdependent relationship between the food industry and agriculture, which does not exist between other sectors.

Contract production regulates the relations between, on the one hand, farmers, and on the other hand, private, cooperatively owned or public companies, so that it replaces the usual spot market. Development over recent decades has been in the direction of more and more contract production, which also applies to a great extent to the poultry sector. In the USA, almost 90 per cent of chicken was produced under contracts as early as the mid-1950s, and the share is still very high (see Martinez, 2007). According to MacDonald (2008), almost 100 per cent of chicken production in the USA is on contract.

In the USA, 90 per cent of chickens are produced in a vertically integrated chain, where an industrial company supplies almost all the inputs for the poultry producer, including day-old chicks, feed, medicine and veterinary control, and purchases the finished chickens for slaughter.

This business model is spreading to Southeast Asia under the auspices of the Thailand-based multinational company, CP Group (see Murphy, 2006). Thailand's poultry sector has experienced strong and significant development in recent decades in the direction of increasing industrialisation and vertical integration. In recent years, the poultry industry has moved away from contract production towards even stronger vertical integration in order to meet the stricter food safety requirements which followed the outbreak of Bird Flu. The vertical integration has largely been backward, which means that it is the poultry slaughterhouses which set the agenda and have the greatest influence.

It is expected that Thailand's poultry sector will continue in the direction of greater industrialisation and vertical integration, while the processing of poultry meat will increasingly become part of the vertical value chain (see NaRanong, 2007).

In Brazil, the world's largest exporter of poultry, significant vertical integration is also occurring and it is estimated that at least 85 per cent of Brazilian chicken production is vertically integrated. This vertical integration has been highlighted as one of the major strengths and competitive advantages of the Brazilian poultry sector (see Desouzart, 2007).

The farmer's role in vertical integration – the example of the USA

The poultry sector is, as previously mentioned, highly vertically integrated in the USA. This means that companies (also called integrators) own and control all real parts of production in the field-to-fork chain, from hatcheries, feed supply, production of day-old chicks, transport to slaughter and production of processed poultry products. The poultry sector is the most integrated agricultural sector in the USA (Taylor and Domina, 2010).

Companies typically own the chickens and make all the important strategic decisions (e.g. the size of chicken houses, layout and equipment, distribution of chicks among individual farmers, feed composition and time of slaughter), while the farmers are responsible for the daily care of the animals. The farmers' authority and opportunities to make independent decisions are thus limited, for better or worse. The companies usually send inspectors / consultants out to the farmers once a week to monitor the farmer's labour, wastage, etc. and to give advice regarding daily operations.

When contract production began in the 1950s, it was primarily in the form of collaboration between feed companies and farmers about bridging finance and credit. Later it was developed into contracts concerning profit-sharing and subsequently contracts based on price relationships between feed and poultry meat.

Today, farmers typically receive a fixed basic payment, which depends on the farmer's relative performance compared to other farmers. There is no longer a free market for live chickens ready for slaughter. Poultry slaughterhouses do not usually receive poultry from farmers who have not signed a long-term contract. Farmers naturally do not have a right to deliver and poultry slaughterhouses are free to choose their suppliers, deliveries, the time of delivery, etc. if they want. This means that the farmers have no real alternative to contract production controlled by companies.

The balance of power in the value chain seems to have shifted in recent decades. There is general agreement that contract production is an important explanation for the high growth and competitiveness in poultry production but, whereas contract production used to be a link in an equal partnership between farmers and poultry slaughterers, it has become more one-sided in recent years in favour of the poultry slaughterhouses.

The increasing size and market power of the poultry slaughterhouses, which is almost oligopolistic in character, together with insufficient cooperation between farmers, has meant that, particularly since the mid-1990s, the poultry slaughter-houses have enjoyed the biggest advantages of contract cooperation (see Vukina and Leegomonchai, 2006).

International investments and foreign ownership

Not only is it trade in poultry meat that is becoming more international, but also investments, ownership, mergers and acquisitions in the poultry industry. There are many examples of the increasing international investments and foreign ownership:

> Since 1995, significant foreign investment has been made in Brazil's poultry sector, and two of the four largest poultry companies now have foreign owners.
>
> In 2009, the Thailand-based CP Group invested in China's largest egg producer. In 2008, the American company, Tyson Foods, established two new subsidiaries in China, and the plan was to produce 20 million chickens and 1.6 million tonnes of fresh chicken meat per year.
>
> The European poultry industry has also been subject to foreign mergers and acquisitions. The Dutch company, Dutch PlusFood Groep, which produces processed poultry products, was bought by one of the major Brazilian poultry slaughterhouses, Perdigão, in 2007. Similarly, the English company, Moy Park, was bought by the Brazilian company, Marfrig, in 2008.
>
> Finally, the Dutch food company, Vion, bought the English company, Grampian Country Food Group, the main activities of which were beef and pork production, thereby resulting in a greater focus on poultry. Today, Vion has a market share of 16 per cent in the UK regarding chicken meat.

All in all, it can be concluded that production, trade and ownership in the poultry slaughterhouse sector is experiencing significant globalisation whereby national borders are becoming less important.

Questions and assignments

9.1 What is 'structure' – in relation to companies in the food value chain?
9.2 What are the major structural trends in the food industry?
9.3 Why is structure so different from country to country?
9.4 Select a company in a food value chain. Describe the structure of the company.
9.5 What is vertical integration? Why is it often important in food value chains?

10 Cooperatives in the food sector

Cooperatives play an important role in food business in many parts of the world. Cooperatives differ from other companies as the owners and users in cooperatives are the same. In the food industry, cooperatives are especially prominent among dairies, slaughterhouses, trading companies and suppliers. Although cooperatives are based on specific principles, and although there are fundamental and structural differences between cooperatives and capital-owned companies, cooperatives are primarily business-oriented companies, where the goal is to create profit in the short and long term for the owners – just like with other types of company.

Cooperatives may face special challenges when it comes to the globalisation of markets. Mergers across borders, foreign investment and production based on raw materials from foreign non-members can be difficult to handle in a cooperative. Cooperatives are under constant change, and new forms of cooperative continue to emerge. New models are developed in order to, e.g., adapt to change and new opportunities, and to meet the challenges posed by, e.g., globalisation. Therefore, alternative models for development and growth have to be created in relation to cooperatives.

What is a cooperative?

There is no universally accepted definition of a cooperative. In general, a cooperative is a business owned and democratically controlled by the people who use its services and whose benefits are derived and distributed equitably on the basis of use. The user-owners are called members.

ICA, International Cooperative Alliance, defines a cooperative as 'an autonomous association of persons united voluntarily to meet their common economic, social, and cultural needs and aspirations through a jointly-owned and democratically-controlled enterprise' (ICA, 2012).

Another widely accepted definition is: 'A cooperative is a user-owned, user-controlled business that distributes benefits on the basis of use' (Center for Cooperatives, 2012). This definition captures what are generally considered the three primary cooperative principles: user ownership, user control and proportional distribution of benefits.

Members benefit in two ways from the cooperative, in proportion to the use they make of it. First, the more they use the cooperative, the more service they receive. Second, earnings are allocated to members.

Principles

The cooperative principles are guidelines through which cooperatives put their values into practice. Cooperatives thus rely on a set of common values and principles that is built into the companies' regulations, and which in practice sets guidelines for the companies' activities and development.

Cooperatives in the agricultural and food sectors often base their regulations on the seven international cooperative principles established by the International Cooperative Alliance (ICA) (see Box 10.1). The principles are also a test of whether a company is qualified to call itself a cooperative according to ICA formulations. The principles have been continuously revised and modernised in line with developments.

***Box 10.1* Cooperative principles defined by International Co-operative Alliance (ICA)**

The co-operative principles are guidelines by which co-operatives put their values into practice.

1st Principle: Voluntary and Open Membership

Co-operatives are voluntary organisations, open to all persons able to use their services and willing to accept the responsibilities of membership, without gender, social, racial, political or religious discrimination.

2nd Principle: Democratic Member Control

Co-operatives are democratic organisations controlled by their members, who actively participate in setting their policies and making decisions. Men and women serving as elected representatives are accountable to the membership. In primary co-operatives members have equal voting rights (one member, one vote) and co-operatives at other levels are also organised in a democratic manner.

3rd Principle: Member Economic Participation

Members contribute equitably to, and democratically control, the capital of their co-operative. At least part of that capital is usually the common property of the co-operative. Members usually receive limited compensation, if any, on capital subscribed as a condition of membership.

Members allocate surpluses for any or all of the following purposes: developing their co-operative, possibly by setting up reserves, part of which at least would be indivisible; benefiting members in proportion to their transactions with the co-operative; and supporting other activities approved by the membership.

4th Principle: Autonomy and Independence

Co-operatives are autonomous, self-help organisations controlled by their members. If they enter into agreements with other organisations, including governments, or raise capital from external sources, they do so on terms that ensure democratic control by their members and maintain their co-operative autonomy.

5th Principle: Education, Training and Information

Co-operatives provide education and training for their members, elected representatives, managers, and employees so they can contribute effectively to the development of their co-operatives. They inform the general public – particularly young people and opinion leaders – about the nature and benefits of co-operation.

6th Principle: Co-operation among Co-operatives

Co-operatives serve their members most effectively and strengthen the co-operative movement by working together through local, national, regional and international structures.

7th Principle: Concern for Community

Co-operatives work for the sustainable development of their communities through policies approved by their members.

Source: ICA (2012)

Recently, in response to changing market conditions, some cooperatives in the USA have experimented with modifying these principles. For example, some cooperatives have used closed membership to maximise efficiency, profitability and the return on member equity investments.

Box 10.2 ICA – International Co-operative Alliance

Founded in 1895, the International Cooperative Alliance is an independent, non-governmental organisation which unites, represents and serves cooperatives worldwide. It is the largest non-governmental organisation in the world.

ICA members are national and international cooperative organisations in all sectors of activity including agriculture, banking, fisheries, health, housing, industry, insurance, tourism and consumer cooperatives. ICA has 267 member organisations from 96 countries, which represent approximately 1 billion individuals worldwide (ICA, 2012).

Historical development

The fundamental ideas behind the cooperative concept as we know it today were formed in the first half of the 1800s. It happened as a reaction to the social problems that had come in the aftermath of industrialisation and the creation of the modern working class.

In 1844, several workers in the factory town of Rochdale in the north of England established the first consumer cooperative. The workers faced miserable working conditions and low wages, and they could not afford the high prices of food and household goods. They decided that, by pooling their scarce resources and working together, they could access basic goods at a lower price.

The organisers formulated, at the same time, the principles and tenets that have since been regarded as the guideline for cooperatives. These principles have been revised and updated, but remain essentially the same as those practised in 1844. From Rochdale, consumer cooperatives spread to the rest of Britain and later to Europe. In France, several social theorists had similar thoughts to Robert Owens and, in Germany in the 1840s, groups emerged based on cooperative partnership to provide peasants with credit.

The spread of the cooperative concept was mainly in the form of consumer cooperatives in the 1800s. In the 1900s, the cooperative concept gained momentum worldwide. Two areas dominated – consumer cooperatives and cooperatives in agriculture.

In the second half of the 1900s, the cooperative concept also spread to a number of developing countries. Here, there was a conscious effort to build the economic company on the basis of the cooperative concept and there was also strong public management. However, experience from developing countries is highly variable.

The significance and spread of cooperatives

The significance and spread of cooperatives has not been precisely documented because, among other reasons, there are many intermediate forms or 'semi-cooperatives'. As illustrated in Box 10.3, there are many examples which indicate that cooperative ownership is widespread – including at the global level.

Box 10.3 **Examples of the significance and spread of cooperatives**

- In Argentina, there are 12,670 cooperative societies with over 9.3 million members.
- In Uruguay, cooperatives produce 90 per cent of total milk production, 30 per cent of honey and 30 per cent of wheat.
- In Poland, dairy cooperatives are responsible for 75 per cent of dairy production.
- In Singapore, consumer cooperatives have 55 per cent of the market in supermarket purchases.
- In Vietnam, cooperatives contribute 8.6 per cent of gross domestic product (GDP).
- In Norway, agricultural cooperatives have 96 per cent of the market for raw milk and 55 per cent of the cheese market, 80 per cent of the timber market, over 70 per cent of the egg and fur markets, and 52 per cent of the seed market.
- Cooperatives provide over 100 million jobs around the world, 20 per cent more than multinational enterprises.
- In Brazil, cooperatives are responsible for 37.2 per cent of agricultural GDP and contribute 5.39 per cent of the country's total GDP.
- Agricultural cooperatives in the EU have an over 50 per cent share in the supply of agricultural inputs and an over 60 per cent share in collection, processing and marketing of agricultural products.
- In Japan, 91 per cent of all farmers are members of agricultural cooperatives.
- In Kenya, cooperatives have 70 per cent of the coffee market, 76 per cent dairy, 90 per cent pyrethrum, and 95 per cent cotton.
- In New Zealand, cooperatives are responsible for 95 per cent of the dairy market, 95 per cent of the export dairy market, 70 per cent of the meat market, 50 per cent of the farm supply market and 70 per cent of the fertiliser market.
- In the USA, the share of all milk delivered to plants and dealers by cooperatives was 86 per cent in 2002, up from 48 per cent in the mid-1930s.

Sources: ICA (2012), COCEGA (2005),
Co-operatives Australia (2012), USDA (2005)

The degree of cooperative organisation in agriculture and the food industry varies significantly from sector to sector and from country to country, which can partly be explained by the different market conditions, which to a greater or lesser degree stimulate cooperative organisation. In the case of cooperatives in agriculture and the food sector, a pattern is apparent in that cooperatives are most widespread in North America, Northern and Central Europe and in Japan and Korea.

Generally, cooperatives – of the formal kind – are most important in the most economically developed countries. Here, cooperatives have a relatively large market share and most farmers are members of one or more cooperatives. Figure 10.1 illustrates the link between farmers' membership of cooperatives and the countries' levels of economic development.

The figure shows a relatively clear trend: cooperatives are less common in the poorest countries, while their prevalence increases concurrently with economic growth.

An important explanation is that the establishment of cooperatives requires a certain level of infrastructure, education and organisation, which is not always present in the least developed countries. It is also noteworthy that the cooperative organisation is particularly prominent in the processing activities which are close to agricultural production in the value chain, or where agricultural goods account for a large proportion of total costs.

Data from the USA show significant correlation between agricultural commodities' share of total costs and the extent of cooperative organisation (see Figure 10.2).

The figure shows the relationship between, on the one hand, agricultural goods' share of total costs and, on the other hand, the extent of cooperative organisation. As can be seen, cooperative organisation is the more widespread, the more important agricultural goods are in respect of the individual product groups. For the product groups where agricultural goods play a relatively minor role, farmers will naturally be less interested in owning the processing link – and vice versa.

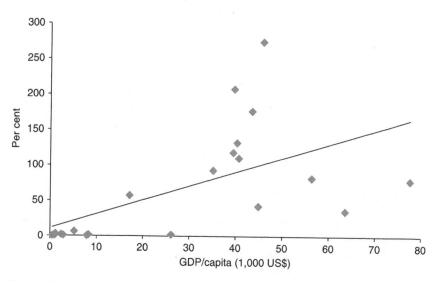

Figure 10.1 Number of memberships of agricultural cooperatives as a percentage of the agricultural population.

Source: Author's presentation on the basis of Zeull and Cropp (2004).

Note: Farmers can be members of several cooperatives at the same time, which is why the percentage can be over 100.

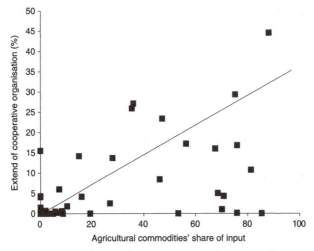

Figure 10.2 Correlation between agricultural commodities' share of input and the extent of cooperative organisation in the US food industry.

Source: Author's presentation on the basis of Rogers (2000).

The significance of the cooperative organisation is likely to develop in a relatively stable manner. Cooperatives are, by virtue of their form of ownership and liability, financially robust and difficult to purchase, and they therefore usually retain their market share over time.

The significance of cooperatives can also change over time. The placement of cooperatives changes in line with a country's economic development, but changed market conditions can also affect the spread of cooperatives.

In many countries there are examples of the disappearance of the cooperative organisation in several sectors, as cooperatives have been bought or out-competed by capital-owned companies. There are, however, also examples of cooperatives spreading to new areas, or increasing their market share at the expense of other types of company. For example, cooperative ownership in the dairy sector is widespread and increasing in several countries (see Figure 10.3).

Differences and similarities

Cooperatives and capital-owned companies have both similarities and differences. Both types of company develop over time and thus it is a recurrent feature that modern cooperatives, in many cases, have developed so that they share many features with capital-owned companies. Generally, there has been a tendency for cooperatives to increasingly focus on business, while non-economic, non-commercial and ideological aspects have become less important. In addition, several hybrid models have developed which are crosses between cooperatives and capital-owned companies, or which contain both cooperatives and capital-owned companies in the same company.

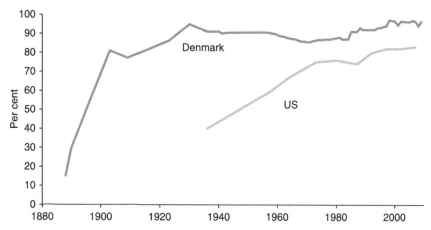

Figure 10.3 Cooperatives' market share in the dairy sector in the USA and Denmark.

Source: Author's presentation based on USDA (2009) and Hansen (2011).

Note: Denmark: Share of milk intake by cooperatives.

USA: Cooperative member milk volume as a percentage of volume sold to plants and dealers.

Cooperatives and capital-owned companies are therefore far from unambiguous company structures and there can be large differences between different types of cooperative, and there can also be big differences from country to country. Despite this, it is possible to identify a number of general and important similarities and differences between cooperatives and capital-owned companies as described in the sections below.

Profit distribution

In cooperatives, a part of the profits remain in the company and equity is used to consolidate. The other part is distributed among the owners – the members – in proportion to their purchases from and sales to the cooperative company. In a dairy cooperative, typically, an amount is paid which is in proportion to the amount of milk that each individual cooperative member has delivered.

Even in a capital-owned company, a part of the profits is used as equity, and a part is paid to the owners as dividends. Dividends are paid in proportion to the amount invested, while the profits of a cooperative are distributed in proportion to deliveries and / or purchases.

The value of the share

In a cooperative, a new member typically joins the company and receives a share of the company for free, while a withdrawing member will similarly not be able to sell his or her share certificate and thus cannot withdraw money from the company. If the cooperative allows a portion of the profits to remain in the company for long-term investments, the shareholders, in the short term, do not receive any significant benefit. The benefits are obtained prospectively in that the investments provide profits for distribution or result in better prices for members' deliveries to the cooperative, etc.

In a capital-owned company, one buys a share in the company (a stake) which can subsequently usually be sold at the market value. Shares typically increase in value if the value of the company increases. The shareholders' value of ownership thus varies continuously with the company's performance and in line with both short- and long-term actions.

Influence

In cooperatives, owners (the members) have influence according to the principle: one man, one vote. Members, therefore, have the same degree of influence, regardless of whether they have a large or small commitment (purchase or sale) to the company.

In a capital-owned company there is a correlation between ownership and influence. The larger the amount of capital invested, the greater the share and influence.

Social dimensions

Almost right from the start, cooperatives have had special social obligations or principles. A desire to create economic development and independence, social improvements and cooperation has been an important foundation for cooperatives. Cooperatives have thus a 'Concern for Community' (see the previously discussed cooperative principles). Capital-owned companies have previously not had the same goals. However, in recent years, increasing interest in Corporate Social Responsibility (CSR) has, to some extent, meant that capital-owned companies have incorporated cooperatives' social principles.

Organisational structure

The organisational structure is largely the same in the two types of company. The structure is the same with regard to the board of directors (elected at the annual general meeting) and the day-to-day management (employed by the board). It is a general rule that the board be composed of members elected at the annual general meeting. The general assembly may also choose board members outside the ownership group. This is typically the case if individuals with special leadership competences, etc. are required.

In a capital-owned company, where shareholders are often large financial or investment funds, pension funds or industrial investors, it is customary to appoint board members who are not necessarily shareholders. In this way, the basis for recruitment is far broader than in cooperatives. Conversely, the board members of a cooperative often have a very keen interest in the company and their economic incentive to ensure the healthy development of the company is significant.

Capital

Cooperatives' equity mainly consists of accumulated retained profits and members' investments. In addition, cooperatives can bring in subordinated loan capital from members or from external lenders. Finally, it can be argued that the members' obligation to deliver acts as a hidden reserve: if the cooperative gets into financial difficulties, it can reduce members' prices, thereby improving profitability. This is one of the reasons that lenders to cooperatives emphasise the members' obligation to supply.

Capital-owned companies can also increase equity through accumulated retained profits and subordinated loan capital, but they can also attract new equity capital by issuing shares. Therefore, capital-owned companies, in principle, have unlimited access to external capital to increase equity.

Ties in relation to resources (raw materials and capital)

In many cooperatives, the shareholders have delivery rights and obligations. This means that members must deliver their entire production – or a predetermined percentage of production – to the cooperative. Delivery rights and obligations are two sides of same coin: members receive a guarantee that they will always have a buyer for their products, which is crucial for, e.g. dairy producers who have daily deliveries. On the other hand, the cooperative has widespread assurance for raw material supply, which is also an important condition for many food companies.

In capital-owned companies, there is no corresponding delivery right and obligation between the company and owners. One can, however, largely accomplish the same through contracts between the company and suppliers, although the same common interests are not present.

The members' delivery right also means that the cooperative cannot control volumes to the same extent as the capital-owned company.

There are many cases of cooperatives also receiving supplies from non-members. The condition here is that the non-member's produce must not generate an additional return to the cooperative and the cooperative's members at the expense of the members' delivery right and that the non-member must not receive the excess payment that members receive.

Profit maximisation

Both cooperatives and capital-owned companies strive for profit maximisation under certain preconditions or restrictions. There is, therefore, no fundamental difference in business practice or economic optimisation. The difference lies primarily in the distribution of profits, in that in cooperatives profits are distributed to the members in proportion to their supplies or trade with the cooperative enterprise, while in the capital-owned companies, profits are distributed among the investors in proportion to the size of their investment.

Advantages and disadvantages of cooperatives vs capital-owned companies

Cooperatives have a number of advantages and disadvantages in relation to capital-owned companies. However, one cannot say in advance that one or the other company structure is optimal, since it depends on the specific situations and market conditions.

A number of significant advantages and disadvantages of cooperatives in relation to equity-owned companies are presented in Box 10.4. In many cases, one seeks to address many of the presented disadvantages by adapting and developing the cooperative structure.

Box 10.4 **Cooperatives: significant advantages and disadvantages compared to capital-owned companies**

Advantages

Strong vertical integration

Through cooperative ownership several links in the value chain can be controlled.

Low transaction costs

The supply chain is effective, and supplies between the links are often at no cost to intermediaries or other sales links.

Security of supply

Both farmers and the cooperative have secure sales and supply.

Relatively small demand for capital

The supply obligation acts as a financial cushion and thus the need for equity is reduced.

Cooperatives are often economically robust

The cooperative structure, with the obligation to supply, etc., means that it is relatively rare that cooperatives go bankrupt.

Market power in the value chain is evened out

Agricultural production typically comes from many small units which individually have weak market power. By standing together in cooperatives, the bargaining power of these small units is strengthened, and it becomes more equal in relation to the other links in the value chain.

Disadvantages

It is difficult to attract equity

The potential for attracting external capital is limited.

Volume control is difficult

Because of members' delivery rights, cooperatives have limited scope for volume control.

Conflicts of interest and dual role

Members' dual role as both owners and suppliers (or customers) can cause conflicts.

Lack of incentives for long-term investments

Since the cooperative owners basically cannot withdraw their share of the value added from the company when they drop out, their economic incentive to leave money in the company for long-term investments and return can be limited.

Limited recruitment base to the board

Positions on the board are predominantly reserved for members, which results in a significantly reduced basis for recruitment.

Ties to produce

Cooperatives may have an implicit or explicit tie to the members' own supply of raw produce, which can cause non-optimal commodity composition.

Focus on value chain around members

Cooperatives will, by virtue of their aim to protect the supply and sales of their members, often focus on the links of the value chain which lie closest to the members. Activities further down the value chain closer to consumers can therefore be assigned a lower priority, even though they may be economically attractive.

Driving forces behind the formation and development of cooperatives

The spread of co-operatives varies depending on a number of market conditions which can make it more or less advantageous to establish – or maintain – cooperatives. In summary, one can say that the following factors promote or influence the spread of cooperatives (the conditions may be more or less interconnected and the list can, therefore, include different aspects of the same problem):

The products constitute a high proportion of the consumer price.

When agricultural commodities constitute a large share of the retail price, the price of the agricultural commodities is a relatively important parameter. Therefore, there will be, *ceteris paribus*, a strong focus on reducing the price of agricultural commodities, which increases farmers' incentive to own and operate businesses where the costs of agricultural commodities account for a large share of the retail price.

Supply and processing activities are close to agricultural production in the value chain.

Companies which are involved in supply or processing in the value chain that is directly in connection with agricultural production are often cooperatively owned. Market power in relation to suppliers and purchasing companies is crucial for competitiveness, and farmers can increase market power by owning and operating these businesses.

There is no or only weak market power in existing supplier associations, etc.

Farmers can often achieve a degree of market power by establishing supplier and producer associations, which have bargaining power over supply and processing companies. Thus, the benefits of establishing a cooperative are less. Conversely, the absence of such supplier and producer associations increases the incentive to establish farmer-owned cooperatives.

There is weak competition in agriculture's supply or marketing stages.

Fundamentally, cooperatives are created because a community comes together to solve a problem of a commercial character, which is important for the community and which, for one reason or another, has not been resolved satisfactorily. If there is insufficient independent competition in the agricultural supply and marketing link, the market does not work properly, and thus the farmers' market conditions are adversely affected. There is thus an incentive to establish cooperatives in these sectors. There are also cases in which the market does not exist (where there is no local demand) and where farmers therefore have formed a cooperative to build an agro-industrial complex.

Farmers need professional, democratic and social skills.

The establishment, organisation and operation of a cooperative require that the members have the right professional, democratic and social skills. Farmers need to understand and respect the common rules and have the ability to cooperate and to recognise that mutual benefits must be present.

Delivery guarantee is important due to daily deliveries.

Agricultural products which are sold daily, or almost daily, require a stable sales organisation and the right to deliver. For a dairy farmer, it is important that the milk can be delivered every day, while it is easier for, e.g., a grain producer to store grain and spend time on evaluating alternative sales opportunities. Therefore, the right to deliver – and thus also the value of being a member of a cooperative – is greater in some sectors than in others.

Cooperative ownership implies growth.

As a general rule, cooperatives have open membership, which means that new members have access and can achieve the same prices, etc. as the existing members. This applies even if the increased volume of produce from the new members leads to a lower return to the cooperative, which occurs because the marginal amount has to be sold on less lucrative markets. Therefore, cooperatives cannot control volumes to the same degree as companies without open membership. The result is that cooperatives often have a built-in mechanism that results in increased growth and increasing market share.

Legislation promotes cooperative ownership.

Legislation can in several areas be a significant driver for the establishment of cooperatives. In several cases, the state supports the formation and development of cooperatives through special arrangements, support or legislation.

Capital structure and needs are relevant.

The cooperative's capital situation, including the cooperative's capital needs relative to the number of members, also has an impact on the spread of cooperatives. If processing activities are highly capital intensive, and if there are very few members, the capital requirement per member will be so large that the cooperative structure will be unsuitable – especially if there is a start-up phase.

New Generation Cooperatives – NGCs

Cooperatives develop over time as a result of influences from society and the market and internal conditions in the cooperative sector and in the cooperatives themselves. A recent change has been the establishment of so-called New Generation Cooperatives, which is often abbreviated as NGCs.

Form, content and development

A large number of New Generation Cooperatives have been established in the USA over the past 20–25 years. These organisations have predominantly exploited niche markets and have been a kind of backlash against the established cooperatives' lack of commitment to exploit new market opportunities. This development can also be interpreted as a reaction to the fact that established co-operatives can have built-in problems regarding the raising of capital, volume control, etc.

NGCs differ notably from traditional cooperatives by having:

- closed membership
- tradable delivery rights.

New members of an NGC must typically make a considerable capital investment in the organisation, as members have to pay for the right to deliver. This delivery right is typically transferable, whereby a member automatically receives a share of the increased value of the organisation. Members' incentives to invest and to make long-term decisions are therefore relatively good in an NGC.

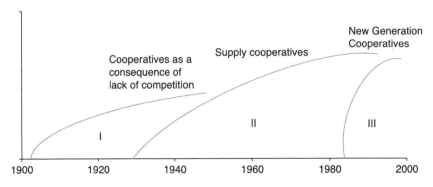

Figure 10.4 The three waves of cooperative establishment in the USA.
Source: Author's presentation based on Fulton (2000).

NGCs solve some problems but create other problems in certain areas. There-fore, they will probably only emerge in specific areas and on the basis of specific needs. The name 'New Generation Cooperative' was originally used regarding a small number of American processing cooperatives with closed membership, which were formed in the 1990s. NGCs can be said to be the third wave of coop-eratives in the USA, as is illustrated in Figure 10.4.

The first wave began at the start of the twentieth century when agricultural markets were being constructed and developed. Farmers established cooperatives in response to a lack of competition and monopoly conditions, which both supply (feed, fertiliser, etc.) and processing companies (slaughterhouses, dairies, etc.) exploited to the detriment of farmers.

The second wave occurred in the 1930s and 1940s, which was mainly a response to inadequate supply from sectors including finance, energy and retail. The unsat-isfactory supply was due to the existing suppliers in the market who focused on more lucrative business sectors than the agricultural sector.

The third wave – New Generation Cooperatives – emerged in the 1990s, and it was a reaction especially from young farmers, who faced new challenges as a result of the liberalisation of agricultural markets and a need to establish special-ised niche markets. However, there are a number of different explanations as to why NGCs emerged during this period. In some cases, the driving force was a need for market information and coordination, while, in other cases, it was the farmers' desire to obtain a larger share of value added in the value chain and thus also have a larger share of the consumer value.

The greater focus on added value illustrates a difference between NGCs and traditional cooperatives, for which market power and coordinated sales were key drivers. In an NGC, the starting point is an effective capacity level where, e.g., machines are utilised optimally or where the market is supplied such large amounts that optimal earnings are achieved. Precisely this level is determined by the amount that members can deliver to the organisation. Membership is thus limited to those members who were the first to purchase delivery rights to the company.

The organisation sells delivery rights during the establishment phase to allocate delivery rights effectively among farmers and to raise capital. Each individual delivery right gives a member the right and an obligation to deliver a given quantity of goods. The size of the delivery right typically varies from member to member, but there is often an upper and lower limit.

The price of the delivery right is initially determined by the organisation's capital requirement divided by the optimum amount of agricultural commodities. Generally, 30–50 per cent of the total capital requirement is covered by contributions from members (Fulton, 2000). Additionally so-called preference shares are issued, where a special group of outside investors are given the opportunity to receive a stake – albeit typically with a ceiling on the annual return and usually without voting rights.

In this way, an NGC finances most of its capital needs in advance, and this also means that large parts of the operating surplus can be returned to the members at year end – in proportion to their deliveries.

Once the establishment phase is over, delivery rights can be traded freely. The market price of the delivery rights will thus reflect the direct and indirect return which future members of the organisation can expect. If the company wants to expand production, new delivery rights can be granted to cover the additional quantity of agricultural commodities. In this way, new members finance the organisation in advance, and thus an NGC does not have the same problem with financing as a traditional cooperative.

Driving forces behind the formation of NGCs

NGCs occurred as a result of changes and pressures both internally in the cooperative sector and externally in society.

The *external* pressure must be viewed in light of the industrialisation of agriculture, the food industry and the whole food chain, which has been occurring for several decades. Partly as a result of the retail sector's development, growth and focus on economies of scale have factors such as uniformity, guaranteed supply, high volumes and 'just-in-time' become very important. Much greater dependence in the value chain has emerged, while vertical integration has been strengthened. Meanwhile, globalisation, global marketing, increased use of brands, private labels, etc. has resulted in a development whereby buyers, to a large extent, go for mass production and large quantities.

Agricultural commodities thus have largely become undifferentiated products which meet a number of general requirements regarding standards, quality and uniformity from customers, particularly the processing industry and ultimately the retail chains. This development has, for the time being, given a lower priority to the individual qualities of produce and diversity, as well as produce's unique qualities in small volumes. Even though retailers continue to develop in the direction of increased concentration and international orientation, there is also a trend for increasing differentiation. Some retailers want to differentiate their products from the products of other retailers and this can be achieved through marketing, packaging and product development – but also by using unique and special qualities of agricultural commodities.

There has been a tendency for food demand to be more varied and differentiated. Organic products, meat from special pigs and alternative choices regarding eggs are some of the many examples of how more and more differentiated agricultural products have become part of the retail selection. In the case of fresh milk, a marked differentiation has occurred in recent years whereby new special varieties have emerged – based on criteria such as cattle breed, delivery time / freshness, animal welfare, geographical origin, producer (including branded and private labels) and fat content. The food industry is also demanding more and more agricultural produce with product-specific characteristics.

Farmers have traditionally established cooperatives especially to ensure greater control over the value chain and to ensure efficient markets, both on the supply and sales side. Farmers joined forces to ensure an effective value chain and to ensure that other companies in the value chain could not establish and exploit excessive market power in relation to a large number of small farms. Community, cooperation and market power through large-scale operations and coordination were therefore the driving force behind the establishment and development of cooperatives for many years.

The establishment of NGCs has also to some extent been a result of an incipient *internal pressure* in the cooperative sector. When cooperatives were created in the nineteenth and twentieth centuries, farmers, and hence the cooperative members, were a relatively homogeneous group. The group had, to a large extent, the same interests in that they all had a common opponent and they were all too small to survive as successfully outside the cooperative. In recent decades, agriculture has become much less homogeneous and farmers have become more specialised.

At the same time, cooperatives are increasingly developing into large organisations, which in the eyes of many farmers 'behave exactly like limited companies and thus lose their independent legitimacy'. The ideological preference for cooperatives thus becomes weaker. Objectively speaking, is it quite natural that cooperatives become 'business and not ideology', cooperatives would not be able to survive in a competitive market if they did not drive the business based on commercial goals.

The trend towards more diversity and less homogeneity can be found in many places in the Western world. This development means that several special interests naturally arise in agriculture, but also greater opportunities for individual farmers – or small groups of farmers – to develop new business areas and niche productions.

Tiered cooperatives

Several of the needs and drivers that may otherwise lead to the formation of NGCs can be satisfied to a large extent by the so-called tiered cooperatives. These organisations handle the differentiated raw material production in particular, which is otherwise a great challenge for cooperatives.

When a cooperative bases its production on differentiated raw produce from members, we are often dealing with a tiered cooperative. Tiered cooperatives can be described as a further development of the traditional cooperative form and there is also, in several areas, a break with the traditional cooperative model and the cooperative's role in relation to members' raw produce production.

There can be significant and fundamental differences between a tiered cooperative and a traditional cooperative. In several areas, tiered cooperatives break with the traditional principles and almost entrenched rights in traditional cooperatives. Consequently there are several factors which need to be carefully considered when establishing a tiered cooperative:

> Differentiated commodity production requires more direct control and it is often necessary to make contracts with larger or smaller groups of farmers.
>
> As the individual members are treated substantially differently in a tiered cooperative, and the members can have very different duties and rights, there is clear potential for conflict between members.
>
> Almost all large cooperatives are, to a greater or lesser extent, considered to be tiered. Specific groups of farmers and suppliers with limited niche production can, in many cases, be included as a defined part of the cooperative.

Tiered cooperatives can be said to be an alternative to NGCs, and there are both advantages and disadvantages to the two alternatives. In tiered cooperatives, it is possible to exploit synergies and economies of scale between the existing cooperative and new differentiated areas. Conversely, it is easier to lose focus, commitment and closeness, and internal conflicts are more frequent in tiered cooperatives.

How cooperatives grow

All businesses must constantly develop to adapt to changes and new conditions and opportunities. This also applies to cooperatives, which in some areas face special challenges in the form of globalisation and access to capital.

It is crucial that adequate models of growth are developed in agricultural and food cooperatives, as these will enable cooperatives to generate further growth despite potential barriers and obstacles. In this section, 12 different models are presented and discussed.

Model 1: The status quo

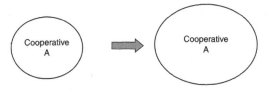

Model 1 represents the status quo whereby the cooperative structure remains unchanged, and no major changes in structure or ownership are implemented. The cooperatives create growth through self-financing and loan finance.

There are many examples of cooperatives which have managed to carve out a national or even international market position in several selected business areas without fundamentally changing the cooperative model. This emphasises that cooperative ownership, growth and globalisation can be combined. Conversely, it must also be recognised that a fully consolidated domestic sector, fewer cooperative members and a growing need for foreign acquisitions to secure growth, the exploitation of economies of scale and market position puts the pure cooperative form under pressure.

Model 2: Growth through foreign members

Growth can also be created by offering membership to foreign farmers who can either be farmers in the countries where the cooperative has foreign operations, or foreign farmers who wish to trade with the cooperative.

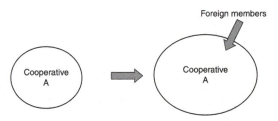

A number of Dutch cooperatives have opened up to foreign members in this way. A number of different motives have been behind this development (see van Bekkum, 2009):

- Some Dutch farmers moved abroad, but several cooperatives wanted to continue to trade with these farmers who now lived in a foreign country, and they therefore continued to be members.
- Some cooperatives engaged in cross-border activities, which were very similar to domestic activities. Therefore, the cooperatives considered it appropriate to give equal rights and benefits to foreign farmers.
- Some cooperatives offered foreign farmers membership in order to support future cooperation with these farmers.
- Some cooperatives had an interest in taking up foreign members in the foreign companies as it strengthened the organisation's profile and goodwill, which was a significant advantage when marketing the company and its services.
- By offering foreign farmers membership, these new members contributed with capital for the further international growth of the cooperative.

There were also a number of intermediate solutions. Cooperatives could, e.g., have farmers as shareholders of foreign subsidiaries. Another solution was to link the foreign farmers to the foreign activities through looser membership, bonuses, discussion groups, etc.

Model 3: Mergers with foreign cooperatives

Model 3 is when cooperatives in two different countries merge.

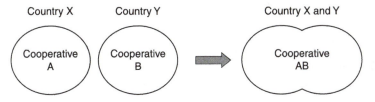

In principle, national and international mergers between cooperatives are alike and the need for finance is in both cases very limited, as only a combination of activities occurs. In practice, however, there are a number of, often very significant, cultural, legal, structural and emotional barriers that can prevent mergers between cooperatives across national borders.

Model 4: Global strategic alliances

In Model 4, cooperatives generate growth, critical mass and market power through cooperation with other national or international companies.

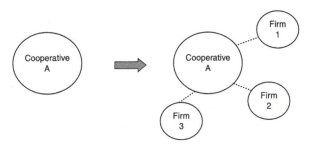

Global strategic alliances are being used more and more often in the globalisation strategy of cooperatives.

Model 5: The cooperative is transformed into a shareholding company

In Model 5 the cooperative members maintain majority shares through common ownership in the shareholding company.

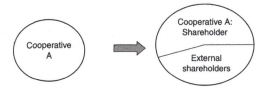

A cooperative can be converted into a public company where the members retain the majority stake, but where, at the same time, room is made for new external shareholders. The conversion can be conducted in order to attract new equity and to finance future international growth, processing, business acquisitions, etc., or, alternatively, it may be a defensive conversion in order to attract equity for the reconstruction of the organisation's activities.

Model 6: Core business units are maintained in the cooperative, while other business units are separated or developed into shareholding companies with external investors

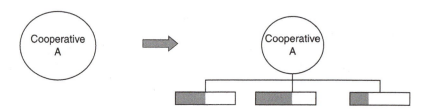

This model has the advantage that risk, earnings and, not least, financing are shared with others. At the same time, the affiliated companies become independent business units, which are easier to measure economically and which obtain an internal focus more easily. Additionally, synergies can also be achieved through the other companies which are joint owners of the affiliated companies.

The precondition which ensures that the model works best is that the companies have to function as separate business units, but that synergies between the affiliated companies or in relation to the cooperative can be exploited. This is also necessary to attract and retain external investors and shareholders in the affiliated companies.

Model 7: A capital-owned company is created directly under the cooperative

This corresponds to a certain extent to Model 6 but, in this case, the cooperative's primary function is to be a parent company of the limited company. The intention is that external investors become joint owners of the limited company.

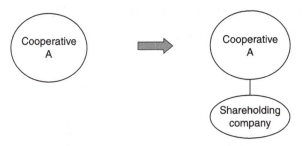

Model 8: The cooperative is sold and transformed into a shareholding company

In this model, the assets are distributed to the former cooperative members as capital or as shares in the new shareholding company.

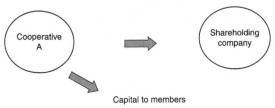

The comprehensive restructuring of the Irish dairy sector has largely occurred on the basis of this model.

Model 9: New Generation Cooperative (NGC)

In general, new members of an NGC have to make a capital contribution to the company to pay for the right to deliver. This right to deliver is often a tradable asset, which means that members receive a part of the added value of the company. Therefore, the members have an incentive to take part in long-term investments in an NGC.

Model 10: Cooperative members contribute to the cooperative in the form of equity loans

Cooperative members, and perhaps also other individuals or investors with a special interest or connection with the cooperative, provide equity loans. The cooperative pays an interest rate which is equivalent to the change in the average share price of a comparable shareholding company.

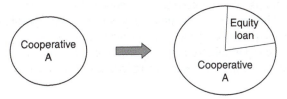

The cooperative thereby ensures additional capital without, at the same time, there being a risk of losing influence, as formal influence does not usually follow subordinated loan capital, which is usually temporary. The disadvantage for the cooperative is that subordinated loan capital as a starting point requires a larger business, as the capital is risky and without security.

Model 11: Diversification – spreading into new business areas

Cooperatives can also create new growth, even on a fully consolidated market with low market growth, by engaging in new Strategic Business Units (SBU) which lie outside the traditional core business area. The cooperative can thus create a greater critical mass, and a number of synergies and economies of scale can be achieved in, e.g., marketing, leadership and innovation.

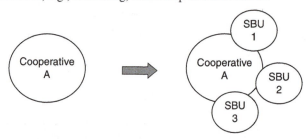

The risks of such diversification are that there is not enough synergy or connection between the new activities and the core activities.

So far, many cooperative societies have been characterised by very little diversification. There has, however, been a high degree of specialisation and focus on a single production area. Integration primarily takes place vertically (increased processing, integration of the supply link, etc.), while diversification into completely new areas is very limited. This particularly applies to cooperatives.

Development in recent years has generally been in the direction of increasing focus and specialisation, and less emphasis on diversification. The emphasis is on becoming larger and stronger in core areas, while the more peripheral areas of business are divested. It is natural that cooperatives, as a result of their ownership structure, historical development and, not least, agriculture's specialisation, focus on the product areas which their members supply.

There are, however, also several examples of large international food companies becoming increasingly diversified, as they spread to several new business areas, but still within the food sector.

Finally, there is also a tendency for cooperatives to redefine their core competences. The concept of competence is not limited to specific products, but to business units, processes, technology or the like. These slightly more abstract definitions make it possible for a cooperative to extend activities into new areas, whilst still exploiting the organisation's unique core competences.

Model 12: Increased value and forward integration

Companies can enhance growth by increasing value added and by moving forward in the value chain, thereby increasing the focus on consumer-oriented products.

The reason for this is that many companies seek to avoid fierce price competition in a bulk market, which is where agricultural commodities and other non-processed goods often end up. This can be done in several ways, including by generating more added value to products, by moving further up the value chain (forward integration) or by producing unique products for industrial use.

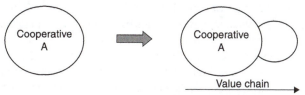

Generally one can see that cooperatives typically emphasise activities near the farmers in the value chain. It is also noteworthy that cooperatives are particularly prominent in processing activities where agricultural goods represent a large proportion of total costs (large share of the consumer price) (see, e.g., Rogers, 2000).

Thus, cooperatives are also typically involved in the first marketing and processing stages as a result of their role as the processing and sales link for their members. However, it is often the case that these links are associated with low margins and little market power (see, e.g., Royer, 2009). As can be seen in Figure 10.5, the cooperatives in the USA have a relatively small market share when it comes to consumer-oriented products in the dairy sector.

The figure clearly shows that cooperative dairies in the USA have a relatively small market share in products which are sold directly to consumers. Economists have tried to find explanations as to why more cooperatives are not integrated into the later stages of the value chain where, e.g., processing and product differentiation

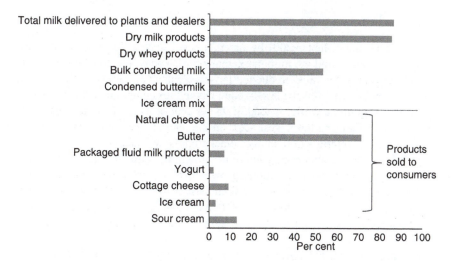

Figure 10.5 Cooperative market share for various dairy products in the USA, 2007.
Source: USDA (2009).

are usually more significant. Most studies reach the conclusion that it is due to the cooperatives' organisation. In particular, the commodity-oriented focus and inadequate opportunities to invest in research, development and marketing are given as the main reasons for the limited integration into the more consumer-oriented part of the value chain (see, e.g., Royer, 2009).

Therefore, the creation of growth by increasing value added and by moving forward in the value chain may well be an opportunity for cooperatives, but there are two major barriers which have to be overcome: strategic orientation towards raw produce supplies and a lack of financing for the necessary capacity building.

In Models 5, 6 and 7, it is assumed that cooperative members do not have special preferences for or advantages from being suppliers of the company. The agricultural products delivered to the company are traded at the 'market price', which in itself may be difficult to quantify. Payments for other assets and values, such as market competences, brands, security of suppliers, etc. are not given to the farmers as a price supplement. However, these assets are priced and capitalised and the value is reflected in the price of the shares, which new investors have to pay for up front.

The aim is to ensure that external investors are quite confident that the company works purely for profit maximisation and that the profit is strictly shared among the owners, in relation to their share of capital invested in the company.

Cases: models to create growth

All 12 models are implemented today in several areas, and often parts of several models are used in a corporate structure. In this section, we will discuss examples of how the models are implemented and used by farmers and cooperative members in order to generate more growth in agri and food industries.

Fonterra

Fonterra was established in 2001 by a merger between New Zealand's two largest cooperative dairies and the milk marketing board. Today, the company accounts for 95 per cent of the milk production in New Zealand and processes milk from 11,000 dairy farmers. It is the largest company in the country and the sixth largest dairy company in the world. A total of 95 per cent of its production is exported, which makes Fonterra the largest actor on the international dairy market. Some 80 per cent of Fonterra's milk intake comes from New Zealand.

In 2007, Fonterra launched an ambitious growth strategy, the aim of which was to expand in a number of international growth markets, including China and India. There was strong demand for fresh milk in these markets, and Fonterra's strategy was to supply them through foreign direct investment in local production. To fulfil the strategy, it was urgent to attract a certain amount of capital from external investors.

In the autumn of 2007, the board of directors at Fonterra proposed to transfer all assets in the company to a new shareholding company and to list the shares on the stock market. The intention was that the cooperative should retain 65 per cent of the shares, members would receive 15 per cent and the remaining 20 per cent would be sold on the stock market.

According to the plan, the members of Fonterra were supposed to vote for the first part of the proposal in May 2010. However, the cooperative members were rather against the plan, so the board of directors chose to postpone it. The resistance among the members was due to three major concerns:

- that the new corporate structure would have a negative impact on their milk price;
- that the cooperative members' share of 65 per cent would be reduced;
- the question of how to pay for capital and milk in a fair way: there was no simple answer to this question.

Fonterra also has other instruments to attract equity capital. Cooperative members are invited to provide equity capital for the company, and the company has already succeeded in attracting a significant amount of money.

The Fonterra case shows that a transfer to a shareholding model might lead to both advantages and disadvantages for farmers. Access to external and equity capital will be possible, but at the same time farmers will have to sacrifice influence and price premiums.

Arla Foods

In 2000, the Danish dairy, MD Foods, merged with the Swedish dairy, Arla. Both dairies were cooperatives, and the new cooperative, Arla Foods, became one of the largest dairies in the world. The creation of Arla Foods was a major example of a merger between two cooperatives from two different countries.

The increased concentration among both retailers and competitors was a major driver behind the merger. The fact that consumers' increasing demand for product innovation, marketing and processing would require larger companies in the dairy sector, was emphasised (see Danish Dairy Board, 2000).

Also, increasing liberalisation and competition on the dairy markets and the enlargement of the EU were major drivers behind the merger. Further, very low growth on the domestic markets made it advantageous to find a foreign partner.

Finally, it was also important that the two dairies were able to supplement and complement each other. The cooperative model and historical origin created a common platform and, through MD Foods' international position, common synergies could be exploited. Arla's export share was only 12 per cent, while MD Foods' was greater than 60 per cent.

Changing corporate structures and the transformation to a shareholding model has been thoroughly discussed in recent years at Arla. However, until now, farmers have decided to retain the cooperative model. Furthermore, at the end of 2010, the members decided to significantly increase the equity capital of the company in order to be able to cope with the corporate strategy, which implied an increase in turnover of 50 per cent within the subsequent five years. The extra equity capital would be obtained by the farmers, who would double the share of the milk price, which they would leave as capital in the company.

DLF-TRIFOLIUM Ltd

DLF-TRIFOLIUM Ltd is an example of a cooperative which is a completely dominant shareholder in a shareholding company.

DLF-TRIFOLIUM Ltd is the world's largest seed company within the breeding, production, sale and marketing of cool season clover and grass seed species. The company is estimated to have a world market share of 20 per cent. The company is based in Denmark and is owned by Danish seed growers through the cooperative DLF AmbA.

DLF AmbA was the main shareholder and the major driver behind the creation of DLF-TRIFOLIUM Ltd. The company was listed on the stock market in 1989 and the cooperative was able to buy up shares and increase its share in DLF-TRIFOLIUM Ltd. The company was then delisted, and today the cooperative owns 95 per cent of the shares. The farmers managed to obtain complete control and ownership and the company experienced significant consolidation and globalisation, as illustrated in Figure 10.6.

The figure shows that the company's share of the world market has more than doubled since the mid-1980s. At the same time, the international activities of the company have increased remarkably since the mid-1990s, and the foreign assets as a percentage of total assets have increased from zero to almost 50 per cent.

In the 1980s, acquisitions focused on increasing the domestic market share, but as consolidation in Denmark matured, a number of foreign acquisitions in Europe were carried out. In 2002, the internationalisation of the company was

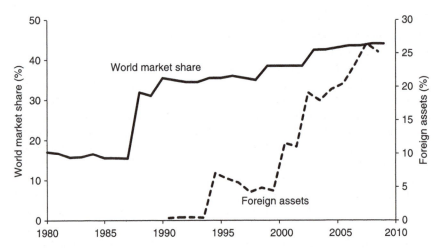

Figure 10.6 DLF-TRIFOLIUM Ltd: share of world market and share of foreign assets.
Source: DLF-TRIFOLIUM (several issues) and Danish Seed Council (several issues).

strengthened, as the company acquired the third largest seed company in Europe, the Dutch Cebeco Seeds Group.

DLF-TRIFOLIUM Ltd. is now almost completely owned by a cooperative and managed as a cooperative. This case illustrates that a mixed corporate model can succeed and that farmers have been able to establish, manage and finance a company that has become the world leader within its business area within a relatively short time.

HKScan

HKScan is one of the leading meat and food companies in Northern Europe, with a domestic market consisting of Finland, Sweden, the Baltic States and Poland. The company produces, sells and markets pork, beef, poultry meat, processed meats and convenience foods. HKScan is a result of a merger between Swedish Meats and the Finnish HK Ruokatalo in 2006. The largest shareholders are shown in Figure 10.7.

The figure shows that LSO Osuuskunta holds 35 per cent of the shares, but almost 70 per cent of the votes. LSO Osuuskunta is a cooperative owned by farmers, who deliver animals for slaughter to HKScan.

In this case, the cooperative has maintained a decisive influence in the share-holding company, despite a rather small percentage of the shares. Similarly, the

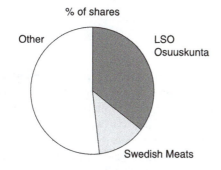

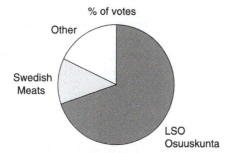

Figure 10.7 The largest shareholders in HKScan: percentage of shares and votes.
Source: HKScan (2010).

former Swedish cooperative members of Swedish Meats have managed to obtain 12 per cent of both shares and votes in HKScan. In addition, there are a number of smaller shareholders, including pension funds and insurance companies.

HKScan is an example of farmers managing to maintain their decisive influence in a share holding company. Furthermore, the shareholding structure has facilitated mergers and investments both nationally and internationally.

Crucial factors and lessons to be learned

The 12 models encompass a number of crucial factors, which need to be taken into account when considering new corporate structures. The cases discussed above illustrate this.

One major shareholder demanding majority

In several models, it is assumed that a group of cooperative members or farmers maintain a decisive influence in the company through a majority of the shares or votes.

Obviously, maintaining the majority of votes without holding the majority of shares requires some kind of concession or payment. However, if you obtain the majority of votes through acquiring the majority of shares, concessions may be unnecessary. Often, external investors prefer to have one major industrial share holder.

The pricing of agricultural products

In cooperatives, the profit generated is returned to members through a price premium on the commodities that members deliver. In a shareholding company, the profit is returned according to the capital that the owners invest. Therefore, a crucial question is how to pay for two very different inputs, capital and agricultural products, in a fair manner.

Fundamentally, a 'market price' should be paid for the agricultural products. Afterwards, the company can decide to distribute the profit to the cooperative members as a price premium per delivered amount of products. In order to be able to attract external investors, there must be very strict procedures for pricing the agricultural products delivered by farmers. However, it can be extremely difficult for large companies to estimate the market price. Increased vertical integration and very high market shares will blur the market prices.

Access to markets and to products

Farmers have an interest in ensuring the sale of their products. In the same manner, agri and food companies have an interest in maintaining their access to agricultural products as raw materials for their processing industry. This mutual interest, which is a cornerstone of cooperatives, can be fulfilled by the drawing up of contracts between farmers and companies. However, contracts of this type are a source of conflict.

The strategic development of the company

A cooperative group of farmers in a shareholding company may primarily strive to ensure optimal sales of their agricultural products. They also have a secondary interest in ensuring that the company generates a large profit. However, the company may decide to move its production and sourcing of agricultural products to a foreign country.

The company's competences within quality, health, vertical integration, marketing, etc. can be transferred to a foreign country and to a foreign plant, which is based on local agricultural products from foreign farmers.

Global off-shoring of agricultural production appears to be an obvious strategy to follow, but farmers and cooperative shareholders will probably oppose this. In any case, the shareholders must be prepared for this conflict in advance.

Transnational mergers between cooperatives can involve cultural, linguistic and structural problems

Merging two cooperatives from two different countries is a challenge. Cooperative members are owners and suppliers, and they may depend heavily on the outcome of the cooperative company. In many cases, farmers and members take an active part in the strategic decisions of a cooperative. These democratic and economic dimensions imply that competing interests often emerge if the group of members is too heterogeneous.

Questions and assignments

10.1 Why does the importance of cooperatives vary from product to product?
10.2 Why does the importance of cooperatives vary from country to country?
10.3 Describe briefly major advantages and disadvantages of cooperatives.
10.4 How will these advantages and disadvantages be affected by the global trends in liberalisation, globalisation, FDI, etc.?
10.5 Why and how may cooperatives change in future?
10.6 Which model(s), from 1 to 12, do you think will be successful?

11 Mergers and acquisitions in the food industry

Drivers and results

The trend towards more mergers and acquisitions, fewer and larger firms and growth and concentration in the food industry does not come about spontaneously, but is, rather, due to a series of driving forces, which may come from the outside world, or from inside companies. At the same time, the drivers can be either active or passive (proactive or defensive). Therefore, in total, there are four groups of drivers.

It is important that these driving forces are determined in each individual case as the basis for decision making and as targets for, e.g., a merger between food companies. There must be a clear aim to grow. Based on analyses of a wide range of mergers and acquisitions in the food sector, approximately 35 different driving forces have been identified which can justify and explain developments so far.

The concrete results of mergers and acquisitions – in hindsight and compared with the expectations prior to the mergers – are mixed and often negative. Based on broad experience, it is possible to identify a number of measures which can make mergers and acquisitions more successful in the future.

Introduction

Mergers, acquisitions and structural development are often not explicit goals as such, but are rather tools for achieving economic advantages – and thus increased revenue – in the short or long term. There are a number of factors which directly or indirectly can facilitate mergers, acquisitions and structural development. Three examples illustrate this:

> First, the retail sector is characterised by high concentration, which means that the food industry's market and bargaining power is limited. The consequence can therefore be that the food industry is forced to undergo similar concentration in the form of mergers and acquisitions.
>
> Second, many companies fear that competitors will quickly catch up on their technological lead, if the technology is easy to copy. In order to exploit technological advantage, it is therefore necessary to accelerate and push marketing and sales as much as possible. Mergers and acquisitions can therefore be a necessary means to increase production and marketing, etc.

Third, significant economies of scale continuously emerge, which encourages a trend towards larger and consequently fewer companies. In order to take advantage of economies of scale as much as possible, thereby maximising profits for owners, it is therefore necessary to grow by way of mergers, acquisitions, investments, etc.

In all cases, these three things – concentration in the retail sector, rapid utilisation of technology and the exploitation of new economies of scale – create a need for increased growth in order to maximise profits. Structural development in the form of mergers and acquisitions in the global food industry has been widespread in recent decades. The general driver, and desired outcome, has been the desire for more efficient production, the exploitation of economies of scale and a stronger market position, which involves aiming for improved earnings in the short or long term.

Overall rationale: improved earnings potential

The primary motive for mergers and acquisitions is, in almost all cases, to increase revenue for the company's owners. The merger is not an end in itself – but a means of generating more revenue in the short or long term. Mergers, acquisitions and structural development can both directly and indirectly generate more revenue: the direct effect is seen when increased volume with a constant gross margin results in greater profits.

The indirect effect is seen when, e.g., the acquisition of a company leads to efficiency improvements, the exploitation of synergies and increased market power, which subsequently results in an increase in income.

However, in some cases, a merger can be an end in itself, while at other times it can be a sub-goal along with other aims.

The general rule is thus that mergers and acquisitions should ensure increased profit – either through better transfer prices for the shareholders or through increased profit, which is then distributed among the shareholders or members.

Motives

There is a range of explanations for mergers and structural development that may represent important motives and reasons for choosing a strategy based on increased growth, concentration and possibly also internationalisation. In each case, the individual company must assess whether the advantages outweigh the increased risk. It is therefore essential to uncover the most important drivers behind mergers, acquisitions and structural development in order to be able to assess the existing opportunities and constraints.

The basic motive is often the desire to use resources in such a way that they create increased earnings in the short and / or long term, which often involves an investment or a cost increase, which only provides a profitable return after a number of years.

There are four fundamental types of motive or explanation for mergers, acquisitions and structural development. It may be *internal* factors in the company or *external* factors that explain growth and structural development. At the same time, there may be a *proactive* explanation, whereby a company anticipates and seeks to exploit new opportunities, or there may be a more passive and *defensive* explanation in that the company may be trying to reduce risks and threats. The various factors which can explain and justify growth and structural development are illustrated in Box 11.1.

The following describes the factors in more detail.

Economies of scale

The concept of economies of scale describes the situation in which a business achieves reduced costs per unit produced by increasing production. The advantages of economies of scale mean that companies become larger.

Box 11.1 Drivers behind growth and structural development in the food industry

	Internal	External
Active	Economies of scale	Access to cheap produce and resources
	Increase in productivity	Vertical integration
	Synergies	Market closeness
	Growth goal	Market share and dominance
	Managerial ambitions	Access to know-how
	Earnings and trade conditions	Liberalisation of capital markets
	Exploitation of know-how and technology	Positioning on an emerging market
	Control of marketing	Favourable purchasing opportunities
	Desire to diversify	Economic growth
	Desire to specialise	Improved infrastructure
	Attract qualified employees	
Passive	Risk spreading	Low market growth
	Protection of know-how and technology	Matching of customers
	Excess capacity	Larger product range
	Seasonal levelling	Removing competitors
	Merging is the last option for survival	Guarantee produce supplies
		Creation of entry barriers
		Competition law
		'Eat or be eaten'
		Investors expect growth

Source: Author's own presentation.

There are several reasons why production costs per unit will decrease with increasing levels of production. Initially, it is significant that the fixed costs of production can often be spread over more produced units. It is often possible to utilise existing production machinery better by, e.g., increasing production without increasing the number of employees and machines. Since the variable costs per unit are unchanged, or perhaps lower, an overall lower cost per produced unit is achieved.

Economies and diseconomies of scale are illustrated in Figure 11.1, which shows the average cost per produced unit in the long term with increasing production.

The figure shows that there is an economic benefit in becoming larger, as the marginal and average costs decline to a given level.

The goal is to achieve the lowest possible average costs in the long term as this means the greatest profit in the long term. This is achieved by reaching the so-called optimal production level. Theoretically, as mentioned above, this involves achieving lower and lower costs per unit produced as the size of the production facilities increases. However, this only applies until a certain level is reached, after which point the economies of scale are exhausted.

The cost curve in Figure 11.1 is not unambiguous, as it can vary from company to company. Some companies can obtain greater benefits by becoming larger,

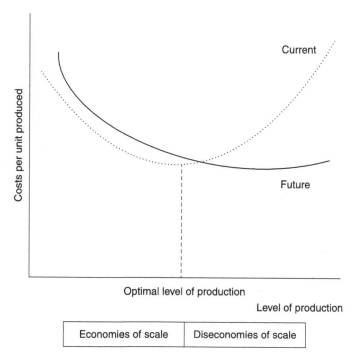

Figure 11.1 Economies and diseconomies of scale.
Source: Author's presentation.

while others have a lower optimum size. In addition, the curve is not stationary, but shifts to the right. The optimal level of production therefore becomes continuously larger and larger, which in turn helps to create growth.

The figure also shows the current and future cost curve. Opportunities to exploit economies of scale are increased by, among other things, technological progress and globalisation. The optimal level of production is thus shifted as shown in the figure, and diseconomies of scale occur much later than before.

Research and development often involves a lot of investment and costs, which enables significant economies of scale. Ollinger and Fernandez-Cornejo (1998) studied the development in the US agro-industry (pesticide industry) and found, among other things, that high research costs have a negative effect on the number of companies in an industrial sector. It also seems that small firms are more affected by these research costs than large firms.

Economies of scale can occur within, e.g., production, advertising, distribution and research and development. Economies of scale can also result in international expansion in the form of exports or foreign investment. The opportunity to advertise internationally will also stimulate the internationalisation of, e.g., brands.

Economies of scale can also emerge as a result of synergies, whereby, e.g., IT, distribution facilities or marketing can be better utilised by increasing sales, including new products in the portfolio and the like.

Many authors highlight economies of scale as being the most important explanation for mergers and acquisitions in the agroindustry (see, e.g., Sparling and van Duren, 2002).

Increases in productivity

As discussed previously, productivity is increasing significantly in the food industry. This continuing opportunity for productivity gains will help to promote mergers and acquisitions in the sector.

The explanation for this is that high productivity gains, together with relatively specific and thus fixed capacity costs – which, in many cases, is precisely the case for agribusinesses and food businesses – means that companies have to increase sales in order to create optimal adjustment. Because, at the same time, growth in demand is limited, this can instead be achieved through mergers and acquisitions.

It is assumed here that there is an annual average productivity increase of 3 per cent. This means that, if a company has constant production, the workforce (or other input factors) must be reduced by at least 3 per cent every year, in order to achieve an optimal adjustment without overcapacity.

Labour is in many cases a relatively fixed resource. In these cases, it is easier to increase productivity through growth than by making redundancies. In this way, the productivity gain will promote the tendency for mergers and acquisitions in the food industry.

At the same time, it also seems that mergers and acquisitions often lead to higher labour productivity (Ollinger *et al.*, 2005, 2006). Therefore, one can say that it is a self-reinforcing process.

Synergies

Synergy benefits and hence increased efficiency are probably the most used argument for mergers and acquisitions. Synergy benefits is, however, a broad term that covers a range of different benefits of mergers, acquisitions, etc.

Synergy basically means that '2 + 2 = 5'. That is, the value of the two combined assets is greater than the value of the two separate assets. Therefore, additional benefits are secured by combining two functions.

Synergy benefits can basically be static or dynamic. The *static* benefits can be in the form of cost reductions, whereby one closes dual functions (one headquarters instead of two) after the merger. Increased earnings may also occur because the two companies can exploit each other's sales and distribution network because bargaining power is increased, or because economies of scale can be better exploited. The static benefits are particularly important in sectors with very high competition, declining prices and excess capacity.

The *dynamic* benefits can, e.g., be larger and better development activities, whereby respective competences are exploited in order to improve long-term competitiveness and hence sales and earnings. The dynamic synergy benefits are important in sectors which are experiencing rapid technological development, i.e. which are development-driven (UNCTAD, 2000).

Growth goal

Many companies have growth as an overall goal. The ambition for growth can be seen in many companies' strategic considerations. It is characteristic that growth is an independent criterion for success. The objectives are emphasised when the company's overall corporate vision and strategies for future development are presented. It is also the hallmark of a number of food companies which seek to grow through international expansion.

Box 11.2 shows specific growth targets for a number of companies in the food and agroindustry:

Box 11.2 Growth as driver in companies

Danone's strategy of 'growth first' was confirmed once again by strong 2010.

Danone (2011)

Our aim is to double the size . . .

Unilever (2012)

Organic growth of revenues of 5 percent or more.

Kraft (2012)

General Mills' long-term growth model

Growth factor	Compound annual growth target
Net sales	Low single-digit
Segment operating profit	Mid single-digit
Earnings per share	High single-digit
Dividend yield	2–3%
Total return to shareholders	Double-digit

General Mills (2012).

Orkla's strategic focus will be on creating growth in its branded consumer goods operations.

Orkla (2012)

Aiming at becoming a leading company in the Asia-Oceania region.

Kirin (2012)

We continue to be outward looking for companies that would allow us to continue to grow.

Smithfield (2012)

Managerial ambitions

The company's leaders can have both economic and personal motives for creating an ever larger concern. Considerable prestige can be associated with being responsible for a large, expanding and possibly international company. At the same time, leaders can even have personal economic incentives to make the company grow, see, e.g. Wai (2003) and Gugler *et al.* (2003). Leaders' ambitions are naturally seldom explicit goals, so it is difficult to estimate their significance.

Earnings and trade conditions

Corporate earnings apparently also affect merger activity. The higher the earnings in the business community, the more mergers occur. High earnings give the acquiring companies greater opportunities to finance their expansion. Conversely, companies which are experiencing bad economic times have less financial strength and they will probably also be less willing to take risks.

Figure 11.2 shows clear correlation between the number of mergers in Europe and the European share price index in the period 1993–2002.

Fluctuations in the share index may be the result of both corporate earnings (internal influence) and the general trade conditions in the economy (external exposure). Figures from the USA show similar correlation between the share price index (here expressed as P/E – Price/Earnings) and the number of mergers over a long period of time (see Figure 11.3).

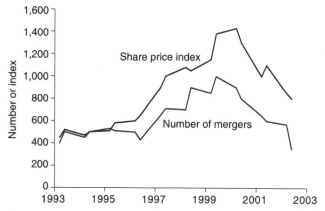

Figure 11.2 Correlation between share index and the number of mergers.
Source: KPMG (2003).

Note: European mergers and Morgan Stanley European share index.

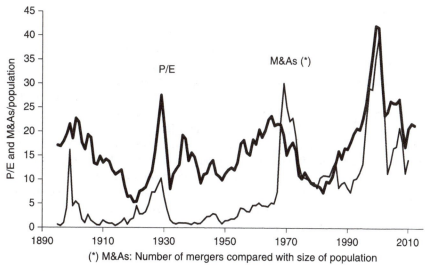

(*) M&As: Number of mergers compared with size of population

Figure 11.3 P/E and the number of mergers and acquisitions in the USA.
Source: Gugler *et al.* (2006) and author's own calculations.

There may be several explanations for this correlation. It is clear that a share price increase will boost optimism, and financial opportunities, among the purchasing companies. An increase in the share price of a firm can be interpreted as the result of good leadership and thus can be the basis for increased growth and acquisitions.

Empirical studies (Gugler *et al.*, 2003) show that acquiring companies have a relatively high share price before a merger or acquisition, but a relatively low share price for a period after a merger or acquisition.

Exploitation of know-how and technology

In a small country, a company, e.g. an abattoir, can have developed a technology that requires a large volume of sales to be profitable. It is therefore necessary to transfer and reuse their technology assets on other markets to remain a technological leader. Joint ventures, licensing or actual production abroad can be possibilities to capitalise on their know-how. In the European food industry, there are several examples of companies which have wanted to reuse and further utilise technology assets through investing in foreign companies.

Control of marketing

Sometimes it may be important for a company to control the entire process from production to sales to the final consumer. If a company, e.g., wants to maintain a strong image regarding service, quality, brand and lifestyle, it will have to invest in comprehensive marketing. It may therefore be necessary for the company to control all the links in the marketing chain in order to support the desired image.

Desire to diversify

It may be the strategic goal of a company to diversify its activities in various markets and with various products. The aim may be to use all its competences or there may be a desire to balance the company's strategic portfolio.

Especially if market growth in the company's current products is low, it may be advantageous for the company to move into other areas where growth is higher and where the company's competitive strengths can be exploited.

The desire to diversify played a significant role in the global wave of mergers in the late 1960s. According Oustapassidis *et al.* (1995), the main motives for mergers in the EU food industry during the period were to diversify investments and to strengthen market position (market share and dominance).

The increasing focus on core activities, however, means that the motive has declined in importance. According to, e.g., Azevedo (1999), the motive to diversify no longer plays a significant role today.

Desire to specialise

In recent years, there has been a trend towards further specialisation and a focus on 'core business', etc. The peripheral business areas are sold off, while the core activities are expanded in the form of organic growth and direct mergers and acquisitions. Thus, the market share and the company's size regarding core activities are increased.

Cadbury Schweppes entered a demerger in 2008, whereby its global confectionery business was separated from its US beverage unit. The food company, Danisco, is an example of a company which has focused on its core activities and has divested its more peripheral activities. The Norwegian chemical company, Yara, also specialised and demerged part of its non-core business within food and agribusiness.

Attract qualified employees

It is considerably easier, *ceteris paribus*, for large and expanding businesses to attract skilled labour. The larger the company, the better it is able to meet the specific needs of future employees. Furthermore, there are more opportunities for employees to work in different departments with different tasks in large companies.

Finally, large companies are also more well known, which means that it is easier for them to attract new employees. A company's corporate image and reputation has an important influence on a jobseeker's choice for future employment.

Risk spreading

The economic cycle never follows the same pattern in all product areas or in all countries. By spreading activities into several markets and / or products, companies can therefore reduce the disadvantages related to changing market conditions. The spreading of risk will often result in growth and investment in new activities, possibly in the form of mergers and / or acquisitions.

Protection of know-how and technology

This motive is defensive, as it is reflects the fear that competitors will narrow the company's technological lead. Especially if the product is easy to copy, it will be necessary for the company to quickly enter major foreign markets in order to reduce competitors' incentives. The significant market expansion will also require growth.

Box 11.3 Demerger

A demerger is a business strategy in which a single business is broken into components, either to operate on their own, to be sold or to be dissolved. A demerger allows a large company, such as a conglomerate, to raise capital by selling off divisions or components that are no longer part of the business's core product line, or to create separate legal entities to handle different operations. It is the converse of a merger or acquisition.

Demergers can have a positive impact on the quality of management as they allow the management of demerged companies to focus on their core business, they make companies easier for investors to analyse (by simplifying the business) and they often demonstrate a management focus on increasing shareholder value.

A demerger may be full or partial. A partial demerger means that the parent company retains a stake (sometimes a majority stake) in the demerged business.

Sometimes a partial demerger will force the market to separately value the business that is demerged, in the expectation that this will lead to a higher sum-of-the-parts valuation of the parent company.

Excess capacity

Excess capacity as a motive for mergers and acquisitions has two dimensions:

> First, general overcapacity in an industrial sector means that structural adjustment and efficiency improvements, as long as we are dealing with more permanent overcapacity, will be necessary. In reality, it transpires that relatively many mergers and acquisitions also occur in sectors with overcapacity. The steel, automobile and chemical industries have been highlighted as sectors with high overcapacity. However, the entire agroindustry also often experiences substantial overcapacity, as there is relatively weak market growth, relatively capital-intensive production and often very specific production plants with few alternative uses. Abattoirs, dairies and agribusinesses have in several cases had significant overcapacity.
>
> The starting point for a company is that overcapacity in the market puts pressure on earnings. After a merger or acquisition, the least competitive plants are closed, the least competent leaders are removed and the administrative set-up is streamlined, etc. The desired result is that the company achieves an increasing market share, while unprofitable resources are removed and the entire sector ends up with reduced capacity.
>
> A study of over 1,000 cases in the USA shows that overcapacity is the most important reason for mergers and acquisitions (see Bower, 2001).
>
> Second, overcapacity gives rise to other types of mergers and acquisitions. The desire to utilise overcapacity often leads the company to consider options for organic growth. Instead of selling free production capacity, and thus perhaps risking that a new competitor will emerge, a company can exploit capacity for other purposes. If there is also a synergy with the already established activities and there is an earnings contribution to the company, it may be an obvious approach, which also results in increased growth. Excess capacity is thereby made usable through diversification and mergers and / or acquisitions.

Box 11.4 Kraft Foods' acquisition of Cadbury

In 2009, the US food company, Kraft Foods, launched a bid for Cadbury, the UK-listed confectionary company. The challenge for Kraft Foods was how to buy Cadbury when it was not for sale.

Initially, Cadbury rejected the offers from Kraft Foods, as management saw no strategic advantage in a merger with the Americans and they believed that the price which was being offered was too low. The management at Cadbury believed more in a strong future as an independent confectionary manufacturer and feared that a merger would result in an 'unfocused conglomerate' with businesses in 'unattractive categories'. As a consequence, Kraft Foods increased its offer, which this time was delivered directly to Cadbury's shareholders, thereby making it a hostile takeover attempt.

Meanwhile, the US confectionary giant Hershey came forward as a potential buyer, like a 'white knight' coming to the rescue of Cadbury from the clutches of Kraft Foods. Hershey was interested in buying Cadbury because it would broaden its access to faster-growing international markets. After a battle that lasted more than 100 days, Cadbury's board of directors said 'yes' to an offer of 840 pence per share, of which Cadbury's shareholders received 500 pence in cash and the rest as Kraft shares, while there was also an extra return of 10 pence per share for Cadbury shareholders. Within hours of Kraft taking control of the British confectioner, the three most senior directors quit, while a significant number of Cadbury managers and executives quit within months of the takeover.

Strategic purpose

Kraft's reason for purchasing Cadbury was to become a global market leader in the confectionary market and to gain access to emerging markets. With the acquisition of Cadbury, Kraft Foods became the world leader in snacks, a category that now accounts for more than half of the company's total revenue.

The combination of Kraft Foods and Cadbury and the economies of scale were intended to provide the scale necessary to grow sales and distribution in new and existing markets, delivering US $1 billion in incremental revenue synergies – in addition to $750 million in cost synergies – by 2013.

From a strategic perspective, the merger of Kraft Foods and Cadbury was supposed to:

- create a strong combined portfolio with leading market positions in the fast-growing confectionery category;
- have a significantly strengthened footprint in developing markets, with enhanced scale;
- benefit from world-class infrastructure in traditional and instant consumption channels; and
- offer meaningful revenue synergies and significant cost savings.

Source: Kraft (2012)

Kraft Foods

Kraft was the world's second largest food company, which manufactured and marketed packaged food products, including snacks, beverages, cheese, convenience meals and packaged grocery products.

Cadbury

Cadbury was the second largest confectionery group in the world. The company manufactured and marketed mainly three kinds of confectionery products – chocolate, gum and candy.

Seasonal levelling

In several areas of the agro and food industry, there are significant seasonal variations, and production plants can be out of operation for very long periods of time. This may be the case for, e.g., sugar factories, but there can also be large seasonal fluctuations for manufacturers of canned and frozen goods, and indeed throughout the fresh produce industry. The opportunity to utilise the free capacity in the low season has, in several cases, been the motive for acquisitions and growth.

Merging is the last option for survival

Merging can also be the only way out for a company in financial crisis. A firm can actively seek to be acquired by, or merge with, another company because it is not possible to continue operating as an independent unit. In this case, therefore, the motive is defensive in nature.

Clearly a company's bargaining situation becomes worse as the possibility for economic survival gradually disappears. Therefore it may be tactically correct to seek a merger or similar as soon as the risk of economic collapse can be discerned.

Many newly started companies which are, e.g., based on new technology or another form of innovation may have the goal to be acquired by another larger company from the very start. The newly established company recognises in advance that it does not have the competences or incentives to develop into an actual concern. The goal is rather to develop a unique product or concept, to demonstrate its technical and commercial opportunities and then to be purchased by another company, which can quickly and effectively exploit the new knowledge.

In the agro and food industries, there are numerous examples of companies having to agree to an acquisition or merger because it is the only way to maintain the maximum value of the company (see Box 11.5).

Box 11.5 From 'merger as the only solution' to 'world leader'

Parts of the Brazilian food industry have undergone major changes since 2005.

In 2006, Sadia, a major Brazilian food company, attempted a hostile takeover of Perdigão, another Brazilian food company. Two bids were submitted. However, both were rejected by a majority of Perdigão's shareholders. Subsequently, Perdigão overtook Sadia to become Brazil's second-largest food company.

In 2008, Sadia made the first loss in its history after bets on the continued appreciation of Brazil's currency went badly wrong following the onset of the global economic crisis. As a consequence, Sadia was forced to seek capital from outside investors. When no investors came forward, a merger was the only solution and the company agreed to discuss a merger with Perdigão. In 2009, the two companies merged, and Brasil Foods (BRF) was established. The vision was to create a Brazilian multinational company which was capable of competing for a leading position on global markets. The merger was completed in 2012.

Brasil Foods is now one of the largest food companies in the world by market capitalisation and is the world leader in the production of proteins, with a 9 per cent share of the international trade in the sector. It is also the largest exporter of poultry meat.

Today, the company is involved in the raising, production and slaughtering of poultry, pork and beef, as well as in the processing and sale of fresh meat, processed products, milk, dairy products, pasta, frozen vegetables and soya bean derivatives. The company's product portfolio includes whole chickens and cuts of chicken, turkey, pork and beef; hams, mortadella, sausages and other smoked products; burgers, nuggets and meatballs; frozen lasagnas, pizzas, cheese breads, pies and vegetables; milk, dairy products and desserts; juices, soy milk and soy juices; margarines; soy bran and refined soya flour, which is also used as animal feed.

Source: Brasil Foods (2012)

Access to cheap produce and resources

In addition to raw produce, we may also be dealing with labour, capital and land. The price of these factors of production varies widely from country to country, and companies often locate labour and technology-intensive production in countries with low wages. This motive is known in several parts of the food sector, which are directly dependent on raw produce supplies from the agricultural or fisheries sector.

The establishment of biotech companies in Asia has also, in several cases, been based on access to highly qualified and cheap labour.

Vertical integration

Vertical mergers occur when a company acquires or merges with another company, which is located immediately before or after the company in the value chain. For example, a company may purchase one of its suppliers or one of its customers. The motive can be to ensure more flexible production planning, lower transportation and transaction costs, smaller reserves, etc.

Furthermore, one can minimise problems regarding asymmetric information and moral hazards which can arise if there is not any kind of vertical integration. Moral hazard can arise if one of the contracting parties – after entering into the contract – has an incentive to do something other than what was agreed. The risk of moral hazard may arise when the contracting party has nothing to lose by taking on greater risk.

These benefits must, however, be viewed in relation to possible disadvantages, e.g. the relationship to other customers can be adversely affected by a forward vertical merger in the sector.

Finally, it should also be mentioned that there are other forms of vertical integration than just mergers. Contract production, strategic alliances, etc. can also be used to ensure or improve vertical integration.

Smithfield Foods, the world's largest pork producer and processor, is an example of a food business which focuses on vertical integration, both forward and backward, as a strategy and, in relation to growth and acquisitions, focuses on vertical integration.

There are also indications that in the food, drink and consumer goods manufacturing and retail sectors there is an increasing focus on supply chain optimisation, particularly in the face of rising commodity prices and sourcing challenges (KPMG, 2012). Here, vertical integration is a way to enhance and secure the supply chain.

The spread of biotechnology in the agro-industrial complex provides an extra new dimension in vertical integration. The rights to use biotech knowledge (intellectual property rights – IPRs) create pressure for either further vertical integration or strategic alliances and contract production. If IPRs are well defined, transaction costs will be relatively small, and thus alliances and contract production will be obvious means to use. If IPRs are not precise or well defined, then vertical integration through mergers and acquisitions may be advantageous.

Market closeness

This motive can also be important for the food sector. If companies gain an advantage by offering fresh milk or fresh meat, it may be advantageous to locate production close to consumers for transportation reasons. Production which is close to customers facilitates better service, which strengthens customer confidence in the company.

Market share and dominance

There is often a connection between earnings and market share. For example, Cotterill (2000) has demonstrated very clear correlation between the concentration of supermarkets and supermarket prices (see Figure 11.4).

The figure shows clear correlation between concentration and price levels. Although price levels can be the result of other factors, it can be established that the correlation is significant and that highly concentrated supermarkets manage to maintain relatively high selling prices.

In practice the correlation means that earnings and profitability increase with increasing market share – to a certain limit. If the market share is high, companies can achieve a more or less dominant position over competitors, suppliers and buyers. Increased growth and market share can thereby directly increase revenue.

Other studies contain evaluations of the relationship between market share and market prices. An analysis from the University of Nebraska (Azzam, 2002) shows, e.g., that mergers in several sectors of the US food industry, in most cases, result in higher consumer prices.

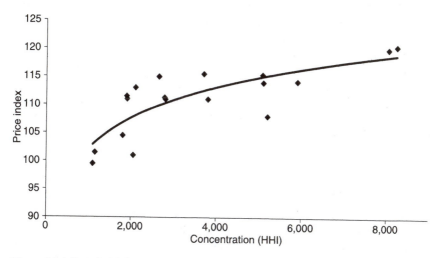

Figure 11.4 Correlation between supermarket concentration (Herfindahl index) and their prices in the USA (1999).

Source: Cotterill (2000).

Newmark (2004) refers to numerous studies of the relationship between concentration and market prices. He emphasises, among other things, that numerous factors, besides concentration, can affect prices, including differences in quality and transportation costs. Therefore, one has to be very careful when concluding that concentration is the cause of higher prices, even if there is a statistical correlation.

Access to know-how

Especially for the very technology-intensive industries, it may be useful to build an international position close to research and development centres. Knowledge in biotechnology, functional foods, process technology and consumer trends can be important know-how, which the food industry could obtain through new investments.

Liberalisation of capital markets

The international capital markets are becoming increasingly liberalised, which has a significant effect on merger and acquisition activity worldwide. In most industrialised countries, capital flows freely across national borders and the same trend is underway in many developing countries. The political and economic liberalisation in, e.g. Central and Eastern Europe and China over the past 10–15 years has played a crucial role in the distribution of the world's total foreign direct investment (FDI).

In 2011, China had the second highest number of foreign investments. Both China and the Central and Eastern European countries have thus experienced a significant increase in foreign investment since the early 1990s (see Figure 11.5).

Since the early 1990s, China and Central and Eastern Europe's role as host countries for FDI has doubled, seen in relation to the world's total FDI. The market orientation of the Central and Eastern European economies in the 1990s also meant that many of the countries' companies were purchased by foreign companies, which would have been unthinkable before the fall of the Berlin Wall. Central and Eastern Europe thus became an important host region for foreign investment.

Positioning on an emerging market

In countries with a market undergoing economic development, companies can establish themselves in order to get ahead of future competition. The aim is to expand while the market is growing rapidly and to simultaneously gather local knowledge and experience and build customer knowledge and dependency, all of which reduce the entry opportunities for subsequent competitors.

It can obviously be difficult to identify the countries or areas which are under development and which at a later date will develop rapidly and become attractive economies. Positioning on a market under development therefore involves a substantial risk that the market will not experience the expected future development.

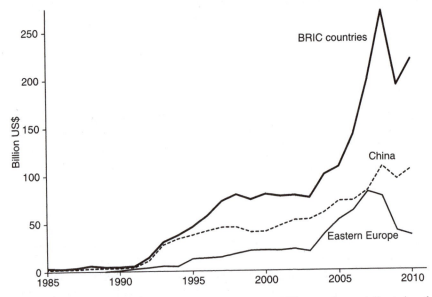

Figure 11.5 Foreign direct investment in China, the BRIC countries and Central and Eastern Europe.

Source: UNCTAD (2012).

However, new countries joining free trade areas or economic unions often implies considerable expectations regarding increased growth and attractiveness. An example is the ongoing expansion of the EU with new members, which has meant that there has been increasing interest in investing in the future new member states (see Figure 11.6).

Spain and Portugal both became members of the EU in 1986. As the figure shows, strong growth in foreign investment in Spain and Portugal occurred in the period before their formal entry. Similar progress is seen in connection with the enlargement of the EU in 2004 when six Central and Eastern European countries joined. Once again, there was a marked increase in foreign investment in the countries upon their accession.

Favourable purchasing opportunities

Mergers and acquisitions can occur when companies are interested in acquisitions or mergers, or when companies are interested in being acquired or taken over. In the food industry, there are numerous examples of floundering companies which have wanted to be acquired.

The purchasing company is likely to have the skills that the ailing company does not. At the same time, the buyer has an opportunity to increase both growth and market share relatively rapidly. The more in difficulty the one company, the

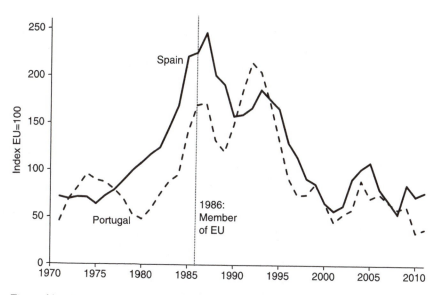

Figure 11.6 Foreign direct investment in Spain and Portugal before and after their entry into the EU.

Source: Author's own calculation based on World Bank (2012b).

more favourable the terms on which the buyer can take over the company – *ceteris paribus*.

Economic growth

The economic situation greatly influences interest in mergers and investment. During economic booms, earnings and willingness to take risks are increased, and thus the interest in expanding and investing becomes correspondingly greater. If one looks at the USA, there is clear correlation between economic growth (business cycle) and the number of mergers in the food industry (see Figure 11.7).

Improved infrastructure

Improved infrastructure, easier and cheaper transport and improved logistics can be an important motive for foreign acquisitions and investments.

Since the mid-1990s, foreign investment in the horticulture industry in several African and Southern and Central American countries has been increasing. The driving force was not access to raw produce, but access to finished consumer goods produced with much lower labour and energy costs. In many cases, the investments were made by European or US investors. A crucial precondition for these investments was that it was possible to send fresh produce from these countries to the European and American markets by air at a competitive price.

Low market growth

Market growth in the agro and food industries is generally low compared to other sectors. Consumption of food does not increase much over time, even with rising income and consumption opportunities. This is significant for the companies'

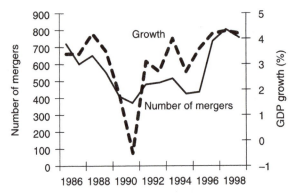

Figure 11.7 Number of mergers in the food industry and GDP growth in the USA.
Source: Author's calculations based on Rogers (2000) and OECD (2012c).

growth opportunities. When market growth is small, it will only be possible to expand considerably by taking market share from other companies. Organic growth therefore implies that other companies give up their market share which, *ceteris paribus*, can be difficult. For this reason, it is often more advantageous to achieve growth through mergers and acquisitions. A low market growth rate will, *ceteris paribus*, facilitate structural development based on mergers and acquisitions.

Matching of customers

Market and consumer-oriented companies must adapt to demand. The retail sector, which is often the food industry's customer, has in recent years been characterised by high concentration and internationalisation (see Figure 11.8). The European retail sector is an example of very intense concentration, with few, but very large retail chains. It is expected that the 10 largest retail chains in Europe will account for 80 per cent of the market by 2020 (see Hampl, 2002).

It is generally the case that the retail sector is most concentrated in the most developed countries (see Chapter 12) and therefore ongoing structural changes will occur in the retail sector in line with economic development.

The food industry has, therefore, to some extent, been forced to follow the same development to preserve the balance of power. In practice this means that mergers

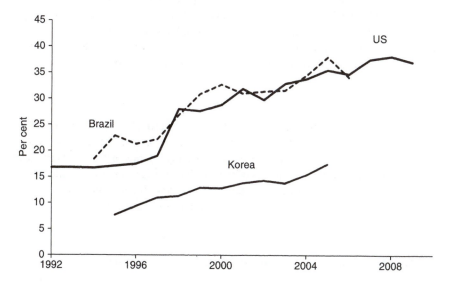

Figure 11.8 Development in concentration in the retail sector in different countries.

Source: USDA (2012e) and Stiegert and Dong (2009).

Note: USA: Top four firms' share of grocery store sales.

Brazil: Concentration rate (CR3) in the Brazilian retail sector.

Korea: National CR4 of conventional supermarket sector.

and investments are often made on the basis of a need to match the ever larger and more global retail chains.

It is thus possible to see very clear correlation between the retailers' and food industry's concentration in the European countries.

Larger product range

Retail increasingly requires that suppliers are fewer, larger and able to offer a full range within individual product categories. The requirement for a wider range often means that companies have to expand production to meet this requirement.

To meet this need, some companies strategically acquire both domestic and foreign companies. The need for foreign acquisitions and investments can occur, e.g., when dairy companies are faced with the demand to supply retail chains abroad with fresh products. In these cases, it is often necessary to invest in the local dairy sector close to retail customers in order to meet demand.

Removing competitors

Through mergers and acquisitions, companies can eliminate competitors, thus reducing competition so that the company can increase the sales price. At the same time, there can of course also be other benefits in the form of rationalisation gains, etc. The desire to eliminate a competitor to reduce competition will rarely be a particularly official motive for good reasons. However, there are examples of mergers and acquisitions in, especially, the dairy and brewery sectors, whereby the desire to eliminate a rival company has been a major motive.

Guarantee produce supplies

Stable access to raw produce through backward vertical integration may also necessitate investments and acquisitions. In such cases we are dealing with a defensive measure to preserve the existing supply of raw produce. There are examples of the securing of supplies of raw produce being a very important motive for investment and acquisitions in the food industry. Such examples are most often found in countries where cooperative organisation is insignificant.

Box 11.6 China's investments in Africa: access to natural resources

In recent years, FDI in natural resources in Africa has been particularly strong. The African continent is rich in natural resources and more than half of FDI inflows have gone into the natural resource sector. Furthermore, Chinese FDI in general and in Africa in particular has risen substantially (see Figures 11.9 and 11.10) and has been increasingly targeting natural resources in Africa in recent years.

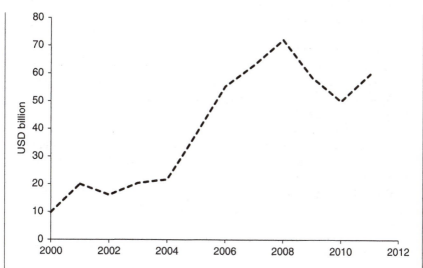

Figure 11.9 FDI flows to Africa.

Source: African Economic Outlook (2012).

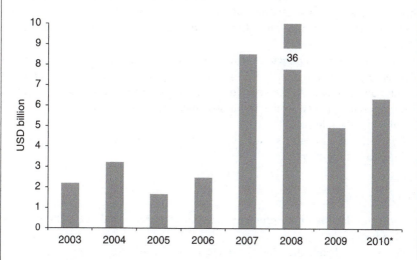

Figure 11.10 China: FDI flows to sub-Saharan countries.

Source: Author's calculations based on UNCTAD (2012) and IMF (2011).

The Chinese Government has identified certain industries and types of project in Africa in which it encourages Chinese enterprises to invest. These include industrial processing, agriculture, natural resources and infrastructure (UNCTAD, 2007). Access to natural resources is an important instrument to support economic development in China.

Access to natural resources is also becoming more and more important, which reflects an increase in demand from China. Substantial investments made or announced recently in Africa are related to this. It is a characteristic of Chinese firms that they seek to secure their natural resources from Africa.

China's investments in Africa have mainly been in manufacturing, resource extraction, construction and other services. China's investments in African agriculture are still insignificant compared to those in oil, gas, mineral resources and infrastructure.

Since 2003, Chinese firms have become very active in investing directly in natural resources in sub-Saharan Africa. Chinese investment in the resource sector extends to many countries and, during 2003–07, Chinese firms were involved in 81 projects in at least 25 countries (IMF, 2011).

Most Chinese enterprises which are investing in natural resource sectors are state owned and receive government grants or loans from state-owned banks.

Creation of entry barriers

The creation of entry barriers means that other or new companies will have difficulty getting in and establishing themselves in the sector. A company has a vested interest in keeping other firms out of the market and this can happen in several ways.

The acquisition of companies which may otherwise be sold to competitors, as well as acquisitions in the supply and purchasing links, can prevent new players coming on the scene. At the same time, increased concentration and the creation of large competitively strong businesses mean that companies lose interest in moving into the market.

Generally, an offensive strategy based on mergers and acquisitions will create and increase entry barriers.

Competition law

Competition law can both promote and restrict mergers and acquisitions in the food industry.

On the one hand, there are concrete examples of national or international competition laws which have forbidden or prevented a merger or an acquisition. In the period 1990–2012, the European Commission banned 22 such mergers, although this only represents less than 1 per cent of the reported cases. In addition, there have also been a significant number of conditional approvals (see European Commission, 2012). Merger control is now practised in over 60 countries.

It is also generally assumed that weak competition legislation creates a favourable basis for mergers, or at least that strong competition regulation hinders overly dominant mergers. Both observations imply that competition law limits the number of mergers.

On the other hand, there are also examples of competition law promoting mergers. Cooperation between companies, which either directly or indirectly aims to restrict competition, is basically prohibited. This ban can, to some extent, be circumvented by merging instead of cooperating. Therefore, there are examples of food companies which have merged instead of entering into strategic cooperation.

'Eat or be eaten'

There are numerous examples of companies which have undertaken mergers or acquisitions to avoid other companies' expansionist plans (see e.g. Graney, 1998; Doyle, 2002; Cook, 2002; Economist.com, 2003).

There can be several reasons for this 'eat-or-be eaten' philosophy:

> First, a company will lose its competitiveness if it does not actively exploit economies of scale and efficiency advantages through mergers and acquisitions. The company will therefore lose market share and earnings, and closure or acquisition by another firm may be the eventual outcome for the company.
>
> Second, it is typically large companies which buy smaller companies. A company which is not growing can therefore gradually lose the ability to decide the nature and form of future ownership. Hostile corporate takeovers usually involve relatively small companies.
>
> Third, the leaders of many companies prefer to remain economically and financially independent rather than be bought (see, e.g., Gorton *et al.*, 2002). Companies can therefore reduce the risk of being bought up by growing and purchasing companies themselves.

Box 11.7 Drivers behind M&As in the Danish agri and food industry

A number of Danish companies in the agri and food industry have been interviewed about their motives behind recent M&As. The answers have been given anonymously and by members of the management team. A major part of the agri and food industry – measured by turnover – was represented in the survey.

A list of 26 different drivers behind M&As were presented to the companies. The companies then ranked these drivers as 'very important', 'medium' and 'less important'. The results are presented in Table 11.1.

As the table shows, 'economies of scale', 'market share and dominance' and 'matching of customers' are the most important drivers behind M&As. It means that internal, external, active and passive drivers are important. In general, the answers from the companies had a rather uniform pattern.

Table 11.1 Ranking of drivers behind M&As in Danish agri and food industry

Most important
1) Economies of scale
2) Market share and dominance
3) Matching of customers
4) Utilisation of know-how and technology
5) Larger product range
6) Growth goal
7) Desire to specialise
8) Positioning in an emerging market

Medium
9) Control of marketing
10) Low market growth
11) Removing competitors
12) Increase in productivity
13) Desire to diversify
14) Protection of know-how and technology
15) Market closeness
16) Creation of entry barriers
17) Economic growth
18) Excess capacity
19) Favourable purchasing opportunities
20) Guarantee produce supplies
21) Competition law

Less important
22) Managerial ambitions
23) Risk spreading
24) Access to know-how
25) Access to cheap produce and resources
26) Liberalisation of capital markets

Source: Author's presentation based on interviews and surveys.

Investors expect growth

Among many financial investors there is a persistent expectation for significant growth in the companies that they can potentially invest in. Increased growth is, *ceteris paribus*, met with increasing share prices. A study of over 1,000 cases in the USA shows that the expectations and motivations of investors were the reasons for mergers and acquisitions in 13 per cent of cases (see Bower, 2001).

Investors are divided into growth and value investors. Growth investors buy shares in companies whose business is growing rapidly, whereas value investors buy shares at a discount. A study by IFII (2012) which was based on the development during the last 10 years shows that value shares (with P/E ratios of 12 or lower) beat growth shares (> 17 per cent increase in earnings) substantially. However, this merely illustrates that growth is a key driver behind the investments made by investors, but that growth is far from being synonymous with good performance in the long term.

Results of mergers

Generally speaking, it can be said that mergers do not succeed to the extent expected by the companies involved.

Studies of whether mergers live up to their initial success criteria give differing results regarding the percentage of businesses which are successful. It is important in relation to the studies to be aware of how this success is measured, as it is clear that some of the differences are due to the way in which success is defined. If the purpose of a merger is a desire for increased growth or, e.g., greater diversification, it is misleading to simply examine earnings before and immediately after a merger (see also Box 11.8.)

Box 11.8 The result of merger – compared to what?

Assessing the results and consequences of a merger will always be difficult and uncertain. A merger often has very long-term effects, and it is impossible to completely isolate the effects of a merger from other internal or external effects. However, it is possible to evaluate the result (i.e. the sum of all the realised benefits) of a merger by comparing a company's profit – before and after a merger – assuming *ceteris paribus*.

One can thus compare the realised result (profit) after a merger with 1) hypothetical profit as if the merger had not taken place; 2) profit before the merger; 3) financial performance as a benchmark of comparable companies; or 4) the forecasted profit after the merger:

1) Result without merger: an expected hypothetical result as if the merger had not taken place.
2) Pre-merger result. Result one year before the merger.
3) Result from an industry benchmark.
4) Expected result. The result according to projections, etc. delivered by the company as a basis for the decision to merge or not.

The actual result compared to alternative comparable results is illustrated in Figure 11.11.

As can be seen in the figure, the result of a merger can be beneficial and contribute positively to the merged companies' earnings, even though the expected result, which was the basis for the decision to merge, is not met.

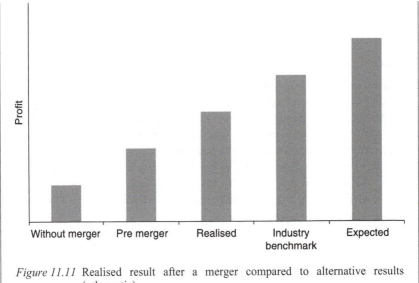

Figure 11.11 Realised result after a merger compared to alternative results (schematic).

Source: Author's presentation.

Since increased profit, in the short or long term, is usually the overall motive, there is general agreement that the return to owners is the best criterion of success. VSC Growth (2011) reviews the success rate of mergers and acquisitions and includes more than 70 technical papers which were reviewed by researchers and academics across the world. The conclusion is that approximately 70 per cent of all mergers and acquisitions fail to achieve expectations and that more than half destroy value.

A study (PA Consulting, 2004) finds that only 23 per cent of all mergers earn back the capital expenses. Furthermore, the share price only increases in 30 per cent of companies after the announcement of the merger. Finally, the expected synergy effects are not realised in 70 per cent of merger cases, while productivity falls in the months after a merger in up to 50 per cent of cases.

KPMG (1999) analysed 700 mergers and acquisitions made during the period 1996–98. A total of 107 companies from all parts of the world were included in the study. The conclusion was, among others, that as much as 83 per cent of mergers and acquisitions do not provide returns for shareholders. Indeed, there is a direct loss in half of the cases.

KPMG (2011) presents the results of five subsequent analyses. There are no major changes in the overall conclusions. However, there is a small relative increase in the number of mergers which add value to businesses. Figure 11.12 shows the extent to which mergers improve or worsen the situation of merging companies in the period 1997/98 to 2007/09. As stated, a relatively constant and moderate proportion of the mergers add value to the businesses. The figure also shows the balance between buyers and sellers in each period.

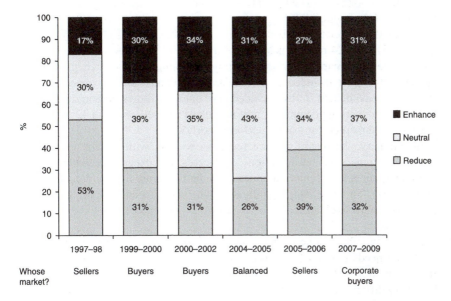

Figure 11.12 Trends in M&A value enhancement.

Source: KPMG (2011).

Various studies by McKinsey focus more on growth after the mergers. Here only 12 per cent of businesses achieve a growth rate that is greater than their competitors. Additionally, only 11 per cent managed to maintain their growth rate in the third quarter after the announcement of the merger (see Bieshaar *et al.*, 2001).

Another study by Deloitte Consulting (2002) shows that the strategic goals of the planned period are only achieved in 32 per cent of all mergers and acquisitions. Furthermore, according to Chamman *et al.* (1998), returns to shareholders in the first 10 years are not achieved in 60 per cent of cases. A study of 300 large mergers and acquisitions conducting during 1995–2001 shows that 61 per cent of the acquiring firms lost money – here measured by the development in share prices relative to the market average after 1 year (BusinessWeek, 2002). Among the main reasons for this are:

- purchase price too high: the company has paid too much compared to the market price because of expectations of additional earnings, which have not been realised;
- a failure to merge and integrate the businesses fast enough;
- cost savings and synergies were overestimated.

Accenture (2012) analysed 500 mergers and acquisitions completed during the years 2002–09. The success of the mergers was measured by calculating the returns to the shareholders of the merged firms relative to the returns of comparable companies. The return to shareholders was measured 24 months after the merger (see Figure 11.13).

This method is relatively objective and measurable, but it is inherently an open question whether 24 months is sufficient to show all the effects of a merger and whether the benchmark group is sufficiently representative. The share price development is therefore included in the standard of reference and it is expected that a future expected benefit is also included. The analysis shows that, in over half of the cases, the merging companies perform relatively well, while in 42 per cent of the cases, the merged companies perform poorly.

In summary, the overall picture seems to be that, with certain reservations due to differences in the definitions of success, the expected economic gains from mergers are not met in more than half of cases (see, e.g., Bieshaar *et al.*, 2001). This is a fact, regardless of whether companies apply growth, or the more 'objective' indicator of a return to shareholders, as the yardstick for success.

Despite the above, one cannot conclude that mergers are generally fiascos. First, one needs to compare with the alternative to a merger or an acquisition. If a competitor had made the acquisition, the alternative would probably have been very different and more negative. Defensive mergers and acquisitions occur, as mentioned earlier, where companies try to reduce risks and threats. In these cases, constant earnings or even a small decline after the merger or acquisition is satisfactory. Second, the merger or acquisition may still be favourable, even

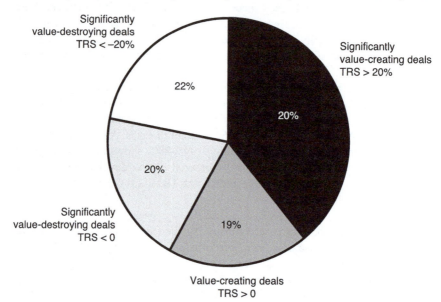

Figure 11.13 Total return to shareholders (TRS) versus industry benchmarks.

Source: Kilde: Accenture (2012).

Note: TRS measured 24 months after deal announced.

though expectations are not completely satisfied. Third, many consequences may be invisible or impossible to quantify. The value of increased market power, for example, is very difficult, and often completely inappropriate, to quantify. Fourth, one can interpret a merger or an acquisition as a long-term investment where it can take several years before any positive effects are discernible. The study by KPMG (1999) presents results one year after a company merger or acquisition, which is a very short and inadequate timeframe.

The conclusion should therefore be:

- that a merger's success or failure should be assessed in relation to the original motives. If the motive was, e.g., defensive, one cannot expect a significant increase in earnings;
- that mergers and acquisitions generally do not provide the owners a market return in the short term;
- that mergers and acquisitions are long-term investments so the total return can only be calculated after several years, and the basis of comparison benchmark (the alternative) can be very difficult to determine;
- that the pros and cons of mergers and acquisitions vary greatly depending on whether they are national or international, whether they are inside or outside the existing core areas, whether they are well planned and whether they are implemented determinedly in the organisation.

Requirements for growing and merging companies

With increasing company size, mergers and acquisitions increase the demands for control, management, financing, etc. Generally, there are several conditions that must be met before a company can create and manage increased growth.

Growth requires additional financing. Venture capital is often necessary to generate growth in the form of acquisitions, investments, etc. If loan capital has to be used, it may be necessary to relinquish influence to other parties. This balance between influence and capital must be carefully weighed.

A certain degree of consolidation and strength is required. Sufficient equity must be created which can withstand economic downturns, competition from other companies, investments in development, etc.

Growth is a strategic decision, which of course must be supported and which must be backed up by tactical and operational plans. There must be agreement and understanding regarding the ends and means.

Specifically for cooperatives it is also the case that, as size increases, so does the distance from the member / supplier to the company. Active ownership must, therefore, be further stimulated, so that the members become involved, to an appropriate extent, in major decisions and provide support for the company's values, mission and goals.

If a company grows from being a small local firm to a global concern, new and different demands will face the board and management. Competences in the area must be continuously developed.

There are, e.g., large differences depending on whether a business is focused on the domestic market, highly export-oriented or internationalised via FDI. Exporting directly to export markets requires completely different competences than producing through companies abroad.

Companies which are experiencing significant growth and development will often be exposed to increased risk in the short term. More choices and gambles must be made if the desired benefits are to be achieved in the longer term. However, there must also be an acceptance that not all gambles will proceed as planned. On the one hand, one should not hastily stop an agreed development plan, simply because not everything is going as planned. On the other hand, one has to follow the development closely, so one is in a position to carry out targeted modifications.

How do mergers succeed? Specific experiences

Growth is increasingly achieved, as previously discussed, through mergers and acquisitions. In this way, growth is achieved more quickly, but also with significantly greater risks.

Based on these observations, among other things, a number of specific studies have been conducted on a large number of companies to investigate their preparation, planning, management and follow-up, etc. in connection with mergers and acquisitions. By comparing these measures with the subsequent economic performance of the companies, it is possible to assess how companies can achieve the best results of mergers and acquisitions.

The studies show that overall there are two different explanations as to why a merger is successful or not: the qualitative and the quantitative parameters.

The qualitative parameters comprise the parts of a merger or an acquisition that have something to do with the corporate culture, information to employees, allocation of new roles regarding responsibility, position in the organisation, etc. The point is that, in order to achieve a successful merger, it is important that management addresses these issues. An important management task is therefore to remove the employees' natural insecurity regarding a merger or an acquisition and to create and communicate a new shared company spirit, with clear visions and strategies.

The acquisition of a previous tough competitor from another country with a completely different corporate culture requires major effort to preserve and exploit the values of the acquired company. Otherwise the company risks decreasing productivity, employees looking for employment elsewhere and the element of uncertainty regarding the new company goals resulting in a failure to realise the synergistic effects, rationalisation gains and economies of scale that looked so neat on paper.

Mergers often go through the same phases or processes. When one is familiar with and can, more or less, predict the individual steps in the process, one is in a better position to anticipate problems and exploit the advantages regarding the qualitative parameters (see Figure 11.14).

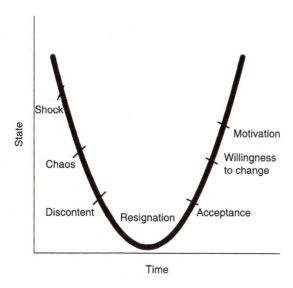

Figure 11.14 The phases of a merger alliance.
Source: Author's presentation based on Lüders (2002).

The first step in the process is often **shock**: the merger can be very unexpected, and often those who were previously competitors are now colleagues.

Chaos may be the next step: a lot of unanswered questions emerge while the usual, familiar surroundings disappear.

The next step may be **discontent**: one cannot get answers to questions, and uncertainty cannot be dispelled.

Next comes a certain degree of **resignation**: one may lose commitment and involvement. Both the negative and positive influence is low.

Gradually, a certain degree of **acceptance** emerges: one comes to recognise that the development cannot be changed and one perhaps begins to focus a little more on the positive and forward-looking aspects of the merger.

Acceptance is strengthened and after a while it grows into **willingness to change**. One goes with the flow and takes co-responsibility and becomes committed to the merger.

The final phase is great **motivation**: the advantages and the potential of the merger dominate. Short- and long-term opportunities help to set the agenda.

The process can clearly vary significantly from company to company and from person to person. Whether we are dealing with a merger of equals, a unilateral acquisition or a completely necessary action, and thus the solution to a serious problem, is also crucial. An important management task is to ensure that the process is as short as possible so that willingness to change and motivation are achieved as quickly as possible.

The quantitative parameters include preparatory activities conducted before the merger or acquisition becomes a reality.

In this context, it is important that the synergy benefits are clarified and defined. One should already have thoroughly investigated, what, how and where potential synergies can be realised. Only if these potential synergies have been previously established, can they be optimally implemented and followed up.

Synergies can in principle manifest themselves in the form of additional earnings and / or reduced costs. The most important synergies which occurred in a number of transnational mergers and acquisitions have been compiled by KPMG (1999) and are presented in Table 11.2.

As can be seen in Table 11.2, most businesses achieve synergies through cost reductions in terms of fewer staff. However, there is considerable disagreement as to which synergy is the most significant.

Chamman *et al.* (1998) believe that the greatest benefits lie on the cost side – especially on the purchasing and supplier side. Bekier *et al.* (2001), however, believe that too much attention has been given to the cost side, and that there are, in fact, no significant profits to be gained. In contrast, they assert that there are great benefits to be gained through increased growth in the form of new markets, etc. Marm *et al.* (2000) assert that a very significant synergy is the potential to increase prices after a merger or an acquisition.

Table 11.2 Synergies from international mergers and acquisitions

Additional earnings	Per cent
New customers	45
New markets	42
Marketing	34
New product development	34
Customer service, etc.	32
Access to new distribution channels	32
New products	29
Effective sales	26
Cost reduction	*Per cent*
Reduction in employees	66
Purchase and trade	60
Supply link	60
Input/supply	48
Production	35
Distribution	32
New product development	32
Outsourcing	25
Research and development	24
Other	8

Source: KPMG (1999).

Note: Percentage figures indicate the percentage of companies that indicated a synergistic effect regarding the relevant area.

Experience also shows that dedicated project management regarding the implementation and utilisation of synergies, follow-up, communication, etc. gives a significantly better result.

Finally, experience also shows that proper due diligence prior to a merger or acquisition is worthwhile as it leads to improved economic performance in the longer term (see KPMG, 1999). Due diligence is often conducted in connection with acquisitions or mergers of companies. The aim of due diligence is to identify the obligations or potential risks that a given company faces, thereby avoiding unpleasant surprises after the acquisition.

In general, the due diligence process can be divided into three parts. The first part is a general market analysis. This is followed by a financial analysis of the company's accounts, balance sheet and tax-related position. The third part is a legal analysis to identify the legal problems that the organisation must tackle. What is common to all three parts is that they facilitate a better understanding of the threats and thereby the costs which the company can expect to encounter in the future.

Due diligence is often costly and time consuming, but it usually turns out to be a good investment. Deloitte Consulting (2002) have compiled six success criteria for an effective acquisition and merger process of which due diligence is a key element:

1) Establish an acquisition and merger strategy that focuses on the real factors for success: increased efficiency, increased market power, etc.
2) Be honest about the strategy: ask yourself why you want a merger or an acquisition. If you cannot give a fair answer, then drop the idea!
3) Focus on the potential synergies in the merger and acquisition process. Calculate the estimated saved costs and increased revenue.
4) Use due diligence as a tool during the merger and acquisition process. Due diligence is not just a financial or legal 'evil', but is something which can have great significance for the ability to merge two organisations.
5) Plan and structure the fusion in advance.
6) Integrate the two organisations as quickly as possible.

Based on many years' experience with company mergers, Accenture (2012) has also compiled a number of success factors for mergers and acquisitions:

Create value
Move beyond integration to focus on customer value and retention in order to realise value.

Manage top 5–10 critical decisions
Focus on decisions that drive value.

Set clear aspirations
Establish clear baselines and set internal stretch targets; manage market expectations around achieving synergies.

Take action

Take advantage of unprecedented opportunity for change: mergers create increased momentum for bold transformational change, but there is a limited window of 18–24 months to achieve synergies.

Ensure frequent communication

Launch a comprehensive and consistent communication strategy immediately.

Address cultural issues early on

Identify desired state dimensions and actively manage employee transition using a transparent and quick appointment process; avoid slow decision making.

Avoid gluttony

Achieve 80 per cent planning certainty and quickly move to 100 per cent implementation.

Implement strong governance and tight process controls

Create a single, strong project management office for integration; manage pace, interdependencies, common processes and releases to avoid overload.

Source: Accenture (2012)

Questions and assignments

11.1 What is the overall motive behind M&As?
11.2 Describe and discuss briefly the drivers behind M&As
11.3 Find recent examples of M&As in the food industry. Describe the drivers behind these M&As.
11.4 'M&As often fail'. Discuss this statement.
11.5 How do M&As succeed?
11.6 Are M&As in the food industry different than those in other industries? Why / Why not?

12 International food business

International food business encompasses the cross-border activities and transactions of food businesses. With increasing globalisation, more and more relations are considered international business. Different models can be employed to explain the internationalisation process, which companies, and specifically food companies, go through. These models can also identify the various drivers, challenges and possible solutions in each step of the process. On the international food markets, and in the intersection between food companies and retail chains, competition increases significantly, which is further intensified by internationalisation. Internationalisation and entry on to international markets are important for food companies. Entry modes can be selected based on a number of criteria, and they are important for the success of the internationalisation process, but also here specific conditions apply in the food sector.

What is 'international food business'?

International food business may be defined simply as food business transactions which take place across national borders. This broad definition includes the very small food companies that export (or import) small quantities to only one neighbouring country, as well as the very large global food companies with integrated operations and strategic alliances around the world.

With increasing globalisation, more and more transactions are taking place across borders. The supply of raw produce, sales, alliances, owners, stakeholders, financing, etc. all have international dimensions, and therefore business is increasingly becoming international.

The food industry and food markets will similarly function in the same way as other sectors and markets. 'International food business' will therefore increasingly become known as simply, 'business'.

However, there are significant conditions in international business, which are particularly important for the food industry. The distinctive structure of the food industry, value chain connections and specific market conditions mean that the discipline of international food business encompasses important elements which need to be included in food businesses' strategic analysis. These elements are discussed in this chapter.

Corporate internationalisation processes

Corporate internationalisation processes have been a subject of great interest for many years. By analysing a company's internationalisation process, it is possible to predict and explain, to some extent, the steps, processes and problems that the company faces. Different alternatives can be highlighted and analysed in advance. This makes the company's internationalisation process more flexible and reduces risks and uncertainties.

Classical internationalisation theories based on experience and a preference for proximity have been developed and modified. However, developments in recent years especially among globally oriented start-up companies cannot be fully explained by classical theories. Many companies now start their international activities when already in the establishment phase and do not follow the traditional steps.

One can divide internationalisation theories into two types:

- step-models where internationalisation is a gradual learning process and where one step is taken at a time: on the basis of the experience gained, the next step is taken and this therefore represents a slow and gradual development. There are several different step-models, but all are based on the premise that a company's internationalisation occurs in stages or steps. A time lapse occurs between each phase, and a degree of maturing or experience building must occur before the next step can be taken;
- strategy models, where companies adapt in order to exploit business conditions optimally: this means that a company operates without special regard to the country of origin; there is no explicit time-related process; and markets, investments and other resources are placed around the world where it is most economically advantageous and where new knowledge can contribute to innovation and growth. This process represents quick and radical development.

The Uppsala internationalisation model

The Uppsala internationalisation model was developed in the 1970s and explains a company's choice of export market and entry strategy. Physical distance is an important variable in the model and it can explain where a business will establish itself.

The Uppsala model shows that companies start their international activities on local markets which are close to home. Subsequently, companies gradually and incrementally enter more distant markets. Thus, internationalisation is a step-wise process, where expansion is like a ripple in the water, with the domestic market as the centre and starting point.

The Uppsala model assumes that learning and experience are the main explanations as to why companies expand internationally. The close, most familiar, and thus less risky, markets are developed first. Internationalisation thus begins on markets that most resemble the domestic market. In this way, experience is gained which can be utilised to progressively expand on more distant markets.

While the market composition changes, the nature of the entry also changes. Companies initially establish themselves through exports, followed by foreign sales businesses, and it is only in the later stages that companies establish production abroad.

However, the Uppsala model also acknowledges that firms can skip steps in the internationalisation process by, e.g., expanding onto distant markets early in the process. A modified Uppsala model is illustrated in Figure 12.1.

In the figure, the internationalisation process is divided into seven steps. With increasing internationalisation, a company's management, commitment and risk also increase, although more opportunities also exist.

The figure only shows some of the key stages of internationalisation. However, there are various intermediate solutions, e.g. licensed production and joint-ventures. The contents of the individual steps are outlined below:

Sales on domestic markets

Most companies start with sales to domestic markets. The fact that domestic markets are still very important is evidenced by the fact that 95 per cent of the food industry's and 85 per cent of total industry's revenue in the USA is generated on the domestic market. Typically, the domestic market is important for the large countries.

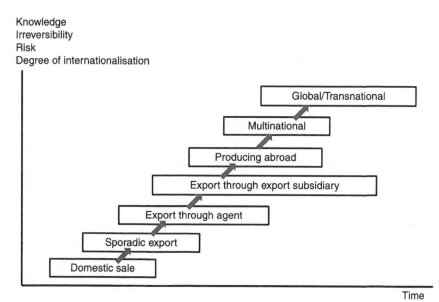

Figure 12.1 Stages in the internationalisation process.

Source: Author's presentation.

Sporadic exports

Sporadic exports can be indirect and *ad hoc* with low involvement from the company. Indirect export means that the company is not investigative regarding its trade with the foreign market. Put simply, indirect export is driven by the importer, which stimulates the export process through orders. Exports are thus characterised by randomness and their size often fluctuates considerably.

Indirect exports are not very demanding for the exporting company, as it does not have to invest any additional capital or commitment to service the export market. Indirect export means that the exporter has no control over marketing and thus has no direct influence on, e.g., the pricing of the product for the final consumer.

Export via an agent, etc.

In this case, exports are more formalised, although they are still relatively indirect. However, if there is a trade agent, the producer has greater influence on sales and has direct contact with the customer.

Sales subsidiary

With a sales subsidiary, export marketing is more active. Investments are made in a foreign sales subsidiary, which ensures more direct control of marketing. With this form of internationalisation, the company is more investigative in its involvement on the market and enters into fixed agreements with importers and distributors where the arrangements, as well as establishing details regarding exports, can include wide-ranging agreements regarding the marketing of the product and pricing policy on the relevant market.

Investment and production abroad

Production now takes place in owned companies abroad. Often, the purpose of foreign production is to supplement the dominant production at home. By producing abroad, the company can free itself from the constraints caused by trade policy measures, while local production in many cases makes it easier to implement precise market adjustment and extensive marketing. Additionally, there may be other considerations related to technical production that call for the transfer of production abroad, such as access to cheaper inputs, specific commodities or easier transportation.

Producing abroad means that a company has to become more involved, which often requires additional investments. Production, however, can be licensed to foreign companies, whereby technology and know-how are transferred to the foreign company so that it can conduct marketing. Licensed production limits the need for capital, but it also limits the extent of the company's control. When a company produces abroad, it is natural to conduct distribution and marketing, which maximises the company's ability to control its activities on the market and to independently implement all the elements in its market strategy.

Multinational

A fully multinational company does not take the home market as the starting point of its operations. Rather, production and sales are dictated by where in the world raw produce and labour are most cheaply obtainable, and where in the world the products can be sold most optimally.

Global/transnational

Just like in the previous step, the company's strategic and visionary planning has an extra dimension.

With global or transnational internationalisation, a company seeks to optimise both sales and investments / assets. The company's entire portfolio is put together and positioned relative to what is advantageous in the individual countries.

The three-phase model

The three-phase model consists of the following three stages or phases of internationalisation:

1) initial international expansion
2) consolidation on the export market
3) global division of labour.

The three phases represent a gradual (step-wise), but phased increase in internationalisation as illustrated in Figure 12.2.

Initial international market expansion

In the first phase of internationalisation, the company is on the verge of moving from being purely domestically oriented to also having international activities. At this stage, three important decisions must be made regarding:

- the international markets to be focused on
- the timing of entry
- how operations are be conducted on the international markets.

The selection of the international markets should be based on analyses of the attractiveness of the markets, including issues such as purchasing power, growth, market access and competition. In many cases, countries are selected which are geographically, culturally and linguistically close to the domestic market, as these markets are considered to be less risky and more secure.

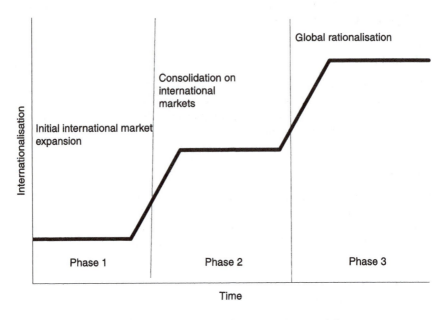

Figure 12.2 The internationalisation stages of the three-phase model.

Source: Author's presentation based on Douglas and Craig (1989).

The timing of entry depends on whether the selected markets are to be exploited simultaneously, or whether market penetration is to take place one market at a time. Factors such as economies of scale, capacity and risk-equalisation can be decisive for the final decision regarding timing.

Entry mode represents a choice between indirect export, licensed production, sales subsidiaries, investments and production abroad, foreign partners, etc. Once again, there are a number of factors within the company and externally in the relevant markets which may be decisive for the decision.

Consolidation on the export market

When a company has established a satisfactory foothold in a number of countries, it will often, in the next phase, focus on growth and expansion. The task therefore consists of developing the market and full penetration, which is often based on the experience acquired in the previous first phase. Entry onto further new international markets is given a lower priority, and the company instead seeks to increase its market position and market share on the international markets where it has established itself in phase 1.

The company focuses on adapting the product and strategy in each country, whereby market share increases and new segments are reached. The process is more based on the individual markets' resources and features than on the strategy of the parent company. Product development can be conducted by, e.g., adapting to the local conditions on the individual markets. Issues such as market and product development, the development or acquisition of new brands and further market segmentation are essential during this phase. The intention is to stimulate market growth and achieve greater market share.

During this stage it is important that the company adapts to the individual international markets so that it can achieve synergies and economies of scale and so that assets and core competences can be utilised optimally.

Synergy benefits can arise from the use, integration and sharing of, among other things:

- marketing costs
- production and distribution facilities
- administrative functions
- research and development
- market knowledge, network, etc.
- brands.

Market and product development and the exploitation of synergies can take place simultaneously: the adaptation or development of new products on a new international market can be achieved by utilising available capacity and resources within the group.

Companies will at some point move out of phase 2 and into phase 3.

Global division of labour

In the third and final phase of internationalisation, companies move towards full global orientation regarding their formulation and implementation of strategy. Therefore, the national orientation disappears and markets become increasingly integrated and interdependent on a global level.

The company focuses on optimising, coordinating and improving the efficiency of its worldwide activities, while identifying and exploiting possible synergies. Thus the company seeks to improve coordination and integration of its plants and units in different countries. This is partly achieved by optimally allocating resources across countries, markets and customer segments in order to optimise earnings at the global level and not solely on a country basis.

The following elements may be included in the process of improving efficiency and coordination:

- product development
- public relations
- distribution
- production
- sourcing

- research and development
- technology
- management.

The goal is to ensure a sustained improvement in efficiency, synergies and economies of scale and to achieve sustained growth with regard to new markets,
new products and further market development. All this necessitates a global
strategy which entails an overall vision and strategy, together with concrete
strategies regarding the individual units, markets, product mix, coordination and
management measures, etc.

Born globals

Over the past decade there have been several examples of companies which
have not followed the traditional steps and processes with regard to their
international activities. These companies start their international activities
very early in their lifetime, from the very beginning or after just a few years.
They soon start exporting to distant markets, develop many different export
markets at once and quickly establish international joint-ventures with no great
experience.

These companies are commonly called 'born globals', but they are also known
as 'new ventures' or 'high technology start-ups'.

Madsen *et al.* (2000) define born globals as 'a manufacturing company with
an export per cent of 25 or more, which has started exporting within 3 years of
its start'.

Cavusgil (1994) has studied the emergence of born globals and concludes that
'gradual internationalisation is dead'. The basis for this conclusion is that all
companies, even small ones and start-ups, have access to knowledge about export
markets and they therefore can base their business on exports right from the very
beginning.

Thus, there is general agreement that born globals cannot be explained in full
by means of the conventional step-models. The following are characteristics of
born globals:

- Management has an explicit focus on internationalisation.
- The company is able to standardise production and sales in a global
  niche.
- Growth, particularly export growth, is generally high.
- The leader's and the founder's personal experience, competence and relation-
  ships are important parameters.
- The founder's international approach and network are of great importance in
  the start-up phase.
- Their unique competences and comparative strengths are developed before
  the company's formal start-up.
- They usually do not receive any public financial support.

There may be several explanations for the emergence of these born globals which do not follow the usual processes of globalisation:

> First, international trade and investment have been significantly liberalised during the past decade. Thus, economic and political barriers to internationalisation have become increasingly reduced.
>
> Second, new technology in transport and communications also promotes international trade and investments. The transportation of products, commodity inputs or finished products for sale, to, e.g., China has become relatively cheap, while it has become considerably easier to communicate with customers, suppliers, intermediaries, partners, etc. on distant markets.
>
> Third, more and more people have international careers and experience with international activities. Their international competences can be quickly exploited in start-ups, which therefore do not need to spend a long time building up their own internal competences. In this way, the process of building-up internal experience is shortened or avoided altogether.
>
> Fourth, relatively many companies are established based on a technological invention. The commercialisation of a technological innovation in a company makes it necessary for even small and start-up companies to quickly enter large foreign markets. Otherwise, competitors will be able to catch up and reduce the company's technological lead. Especially if the product is easy to copy, it is necessary for the company to expand onto international markets quickly to remove the incentive for competitors.

Also, if a new product has a short lifecycle, international market expansion may be necessary to generate sufficiently large sales, which will also promote the establishment of born globals.

Retail market power

Retail's power, position and development have a significant influence on the food industry's strategic choices. There are numerous examples of food companies which have implemented significant initiatives just for the sake of their existing or potential retail customers. This is supported by several factors.

First, it turns out that many mergers and acquisitions in the food industry are precisely motivated by increasing concentration in the retail link (see Chapter 11).

Second, a study conducted among the leaders in the European food industry shows that concentration in the retail sector is perceived as an important and real threat out of all the challenges which face the food industry (KPMG, 2000). According to the study, business leaders in particular expect challenges to come from the side of retail. A figure of 83 per cent of surveyed leaders expect that a relative strengthening of the retail link, caused by, among others, the entry of large multinational chains, represents a high or moderate threat to the food industry's future earnings.

In the food industry, there is general agreement that the retail trade's increasing market power means that retailers can more or less dictate the terms of trade, including pressurising prices and demanding support for marketing. The result is reduced growth and earnings in the food industry.

Pressure from retailers is especially experienced in the form of a demand for very low prices (discount). More than 70 per cent of the food industry experiences this as the greatest pressure from retailers. Also, retailers' increasing internationalisation is perceived as a threat, especially for the more locally oriented food companies.

Another large study covering a number of major food companies in Europe, America and Asia shows that three-quarters of food businesses fear the increasing power of retailers (see Grievink *et al.*, 2003).

During the 1990s, there was a general tendency for the retail industry to become increasingly focused on sales outside the domestic market. There has been a significant increase in foreign sales among the major retail chains (see Figure 12.3).

As seen in the figure, there is a relatively clear increase in international activities. The development has been significant over the last decade during which time globalisation has really taken off.

The increasing international orientation of the retail chains has also given them a competitive advantage. New economies of scale have been exploited, and new international supply channels have been developed.

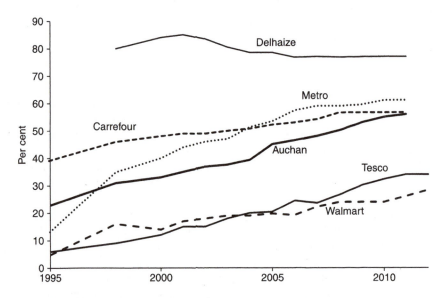

Figure 12.3 Selected retailers' sales outside the domestic market (per cent).

Source: Author's presentation based on the companies' annual reports.

Third, the increasing proliferation of private labels (retailers' own brands) in recent years has intensified competition on the market, which has greatly necessitated increased concentration in the food industry.

Implications for the food industry

The structural development of the retail industry is of great significance for the food industry. Initially it has a direct impact in the form of changes to market power and the market equilibrium. This then results in specific adaptations in the food industry.

The retail sector has undoubtedly achieved a much stronger negotiating position with regard to its suppliers and customers. This strengthened bargaining position has given the large retail chains significant economic advantages which have forced the smaller retailers out of the market and have led to cheaper goods from suppliers. This in turn has given the strongest retail chains economies of scale and opportunities for further expansion, which represents the start of a vicious spiral.

Aconis (2004) notes that, e.g., 'The revolution is long over. Retail has triumphed.' Hansen (2004) introduces the term 'the Wal-Mart effect', as an example of increasing concentration. At the same time, he notes that the Wal-Mart effect means that ever larger retail chains can now dictate the purchase price to producers, which can be a threat to the existence of many producers.

Globalisation and the advantages and opportunities of international marketing will further increase economies of scale for the retail chains. Concentration in the retail industry has thus in several areas had a significant influence on the food industry.

There are examples of structural developments in the food industry which have occurred to better match the ever larger retail chains. A certain size, product range, market position, etc. are necessary in order to be an equal partner and seller to the retail chains. In many cases the food industry's globalisation has occurred in order to be close to the major international retail chains.

Clearly a highly concentrated retail sector in a country can have an extremely negative effect on earnings in a weak, disorganised food industry with a poor structure. Normally, small food businesses in particular will be exposed and will find it difficult to withstand the pressure from retailers' increasing market power.

In the long term, the effect will be that even efficient food companies will not be able to yield interest on large development investments. Retailers' demand for low prices forces food companies to adjust production to fit short-term marginal costs. In an assessment of the effects of retail's increasing concentration and market power, Dobson (2003) concludes that even large food producers may be deterred from investing in new products and methods, because retail's market and negotiating power results in such low product prices that such investments are unprofitable.

A company can get into a very poor position if it is very dependent on one or two retail chains. Retail chains can threaten to block a supplier's access to their shelves, which does considerably more damage to the supplier than it does to the retail chains. Thus, companies can be forced to accept retail chains' demands regarding prices, etc.

Dobson (2003) takes the view that retail's increasing concentration has been a major cause of the structural change in the food industry toward fewer and larger companies, and the lack of investment in new methods and products in the food industry.

Adaptation options

There are different ways in which the food industry can adapt to or exploit the development in the retail sector. What is optimal in each case depends on a number of factors including, e.g., the company's size and strategy. Overall, there are three opportunities:

> First, the food industry can fight back and develop its own strong brands, grow in size, etc., so that the companies become indispensable and equal suppliers to the retail chains.
>
> Second, the food industry can choose to cooperate with retailers, i.e. if you can't beat them, join them!
>
> Third, the food industry can choose niche markets where retailers are not so focused, or where retailers have just opened up for local niche products, etc.

Often a company can decide to adopt all three options at once.

Production of private labels for retailers

The food industry can choose to produce the retail chains' own brands. It is often possible for a company to produce its own branded products and modified products simultaneously as private labels. Sometimes the products may directly compete with each other on the shelves in stores. This can be an attractive strategy, as in this way a company can satisfy the different needs of two consumer segments. Conversely, a company can find itself in a dangerous situation if a retail chain is an important customer and a competitor at the same time.

This is reflected in the fact that many retailers do not allow large brand producers to produce private labels for them. Carrefour prefers smaller companies, which are much more flexible, to produce their private labels (see Saveuse, 2003).

Especially if a company is operating on a market where the share of private labels is expected to increase in the future, it may be advantageous to obtain a share of this growth area.

Closer cooperation with retail chains

Production and marketing can also be conducted in the form of formalised cooperation. There are many examples of long-term collaboration between food companies and retail chains, whereby a product's design, concept, development, etc. are decided together.

Cooperation can be based on the retail chain's very close contact with consumers, which provides valuable knowledge about demand. Meanwhile, food companies have unique knowledge regarding production conditions. This combination of market and product competence can thus be exploited for mutual benefit.

The retail chain receives a unique product, possibly as their own brand, which can result in the retailer gaining an image in the eyes of consumers and a competitive profile relative to its competitors. At the same time, the company gains market access and ensures sales for a certain period.

Although a company has to invest in product development as part of private label cooperation, the investment would have been much greater, and riskier, if the company had had to develop and market its own brands.

Collaboration between a producer and a retail chain leads to the emergence of an interdependent relationship, which can be both a strength and a weakness. The strength lies in the fact that it is possible for the partners to exploit each other's different competences, while the weakness is that it is possible for one of the partners, in the long term, to abuse the agreement to the detriment of the other. If the retail chain terminates the cooperation, the company loses significant sales and perhaps also considerable development investments that are tied to the product.

Development of own strong brands

Food businesses may also choose to take up the fight and develop and / or maintain their own strong brands. By producing and selling branded products, the price premium accrues to the producer, who achieves more control over the product, and becomes less reliant on the retail chains. Conversely, this strategy involves considerably greater development and marketing costs and thus also risk as brands require substantial investment in marketing in order to maintain the higher market price.

Low-cost strategy

The development of own-branded products and collaboration with retailers to develop private labels often entails high costs. An alternative therefore is to refrain from producing branded products or to become involved in private label cooperation and to instead produce cheaply for the market.

Match the retail chains in size

Food companies can aim to grow in size so that they can fully match the retail chains. The increasing size of retail chains has been an important argument for larger and larger units in the food industry. Countries with a concentrated retail sector also have a concentrated food industry, so there is apparently a connection.

Match the retail chains geographically

Food producers can place plants, distribution, development etc. close to the major retail chains to be close to key customers and to be a major supplier in the increasing globalisation.

Alliances with competitors

A food company can make alliances with other companies (competitors or colleagues) in order to strengthen their market power over the retail sector.

Forward integration

The food industry can move further up the value chain and become more involved in retail in order to share in the profits in the sector. However, this is probably only a realistic option if competition is relatively low in the retail sector. The food industry does not really have the necessary skills to achieve high earnings in the retail sector.

Direct sales

Direct sales between the food industry and the consumer is also an option that is used, albeit to a very limited extent. If the direct sales reach a significant level, the food industry becomes a competitor with its own customers, i.e. the retail sector. A study among large food companies and retail chains in several countries (Grievink *et al.*, 2003) also focuses on this relationship and on the companies' fears of retailers' reaction. However, the majority of the food companies do not deny that at some point they intend to deliver directly to consumers. Conversely, the majority of retailers think that this is unlikely to occur.

Niche orientation

The food industry can focus on niches where private labels are not as prominent, or where competition between the big brands is not so intense. The food industry can also focus on other niches where the market's size, growth or earnings are so low that competition is not so intense.

By focusing on niches, a company can often achieve a large market share in a particular area and thereby gain significant market power.

Segmentation – specialisation in product areas

Several large supermarket chains say that they deliberately give small local suppliers space on their shelves. This proliferation of many suppliers allows even small companies to gain access to the big chains. Regional label is one such example.

Private labels

Private labels are products that are developed, branded and marketed by retailers rather than food manufacturers. Retailers develop and sell private label products in order to make their retail proposition more attractive to consumers by enhancing product choice and value for money.

Development

Private labels have been gaining ground at the expense of food industry brands and private labels' market share has grown steadily in recent decades. In the EU, private labels account for 23 per cent of the grocery market, while the sale of private labels is growing by 4 per cent per year on average (European Commission, 2011). Table 12.1 shows the market shares of private labels in the fast-moving consumer goods in various countries.

As can be seen from the table, the market share of private labels is increasing in almost all countries. It is also apparent that private labels are most prevalent in the economically most developed countries.

Many other studies show the same picture. It is also striking that private labels are most prevalent in the countries in the EU, where retail is most concentrated. This shows that the stronger the retail sector, the greater the potential it has to use its own brands.

Table 12.1 Market share for private labels in fast-moving consumer goods (FMCG) (%)

	2008	*2009*	*2011*
France	31	33	37
Germany	37	36	37
Great Britain	46	46	46
Italy	7	8	8
Spain	33	32	35
Netherlands	33	34	38
Poland	n/a	16	21
Romania	4	4	9
Russia	3	1	2
Ukraine	0	0	1
USA	18	18	18
Mexico	2	2	1
Argentina	4	5	5
Brazil	<1	<1	<1
Peru	<1	<1	<1
Chile	4	5	7
China	<1	<1	<1
India	1	1	1
Thailand	0	2	3
Korea	3	5	3

Source: Europanel (several issues) and author's calculations.

There is also a tendency for the character of branded and private labels to change. Private labels have previously been primarily characterised by low prices and quality. However, gradually private labels have emerged which have been positioned as 'premium' brands in order to directly compete with established brands, but possibly also to build up the retail chain's image.

Thus premium and mainstream private labels are gaining market share along with discount private labels. All in all, it is expected that the group of mainstream private labels will have gained a market share of 30 per cent by 2025 and will thus be the largest group of brands (see Figure 12.4).

As can be seen in the figure, a marked increase in private labels' market share is expected. The market share is expected to increase from 31 per cent in 2010 to 53 per cent in 2025.

The group of value private labels and hard discounts is expected to continue to gain increasing market share. Value private labels are an attempt by the supermarkets to counter competition from the 'hard discount' stores. Value private label products are priced at approximately 50 per cent of the price of established brands, and they thus help to draw customers from discount stores to the supermarket chains.

Mainstream private label products are typically products which are similar to traditional brands, but which are 20–30 per cent cheaper. It is important for the retailer that these products are placed close to the brands and that the goods are comparable, because it strengthens the retailer's bargaining power over producers

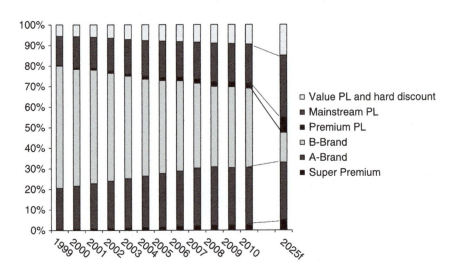

Figure 12.4 Private label market share in developed countries (most notably Western Europe, USA and Australia).

Source: Rabobank (2012).

Note: PL = Private label.

of the brands, while it also makes the private label products more attractive in the eyes of consumers.

It is also noteworthy that A-brands are expected to retain their market share until 2025. Neither the retail sector nor consumers can do without these strong brands. Consumers need A-brands as a benchmark to assess the supermarket's price competitiveness, while retailers need A-brands as a price and quality anchor for each product category.

However, it seems that B-brands (secondary and weaker brands) will continue to be under pressure and will continue to lose market share in the future. Therefore, continuing polarisation between low- and high-price products will occur, while the middle group of weaker and secondary brands will come under threat. Also, it seems that competition between private labels and brands, and thus also competition between retail chains and food companies, will be intensified.

Explanations

There may be several other explanations as to why private labels are gaining so much ground.

Box 12.1 What are private labels and brands?

Private labels are the supermarkets' own brands, which bear the chain's name or a name owned by the chain. The producer's name does not appear, or only very discreetly. As a producer of private labels, there are virtually no marketing costs and the producer is therefore able to offer the products at a price that is typically 15–20 per cent below the price of a brand name equivalent. This lower price is necessary in order to compete with brand product producers. Therefore, the price of private labels in the consumer link is low, but more than the discount level. Correspondingly, the quality is not the highest, although there is a general tendency for the quality difference to become less and less.

There are several different types of private label depending on the branding and marketing which the supermarket chains decide to conduct. The simplest types of good simply bear the chain's name and do not involve any real marketing costs. At the other end of the scale are the retail chain's actual brand products (premium label) where marketing of the name is on a par with the producer brands.

Brands (company label) are the company's brands, which retain their identity throughout the process to the ultimate end user. These are often a little more expensive and the company is mainly responsible for marketing and promotion. Brands often require significant investment in marketing in order to maintain the higher market price. Normally, brands are connected with higher quality.

First, retailers have gained significantly greater market power in recent decades. This has occurred at the expense of both wholesalers and producers. The increased market power in the vertical chain, together with more intense competition horizontally makes it natural for the retail chains to develop new competitive parameters. Private labels are thus a means for a retailer to both improve its negotiating situation with regard to producers and to compete with other retail chains.

Products can be differentiated, and the market made less transparent. At the same time, retailers are no longer reliant on the corresponding differentiation among suppliers.

In the food sector, there are examples of supermarket chains developing their own brands of dairy products. When these private labels become established, the supermarkets are largely free to choose suppliers for private label production, which strengthens their negotiating position considerably compared to having to negotiate with a producer of branded dairy products.

Second, retailers now have greater opportunities to integrate customer-oriented values. A high level of service and experience in the supermarkets supplemented by various bonus schemes makes it possible to build customer loyalty to the supermarket. The same loyalty to the store cannot necessarily be built up based on a single specific product, even if is marketed as a brand.

Studies show that precisely the chains' own brands, private labels, are often decisive in a customer's choice of shopping location.

Third, retail has achieved a very valuable position close to the consumer. In contrast, the producer is positioned several stages earlier in the process and thus has a weaker sense of consumer composition, reactions, etc., which is also to the comparative benefit of private labels. Through this close connection to customers, retail chains are able to collect exact market information which can be used in the marketing of private labels.

There are areas where private labels are not very widespread, apparently because they are not yet attractive to retail chains.

First, these are especially areas in which large investments have already been made to establish brands. Consequently, there are significant entry barriers which keep others out.

Second, products that require a high degree of ongoing development are also less attractive as private labels.

Third, poor earnings for existing brands will also help keep new private labels off the market.

Finally, it turns out that a weak retail sector has difficulty developing private labels. The explanation is that the retail link must have a certain degree of market power to be able to trade with private labels.

These explanations for the increasing spread of private labels reinforce the expectations that the current trend will continue.

Retailers want to use private labels to compete for customers and it is expected that competition in the retail sector will intensify in the coming years. In addition, retail's position will be further strengthened. The close proximity of consumers and the high concentration and establishment of national and international alliances will together increase the power and bargaining position of the retail sector.

At the same time, the big brand names have a strong foothold in the international markets. Therefore, the development is likely to be that the two–three largest brands in each product area will consolidate or expand their market share and private labels will also gain market share, while secondary brands will be more or less out-competed.

The food industry's production of private labels

As previously discussed, food companies may also gain an advantage by focusing on the production of private labels in the retail chain's name. Long-term collaboration between food companies and retail chains where the partners are jointly responsible for the product design, concept, product development, etc. is common.

Cooperation can be based on the retail chain's very close contact with customers, which provides valuable knowledge regarding demand. At the same time, food companies hold unique knowledge regarding production conditions. This combination of market and product competence can thus be exploited for mutual benefit. The retail chain receives a unique product with its name, which can result in the retailer gaining an image in the eyes of consumers and a competitive profile relative to its competitors. At the same time, the company gains market access and ensures sales for a certain period.

Although a company has to invest in product development as part of private label cooperation, the investment would have been much greater, and riskier, if the company had had to develop and market its own brands. Especially for small businesses or small business areas, the establishment of own brands on an already brand-dominated market can be an impossible task, while the production of private labels can be a relevant alternative.

Collaboration between a producer and a retail chain leads to the emergence of an interdependent relationship, which can be both a strength and a weakness. The strength lies in the fact that it is possible for the partners to exploit each other's different competences, while the weakness is that it is possible for one of the partners, in the long term, to abuse the agreement to the detriment of the other. If the retail chain terminates the cooperation, the company loses significant sales and perhaps also considerable development investments that are tied to the product.

For many companies, it is not a question of one or the other, but both, in that they produce their own company brands and private labels for the supermarket chains.

Global strategic alliances

Global strategic alliances have been called the newest form of internationalisation. It is also noteworthy that the entry into global strategic alliances has been increasing over the past decade. Furthermore, it is expected that global strategic alliances will become more prominent in future as a means to survive on global markets. UNCTAD (2005a, 2005b) shows that internationalisation through strategic alliances has grown rapidly in importance. It is also expected that they will be important in the future, although transnational corporations do not assign a major role to strategic alliances.

A global strategic alliance (GSA) is cooperation between companies from different countries in order to achieve a common goal. GSA can be defined as:

> Long-term contract cooperation between companies in different countries which make resources (labour, capital, technology, know-how) available for mutual use, so that identified common goals can be achieved most effectively.

The basic purpose of entering into a GSA is the desire to improve the participating companies' competitiveness in the long term. This presupposes that all partners in the collaboration can offer something valuable, e.g. technology and market access.

Common forms of internationalisation such as exports and sales companies can have limitations, especially in light of recent technological, economic and political changes in the corporate world. In contrast, a genuine global strategic alliance differs in several ways from this:

- There is extensive cooperation within a long-term strategy to achieve overall market strengths and advantages.
- Each company has specific strengths, which it shares with its partner. Both parties have to gain knowledge in order to achieve optimum cooperation.
- All partners have globalisation as an important vision.

GSAs have proven to be both a success and a failure. There are examples of large international companies entering into strategic alliances which have not achieved the desired objectives and where, after several years of disappointment and wasted work, it has been necessary to terminate the cooperation. Conversely, there are also success stories whereby the participating companies have all contributed valuable knowledge, resulting in significant mutual benefit.

Box 12.2 shows examples of global strategic alliances where food companies are participants.

Box 12.2 Global strategic alliances

Novozymes (Denmark) and DSM (the Netherlands) formed a strategic alliance in 2001. DSM is responsible for sales, marketing and distribution of Novozymes' feed enzymes. Novozymes is responsible for product development and R&D. The two companies had different but complementary competences: Novozymes in enzyme screening, strain development, formulation and production; DSM in animal nutrition, feed technology, and sales and marketing.

In parallel with this, DSM has formed a second-generation ethanol joint venture with American Poet, which is a significant customer of Novozymes.

General Mills and Nestlé have formed a strategic alliance, through a firm (joint-venture) called Cereal Partners Worldwide (CPW). General Mills and Nestlé do not compete directly with each other in this joint venture and common strengths are utilised. General Mills has technical excellence and Nestlé has a worldwide presence and brands, together with a local market and distribution knowledge.

The driving force behind the formation of global strategic alliances is often resource utilisation: individual companies do not have the necessary resources to exploit the opportunities that continually arise. GSAs often result from recognition that an individual company is unable to cope with challenges satisfactorily. This is also the case in the biotech sector, where cooperation in research and development, the exploitation of licences and patents, etc. is becoming increasingly significant. Cross-ownership, cooperation and alliances between competitors in the global food industry are also becoming increasingly important.

The next step in the development of global strategic alliances can be corporate consortiums. Corporate consortiums are groups of companies from different industrial areas and from different countries which emerge as a singular and very large unit to achieve a common target. Therefore, it involves super alliances between what were already large companies. These super alliances achieve huge economic, market and political power. Since super alliances have many different home countries, they are in many cases regarded as national or local companies, which can also have significant benefits.

Entry mode

Entry mode, i.e. how a company enters an export market, is an important choice for a business. For food companies, the entry mode has special and important dimensions, e.g. trade barriers, vertical integration in the value chain, access to raw materials, transportation problems, form of ownership and continuous quality control, which represent some of the important challenges which food companies in particular need to consider when choosing the form of internationalisation.

As previously mentioned, there are several different types of internationalisation and the choice of entry strategy in each individual case depends on many different factors. Issues concerning the product, the company, the market and trade policy are crucial in this context.

Factors influencing entry modes

Conditions internally in the company and in its business environment can influence the form of internationalisation which is most suitable in a specific case. These conditions are outlined in Figure 12.5.

The product

If the product requires a lot of service both before and after the sale, it will often be advantageous to follow the product all the way to the final consumer. Therefore, it will be necessary to be present on the market in the form of, e.g., a sales office. Similarly, issues such as transport costs and storage requirements will be crucial as to which type of internationalisation is the most advantageous.

The company

The choice of which internationalisation strategy to adopt must be supported by the necessary company-related framework. One of the essential frameworks for direct investment is adequate and patient capital, because it is possible that several years may pass before the investment yields a profit.

Similarly, direct forms of export require that the company understands how the foreign market functions in order to be able to create an appropriate strategy for entering the relevant market. Managing a company with production units, joint ventures, etc. abroad requires much more, and different, management resources than leading a company that produces exclusively for the domestic market.

If the company has established effective marketing in the home country, it may be advantageous to exploit this, instead of investing in a similar function

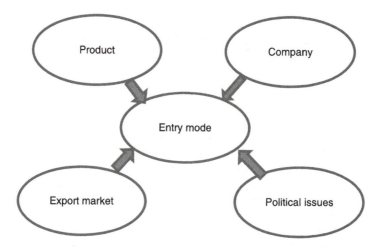

Figure 12.5 Conditions which influence the form of internationalisation.

Source: Author's presentation.

abroad. Here, it is optimal to invest in direct exports, which are based in the home country.

Other factors such as the company's size, financial strength, breadth of product range, form of ownership, willingness to take risks, etc. are also of great importance in this context.

The export market

Several features of the export market may influence the entry strategy, including:

- the extent and distribution of customers
- customer needs, wants and preferences
- the market's economic level and development.

If a company sells to a few very large customers, direct contact with the customers is necessary. If, conversely, a company has a very large and dispersed group of customers who buy frequently, but in small quantities, it is more advantageous to sell through an agent or wholesaler.

Some markets are so poorly developed that there is no satisfactory distribution apparatus which may be used. In this case, it may be advantageous to invest in a sales subsidiary in order to ensure the desired entry on to the market.

Political conditions

Trade policy and economic and legal conditions can also favour one or another form of entry onto a market. The following conditions may be relevant:

- import barriers
- currency rules
- favouring foreign investment in the country
- rules for the purchase and sale of companies abroad
- possibility to bring home profits from a company abroad.

Many factors must be taken into consideration when attempting to identify the optimal entry strategy. Table 12.2 outlines some of the key issues that may be relevant for a food company's entry onto an international market.

The table contains six different entry modes. Furthermore, a number of conditions or factors that are different in each entry mode situation are presented. Based on the table, a screening process can be conducted, which may be the first step in the selection process.

OLI theory

John Dunning's OLI theory is a major cornerstone in the understanding of corporate internationalisation processes. According to Dunning (1980), there are

Table 12.2 Comparing various entry modes

	Agent/Distributor	Representative office	Licensing	Joint venture	Acquisition	Wholly owned subsidiary
Up-front investment	Low	Low/medium	Low	Medium	High	High
Reversibility	Medium/high	High	Medium	Low/medium	Low	Low
Speed of entry	Quick	Low	Medium	Quick	Quick	Slow
Market penetration	Medium/low	Low	Medium/low	Medium/high	High	Medium
Control of market	Low/nil	Low	Nil	Medium	High	High
Control of production	High	High	Low	Medium	Medium	Medium
Political risk exposure	Low	Low	Low	Medium	High	High
Technological leakage	Low	Low	High	Medium/high	Low	Low
Managerial complexity	Low	Medium	Low	High	High	High
Potential economic risk	Low	Low	Low	Medium	High	High
Trade barriers avoidance	Low	Low	High	High	High	High
Utilisation of comparative advantages globally	Low	Low	Medium	High	High	High
Preference for domestic producers	High	High	Medium	Low	Low	Low

Source: Lasserre (2003) and author's own study.

three factors that influence whether a company chooses to establish itself and produce internationally or not. Dunning has combined these three factors in the eclectic paradigm, OLI theory.

The theory consists of the elements Ownership advantages; Location advantages; and Internalisation advantages, all of which describe the competitive advantages for a company on an international market in relation to its foreign competitors. It's called the eclectic paradigm as it is a combination of parts of a variety of economic theories.

Ownership advantages

First, the investing multinational food company has to be in possession of one or more ownership advantages. These may consist of, e.g., either a company's assets or particular transaction advantages. Also, factors such as brands, patents, management systems and production processes may be ownership advantages. Ownership advantages are thus the strengths that help make a company competitive on international markets.

Food companies may have specific ownership advantages when it comes to raw material supply, vertical integration, value chain management, innovation, economies of scale, market position, etc.

Location-specific variables

Second, the host country must be in possession of one or more location-specific variables. These can be on the input side in the form of specific factors of production, cheap inputs or the availability of specific technologies, or they can be on the output side in the form of a large and attractive market. However, there may also be institutional or structural factors such as the protection of markets (trade barriers), which can often be an important aspect for food companies.

If there are localisation advantages associated with the relocation of a part of production to a trade country (special competitive advantages), it can be advantageous to split the value chain between the home country and the host country. In this way, the part-production is localised in accordance with the countries' resources, whereby owner-specific advantages are exploited in a limited geographical area.

Internalisation incentive advantages

Third, internalisation incentive advantages must be present for the establishment of a company internationally. This means that it must be advantageous to retain full control of operations rather than reducing risk by entering into a contractual relationship (a joint-venture, a licensing agreement or similar). Therefore, there have to be economic benefits to maintaining international activities as part of the company, rather than allowing external partners to perform them. For a food company, the issue of transaction costs may be important in this context.

Price transmission in the value chain

Two important factors characterise the food industry compared to other industrial sectors:

> First, commodity prices have become more internationally oriented, and they have become much more volatile.
>
> Second, the vertical integration in the value chain plays a major role.

These two factors together are important for price transmission, which takes place in the food industry: when commodity prices vary greatly, as they do during, e.g., food crises, the price fluctuations spread to the subsequent link in the value chain and eventually affect consumer prices. This means that price volatility on agricultural commodity markets affects all the links in the value chain, to varying extents and with a greater or lesser time lag.

Thus, there are examples of even large companies in the agri and food industries not being able to handle price volatility and being forced to close. These companies have not been able to pass on the price increases, in whole or in part, to the subsequent link in the value chain or they have not made the necessary price hedging in time.

There are also examples of price transmission in the value chain being asymmetric, significant lags or the development of prices in the downstream link in the value chain being too large in relation to what can readily be explained by the price increase in the previous link. This imperfect price transmission is often a sign that the food markets are imperfect; that the market does not work perfectly or optimally. This is a phenomenon that occurs on important national and international food markets. Peltzman (2000) highlights that asymmetric price transmission is more the rule than the exception.

Thus, price transmission along the food chain is often delayed in the EU. Based on empirical studies, which have typically been conducted during and after large commodity price increases, it is possible to divide the process in the value chain into several phases.

In the first phase, the farmers' prices increase. In the second phase, the farmers' prices decrease, while food prices continue to rise. In the third phase, food prices decrease, while retailers' prices continue to increase and, finally, in the last phase, prices stabilise.

It is possible to identify these four phases during and after the food crisis of 2007–08 (see Figure 12.6).

The figure shows the four phases during and after the food crisis of 2007–08 (see, e.g. the European Commission, 2009b):

- *Food price crisis* (August 2007–February 2008): agricultural commodity prices increase sharply by 16 per cent in 10 months. As a consequence, food producer and consumer prices increase in the same period.

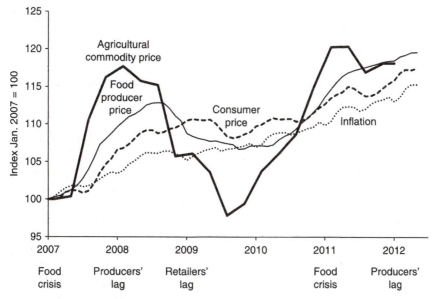

Figure 12.6 Price developments in the European food chain case.

Source: Author's calculations based on Eurostat (2012).

- *Producers' lag* (March 2008–August 2008): commodity prices start declining, but producer prices and consumer prices continue to increase in the period, albeit at a slower pace.
- *Retailers' lag* (September 2008–February 2009): commodity prices continue their sharp decline, and producer prices start declining. However, food consumer prices are still on the rise in the period and only start to stabilise from March 2009 onwards and begin to decline in May 2009.
- *Stabilisation* (February 2009–July 2009): prices in the chain stabilise, and consumer prices start to decline in May 2009.

The price of agricultural commodities began to increase again in mid-2009, which put a stop to the decline in consumer prices. In fact, consumer prices began to rise again, and the price adjustment in the retail link was very fast.

Box 12.3 presents an example of price transmission in a value chain in the food sector.

All in all, there are signs that price transmission in food product chains is an important area of focus. Price adjustment is far from effective, and ensuring effectiveness in the food chain is essential for increasing competitiveness for the benefit of the whole sector.

There may be several explanations as to why price transmission in food product chains is, in general, often ineffective. In a review of the literature, Vavra and

Goodwin (2005), conclude that market power is often perceived as the main potential cause of asymmetric price transmission, although other possible causes for imperfect price transmission are also discussed.

Box 12.3 **Price transmission in grain–flour–bread–value chain: a Danish case**

Since 2007, grain prices have been very unstable following two food crises (see Chapter 2). Grain is a basic input in the agricultural and food sector and, therefore, changes in the price of grain affect many of the subsequent stages in the value chain. Change in grain prices is an important factor for the development of both the supply and prices of poultry and pork.

Also, when it comes to grain-based foods there are clear price spillovers. The price of flour, bread, etc. is directly affected by changes in the price of bread grain. Price fluctuations for these grain-based foods are typically less than price fluctuations for grain itself, since grain costs only represent a small part of the final sales price. In the case of bread, grain costs often only constitute 5 to 20 per cent of the retail price. Because the raw materials' share of the final sales price decreases as one moves forward in the value chain, price volatility as a result of fluctuations in the price of raw produce also decreases as one approaches the consumer link.

The correlation between grain and bread prices is shown in Figure 12.7 – with the development in Denmark as an example.

The figure shows that the prices of bread rose rapidly (approx. 15 per cent) after the increases in the price of grain in 2007. Since grain costs only account for approximately 5 per cent of the price of bread, there was a relatively sharp

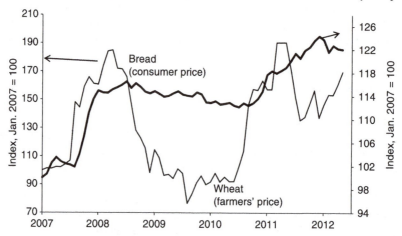

Figure 12.7 Farmer prices for bread wheat and consumer prices for bread in Denmark.

Source: Author's calculations based on Statistics Denmark (2012 and several issues).

increase in the bread price. When the grain price subsequently decreased, the decrease in the price of bread was delayed and relatively modest.

The same process occurred after the food crisis and grain price increases in 2010: the price of bread increased relatively quickly (time-lag of 1–3 months) and substantially, while the subsequent fall in prices, as a result of a decline in the grain price, was delayed (7 months) and relatively modest.

The figure thus shows that there are signs of irreversibility, time-lags and an overreaction with regard to price transmission in this grain–bread value chain.

Grain passes through several links in the value chain (see Figure 12.8). The grain is sold to grain companies which then sell it to millers, who grind the grain into flour. Then the flour is sold to bakeries for further use or to the retail link for sale to final consumers. The bakeries produce bread which is then sold either directly to consumers or to retailers. The grain must therefore pass through at least three–four links before it reaches the end users, i.e. the consumers. Therefore, the price is set (sale and purchase price) many times in the value chain. The development of the price is presented in Figure 12.9.

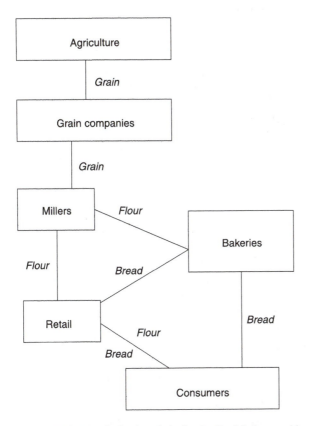

Figure 12.8 A typical value chain for the Danish flour and bread sector.

Source: Author's presentation.

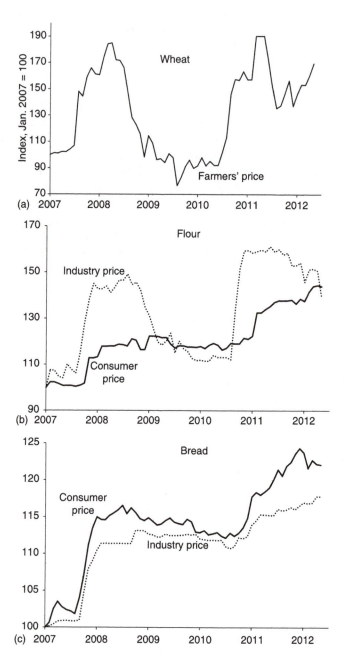

Figure 12.9 Price transmission in the Danish grain–flour–bread value chain.

Source: Author's calculations based on Statistics Denmark (2012 and several issues).

Note: Industry = processing companies.

The figure shows that price fluctuations decrease as one moves forward in the value chain. One can also see that the price increases occur relatively quickly and are significant, while the price decreases are smaller and significantly slower as one moves forward in the value chain.

This irreversible, delayed and sometimes excessive price transmission may be a sign of market imperfection and increasing profits. Based on the price developments in 2007–09, the Danish competition authorities conclude that the price increases in the retail link could not be entirely explained by commodity price increases. Rather, the increasing profit margins in the value chain, especially for mills and supermarkets, were the cause of increasing consumer prices (Danish Competition Authority, 2008, 2009).

International competitiveness of food industries

The food industry's international competitiveness can be considered as a measure of companies' ability to increase market share, create profitability, continue to develop and on the whole achieve objectives on a global and open market. To become internationally competitive is therefore crucial in international food business. It is also important to identify the factors that create international competitiveness and to establish empirical and comparable measures of food businesses' international competitiveness.

The food industry's international competitiveness is crucial for both business economics analyses and for companies' strategic business development plans.

The food industry's international competitiveness can be analysed in two different ways:

First, an internal and external analysis of the sector's framework conditions is conducted – business environment and competitive factors – which is an analysis of the factors that influence and create international competitiveness. It is an ex-ante analysis, which can highlight the causes of subsequent development.

By identifying these factors, one can also attempt to improve conditions in order to improve international competitiveness. At the same time, food companies position themselves geographically, where the factors are optimal for them.

The weakness of this method is that the significance of the factors can vary from company to company, and the actual influence of the factors in the short and longer term can always be discussed.

Second, it is possible to analyse the food companies' international performance as a measure of the effect of international competitiveness: companies or sectors that are developing relatively positively have been able to exploit their international competitiveness. Therefore, one can use the companies' earnings, growth, consolidation or market share as a direct expression of, or result of, international competitiveness. In this case, we are dealing with ex-post analysis.

Business environment and competitive factors

The internal and external analysis describes the factors in the company and in the economic, political and market environment that influence international competitiveness; the factors' importance has to be assessed. In many cases, a SWOT analysis can be used as a model for gathering and structuring data (see Chapter 13).

Business environment and competitive factors can also be very different when it comes to measurability. Some factors are easily measurable, e.g. concentration, exchange rate and tax conditions, while others are very difficult to measure, e.g. innovation and competence. In addition, factors such as taxes and duties are a disadvantage for a sector, but these taxes and duties directly or indirectly finance public services such as teaching and research and development, which can be very advantageous for the sector. It is necessary to look at both aspects, but the positive effects can be much harder to identify, let alone quantify, than the negative effects for the sector.

Some factors may be difficult to quantify, such as leadership skills, motivation and willingness to change. In these cases it may be necessary to supplement the analysis with interviews with experts in business and academia. Their experience and knowledge can thus be included in an overall index.

Competition parameters such as 'knowledge transfer between companies and universities', which may be important parameters for an expanding international food company, can therefore be quantified in this way (see Figure 12.10).

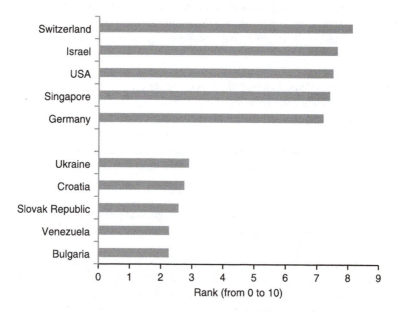

Figure 12.10 Knowledge transfer between companies and universities.

Source: IMD (2012).

Note: Top five and bottom five (the five best and five worst).

The data are from the IMD's *World Competitiveness Yearbook*, which contains numerous analyses and benchmarking results of countries' international competitiveness based on both qualitative and quantitative data. Their analysis consists of data from 59 countries and includes 327 criteria (factors) for each country. It also emphasises that there are many and different types of framework condition.

Performance

A company's international competitiveness can, as previously mentioned, also be determined by comparing performance. Performance can be viewed in several different ways, but basically one needs to assess a company's performance in relation to the goals set by the company. Therefore, if a company is focusing on earnings, then its performance should be measured against this. However, in most cases, key performance indicators such as earnings and market share will be indicators for most of the goals that companies have.

Box 12.4 shows the indicators that were used in an analysis of the European food industry's international competitiveness.

Box 12.4 Competitiveness indicators for European food industry

In 2007 the European Commission published a report, 'Competitiveness of the European Food Industry. An economic and legal assessment'. The selected indicators to quantify the competitiveness of industry which were used in the report were:

- *growth value added* of a specific industry in the total food industry: this reflects the competition for product factors between different industries within a country;
- the *Balassa index*: this index reflects the specialisation level in one category of goods from one country;
- growth of the *export share on the world market*: this performance indicator reflects the outcome of the competitive process;
- growth of *labour productivity*: this affects the unit labour costs and, in this way, the relative prices;
- growth of *value added*: this reflects the industrial dynamism.

Source: European Commission (2007).

The Balassa index of revealed comparative advantage, which is a widely used indicator, shows the relationship between the individual products' world market share and the average for all products. If the index of comparative advantages is > 1, then we are dealing with a comparative advantage.

Table 12.3 presents the index of comparative advantage for different products and countries. The table shows the specific areas (countries and products) which have high comparative advantages.

Table 12.3 Index of comparative advantage for different products and countries (2009)

	Agricult. Products, Total	Food Excl. Fish	Beverage Total	Coffee+Tea+Cocoa	Fruit+Vegetables	Bananas	Cereals	Rice	Sugar	Total Meat	Pig Meat	Poultry Meat	Dairy Products	Butter	Cheese
Argentina	6.3	5.5	2.2	0.8	3.3		9.8	3.4	3.3	5.0		2.5	2.6	1.6	1.5
Brazil	4.6	4.7	0.1	5.8	1.4	0.4	1.7	1.2	32.8	9.5	3.2	18.7	0.3	0.1	0.1
Canada	1.3	1.6	0.4	0.6	1.1		3.1			1.4	2.4	0.5	0.1		0.1
Chile	1.9	2.0	4.5	0.2	6.0	0.5	0.6		1.3	1.6	2.6	2.2	0.5	0.1	0.3
Mexico	0.9	0.9	2.1	0.7	2.3	0.5	0.3	1.4	1.3	0.3	0.4		0.1		
USA	1.3	1.4	0.5	0.4	1.1	0.5	2.6	0.1	0.1	1.3	1.4	2.0	0.4	0.2	0.2
Australia	1.9	1.9	2.2	0.3	0.7		4.6		0.3	4.1	0.3	0.1	2.4	3.1	2.0
New Zealand	7.0	8.3	5.3	0.5	4.4				0.3	16.8	0.1	0.4	46.0	102.4	19.1
China	0.3	0.3	0.1	0.2	0.7		0.1	0.3	0.0	0.2		0.4			
India	1.3	1.0	0.1	2.0	1.0	0.2	2.8		0.1	1.0	0.2		0.2	0.3	
Indonesia	2.3	2.3	0.1	4.2	0.4								0.2	0.1	
Japan	0.1	0.1	0.1												
Philippines	0.9	1.0	0.2	0.1	2.0	14.1	1.8	0.0	1.4	0.1	0.1	0.3	0.6		0.1
Republic of Korea	0.1	0.1	0.2	0.2	0.1	0.0			0.2	0.0	0.1				
Russia	0.3	0.4	0.2	0.3	0.1		5.4	0.1	0.1	1.5	0.1		0.2	0.1	0.1
Thailand	1.8	1.7	0.5		1.5	0.1		23.3	7.1			5.4	0.2		
Turkey	1.4	1.6	0.3	0.9	4.1		1.2	0.1		0.2		0.8	0.5		
Viet Nam	1.3	1.1	0.1	6.4	1.8	0.1	4.4	19.9		0.1	0.2				0.5

(Continued overleaf)

Table 12.3 Continued.

	Agricult. Products, Total	Food Excl. Fish	Beverage Total	Coffee+Tea+Cocoa	Fruit+Vegetables	Bananas	Cereals	Rice	Sugar	Total Meat	Pig Meat	Poultry Meat	Dairy Products	Butter	Cheese
Egypt	2.6	3.0	0.1	1.0	6.9	0.9	3.5	14.4	3.3	0.1		0.2	4.6	1.1	10.1
Kenya	7.3	2.4	2.0	45.7	6.3		0.4	0.2	0.2	0.4	0.8		0.7	0.5	
South Africa	1.2	1.1	2.6	0.3	2.7		1.3	0.2	3.6	0.3	0.1	0.2	0.3	0.2	0.1
Belarus	1.4	1.8	0.2	0.2	0.4		4.7	0.9	6.7	3.4	2.4	1.0	10.9	29.0	10.2
Bulgaria	2.2	2.4	1.1	0.8	1.3	0.1	0.6	0.1	2.2	1.1	0.2	2.8	1.6	0.9	2.4
Denmark	2.3	2.4	1.4	0.5	0.4	0.6	2.3	0.1	1.6	6.6	15.8	2.0	5.4	7.6	8.0
France	1.6	1.5	4.6	1.0	0.9	0.6	0.4	0.1	1.9	1.2	1.2	1.5	3.0	1.6	3.9
Germany	0.8	0.7	0.8	1.1	0.4	0.4	0.4	1.3	0.4	1.1	1.9	0.7	1.6	0.8	1.8
Italy	1.1	1.1	2.7	1.0	1.5	0.4	0.2	0.2		0.8	1.3	0.5	1.2	0.2	2.7
Netherlands	2.0	1.8	1.4	1.8	2.3	0.1	0.7	0.1	0.3	2.2	1.9	2.6	2.9	3.3	3.0
Poland	1.4	1.5	0.6	1.6	1.6	0.2	0.3	0.3	0.6	2.5	2.1	3.2	2.4	1.1	2.1
Spain	1.9	2.2	2.4	0.8	5.0		0.3	0.3	0.2	2.1	4.9	0.5	1.0	0.6	0.6
Ukraine	3.1	3.9	1.8	2.2	0.9		14.0	0.0	0.2	0.3		0.3	2.6	0.2	4.2
United Kingdom	0.8	0.6	3.8	0.7	0.3	0.2	0.4	0.1	0.7	0.7	0.4	0.8	0.8	0.7	0.7

▢ = Coefficient > 5

Source: Author's calculations based on FAO (2012).

Questions and assignments

12.1 What is a company's internationalisation process?

12.2 Present and discuss briefly different internationalisation models. Why may companies become international in different ways?

12.3 How are internationalisation models changing? Is gradual internationalisation dead? Why / Why not?

12.4 Why is the retail sector important for the food industry? How can the food sector react to increasing retail market power?

12.5 Private label: what is the market share of private labels? How is the trend? What are the implications?

12.6 Global strategic alliances: what are the advantages and disadvantages? Find and comment on other examples of global strategic alliances.

12.7 Why is entry mode important? Which factors may determine entry mode? How?

12.8 What is price transmission in the food value chain?

12.9 How can you measure the international competitiveness of a food company?

13 Models and methods in international food business

When analysing the economic and structural conditions in the food industry and on food markets, it is often advantageous to use systematic models and methods. This ensures a common framework of analysis and that all the significant conditions are included. Models and methods are typically developed on the basis of theoretical analyses and empirical studies and therefore they create a reliable and useful basis for strategic decisions in companies.

When using these common models and methods, it is also possible to make comparisons between the different studies. The basis for comparison is the same, which makes the results more useful and valid. The models and methods have very different aims and uses: some can shed light on competitive conditions; some can be used as a framework for future growth; while others can be used to describe a company's environment or market potential, etc.

The complexity of the models and methods varies substantially. Some are based on complex relationships and encompass many different aspects and dimensions of business or market conditions, while others are based on simple principles and are more focused. This chapter presents some of the common methods and models that can be used to analyse the food industry and food markets in a national and international perspective.

Porter's Five Forces

Porter's Five Forces is a framework to analyse industry and business strategy development which was created by Michael E. Porter at the Harvard Business School in 1979.

The model is used to gain an overview of the competitive situation in a given market. The model takes five forces into account, each of which influences competition in a given industry. The model is a good tool to gain insight into how a sector operates and what factors influence competition.

The model is also very relevant for the food industry. Negotiating strength in relation to suppliers and customers is important for the food industry, since trade is considerable and sustained. There are often many competing companies on the market and, with increasing globalisation and liberalisation, pressure from

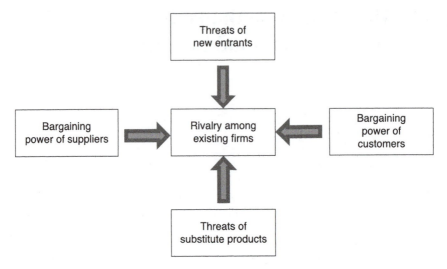

Figure 13.1 A graphical representation of Porter's Five Forces.

Source: Porter (1980).

potential new entrants on the market is significant. The five forces which affect competition in a business sector according to Porter's model are presented in Figure 13.1.

As the figure shows, the five forces are connected.

The five forces are crucial for the future competitive ability of individual companies in the food industry: the internal competition between companies in the food industry, a company's relative strength with regard to its raw produce suppliers and the retail sector, new foreign competitors and the threat of substitute products are all examples of the forces that can affect competition.

The threat of new entrants

If a particular market is characterised by weak competition and significant earning potential, it will soon attract new businesses. Thus the supply to the market will increase, which will reduce price and earnings. Therefore, a company which is already on the market has an interest in preventing new players from emerging on the market. There are several ways of restricting the access of new competitors to the market:

- Economies of scale: this means that unit costs can be kept low so that the selling price can be maintained at a competitive level.
- Product development: developing new and unique products (or brands) supported by effective marketing makes it more difficult for competitors to gain a share of the market.

- Large capital requirements: highly capital-intensive industries often have a rather protected existence, as potential new competitors cannot meet the capital requirements.
- Alliances with customers: when a company enters into close cooperation with its customers with regard to product development, marketing, etc., the customers become more or less tied to the company, thereby creating a kind of mutual dependency. If a customer switches to a new competitor in the market, it will require significant resources to establish new collaboration. This will also make it harder for potential competitors to enter the market.
- No access to distribution channels or commodities: an effective shield against foreign competition is if a foreign company cannot use the existing distribution system.
- Other cost advantages: access to raw produce, vertical integration via cooperative organisation, a favourable location and government grants, are examples of other barriers against foreign entry.
- Competitor reaction: a new and dangerous competitor on the market can expect to be met by a price war, which will, sooner or later, make the competitor abandon the entry. The mere fear of a competitor's reaction or experience from previous attempts can in itself be an effective shield against foreign competitors.

The threat of substitute products

The threat of substitute products (products that are similar and can thus replace existing products) is also one of the forces that can affect competition. In particular in research-intensive industries (pharmaceuticals, etc.), the emergence of new, better or cheaper products can decisively weaken the competitiveness of existing companies. Also, genetic engineering and food technology can result in a threat from substitute products.

Customers' bargaining power

The food industry's products can have several different customers, but the customer is usually the retail sector. In this case, the retail sector seeks to achieve a better market position than the food industry in order to be able to dictate, or at least have a significant influence on, prices and other trading conditions. The retail sector can attempt to improve its market power in several ways:

- by making the supplier crucially dependent on deliveries to the specific customer;
- by demanding standard or bulk goods: these products are homogeneous, and therefore the price is relatively low; at the same time, it is easier to switch suppliers if this proves to be advantageous;

- through backward integration, i.e. acquisitions in the industry, alliances, contract manufacturing, etc.

Suppliers' bargaining power

The relative strength of suppliers of raw produce can also greatly affect competition. Suppliers can achieve higher prices for their commodities if they have a stronger market position than their customers. Suppliers can increase their market power in several ways:

- by organising into fewer larger units;
- by producing specialised and heterogeneous goods which are indispensable for customers;
- through forward integration in, e.g., the food industry, which will create a new competitor on the market and an alternative customer for the supplier's goods.

Rivalry among existing companies

Between companies in a given sector there will always be healthy or unhealthy competition. Competition is healthy when it constantly forces companies to be market oriented and to keep a step ahead of competitors. However, competition is unhealthy for businesses when it leads to price wars and market instability. Competition, or rivalry, between existing businesses may be intense or weak. The following factors can increase competition in an industry:

- *Low market growth*. On a market with low growth in sales, many companies will try to increase their growth by taking market share from competitors. This is very much the case in the food sector.
- *High fixed costs*. Companies with substantial investments in production plants, etc., and thus high fixed costs, are forced to fully exploit capacity to cover fixed costs. If excess capacity arises, the company will seek to increase production, which will result in decreasing prices and profits.
- *Production of standard products*. If the company produces homogeneous standard products, along with other similar producers, customers can play the producers against each other, thereby increasing competition and applying downward pressure on prices.
- *Ambitious companies*. Companies with high ambitions regarding growth, market strength and expansion often contribute to high competition in a sector. Since earnings are not necessarily the main immediate goal for the company, low profits in order to maintain or increase market share may be acceptable. This will mean that the market will become unstable and will be characterised by low earnings, because the company is not responding in an economically rational way, or because the company is following long-term growth targets.

SWOT analysis

A SWOT analysis is often used as a simple, clear and very useful model for the strategic development of companies and organisations. SWOT is an abbreviation of the words: Strengths, Weaknesses, Opportunities and Threats.

Strengths and weaknesses are internal conditions, while opportunities and threats represent external factors in the surrounding business environment. Figure 13.2 shows a typical SWOT matrix.

The procedure for a SWOT analysis is as follows:

In step 1, the relevant conditions which are important in the particular case need to be identified.

It should be noted that the selection and assessment of the factors in a SWOT analysis can be very subjective. There is no clear method for identifying the factors, as it always depends on an individual analysis, and two people are unlikely to reach the same SWOT conclusion, even though they may be using the same data. Therefore, a SWOT model is not definitive and it is therefore not an immediate basis for decision making, unless there is general agreement regarding the model's content and implications.

In step 2, the individual factors should be prioritised in relation to their importance by weighting each, which increases the explanatory power and validity of the model. Box 13.1 presents examples of some of the factors typically used in a SWOT analysis.

In step 3 – once the factors have been selected and weighted, they are placed in a SWOT matrix.

SWOT models can be used in several ways:

First, the model helps to highlight and aid understanding regarding a company's strength and competitive position by focusing on the four categories,

	Positive	Negative
Internal origin	Strengths	Weaknesses
External origin	Opportunities	Threats

Figure 13.2 SWOT matrix.

Source: Author's presentation.

Box 13.1 Examples of factors in a SWOT model for food companies

Strengths	Weaknesses
- Technological advantages - Brands - Capital - Management - Economies of scale	- Weak brands - Access to distribution - Too few new products - Weak market and negotiating power - Little equity
Opportunities	Threats
- Trade liberalisation - Changes in customer preferences - Technological progress - Changes in economic policy, etc. - Changes to the tax system - Financial booms - New distribution channels	- Trade barriers - Changes in customer preferences - Technological progress - Changes in economic policy, etc. - Recession - New distribution channels

namely the company's internal strengths and weaknesses and its external opportunities and threats.

Second, the actual process of identifying the factors in the four categories is important and fruitful. Through joint brainstorming within the organisation it is possible to identify new opportunities or threats.

Third, the SWOT analysis can lead directly to action.

Overall, the SWOT matrix is a tool for developing strategies through the inclusion of the factors which were identified in the initial steps of the SWOT analysis. This is done by combining the identified factors and developing strategies which maximise the effect of the company's strengths and opportunities, and minimise the effect of its weaknesses and threats. In concrete terms this means:

- Internal strengths have to be better utilised, developed, renewed, upgraded, etc.
- Internal weaknesses can be addressed in several ways. Either the main weaknesses must be improved, or the company's marketing department can try to manoeuvre so that the weaknesses have as little impact on the business as possible.
- Opportunities must be exploited if the company has, or can develop, the necessary resources.
- Threats must either be converted to opportunities (through internal build-up of resources in the company) or must be avoided or rendered insignificant by moving into the segments where the threat is less significant.

The SWOT analysis can also be used in conjunction with other models and methods, including PESTLE and Porter's Five Forces.

Ansoff's product / market matrix

Ansoff's growth model (also called Ansoff's product / market matrix) is a tool to define a strategy for a company's product and market growth.

The starting point of Ansoff's growth model is that a company's growth initiatives depend on whether new or existing products are introduced onto new or existing markets.

The growth matrix, therefore, divides the segments up in relation to whether the markets and products are existing or new (see Figure 13.3).

In each of the four quadrants is a growth strategy which defines the possible framework for a company's expansion:

> *Market penetration* is the growth strategy which is used by a company when it decides to market an existing product on an existing market. Market penetration means that growth is only achieved by increasing market share, which can be achieved by:

- increasing marketing
- paying more attention to existing customers
- establishing entry barriers to prevent new competitors on the market
- pushing competitors out of the market
- acquisition of competitors.

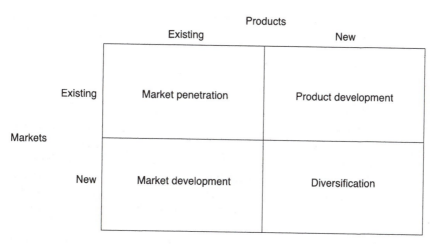

Figure 13.3 Ansoff's product / market matrix.

Source: Author's presentation based on Ansoff (1957).

An entry mode strategy is based on 'business as usual'. The focus is on existing and well-known products, and markets about which the company already has good information. Therefore, this strategy does not require major investment in market research.

Market development is the growth strategy that a company uses when it wants to sell an existing product on a new market. Once again, there is a series of concrete measures which a company can use to achieve this strategy:

• penetration of new geographical markets (internationalisation);
• penetration of a new market segment with a new target group, but in the same geographical area; this can be achieved through, e.g., new distribution channels;
• new applications of the product: the product can be used in new ways, but on the same market.

Product development means that the company introduces new products on existing markets. This is assuming, of course, that there is an actual or potential need and that the company has the right competences to meet the need. Product development may in principle be based on two competency considerations:

• existing competences, which can be technological, market-related or managerial, etc. in nature;
• new competences, where the company is considered to be well placed to build and develop the necessary new competences.

Diversification is a growth strategy where a business markets new products on new markets. It is inherently the most risky of the four growth strategies. There may be two types of diversification; related and unrelated (see Chapter 9).

The Boston Matrix

The Boston Matrix (also called the BCG Matrix and the Boston Consulting Group Portfolio Analysis Diagram) is a portfolio model to manage the business area, products, divisions or the 'strategic business units'. The company's business areas are placed on a diagram in relation to market attractiveness (measured by market growth) and the company's relative competitiveness (as measured by market share compared with the main competitor). The matrix is shown in Figure 13.4.

The starting point is that business areas or products have a life-cycle, which starts in the upper right-hand corner and finishes in the bottom right-hand corner; the equivalent of travelling from 'question marks' to 'dogs'.

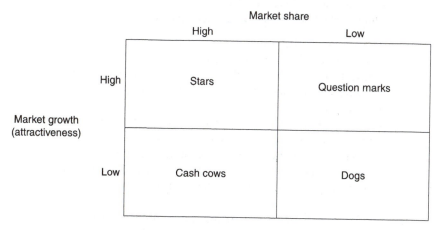

Figure 13.4 Boston Matrix.

Source: Author's presentation based on Henderson (1970).

Stars are high growth areas and products that have a relatively strong competitive position on the market. These segments often require substantial investment to support growth and market share. Eventually, market growth will decline and, if the company manages to maintain the high market share, the products become cash cows.

Cash Cows are low-growth segments of which the company has a relatively large market share. These are saturated market segments which do not require heavy investment. Cash cows need to be supported so that they can continue to generate profits and liquidity to be used for the stars segments.

Question marks are segments where the company has a low market share, but where market growth is high. These segments have potential, but they also require considerable investment if market share is to be taken from competitors who are already on the market.

The task therefore involves selecting the segments to be pursued and which also fit with the company's corporate strategy and competences. Some segments should be developed into stars, while others should be abandoned.

Dogs are segments or products where both market growth and market share are small. This means the segments neither require nor earn much money. However, dogs often tie up resources, e.g. capital, management and focus, in an area that at first seems to have no potential. Therefore, the segment is rarely a real asset to the company in the short or long term.

Placing the business areas on the four squares helps visualise the current distribution of the company's portfolio. Then the company:

* analyses the portfolio and decides which areas should receive more or fewer resources in terms of capital, etc.;

- develops growth strategies to add new products and business units to the portfolio for which the company has four strategic options:

  1) Increase the market share, which can be achieved through marketing, improving quality, reducing prices and through the acquisition of competitors and possibly their subsequent closure. These strategic measures are appropriate for moving a product from being a question mark to a star.

  2) Maintenance. This involves maintaining the current position in the matrix, which may be the case for, e.g., cash cows.

  3) 'Harvesting / milking'. Here, the company reduces its investments in the product in order to maximise short-term earnings and generate cash flow. It may involve, e.g., a product moving from being a star to a cash cow.

  4) Liquidate. A business can be liquidated through a phasing-out or an actual sale. This means that the resources can then be used in other areas, e.g. to move products from being question marks to stars.

Once the company has classified all its segments in the Boston Matrix, the portfolio should be continuously adjusted so that it fits optimally with the company's competences and supports the most attractive business opportunities. The Boston model can be used to ensure that the following important situations pertain:

- The company has stars in its portfolio which can take over when the existing cash cows disappear.
- The company has cash cows in the portfolio in order to constantly generate profits and cash flow to other areas in the portfolio.
- Question marks are constantly nurtured. Question marks are the first link in the 'food chain', and it is therefore important that this area is constantly developed in order to provide the company with future attractive business areas.

Many food companies have explicit growth targets, and the Boston Matrix can be used to ensure balanced development. Growth must occur in the strategically appropriate segments, and new products and markets must be developed, while, at the same time, the entire product portfolio has to be adapted and developed. For this purpose, the Boston Matrix is a useful tool.

The GE model

In the late 1960s and early 1970s, General Electric (GE), a large US company with significantly diversified activities, was unsatisfied with the financial results it had achieved via a number of investments in various business areas. Therefore, management analysed a number of new concepts and techniques as tools for their strategic planning. They became interested in the Boston model, which in many ways was a useful tool for visualising and positioning the portfolio composition.

GE therefore asked McKinsey & Co. to develop a portfolio model which was broader than the Boston model. In 1971, McKinsey & Co. developed a method to identify and organise the future earnings potential of the strategic business areas. This method became known as the GE model.

The GE model (also called The McKinsey / General Electric Matrix) is, like the Boston Matrix, a portfolio model which identifies the various business areas and groups them for the subsequent formulation of strategy. In many ways, the GE model is a development of and improvement on the Boston Matrix. The GE model also has two dimensions, namely the company's strengths and competitiveness, and the market's attractiveness (growth).

Compared to the Boston Matrix, in the GE model 'market growth' is replaced by 'market attractiveness' and 'market share' by 'competitive position' (competitive strength). Therefore the terms are more accurate and comprehensive, but are far more difficult to quantify. The matrix is divided into nine cells as opposed to the four cells of the Boston Matrix (see Figure 13.5).

Market attractiveness and competitive position encompass many different conditions which have to be determined in each case. Box 13.2 lists some of the factors that can affect market attractiveness and competitive position.

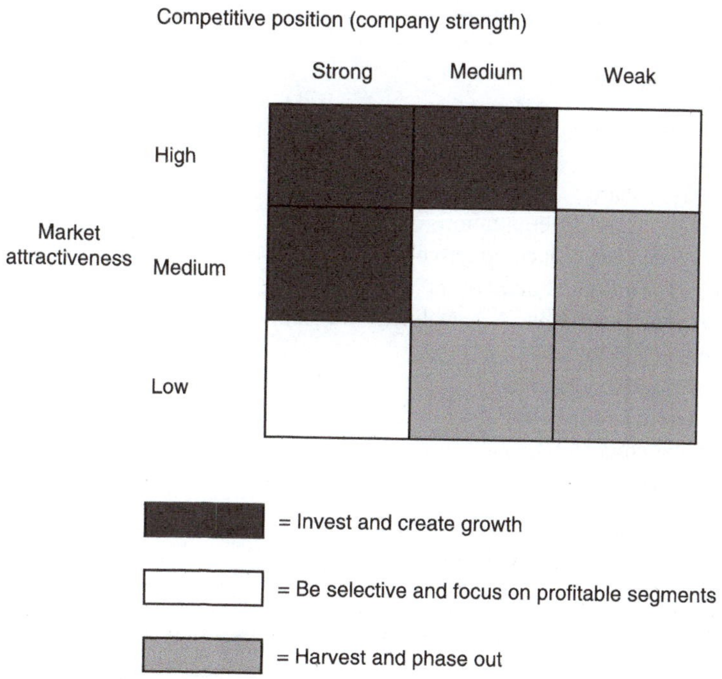

Figure 13.5 The GE model.

Source: Author's presentation based on McKinsey (2008).

Box 13.2 Examples of factors in the GE model

Market attractiveness

Factors contributing to a market's attractiveness are:

- the market's size
- market growth
- purchasing power
- intensity of competition:

  with competitors
  with suppliers
  with customers

- distribution and infrastructure
- coverage
- public subsidies, co-financing schemes, etc.
- synergies with other markets
- entry barriers (existing and future)
- legislative conditions
- economic and political conditions (see PESTLE analysis)
- overall risk and uncertainty.

Competitive position

Factors contributing to a company's competitive position are:

- market share
- potential for differentiation
- potential to produce effectively
- costs relative to competitors
- technological capacity, capability and lead
- image and brand
- distribution channels
- economies of scale
- management
- alliances

  horizontal (with competitors and / or colleagues)
  vertical (suppliers, customers, etc.)

- capital (ability and willingness to invest)
- exploitation of synergies with other parts of the company.

The quantification and positioning is conducted as follows. First, the relevant factors which are crucial for market attractiveness and competitive position have to be identified. The factors are weighted according to their relative importance. Each factor is then given a value depending on its specific market attractiveness and competitive position.

For example, market attractiveness (MA) is calculated as follows:

$$MA = \text{factor value}_1 \times \text{factor weighting}_1$$
$$+ \text{factor value}_2 \times \text{factor weighting}_2$$
$$+ \text{factor value}_n \times \text{factor weighting}_n$$

The factors 1 to n are the market's size, market growth, etc., selected according to the importance in the concrete case and assigned an appropriate weighting. The company's competitive position is calculated according to the same principle.

There are basically three strategic options:

- Best position – invest and create growth (the company must grow in order to achieve a good position on the market).
- Middle position – be selective and focus on profitable areas (the company must manage profitability).
- Worst position – harvest and phase-out (the company must harvest, reduce investments and finally withdraw from the market).

Figure 13.6 shows the specific strategic measures in each of the nine cells.

The PESTLE analysis

PESTLE stands for: **P**olitical, **E**conomic, **S**ocial, **T**echnological, **L**egal and **E**nvironmental.

		Competitive position (The company's strengths)		
		Strong	Medium	Weak
Market attractiveness	High	Protect position and grow as quickly as possible	Invest in order to grow and become market leader	Grow selectively in relation to possible special competitive advantages
	Medium	Grow selectively within the most profitable segments	Be selective and focus on profitable segments	Limit growth or harvest
	Low	Protect position. Focus on profitable segments	Strive to survive in the most profitable segments	Give up Sell

Figure 13.6 The GE matrix with strategic measures.

Source: Author's presentation based on McKinsey (2008).

A PESTLE analysis forms part of the external analysis a company conducts when performing a strategic analysis or market research. PESTLE provides an overview of the different macro-environmental factors that the company has to take into consideration. It is a useful strategic tool for understanding market growth or decline, business position and potential, and the future direction of operations. A PESTLE analysis is also a useful tool to evaluate the attractiveness of a market.

PESTLE analyses are generic methods which can be used in any business industry. However, some factors will be more relevant in some industries than in others. Examples of the components in a PESTLE analysis, with special emphasis on the food industry, are presented below:

Political factors include government policies, such as the degree of intervention in the economy and markets. Political factors such as tax policy, health policy, trade restrictions and political stability may be of specific relevance for food industry firms. Political factors may also include industry support, which can be very important in the agricultural and food sector.

Economic factors include macro-economic factors such as economic growth, interest rates, exchange rates and inflation. Economic growth is an important indicator of the economic situation and therefore also of market potential. Interest rates, which in many instances co-vary with exchange rates, can affect a company's cost of capital. The level and stability of interest rates may influence the investments of firms and hence their growth and expansion.

Social factors also affect food companies, whether they export or invest and produce on international markets. Social factors include conditions such as household size, age and income distribution, population growth, worker motivation, female labour force, religion and consumption habits. In particular, consumption habits may be crucial for a food company which is entering a new international market. Life-style trends, demand for convenience food and food service are also important social factors for the food industry.

Technological factors include R & D, technological processes, e-commerce, the use of Internet technology and infrastructure. Technology can be an important parameter for export opportunities to a given market, but technology can also be a driver for foreign direct investment and global offshoring. Access to technology has, on several occasions, been an important motive for international mergers and acquisitions in the food industry.

Legal factors include the legislation that exists on the market. Food legislation, requirements and control regarding food, veterinary precautions, etc. can be very important parameters for the food industry. For food companies which are planning foreign direct investment, labour market legislation and competition legislation can also be of importance.

Environmental factors include a number of ecological and environmental aspects. Reuse and recycling, rules on packaging, water and climate impacts may be important environmental factors for the food industry. Environmental values of customers, from the market and from stakeholders / investors may also be important factors.

The PESTLE analysis has been further developed and extended (see Box 13.3).

Box 13.3 Extended and similar analyses

- PESTLIED: Political, Economic, Social, Technological, Legal, International, Environmental, Demographic
- STEEPLE: Social, Technological, Economic, Environmental, Political, Legal, Ethical
- STEEPLED: Social, Technological, Economic, Environmental, Political, Legal, Ethical, Demographic
- STEER: Socio-cultural, Technological, Economic, Ecological, Regulatory
- SLEPT: Social, Legal, Economic, Political, Technological.

The Blue Ocean Strategy

The Blue Ocean Strategy is a management concept which was formulated by Professor W. Chan Kim and Renée Mauborgne from the INSEAD business school in France. The aim of the Blue Ocean Strategy is to find and develop a strategy for the company that makes it unique on the market. Instead of focusing on the traditional competitive parameters such as price competition, Blue Ocean companies seek to create market advantages through creativity and innovation.

The Blue Ocean Strategy may be a significant inspiration for many food companies, as agricultural and food products often belong to a homogeneous group, where product differentiation and innovation is limited and where price is an important competitive parameter.

The starting point for the Blue Ocean theory is that no business or industry is constantly successful. Companies must avoid traditional and constant patterns of action, but instead continuously – and in a dynamic process – rethink the way they market, sell and communicate on their market. Companies must be pioneers and be innovative as a way to find and develop their unique business.

Once a company has a unique business, competition from other companies or from other products becomes very limited. In contrast, the red ocean market is characterised by intense competition, which is a situation that many food companies are familiar with. The blue ocean symbolises a unique market position where competition is minimal.

The concepts and ideas behind the Blue Ocean Strategy are not completely unique or new. In a way, the Blue Ocean Strategy is a memorable metaphor which attempts to brand a set of previously existing concepts and frameworks.

Box 13.4 **The metaphor of red and blue oceans describes the market universe**

Red oceans

Red oceans are existing and familiar industries and markets. The industry and market boundaries are relatively fixed and they are more or less accepted by market players. Companies seek to grow, not by expanding the market, but by taking market share from competitors. This internal cannibalisation means that the market space is crowded, and thus the potential for profits and growth is reduced. Products are homogeneous commodities; there is bloody competition and hence the name, red oceans.

Blue oceans

Blue ocean companies, in contrast, create new markets and new demand. The market is expanding by new – and unknown – segments, and products, services, etc. are developed. When the market grows, and when companies obtain their own unique markets, competition is weak. The focus is on creating growth through market research, market development, innovation and unique segments – and not through taking market share from competitors on existing markets (Kim and Mauborgne, 2005).

Questions and assignments

13.1 Select a food company of your own choice. Use Porter's Five Forces to describe the competitive situation of the company.

13.2 Select a food company of your own choice. Use the SWOT model to describe a strategic development of the company.

13.3 Give examples of food companies using Ansoff's growth model.

13.4 Give examples of food companies using the Boston Matrix.

13.5 Describe the main content of the GE model.

13.6 What is the purpose of a PESTLE analysis?

13.7 How can the concept of Blue Ocean Strategy be used in other models?

Bibliography

ABARE (Australian Bureau of Agricultural and Resource Economics) (2008): *Australian commodities*. March quarter. Vol. 15. No. 1. Available online at: http://adl.brs.gov.au/data/warehouse/pe_abare99001419/ac_mar08_full.pdf

Abler, D. (2010): 'Demand Growth in Developing Countries'. OECD Food, Agriculture and Fisheries Working Papers, No. 29, OECD Publishing. http://dx.doi.org/10.1787/5km91p2xcsd4-en.

About.com (2012): US Foreign Policy. ' http://usforeignpolicy.about.com/od/introtoforeignpolicy/a/What-Is-Globalization.htm.

Accenture (2012): 'Who Says M&A Doesn't Create Value?', *Outlook*. No.1. www.accenture.com/SiteCollectionDocuments/PDF/Accenture-Outlook-Who-says-MA-doesnt-create-value.pdf.

Aconis, Anthony (2004): 'Detailhandlen har sejret', *Berlingske Tidende*. p. 2.

Adenäuer, M., Louhichi, K., de Frahan, B. H. and Witzke, H. P. (2005): 'Impact of the "Everything but Arms" Initiative on the EU Sugar Sub-sector'. CAPRI Working Paper 05–03. www.ilr.uni-bonn.de/agpo/rsrch/dynaspat/pap05–03.pdf.

African Economic Outlook (2012): Direct Investment Flows. www.africaneconomicoutlook.org/en/outlook/external-financial-flows/direct-investment-flows.

Agriculture and Agri-Food Canada (2007): Profile of The Canadian Chicken Industry. www4.agr.gc.ca/AAFC-AAC/display-afficher.do?id=1184612239436&lang=eng#sec55.
—— (2012): Consumers. Spending on Food and Beverages. www4.agr.gc.ca/AAFC-AAC/display-afficher.do?id=1170942402619&lang=eng#n2.

Aksoy, M. Ataman and Beghin, J. C. (eds) (2005): 'Global Agricultural Trade Policies', *Global Agricultural Trade and Developing Countries*. The World Bank. Washington.

Aksoy, M. Ataman and Hoekman, Bernard (eds) (2010): *Food Prices and Rural Poverty*. The World Bank. New York.

Anderson, Kym (1987): 'On Why Agriculture Declines with Economic Growth', *Agricultural Economics*. Vol. 1. pp. 195–207.

Ansoff, Igor (1957): 'Strategies for Diversification', *Harvard Business Review*. Vol. 35. No. 5, Sep–Oct. pp. 113–24.

Arlimentos Argentinos (2012): Producción Argentina de Leche – serie mensual. www.alimentosargentinos.gov.ar/contenido/sectores/lacteos/estadisticas/01_Nacional/serie/Prod_Mensual_2.htm.

Asmussen, Christian Geisler, Pedersen, Torben and Petersen, Bent (2005): 'How Do We Capture "Global Specialization" When Measuring Firms' Degree of Internationalization?' Copenhagen Business School, SMG WP 7/2005. http://openarchive.cbs.dk/bitstream/handle/10398/7480 cbs%20forskningsindberetning%20smg%2027.pdf? sequence = 1.

Attac (2012): What is Attac? www.attac.org/en/what-attac.

Azevedo, Joao (1999): 'Why Do Companies Merge? Merger Motives and Determinants'. Helsinki University of Technology. www.tuta.hut.fi/studies/Courses_and_schedules/Isib/TU-91.167/Old_seminar_papers/azevedo_joao.pdf.

Azzam, Azzeddine (2002): 'The Effect of Concentration in the Food Processing Industry on Food Prices', *Cornhusker Economics*, Lincoln: University of Nebraska.

Balcombe, Kelvin (2009): The Nature and Determinants of Volatility in Agricultural Prices. Technical Report to FAO. http://mpra.ub.uni-muenchen.de/24819/1/MPRA_paper_24819.pdf.

Bayrak, Okan (2002): Valuation of Firms in Mergers and Acquisitions. www.fic.wharton.upenn.edu/fic/cmbt/Okan%20Bayrak.ppt.

Bekier, M. M., Bogardus, A. J. and Oldham, T. (2001): 'Why Mergers Fail', *The McKinsey Quarterly*. No. 4. pp. 6–9.

Bekkum, O. F, and van Dijk, G. (1997): *Agricultural Co-operatives in the European Union, Trends and Issues on the Eve of 21st Century*. The Netherlands Institute for Co-operative Entrepreneurship, Assen, The Netherlands.

Bergman, Edward M. and Feser, Edward J. (2007): *Industrial and Regional Clusters: Concepts and Comparative Applications*. Available online at: http://www.rri.wvu.edu/WebBook/Bergman-Feser/chapter1.htm

BIAC (2011): Price Volatility in Food and Agricultural Commodity Markets. www.biac.org/statements/agr/11_06_PriceVolatilityinFoodandAgricultural-Commodity Markets.pdf.

Bieshaar, H., Knight, J. and van Wassenaer, A. (2001): 'Deals that Create Value', *The McKinsey Quarterly*. No. 1. pp. 65–73.

BIS (several years): *Quarterly Review*, Bank for International Settlements.

——— (2011): Foresight Project on Global Food and Farming Futures Synthesis Report C1: Trends in Food Demand and Production. Department for Business Innovation and Skills. www.bis.gov.uk/assets/foresight/docs/food-and-farming/synthesis/11–621-c1-trends-food-demand-and-production.

Bower, Joseph L. (2001): 'Not All M&As Are Alike – and That Matters', *Harward Business School. Working Knowledge*. 2nd April. http://hbswk.hbs.edu/item.jhtml?id=2123&t = finance&noseek = one.

BP (2012): Biofuels. www.bp.com/sectiongenericarticle800.do?categoryId=9037217&contentId=7068633.

Brasil Foods (2012): www.brasilfoods.com.

BusinessWeek (2002): October.

Cavusgil, S. T. (1994): 'A Quiet Revolution in Australian Exporters', *Marketing News*. Vol. 28. No. 11. pp. 18–21.

Center for Cooperatives (2012): University of Wisconsin-Madison. www.uwcc.wisc.edu/whatisacoop.

CEPII (2004): Regionalism and the Regionalisation of International Trade, Gaulier, Guillaume, Jean, Sébastien and Ünal-Kesenci, Deniz. www.cepii.fr/anglaisgraph/workpap/summaries/2004/wp04-16.htm.

Chapman, T. L., Dempsey, J. L., Ramsdell, G. and Bell, T. E. (1998): 'Purchasing's Big Moment – After a Merger', *The McKinsey Quarterly*, No. 1. pp. 57–65.

Chichava, S. (2010). China in Mozambique's Agriculture Sector: Implications and Challenges. Celebrating the 10th Anniversary of the Establishment of the Forum on China-Africa Co-operation (FOCAC). Available online at: http://www.iese.ac.mz/lib/noticias/2010/China%20in%20Mozambique_09.2010_SC.pdf

CIA (2012): The World Factbook. www.cia.gov/library/publications/the-world-factbook/fields/2129.html.

CME Group (2012): www.cmegroup.com.

Cochrane, W. (1958): *Farm Prices, Myths and Reality*, Minneapolis: University of Minnesota Press.

Cook, Dan (2002): 'WLL's Reward: Consolidation', *The Business Journal* – Portland. http://portland.bizjournals.com/portland/stories/2002/01/28/editorial2.html.

Co-operatives Australia (2012): Humanizing the Economy Through Co-operatives. www.australia.coop/ca/index.php/articles/publications/458-humanizing.

Cotterill, Ronald W. (2000): 'Continuing Concentration in the US: Strategic Challenges to an Unstable Status Quo', in Ramsay, Bill (ed.), *The Global Food Industry. Strategic Directions*. Financial Times.

COGECA (2005): *Agricultural Co-operatives in Europe. Main Issues and Trends*. COGECA. Brussels.

Coriolis (2010): Fonterra and the New Zealand Dairy Industry: Options Going Forward. A discussion document.

Crawford, Jo-Ann A. and Fiorentino, Roberto V. (2005): 'The Changing Landscape of Regional Trade Agreements'. Discussion Paper No. 8, World Trade Organisation.

Damuri, Yose Rizal (2009): 'How Preferential are Preferential Trade Agreements? Analysis of Product Exclusions in PTAs'. Swiss National Centre of Competence in Research, Working Paper Number 2009/30. http://phase1.nccr-trade.org/images/stories/publications/IP3/yose_2009-30 Paper_Product_Exclusions.pdf.

Danish Agriculture and Food Council (2012): Dairy Statistics. www.lf.dk/Tal_og_Analyser/Aarstatistikker/Mejeristatistik/Mejeristatistik_2010.aspx.

Danish Competition Authority (2008): Fødevarepriser. October. www.kfst.dk.

—— (2009): Fødevarepriser – Prisudviklingen på mælk, smør og brød Konkurrence-analyse. February. www.kfst.dk.

Danish Dairy Board (several years): Mejeristatistik (Dairy Statistics).

—— (1982): Dansk Mejeribrug 1882–2000.

—— (2000): UgeNyt No. 14. 6 April (Mejeriforeningen).

Danish Seed Council (several issues): *Annual Reports*. www.seedcouncil.dk.

Danone (2011): Danone 10. Danone Essentials in 2010. Available online at: http://danone10.danone.com/uk

Dansk Landbrug (several years): Agriculture in Denmark.

DCANZ (2012): New Zealand Milk Production. www.dcanz.com/files/New%20Zealand%20Milk%20Production%202011.pdf.

Deboo, Martin (2000): 'Concentration in the European Food Market', in Ramsay, Bill (ed), *The Global Food Industry. Strategic Directions. Financial Times Retail & Consumer*. London.

DEFRA (Department for Environment, Food and Rural Affairs) (several issues): *Family Food*. www.defra.gov.uk.

de Groot, N. S. P. (1998): Floriculture Worldwide. Trade And Consumption Patterns. www.agrsci.unibo.it/wchr/wc1/degroot.html.

De Hoyos, Rafael and Leseem, Rebecca (2008): Food Shares in Consumption: New Evidence Using Engel Curves for the Developing World. https://mywebspace.wisc.edu/rlessem/web/engel.pdf.

Dekker, Wout (2003): 'Power Resides Where the Information Is Unique. (Nutreco)', in Grievink, Jan-Willem, Josten, Lia and Valk, Conny (eds), *State of the Art in Food. Financial Times Retail & Consumer*. London.

Deloitte Consulting (2002): Solving the Merger Mystery. Maximizing the Payoff of Mergers and Acquisitions. *Financial Times*, Feb 12, 2002.

De Schutter, Olivier (2009): World Set for New Food Crisis in 2010, UN Warns. www. euractiv.com/cap/world-set-new-food-crisis-2010-un-warns/article-187695.

Desouzart, Osler (2007): Structural Changes in the Brazilian Poultry Sector 1995 to 2005. www.fao.org/ag/AGAinfo/home/events/bangkok2007/docs/part1/brazil_.pdf.

Devlin, R. and Estevadeordal, A. (2004): 'Trade and Cooperation: A Regional Public Goods Approach', in Estevadeordal, A., Frantz, B., Nguyen, T.R., (eds), *Regional Public Goods: From Theory to Practice*, Washington, DC: Inter-American Development Bank.

DLF-TRIFOLIUM (several issues): *Annual Reports*. www.dlf.com.

Dobson, P. (2003): 'Retailer Buyer Power in European Markets: Lessons from Grocery Supply'. Business School Research Series, Paper 2002:1.

Donoso, Ignacio, Shadbolt, Nicola and Bailey, William (2004): 'The Internationalization of Agricultural Co-operatives – A Source of Conflict?' www.ifama.org/conferences/2004 Conference/Papers/Shadbolt2002.pdf.

Donoso, Ignacio, Rudzki, Romuald, Shadbolt, Nicola and Bailey, William (2003): 'The Internationalization of Agricultural Co-operatives: Critical Factors in Development'. Agribusiness Perspectives Papers, Paper 61 ISSN 1442–6951.

Douglas, Susan P. and Craig, C. Samuel (1989): 'Evolution of Global Marketing Strategy: Scale, Scope and Synergy', *Columbia Journal of World Business*. Fall. pp. 47–59.

Doyle, Bill (2002): Global Trends Affecting the Fertilizer Industry. Speech to Ag. Retailers Association. PotashCorp. www.potashcorp.com/media/pdf/investor_relations/speeches/ara_speech_02.pdf.

Dunning, J. H. (1980): 'Toward an Eclectic Theory of International Production: Some Empirical Tests', *Journal of International Business Studies*, Vol. 11. No. 1. pp. 9–31.

eatoutmagazine (2009): Eating out in the UK. www.eatoutmagazine.co.uk/online_article/ Eating-out-in-the-UK/8006.

Ebneth, Oliver and Theuvsen, Ludwig (2005): Internationalization and Financial Performance of Cooperatives – Empirical Evidence from the European Dairy Sector. International Food and Agribusiness Management Association, 15th Annual World Food and Agribusiness Symposium and Forum. June 25–28. Chicago, IL.

ebst (2003): Mapping of Danish Clusters (in Danish). www.ebst.dk/file/1589/kortlaegning_ kompetenceklynger.pdf.

Economist.com (2003): Corporate Strategy. Who Gets Eaten and Who Gets To Eat. www. economist.com/globalExecutive/thinking/displayStory.cfm?story_id = 1936305.

EPI (2011): Corn Production and Use for Fuel Ethanol in the United States, 1980–2010. www.earth-policy.org/datacenter/xls/book_wote_ch5_3.xls.

ETC (several years): Who Will Control the Green Economy? www.etcgroup.org.

Europanel (several issues): Key Indicators. http://www.europanel.com/keyfacts.php.

European Cluster Observatory (2012): www.clusterobservatory.eu.

European Commission (several years): Agriculture in the European Union. Statistical and economic information. Published by The European Commission. Brussels.

—— (2007): Competitiveness of the European Food Industry: An Economic and Legal Assessment. http://ec.europa.eu/enterprise/sectors/food/files/competitiveness_study_en.pdf.

—— (2008): High Prices on Agricultural Commodity Markets: Situation and Prospects – A Review of Causes of High Prices and Outlook for World Agricultural Markets. July. Brussels.

—— (2009a): Historical Price Volatility. http://ec.europa.eu/agriculture/analysis/tradepol/commodityprices/volatility_en.pdf.

—— (2009b): Analysis of Price Transmission along the Food Supply Chain in the EU. http://ec.europa.eu/economy_finance/publications/publication16067_en.pdf.

—— (2011): The Impact of Private Labels on the Competitiveness of the European Food Supply Chain. http://ec.europa.eu/enterprise/sectors/food/files/study_privlab04042011_en.pdf.

—— (2012): Statistics. http://ec.europa.eu/competition/mergers/statistics.pdf.

Eurostat (2012): Food Supply Chain – Price Indices. Available online at: http://appsso.eurostat.ec.europa.eu/nui/show.do?dataset=prc_fsc_idx&lang=en

Evans, L. T. (1998): *Feeding the Ten Billion – Plants and Population Growth*, Cambridge: Cambridge University Press.

Ewans, Alex (2008): 'Rising Food Prices: Drivers and Implications for Development', in Chatham House Briefing Paper, April. www.chathamhouse.org.uk/publications/papers/view/-/id/612.

Ezekiel, M. (1938): 'The Cobweb Theorem', *Quarterly Journal of Economics*. Vol. 52, No. 2 (Feb., 1938) pp. 255–280.

FAO (1971): *Agricultural Commodity Projections 1979–80*. Vol. III. Rome.

—— (2010a): Agricultural Futures: Strengthening Market Signals for Global Price Discovery. www.fao.org/fileadmin/templates/est/COMM_MARKETS_MONITORING/Grains/Documents/ConferenceRoomSeries2.pdf.

—— (2010b): 'Price Volatility in Agricultural Markets. Economic and Social Perspectives'. Policy Brief 12. www.fao.org/docrep/013/am053e/am053e00.pdf.

—— (2010c): 'Economic and Social Perspectives'. Policy Brief 9. June. www.fao.org/docrep/012/al296e/al296e00.pdf.

—— (2011): Price Volatility in Food and Agricultural Markets: Policy Responses. www.ifad.org/operations/food/documents/g20.pdf.

—— (2012): *FAOSTAT*. http://faostat.fao.org/site/339/default.aspx.

FAO *et al.* (2011): Price Volatility in Food and Agricultural Markets: Policy Responses. Policy Report, including contributions by FAO, IFAD, IMF, OECD, UNCTAD, WFP, the World Bank, the WTO, IFPRI and the UN HLTF. www.ifad.org/operations/food/documents/g20.pdf.

Farm Foundation (2009): What's Driving Food Prices? www.farmfoundation.org/news/articlefiles.

FDC (several issues a): *Andelsbladet*. (Federation of Danish Cooperatives).

—— (several issues b): *Annual Report*. (Federation of Danish Cooperatives).

Federal Reserve Economic Data (2012): Spot Oil Price: West Texas Intermediate (Oilprice). http://research.stlouisfed.org/fred2/graph/?s[1][id] = OILPRICE.

Financial Times (2008): Europe's CAP the 'Answer' to Food Crisis. 27th April.

Fisch, J. H. and Oesterle, M.-J. (2003): 'Exploring the Globalization of German MNCs with the Complex Spread and Diversity Measure', *Schmalenbach Business Review*. Vol. 55 (January). pp. 2–21.

FOI (2007): Danish Agricultural Economy in 2007. www.foi.life.ku.dk/Publikationer/Rapporter/~/media/foi /docs/publications/Reports/Agricultural%20Økonomi/2007.ashx.

FORA (2010): The Danish Agricultural and Food Cluster in an International Perspective (in Danish). www.fvm.dk/Default.aspx?ID=18480&PID=167616&year=&NewsID-=6078.

Fortenberry, T. Randal and Park, Hwanil (2008): 'The Effect of Ethanol Production on the US National Corn Price'. University of Wisconsin-Madison, Department of Agricultural & Applied Economics, Staff Paper, No. 523.

Fulton, Murray (2000): New Generation Co-operatives. http://usaskstudies.coop/pdf-files/ What_Are_NGCs.pdf.

G20 (2011): Action Plan on Food Price Volatility and Agriculture. Ministerial declaration. http://agriculture.gouv.fr/IMG/pdf/2011-06-23 - ActionPlan VFinale.pdf.

GATT (1979): Differential and More Favorable Treatment Reciprocity and Fuller Participation of Developing Countries (Enabling Clause). Findes f.eks. på: www.worldtradelaw. net/tokyoround/enablingclause.pdf.

GCSP (2006): Definitions of Globalization: A Comprehensive Overview and a Proposed Definition. Geneva Center for Security Policy. By Dr. Nayef R. F. Al-Rodhan and Gérard Stoudmann. www.sustainablehistory.com/articles/definitions-of-globalization.pdf.

General Mills (2012): A Portfolio for Global Growth. Annual Report 2011. www.generalmills. com/en/Company.aspx.

Golup, Stephen S. and McManus, Jeffery (2008): Horticulture Exports and African Development. UNCTAD. www.unctad.org/sections/ldc_dir/docs/ldc2009#_011_golub&mcmanus _en.pdf.

Gorton, Gary, Kahl, Matthias and Rosen, Richard (2002): Eat or Be Eaten: A Theory of Mergers and Merger Waves. www.personal.anderson.ucla.edu/matthias.kahl/gorton_ kahl_rosen.pdf.

Graney, Brian (1998): Oil Consolidation and Thoughts on Global Competition. www.fool. com/DRIPPort/1998/dripport981202.htm.

Grievink, Jan-Willem (2003): The Changing Face of the Global Food Supply Chain. Conference on Changing Dimensions of the Food Economy: Exploring the Policy Issues. Haag.

Grievink, Jan-Willem, Josten, Lia and Valk, Conny (2003): *State of the Art in Food. The Changing Face of the Worldwide Food Industry*. Elsevier Business Information, Meppel, The Netherlands.

Gugler, Klaus, Mueller, Dennis C. and Yurtoglu, B. Burcin (2006): The Determinants of Merger Waves. University of Vienna. 48 pp. http://mailbox.univie.ac.at/~yurtogb5/ Workshop/merg-det.pdf.

Haagsma, Rein and Koning, Niek (2005): 'Endogenous Norms and Preferences and the Farm Income Problem', *European Review of Agricultural Economics*. March. Vol. 32. No. 1. pp. 25–49.

Hampl, Peter von (2002): *Internationale strategische Allianzen im Handel*, European Marketing Distribution AG.

Handy, Charles, R., Kaufmann, Phil and Martinez, Steve (1996): 'Direct Investment is Primary Strategy to Access Foreign Markets', *Food Review*. May. pp. 6–12.

Hannah, Leslie and Kay, J. A. (1977): *Concentration in Modern Industry. Theory, Measurement and the UK Experience*, London: MacMillan.

Hansen, Henning Otte (1993): 'Agriculture and Economic Trade Blocs' (in Danish), *økonomi og Politik*. No. 1. pp. 47–58.

—— (1997): *Globalisering: Internationalisering af landbruget og fødevareindustrien*, DSR-Forlag. Copenhagen.

—— (2005): *Vækst i Fødevareindustrien. – Vækst, fusioner, strukturudvikling, globalisering og koncentration i det agroindustrielle kompleks – i Danmark og globalt*, Handelshøjskolens Forlag. Copenhagen.

—— (2011a): *Andelsselskaber i udvikling. Andelsbevægelsens evne til forandring og omstilling i landbrugets udvikling fra den lokale til den globale landsby*, Handelshøjskolens Forlag. Copenhagen.

—— (2011b): 'Agricultural Subisidy Schemes. Price and Support Systems in the Agricultural Policy', *Encyklopedia of Dairy Science*. 2nd edition. Vol. 4. pp. 286–94.

—— (2012): *Dansk gartneri og Den Grønne Vækstklynge. Udfordringer og strategiske udviklingsmuligheder*, Handelshøjskolens Forlag. Copenhagen.

Hansen, Rasmus Bech (2004): 'Wal-Mart-effekten truer mærkevarer', *Berlingske Tidende*. 23rd November.

Hansen, Svend Aage (1983): *økonomisk vækst i Danmark. Bind II: 1914–83*.

HCDA (2012): The Horticultural Crops Development Authority. www.hcda.or.ke/tech/index.php.

Heady, Derek and Shenggen, Fan (2010): Reflections on the Global Food Crisis. How Did It Happen? How Has It Hurt? And How Can We Prevent the Next One? IFPRI, Research Monogram 165.

Held, D., McGrew, Anthony, Goldblatt, David and Perraton, Jonathan (1999): 'Global Transformations: Introduction', in Held *et al.*, *Global Transformation: Politics, Economics, and Culture*, Palo Alto, CA: Stanford University Press.

Henderson, Bruce D. (1970): 'The Product Portfolio'. *BCG Perspective Series*. Available online at: https://www.bcgperspectives.com/content/classics/strategy_the_product_portfolio/

Henriksen, Ole Bus and Ølgaard, Anders (1969): Danmarks Udenrigshandel 1874–1958. Studier fra Københabns Universitets Økonomiske Institut, Nr 2.

Hernandez, Manuel A., Robles, Miguel and Torero, Maximo (2010): Fires in Russia, Wheat Production, and Volatile Markets. Reasons to Panic? IFPRI.

Hertel, T. W. and Martin, W. (2000): 'Liberalizing Agriculture and Manufactures in a Millenium Round: Implications for Developing Countries', *World Economy*. No. 23. pp. 455–70.

Heston, Alan, Summers, Robert and Aten, Bettina (2009): Penn World Table, Center for International Comparisons of Production, Income and Prices at the University of Pennsylvania. August.

Hines, C. (2002): *Localization: A Global Manifesto*. Oxford: Earthscan.

HKScan (2010): Annual Report. www.hkscan.com.

Hofstede, G. (1993): 'Cultural Constraints in Management Theories', *Academy of Management Executive*. Vol. 7. No. 1. pp. 81–94.

Hornsberger, Kusi, Ndiritu, Nick, Ponce-Brito, Lalo, Tashu, Melesse and Watt, Tijan (2007): Kenya's Cut-Flower Cluster. www.isc.hbs.edu/pdf/Student_Projects/Kenya_Cut-FlowerCluster_2007.pdf.

Huang, Kuo S. (2003): Food Manufacturing Productivity and its Economic Implications. USDA ERS, Technical Bulletin No. 1905. www.ers.usda.gov/publications/tb1905.

Huffman, Wallace E. and Evenson, Robert E. (2001): 'Structural and Productivity Change in US Agriculture, 1950–82', *Agricultural Economics*. Vol. 24. pp. 127–47.

IATP (2008): Commodities Market Speculation: The Risk to Food Security and Agriculture. www.tradeobservatory.org/library.cfm?RefID=104414.

IBRD (1973): *World Bank Atlas*. Washington, DC.

ICA (2012): Statistical Information on the Co-operative Movement. www.ica.coop/coop/statistics.html.

Ietto-Gillies, G. (1998): 'Different Conceptual Frameworks for the Assessment of the Degree of Internationalisation: An Empirical Analysis of Various Indices for the Top 100 Transnational Corporations', *Transnational Corporations*. No. 7. pp. 17–39.

IFC (2004): Clusters 2.0: The Local Reality of Globalization. By James Gollub, Senior Vice President, ICF Consulting. www.icfi.com/Markets/Community_Development/doc_files/clusters-globalization.pdf.

IFII (2012): Growth or Value? The Surprising Answer. Institute for Individual Investors. www.ifii.com/articles/613423987/growth-or-value-the-surprising-answer.

IFPRI (2002): Green Revolution – Curse or Blessing? www.ifpri.org/sites/default/files/publications/ib11.pdf.

—— (2008): 'Feed the World? We are Fighting a Losing Battle, UN Admits', the *Guardian*. www.guardian.co.uk/environment/2008/feb/26/food.unitednations.

—— (2009): 'When Speculation Matters'. IFPRI: Miguel Robles, Maximo Torero and Joachim von Braun. Issue Brief 57. February. www.ifpri.org/sites/default/files/publications/ib57.pdf.

—— (2012): Has the Growth in Biofuels Helped Drive up Food Prices? www.ifpri.org/book-774/ourwork/researcharea/bioenergy/bioenergy-faqs#faq7.

IMD (2012): World Competitiveness. www.worldcompetitiveness.com.

IMF (1997): *World Economic Outlook*. May. Globalization. Opportunities and Challenges.

—— (2011): 'New Growth Drivers for Low-Income Countries: The Role of BRICs', prepared by the Strategy, Policy and Review Department, Washington, DC.

Irwin, S. H. and Sanders, D. R. (2010): 'The Impact of Index and Swap Funds on Commodity Futures Markets: Preliminary Results'. OECD Food, Agriculture and Fisheries Working Papers, No. 27, OECD.

Johnson, D. Gale (1973): *World Agriculture in Disarray*. MacMillan London.

Jose Graziano da Silva (2012): 'Corn Prices Rise Worldwide Due to US Ethanol Policy, FAO Says', Bloomberg.com. 22nd January.

Ketels, Christian and Örjan, Sölvell (2007): Europe INNOVA Cluster Mapping Project. Available online at: http://www.europe-innova.eu/web/guest

Kim, W. Chan and Mauborgne, Renée (2005): *Blue Ocean Strategy. How to Create Uncontested Market Space and Make the Competition Irrelevant*. Harvard Business School Press.

Kirin (2012): Kirin Strategy. www.kirinholdings.co.jp/english/company/strategy/index.html.

Kompetenznetze Deutschland (2008): Internationalization of Networks – Barriers and Enablers. Study: Empirical Analysis of Selected European Networks. www.comp-era.net/General%20News/Document%20Library/study_internationalisation_english_VDIVDE.pdf.

Kotler, Philip and Armstrong, Gary (2010): *Principles of Marketing*. 13th edition. London: Pearson.

KPMG (1999): Unlocking Shareholder Value: The Keys to Success. Mergers and Acquisitions. A Global Research Report.

—— (2000): Europe's Recipe for Success . . . Innovate and Consolidate. A Survey of European Food Processors. KMPG Corporate Finance.

—— (2003): Beating The Bears. Making Global Deals Enhance Value in the New Millennium. June.

—— (2011): A New Dawn: Good Deals in Challenging Times. www.kpmg.com/DK/da/nyheder-og-indsigt/nyhedsbreve-og-publikationer/publikationer/advisory/transaction-services/Documents/a-new-dawn.pdf.

—— (2012): Global M&A in Consumer Markets: Pursuing Growth in an Uncertain World. www.kpmg.com/Global/en/IssuesAndInsights/ArticlesPublications/mergers-acquisitions-consumer-markets/Documents/mergers-acquisitions-consumer-marketsv2.pdf.

Kraft (2012): www.kraft.com.

Kuznets, S. S. (1966): *Modern Economic Growth: Rate, Structure and Speed*. New Haven: Yale University Press.

Landbrugsraadet (several years): Landbrugseksporten.

Larry, Martin (1981): Economic Intervention and Regulation in the Beef and Pork Section. Economic Council of Canada.

Lasserre, Philippe (2003): *Global Strategic Management*. Basingstoke: Palgrave.

Learning Africa (2010): Flower Growing in Kenya. www.learningafrica.org.uk/downloads/casestudy_flowers.pdf.

Lee, David (1995). 'Western Hemisphere Economic Integration: Implications and Prospects for Agricultural Trade', *American Journal of Agricultural Economics*. Vol. 77. December. pp. 1274–82.

LF (2012): Danish Dairy Industry. www.agricultureandfood.dk/Danish_Agriculture_and_Food/Danish_dairy_industry.aspx.

Lipsey, R. G. (1960): 'The Theory of Customs Unions: A General Survey', *Economic Journal*. Vol. 70. September. pp. 496–513.

Lüders, Steffen (2002): Change Management ved fusioner. www.a-2.dk/pdf/mannov.pdf.

Madsen, T. K., Rasmussen, E., and Servais, P. (2000): 'Differences and Similarities between Born Globals and Other Types of Exporters', *Advances in International Marketing*. Vol. 10. pp. 247–65.

McDonald, Frank and Vertova, G. (2002): 'Clusters, Industrial Districts and Competitiveness', in McNaughton, R. and Green, M. (eds), *Global Competition and Local Networks*, London: Gower.

MacDonald, James M. (2008): The Economic Organization of US Broiler Production. Economic Information Bulletin No. 38. June .

MacDonald, James M., Ollinger, Michael, Nelsen, Kenneth E. and Handy, Charles R. (2000): Consolidation in US Meatpacking. Economic Research Service, USDA. Agricultural Economic Report No. 785.

McKinsey (2008): Enduring Ideas: The GE-McKinsey Nine-box Matrix. www.mckinsey-quarterly.com/Enduring_ideas_The_GE-McKinsey_nine-box_matrix_2198.

MAFF (1974): *National Food Survey, 1973. Annual Report on Food Expenditure, Consumption and Nutrients Intake*. London: Ministry of Agriculture, Fisheries and Food.

Mahajan, Sanjiv (2006): 'Concentration Ratios for Businesses by Industry in 2004', *Economic Trends*. Vol. 635. October. pp. 25–47.

Manning, L. and Baines, R.N. (2004): 'Globalisation: A Study of the Poultry-meat Supply Chain', *British Food Journal*. Vol. 106. No. 10/11. pp. 819–36.

Markham, Jerry W. (2002): *A Financial History of the United States*. Volume III. M. E. Sharpe, Inc. USA.

Marn, Michael V., Moffit, Jamie, Swinford, Dennis D. and Zawada, Craig C. (2000): 'The Hidden Value in Postmerger Pricing', *The McKinsey Quarterly*. No. 4. pp. 39–45.

Martin, Will and Mitra, Devashish (2000): *Productivity Growth and Convergence in Agriculture and Manufacturing*. World Bank and Florida International University.

Martinez, Steve W. (1999): Vertical Coordination in the Pork and Broiler Industries. Implications for Pork and Chicken Products. Economic Research Service/USDA Report No. 777. 39 pp.

—— (2007): *The US Food Marketing System: Recent Developments, 1997–2006*. ERR-42. US Dept. of Agriculture, Econ. Res. Serv. May.

Murphy, Sophia (2006): 'Concentrated Market Power and Agricultural Trade Ecofair Trade Dialogue'. Discussion Papers. www.tradeobservatory.org/library.cfm?refid=89014.

My Decker Capital (2010): Beer Industry in China. December. Available online at: http://mydeckercapital.com/.Documents/20101201_MDC_Beer_Industry_in_China.pdf

NaRanong, Viroj (2007): Structural Changes in Thailand's Poultry Sector and its Social Implications. www.fao.org/ag/AGAinfo/home/events/bangkok2007/docs/part1/1_4.pdf.

Narrod, Claire, Tiongco, Marites and Costales, Achilles (2007): Global Poultry Sector Trends and External Drivers of Structural Change. www.fao.org/ag/AGAinfo/home/events/bangkok2007/docs/part1/1_1.pdf.

Newmark, Craig M. (2004): Price-Concentration Studies: There You Go Again. Prepared for the DOJ/FTC Merger Workshop, 'Concentration and Market Shares' panel. North Carolina State University.

Nielsen, Chantal Pohl (2003): Regional and Preferential Trade Agreements: A Literature Review and Identification of Future Steps. Fødevareøkonomisk Institut, Report No. 155.

Nomura (2010): 'The Coming Surge in Food Prices', *Global Economics and Strategy*. September. www.nomura.com/europe/resources/pdf/080910.pdf.

Nyangweso, P. M. and Odhiambo, M. O. (2004): *Exporting Kenya's Horticultural Products: Challenges and Opportunities in the 21st Century.*

OECD (1992): *Agricultural Policies, Markets and Trade: Monotoring and Outlook 1993.* 'Annex III – Assistance to OECD Agriculture', Paris: OECD Publishing.

—— (1992): OECD Economic Studies. No. 18/Spring. Paris.

—— (1995): Technological Change and Structural Adjustment in OECD Agriculture.

—— (2001): Regional Integration Agreements. www.oecd.org/dataoecd/39/37/1923431.pdf.

—— (2005): 'Regional Trade Arrangments and the Multinational Trading System: Agriculture'. OECD Trade Policy Working Paper No. 15.

—— (2007): Competitive Regional Clusters: National Policy Approaches. Policy brief. May 2007. Available online at: http://www.oecd.org/gov/38653705.pdf

—— (2012a): OECD.stat. SDBS Structural Business Statistics (ISIC Rev. 3).

—— (2012b): Agriculture and Fisheries. Statistics. www.oecd.org.

—— (2012c): Economic Outlook. Available online at: http://www.oecd-ilibrary.org/economics/oecd-economic-outlook-volume2012-issue-1_eco_outlook-v2012-1-en

OECD-FAO (2009): Agricultural Outlook. 2009–18.

—— (2010): Agricultural Outlook. 2010–19.

—— (2011): Agricultural Outlook. 2011–20.

Ollinger, M. and Fernandez-Cornejo, J. (1998): 'Sunk Costs and Regulation in the US Pesticide Industry', *International Journal of Industrial Organization*. No. 16. pp. 139–68.

Ollinger, Michael, MacDonald, James and Madison, Milton (2000): Structural Change in US Chicken and Turkey Slaughter. Economic Report No. AER787. November. www.ers.usda.gov/publications/aer787

Ollinger, Michael, Van Nguyen, Sang, Blayney, Don, Chambers, William and Nelson, Kenneth B. (2005): Structural Change in the Meat, Poultry, Dairy, and Grain Processing Industries. USDA ERS, Economic Research Report No. ERR3. April.

—— (2006): Food Industry Mergers and Acquisitions Lead to Higher Labor Productivity. Economic Research Report. USDA, No. 27.

Organic World (2012): Global Organic Farming Statistics and News. www.organic-world.net/statistics-data-tables-excel.html#c6206.

Orkla (2012): www.orkla.com.

Oustapassidis, K., Banterle Alessandro and Briz, Julian (1995): 'A Review of Some Preliminary Data Relating to Structural Change within the European Food Industries and Factors Affecting It'. Discussion Paper No. 9, in *Structural Change in the European Food Industries*. Brussels, European Union. p. 27.

Oxford Research (2008): Cluster Policy in Europe. A Brief Summary of Cluster Policies in 31 European Countries. Europe Innova Cluster Mapping Project. www.clusterobservatory. eu/upload/Synthesis_report_cluster_mapping.pdf.

PA Consulting (2004): Realising the Value of Acquisitions. A Comparative Study of Post-acquisition Integration Practices.

Peltzman, S. (2000): 'Prices Rise Faster than They Fall', *Journal of Political Economy.* Vol. 108. No. 3. pp. 466–502.

Persson, Martin, Sabanovic, Adis and Wester, Henrik (2007): Is Cluster Theory in Need of Renewal? Porter's Diamond Revised. University essay from Kristianstad University, Department of Business Studies. http://eprints.bibl.hkr.se/archive/00002001/01/c-uppsats_absolute_final.pdf.

Porter, Michael E. (1980): *Competitive Strategy*, New York: Free Press.

—— (1990): *The Competitive Advantage of Nations.*

—— (2006): 'Q&A with Michael Porter', *BusinessWeek.* August 2006. www.businessweek. com/magazine/content/06_34/b3998460.htm.

—— (2008): Clusters, Innovation, and Competitiveness: New Findings and Implications for Policy. January. www.isc.hbs.edu/pdf/20080122_EuropeanClusterPolicy.pdf.

Pouch, T. (2005): Brazil, the Largest World Exporter of Poultry Meat. Chambres d'Agriculture, No. 940.

Rabobank (2011): Private Label vs Brands. An Inseparable Combination.

—— (2012): Producing both Brands and Private Labels. Rabobank Industry Note No. 322. May.

Radetzki, Marian (2006): 'The Anatomy of Three Commodity Booms', *Resources Policy.* Vol. 31: pp. 56–64. www.radetzki.biz/rapporter/ThreeBooms_71.pdf.

ReD Associates (2008): Brugerorienteret Fødevareforskning. Et studie af innovation-spraksis i fødevarebranchen og forskningsmiljøernes brugerpraksis. For Vitus Bering Danmark.

Rehber, Erkan (1998): 'Vertical Integration in Agriculture and Contract Farming'. Working Paper 46, Institution Regional Research Project NE-165. University of Minnesota.

Renard, Mary-Francoise (2011): China's Trade and FDI in Africa, Series No. 126. African Development Bank, Tunis, Tunisia.

RIRDC (Rural Industries Research and Development Corporation) (1997): Sustainability Indicators for Agriculture. Farm Management 500.

Ritson, Christopher (1977): *Agricultural Economics. Principles and Policy.* London: Crosby Lockwood Staples.

Rogers, Richard T. (2000): Structural Change in US Food Manufacturing, 1958 to 1997. Presentation for 'The American Consumer and the Changing Structure of the Food System'. 4th–5th May. Washington, DC, and Arlington, VA.

Royer, Jeffrey (2009): Business Strategies for Cooperative Competitive Positioning. Workshop arranged by COGECA on 'Long-term Governance and Development Strategies for European Agri-cooperatives'. 19th May. Brussels.

Rumelt, R. P. (1982): 'Diversification Strategy and Profitability', *Strategic Management Journal.* Vol. 3. pp. 359–370.

Sandrey, Ron (2006): 'Trade Creation and Trade Diversion Resulting from SACU Trading Agreements'. tralac Working Paper. No. 11/2006. www.tralac.org/scripts/content.php? id=5211.

Saveuse, Joël (2003): 'Big Manufactures Have To Show the Same Flexibility as the Small Ones', in Grievink, Jan-Willem, Josten, Lia and Valk, Conny (eds), *State of the Art in Food.* Meppel, The Netherlands. Elsevier Business Information.

Saxenian, A. (1994): *Regional Advantage: Culture and Competition in Silicon Valley and Route 128*. Cambridge, MA: Harvard University Press.

Scherer, F. M. and Ross, D. (1990): *Industrial Market Structure and Economic Performance*, 3rd edition. Boston: Houghton Mifflin.

Schultz, T. W. (1945): *Agriculture in an Unstable Economy*. New York: McGraw-Hill.

Seale, J. L., Jr. and Regmi, A. (2006): 'Modeling International Consumption Patterns', *Review of Income and Wealth*. Vol. 52. pp. 603–24.

Sisodiya, Amit Singh (2004): Mergers and Demergers – Concepts and Cases. Investment Banking Series. ICFAI University.

Smithfield, (2012): Smithfield Foods, Inc. Recent Material Event. www.hotstocked.com/10-k/smithfield-foods-inc-SFD-657022.html.

Sölvell, Örjan (2008): *Clusters Balancing Evolutionary and Constructive Forces*. Stockholm. Available online at: http://www.cluster-research.org/redbook.htm

Sparling, David and van Duren, Erna (2002): 'Putting Globalization and Concentration in the Agri-food Sector into Context', *Current Agriculture, Food & Resource Issues*. No. 3. pp. 29–48.

Statistics Denmark (several issues): *Statistical Yearbook*.

—— (2012): Special Data Delivery. Available online at: http://www.dst.dk/pukora/epub/upload/16251/sty2012.pdf

Stiegert, Kyle W. and Dong, Hwam Kim (2009): Structural Changes in Food Retailing: Six Country Case Studies. www.aae.wisc.edu/fsrg/publications/Monographs/!food_retailingchapter3.pdf.

Sullivan, Daniel (1994): 'Measuring the Degree of Internationalization of a Firm', *Journal of international Business Studies*. Vol. 25. pp. 325–342.

Tangermann, Stefan (2011): 'Policy Solutions to Agricultural Market Volatility: A Synthesis'. Issue Paper No. 33. ICTSD. http://ictsd.org/downloads/2011/06/tangermann-price-volatility-and-policy-options.pdf.

Taylor, C. Robert (2004): The Many Faces of Power in the Food System. Auburn University. www.ftc.gov/bc/mergerenforce/presentations/040217taylor.pdf.

Taylor, C. Robert and Domina, David A. (2010): Restoring Economic Health to Contract Poultry Production. Report prepared for the Joint US Department of Justice and US Department of Agriculture/GIPSA Public.

Thomson, Robert (2009): World Agriculture in Perspective. www.ifma17.org/presentations.html.

Timmer, C. Peter (2009): Did Speculation Affect World Rice Prices? ftp://ftp.fao.org/docrep/fao/011/ak232e/ak232e00.pdf.

Transparency International (2012): The 2011 Corruption Perceptions Index. http://cpi.transparency.org/cpi2011.

UN (2012): *COMTRADE*. http://comtrade.un.org.

UNCTAD (several years): World Investment Report.

—— (2000): World Investment Report 2000: Cross-border Mergers and Acquisitions and Development. Available online at: http://unctad.org/en/Docs/wir2000_en.pdf

—— (2005a): Prospects for Foreign Direct Investment and the Strategies of Transnational Corporations. 2005–8. http://unctad.org/en/docs/iteiit20057_en.pdf.

—— (2005b): World Investment Report 2005. Transnational Corporations and the Internationalization of R&D. http://unctad.org/en/docs/wir2005_en.pdf.

—— (2005c): Effects of the 'Everything but Arms' Initiative on the Sugar Industries of the Least Developed Countries. Report by the UNCTAD Secretariat. http://unctad.org/en/docs/ditccom20046_en.pdf.

—— (2006): World Investment Report 2006: FDI from Developing and Transition Economies: Implications for Development. Available online: http://unctad.org/en/Docs/wir2005_en.pdf

—— (2007): Asian Foreign Direct Investment in Africa. Towards a New Era of Cooperation among Developing Countries. http://unctad.org/en/docs/iteiia20071_en.pdf.

—— (2009): The Global Economic Crisis: Systemic Failures and Multilateral Remedies. www.unctad.org/en/docs/gds20091_en.pdf.

—— (2011): World Investment Report 2011. Available online: http://www.unctad-docs.org/files/UNCTA_WIR2011-Full-en.pdf

—— (2012): UNCTADSTAT. Foreign Direct Investment. http://unctadstat.unctad.org/ReportFolders/reportFolders.aspxhttp://unctadstat.unctad.org/ReportFolders/report-Folders.aspx.

UNCTAD/DITE (2008): Integrating Developing SMEs into the Global Economy. Fulvia Farinelli. www.unido.org/fileadmin/import/75394_070913_Sess1201_Faranelli UNCTADGVCs.pdf

Unilever (2012): www.unilever.com.

UN News Center (2009): Food Price Fluctuation Driven by Financial Speculation. 19th March.

USDA (several years): Agricultural Statistics Annual. National Agricultural Statistics Service.

—— (1997): The Structure of Dairy Markets: Past, Present, Future. AER-757. September. Available online: http://usda01.library.cornell.edu/usda/ers/dairymarkets/AER757.pdf

—— (1998): Regional Trade Agreements and US Agriculture. Mary E. Burfisher, and Elizabeth A. Jones. Agricultural Economics Report No. AER771. November.

—— (2005): Cooperatives in the Dairy Industry. Cooperative Information Report 1, Section 16. www.rurdev.usda.gov/rbs/pub/cir116.pdf.

—— (2009): Marketing Operations of Dairy Cooperatives, 2007. Research Report 218. By K. Charles Ling. www.rurdev.usda.gov/rbs/pub/RR218.pdf.

—— (2010a): International Food Consumption Patterns. www.ers.usda.gov/Data/InternationalFoodDemand.

—— (2010b): Former Soviet Union Region To Play Larger Role in Meeting World Wheat Needs. www.ers.usda.gov/AmberWaves/June10/Features/FSUWheat.htm.

—— (2011a): US and Foreign Wheat Prices. www.ers.usda.gov/Data/Wheat/Yearbook/WheatYearbookTable20-Full.htm.

—— (2011b): World Markets and Trade. August 2009.

—— (2011c): International Food Consumption Patterns. www.ers.usda.gov/Data/InternationalFoodDemand.

—— (2011d): Food CPI and Expenditures: Table 10. www.ers.usda.gov/Briefing/CPIFood AndExpenditures/Data/Expenditures_tables/table10.htm.

—— (2012a): *Wheat Data*. Yearbook. www.ers.usda.gov/Data/Wheat/Yearbook/Wheat YearbookTable20-Full.htm.

—— (2012b): Foreign Agricultural Service. Grains. www.fas.usda.gov/grain.

—— (2012c): Cooperatives. Historical Data. Cooperative Memberships and Sales, 1913–2007. www.rurdev.usda.govBCP_Coop_DirectoryAndData.html.

—— (2012d): Cooperatives. Marketing Operations of Dairy Cooperatives. Cooperative Member Milk by Farm location, Number of Producers, and Milk per Producer. www.rurdev.usda.gov/BCP_Coop_Data_DairyMarketing.html.

—— (2012e): Food Marketing System in the US: Food Retailing. www.ers.usda.gov/ Briefing/FoodMarketingSystem/foodretailing.htm.

USDL (2011): Bureau of Labour Statistics. Multifactor Productivity Measures for Manufacturing Industries in Selected Periods, 1987–2009. www.bls.gov/news.release/prod5. t03.htm.

van Bekkum, O. F. (2009): Cooperative Champions or Investor Targets? The Challenge of Internationalization and External Capital, 2009. www.lf.dk/Aktuelt/Publikationer/~/ media/lf/Aktuelt/Publikationer/Landbrug/VanBekkum_DK-Study_ CoopChampions_18Dec09.ashx.

Vavra, P. and Goodwin, B. K. (2005): 'Analysis of Price Transmission Along the Food Chain'. OECD Food, Agriculture and Fisheries Working Papers, No. 3, OECD Publishing.

Viner, J. (1950): *The Customs Union Issue.* New York: The Carnegie Endowment for International Peace.

VSC Growth (2011): Mergers and Acquisitions: Part 1. 2011 Research Project. Steeve Coote, Director, VSC Growth.

Vukina, Tomislav and Leegomonchai, Porametr (2006): 'Political Economy of Regulation of Broiler Contracts', *American Journal of Agricultural Economics.* Vol. 88, December. pp. 1258–65.

Wai, Chan Hon (2003): Recent Trends on the UK Merger Activities. www.armchaireconomist. com/frame.htm.

Wall Street Journal (2008): Russian Export Ban Raises Global Food Fears. 5th August.

WATT Poultry USA (2010a): Top Poultry Companies. February. Available online: http:// www.wattpoultryusa-digital.com/poultryusa/201002?pg=3#pg21

—— (2010b): Executive Guide to World Poultry Trends. Available online: http//poultry-productionnews.blogspot.dk/2010/10/2010-watt-executive-guide-to-world.html

Wee, Kee and Arnold, Katrin (2009): 'Transnational Corporations in Floriculture'. Paper prepared for World Investment Report 2009.

World Bank (2005): Global Economic Prospects. Trade, Regionalism, and Development. Available online: http://siteresources.worldbank.org/INTGEP2005/Resources/gep2005. pdf

—— (2007a): *Reforming Agricultural Trade for Developing Countries. Volume Two. Quantifying the Impact of Multilateral Trade Reform.* Alex F. McCalla and John Nash (eds). New York: The World Bank.

—— (2007b): Snapshot Africa – Kenya Benchmarking FDI Competitiveness. Available online: http://www.fdi.net/documents/WorldBank/databases/snapshot_africa/docs/ snapshot_africa_kenya.pdf

—— (2007c): World Development Report 2008. Agriculture for Development. Available online: http://siteresources.worldbank.org/INTWDR2008/Resources/WDR_00_book. pdf

—— (2008): 'A Note on Rising Food Prices'. Policy Research Working Paper 4682. Donald Mitchel.

—— (2010): 'The Impacts of Biofuel Targets on Land-Use. Change and Food Supply'. A Global CGE Assessment. Policy Research Working Paper 5513.

—— (2012a): Historical Commodity Prices. http://blogs.worldbank.org/prospects/category/ tags/historical-commodity-prices.

—— (2012b): World Bank Indicators.

World Food Programme (2009): Financial Speculation and the Food. By economic historian Peter Timmer. www.wfp.org/stories/dr-timmer.

World Poultry (2003): European processing Companies Search for Expansion. Reed Volume 19, No. 2.

WTO (2002): Regional Trade Integration under Transformation. Regional Trade Agreements Section. Trade Policies Review Division. WTO.

—— (2009): Lamy: The World Needs a Shared Vision on Food and Agricultural Trade Policy. 10th May. www.wto.org/english/news_e/sppl_e/sppl124_e.htm.

—— (2011): World Trade Report 2011. www.wto.org/english/res_e/booksp_e/anrep_e/world_trade_report11_e.pdf

—— (2012a): International Trade Statistics. 2010.

—— (2012b): www.wto.org.

Wusheng, Yu and Jensen, Trine V. (2005): 'Tariff Preferences, WTO Negotiations and the LDCs: The Case of "Everything But Arms" initiative', *The World Economy*. Vol. 28. pp. 375–405.

Yago, Glenn (1999): Surfing the Merger Waves: Is California Losing? www.milkeninstitute.org/publications/publications.taf?function=detail&ID = 117&cat = Arts.

Yasushi, UEKI (2006): 'Export-Led Growth and Geographic Distribution of the Poultry Meat Industry in Brazil'. Institute of Developing Economies, Discussion Paper No. 67.

Yip, George S. (1992): *Total Global Strategy*, Upper Saddle River, NJ: Prentice-Hall.

Ylä-Anttila, Pekka (2008): Clusters and Cluster-based Policies. Comments and Finnish Experiences. www.temtoimialapalvelu.fi/files/512/Yla-Anttila_2.klusterisminaari_Feb_08.pdf.

Zeull, K. A and Cropp, R. (2004): Cooperatives: Principles and Practices in the 21st Century. http://learningstore.uwex.edu/assets/pdfs/A1457.PDF.

zu Köcker, Gerd Meier (2008): Barriers, Enablers and Current Trends in Internationalisation of Networks. Agency Competence Networks Germany. www.kompetenznetze.de/service/nachlese/medien/internationalisation-of-networks.pdf.

Index

Note: Page numbers in **bold** are for figures, those in *italics* are for tables.

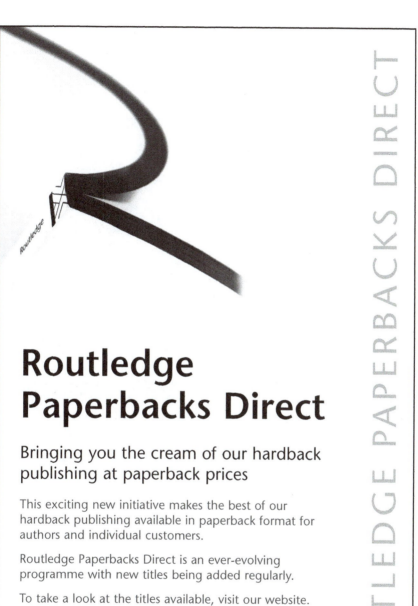